Major Economic Issues

Marilu Hurt McCarty
Georgia Institute of Technology

Scott, Foresman and Company   **Glenview, Illinois**

Dallas, Texas   Oakland, New Jersey   Palo Alto, California   Tucker, Georgia

London, England

Library of Congress Cataloging in Publication Data

McCarty, Marilu Hurt.
   Major economic issues.

   Includes bibliographies and index.
   1. United States—Economic conditions—1981-
2. United States—Economic policy—1981-   . 3. Labor
productivity—United States. 4. Economics. I. Title.
HC106.8.M35   1984   330.973'0927   83-20061
ISBN 0-673-15474-2

1 2 3 4 5 6 - KPF - 88 87 86 85 84 83

Preface

Many students complete their coursework in economics without ever relating economic theory and analysis in a fundamental way to events and decisions in their own experience. If the economics is remembered at all, it is frequently relegated to that body of knowledge for which the student sees no practical applications. This text will provide the reader with a clearer appreciation of how to use economic principles in decision making for personal and business problems as well as for evaluating questions of national or international magnitude.

Each economic issue and policy measure discussed in the text is evaluated as it relates to worker productivity and the goal of raising real per capita incomes and living standards for the nation as a whole. After describing each problem and its consequences for worker productivity, the text explains the economic principles at work and current and proposed policy measures for dealing with the problem. Finally, the reader is asked to consider whether the resulting change in worker productivity reduces or enhances the equity of our economic system.

Topics are taken up in logical sequence according to their contribution to the underlying theme and according to the theoretical principles they illustrate. Chapter 1 describes how the goal of increased productivity is related to the even more fundamental goal of increased individual freedom and dignity. Chapter 2 investigates the process of saving and investment and the motives and rewards for doing so. Chapter 3 looks at the consequences for productivity of changes in the availability of energy, and Chapter 4 focuses on the costs and benefits of defense production. Chapter 5 investigates the responsibilities of government, particularly with respect to government's role in promoting efficiency in production, equity in distribution, and production of positive externalities.

Chapter 6 considers the urgent questions associated with economic growth — the benefits of growth for achieving improved efficiency and equity and the potential problems of growth in terms of negative externalities. Chapters 7 and 8 deal with labor markets, income, and income distribution and consider the efficiency of government policies dealing with total employment and wage-price inflation. Chapters 9, 10, and 11 deal with efficiency, equity, and externalities associated with health care, agriculture, and transportation, particularly with respect to the effects of government policies in these sectors on the productivity of our economic system. Chapter 12 considers the economics of international trade and finance, along with the effects of recent exchange rate fluctuations.

Chapter 13 summarizes and integrates the concepts developed in the preceding chapters. The emphasis is on the politics of economic policymaking and the difficulty of achieving efficiency and equity in a democratic society influenced by special interests. Particular attention is paid to the macroeconomic problems of inflation and unemployment and the various policy tools for combating them.

A real effort has been made to make this text *interesting*. A wealth of detailed information has been included to enliven the descriptive passages. Anecdotes and historical references help the reader relate the subject matter to familiar ideas and experiences. The analytical passages are written in clear and simple language. Numerous graphs are included to amplify the explanations. Mathematical Supplements are set apart for optional use. The mathematical explanations are easily understood and relevant for a wide range of applications. Special Cases encourage independent thinking on subtopics related to the major issues: the threatened water shortage, gasohol production, the B–1 controversy, world hunger, and New York City's fiscal problems are examples. Each chapter includes numerous questions and exercises, as well as a complete, alphabetized glossary of terms.

Seldom have economic issues so clearly dominated public attention. Equipping citizens with the practical and conceptual tools for rational debate is an essential and challenging endeavor. I am grateful for the opportunity to contribute to that effort and welcome suggestions for strengthening this text.

Marilu Hurt McCarty

Acknowledgements

I would particularly like to thank these reviewers for their constructive suggestions and comments:

Richard J. Agnello, University of Delaware
Kenneth S. Arakelian, University of Rhode Island
Fred Bowen, Norfolk State University
Wallace B. Broome, Rhode Island Junior College
Michael G. Ellis, New Mexico State University
L. W. Gallup, Oklahoma City University
Patricia Garland, Northeast Louisiana University
S. M. Ghazanfar, University of Idaho
Shiv K. Gupta, Findlay College
Mark G. Johnson, Lakeland Community College
Donald A. Moore, California State University
John Photiades, University of Montana
Martin L. Primack, San Jose State University
James Starkey, University of Rhode Island
Robert P. Volyn, Wagner College
J. Holton Wilson, University of Montana
Arthur G. Woolf, University of Vermont

Contents

3   Energy, Productivity, and Income
Where Will We Get the Power?   56

10 Feeding the World's People: The Agricultural Sector
Will We Have Enough?

11 Regulated Industries: The Transportation Sector
What's the Best Way to Go?   271

12 U.S. Global Interests: The International Economy
How Shall We Share the Pie?   297

CHAPTER ONE

Foundations of the U.S. Economic System

What Are the Trade-offs?

LEARNING OBJECTIVES

- To consider how an individual's health, happiness, and personal freedom are related to the health and happiness of the community.
- To understand how the market system provides incentives for certain kinds of behavior beneficial to the community as a whole.
- To use a production function as a model of the relationship between resources and total production of material wealth.
- To note the relationship between worker productivity and real per capita income.
- To understand the circumstances that reduce efficiency and equity in our economic system and the actions of government that promote efficiency and equity.

Many people have a mistaken view of economics and economists. Since economics has to do with money, things, work, profit, mathematical equations, and other mundane topics, some people tend to think of it as a worldly subject, concerned only with the material side of life. In their view, focusing on buying and selling, producing and consuming, saving and investing makes economics somehow "unclean" in the catalogue of academic subjects—far below the lofty ranks occupied by philosophy, history, literature, and the physical sciences.

Economics does include such earthy topics, of course. But it would be wrong to focus so completely on these material topics and to forget the main concern of the subject. The main concern of economics and economists is to understand and promote conditions that enhance human health and happiness and that allow the personal freedom to develop each person's own capacities in any way he or she chooses.

A course in economics is not complete if students learn only the material facts and mathematical equations painstakingly developed and handed down by scholars of the past. It is complete only if students can apply what they have learned in ways that improve the nonmaterial aspects of their lives as well as the material ones. The best economists know this. The giants of economic theory and policy have always looked beyond their equations and graphs for the real human meaning of economics. Beyond their **economic models,** many economists are really "closet philosophers."

The goal of this text is to bring the principles and procedures of economics together with their implications for the quality of human life. Toward this purpose, we will focus on some of the major issues faced by today's economies. Achieving dependable food supplies, guaranteeing adequate defense, and providing for dependent citizen groups are examples of serious economic issues with implications for human health, happiness, and personal freedom. We will consider all these and more. In each case, we will begin by describing the problem. Then we will analyze the economic forces that contribute to the problem and might be used to bring about a solution. Finally, we will consider the political context in which policies for solving economic problems must be debated.

Throughout our discussion we will use the tools of the economist to broaden and simplify the explanation. We will find that equations, tables, and graphs can convey important information that would otherwise require lengthy explanation. We will find also that issues can seldom be classified simply as **microeconomic** (concerning only the individual economic unit) or **macroeconomic** (concerning only the economic system as a whole). Indeed, problems that concern individual economic units must also concern the entire economic system. Therefore, we will look at each issue in terms of its implications at both levels of economic analysis.* The result should be a fuller sense of the relevance of economic theory to the student's own life.

In this first chapter, we will consider some of the philosophical foundations of the economic system of the United States and the kinds of policies that have been established for affecting our system. First, we will examine the broad

---

*The reader will discover no single chapter focusing on the macroeconomic issues of inflation or unemployment. In fact, these topics are central to *all* economic issues and will be treated as central themes of *all* chapters.

consequences of our economic philosophy in terms of our own wellbeing. Then we will look at the consequences of current developments for the nation's future economic health.

ADAM SMITH'S LEGACY

The economic philosophy that underlies the U.S. economic system was first described by Adam Smith in his great book *The Wealth of Nations*. Adam Smith wrote about an economic system in which economic decisions are made in markets. Markets are places where buyers and sellers come together to exchange goods and services.* By offering higher prices for the most wanted goods and services, buyers encourage sellers to produce more of such items for sale. Then the expectation of profit leads to economic development and rising material standards of living. Free trade helps transmit technical knowledge among producing groups the world over.

On the surface, *The Wealth of Nations* seems to focus only on the material side of life. Underlying its material concerns, however, was Adam Smith's more fundamental concern with human health, happiness, and personal freedom.

In his first major work, *The Theory of Moral Sentiments,* Adam Smith described how social systems develop. There is a kind of fellow-feeling, he said, that influences relationships between people in any community. People's ability to "put themselves in someone else's shoes" creates a bond of sympathy with their neighbors and guides them to behave in ways helpful to the community as a whole. Acts that would be harmful to the community do not necessarily call for rules and regulations. The disapproval of the community will normally be strong enough to discourage the kinds of behavior that would threaten the health or safety of the social system.

In Smith's ideal society three human characteristics would be in such perfect balance that coercive government would not be necessary:

1. *Self-interest* would encourage people to produce goods and services for personal gain, thus raising material standards of living for all.
2. *Justice* would govern personal relations with others, ensuring equity, or fairness, in economic activity.
3. Finally, *benevolence* would grow out of people's association with the larger social group, leading to feelings of patriotism and a sense of shared responsibility for all the world's people.

Surely, Smith's ideal society is worth achieving. In fact, according to Smith, the **market system** can help bring it about. The market system makes freedom possible. It substitutes *internal* drives and motivations for *external* rules and

*Modern communication facilities make it possible for buyers and sellers to "come together" over wide distances.

regulations. When people are encouraged to use their energies productively, they need no legal (nor religious) coercion to ensure acceptable behavior. Furthermore, their fellow-feeling will restrain most kinds of behavior that would be unhealthy for the community as a whole.

Much of Adam Smith's optimism about increasing freedoms under the market system was based on his belief in economic growth. Market incentives would promote maximum levels of production for the community, he said, bringing higher standards of living for the people and a greater capacity for benevolence toward others. Then, growing material abundance would strengthen democratic institutions throughout the world.

An Evaluation

Much of what Adam Smith foresaw has indeed come to pass. Our own history provides evidence of the parallel growth of material wealth along with personal freedom. The American colonists could enjoy personal freedoms because of the vast wealth of resources of the American continent. Advances in technology over the years since the colonial period have helped extend the benefits of freedom to more and more segments of American society.

In contrast, many poorer nations of the world suffer both economic and political deprivation. Lacking the material wealth necessary for a healthy life, their citizens are unable to develop their productive capabilities fully, to ensure justice in economic relationships, and to exercise benevolence toward others.

If poverty and lack of freedom go hand in hand, rapid economic change poses other dangers. In rapidly changing times, the fellow-feeling that normally guides human relationships can become confused, and the balance between self-interest, justice, and benevolence can become distorted. Whatever natural forces toward order and tranquility exist may fail, and citizens may call for new forms of government control.

The most common example of a failure of natural order occurs in wartime. Wartime dangers may lead governments to limit freedoms in certain ways: in the kinds of jobs citizens must perform and the places they may travel. Wartime scarcities may lead governments to establish rules regarding the things citizens may buy. Without such controls the hardships of war might be shared so unequally that citizens would begin fighting among themselves. In general, we Americans accept new rules and regulations in wartime, but we expect to see our freedoms restored as soon as the emergency is past.

Adam Smith foresaw other problems for a free market economy. He realized that access to material wealth would differ among groups in the economic system. Differences in ownership of wealth would make for differences in living standards. Some groups might enjoy power to exclude others from the market, and thus from the fruits of economic growth. These kinds of circumstances would call for government policies to produce and distribute material wealth and to minimize the effects of market power.

Adam Smith's insights have had extraordinary significance for Western nations, and particularly for the United States. If future policies are to be governed by the policies he described, it is important to understand completely the scope of his reasoning. Smith called for the fullest development of personal freedoms in economic and political life — the maximum incentives to use individual initiatives to promote ends desired by all of us. But — and this point is often overlooked—the fullest development of personal freedoms is possible only in the context of *and for the sake of* the community as a whole. Thus, personal freedom is possible only if the community as a whole is healthy. It is the "oneness" of the community that makes possible the "wholeness" of the individual.

REAL PRODUCTION AND INCOME

Material prosperity is basic to Adam Smith's projections of the good life. Material prosperity makes possible the fullest development of human potential and the maximum capacity for personal freedom. Achieving material prosperity depends first of all on the quality and quantity of resources available for producing goods and services. **Productive resources** can be classified into four broad groups:

1. *Land,* the original and nonreproducible gifts of nature, including farmland, rivers, virgin forests, and minerals;
2. *Labor,* the purposeful work of human beings, both physical and mental;
3. **Capital,** produced means of production, including buildings, machines, tools, and equipment;
4. **Entrepreneurship,** the organizational and managerial system for combining other resources into a productive enterprise. An "entrepreneur" assumes the risks and makes the decisions that cause production to take place.

Technical and social conditions within an economic system determine how effectively it uses its resources for producing some quantity of goods and services. The total quantity produced during any period of time is **real income** for the society and is available for distribution among those who have contributed to production (either through their own labor or through ownership of other resources). Finally, the character of production and the system of distribution determine the living standards for the people.

Adam Smith's theory of production can be expressed in the form of an *economic model.* A model is a simplified view of reality in which relationships among **economic variables** are first described verbally, and then expressed algebraically and graphically. Economic variables are the physical and financial elements that interact to yield economic results. For example, the number of people at work is an economic variable that affects total production of goods and services. The supply of money is an economic *variable* that affects incentives to borrow and spend.

Figure 1–1

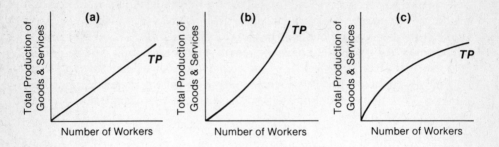

The relationship between economic variables is often stated in the form of an algebraic expression called a **function**. In the first example above, total production of goods and services is a *function* of the number of people working.* Stated algebraically:

$$\text{Total Production} = \text{function (number of workers)} \quad \text{or}$$
$$TP \qquad = \quad f\,(N)$$

This is the same as saying that Total Production *depends* on numbers of workers employed. Thus, production (*TP*) is the *dependent variable* and the number of workers (*N*) is the *independent variable*. The precise form of the relationship between the dependent and independent variable is determined by technical and social conditions in the economic environment.

A **production function** can also be shown graphically. The graphs in Figure 1–1 are alternative forms of production functions. On each graph the number of workers (*N*) is measured on the horizontal axis, and total production (*TP*) on the vertical axis. The line on the graph indicates the total quantity of goods and services that can be produced with various quantities of workers.

The production function in Figure 1–1a rises in a straight line. The constant slope indicates equal changes in total product (*TP*) for each unit change in number of workers (*N*). The production function in Figure 1–1b rises with an increasing slope, indicating greater and greater changes in total product for each unit increase in number of workers. What does the production function in Figure 1–1c indicate?†

Most production functions take none of the forms shown in Figure 1–1 but are believed to take the form shown in Figure 1–2. The production function in Figure 1–2 is drawn to describe the behavior of production in the **short run**. The short

---

*Total production depends on factors other than labor, as we have seen. To begin, we will concentrate only on the contribution of labor. Then we will include the influence of other factors.

†The decreasing slope of the production function in Figure 1–1c indicates smaller and smaller changes in total product for each unit increase in number of workers.

run is a period of time during which one or more of the economic resources described on page 5 remain constant. In general, the quantity of land and capital equipment, as well as the level of technology and other economic and social conditions, are relatively constant in the short run. Thus, over some period of time when these conditions remain constant, various numbers of workers (N) can be used to produce some quantity of goods and services (TP) shown as the production function.

The production function in Figure 1–2 has certain distinctive characteristics. Look carefully at Figure 1–2 and locate the portion of the production function for which each of the following is true:

1. For any period of time in which all other economic variables are unchanged, an increase in workers from zero to some number N' causes Total Product to increase by greater and greater amounts. (We know this because the production function has an increasing slope over this range.) The reason has to do with the proportion of workers relative to the constant supply of other resources available in the community: usable land and capital equipment in the form of buildings and machines. Under existing technical, social, and political conditions there is some number of workers (N) that represents the **optimum proportion** of labor to available land and capital resources.* Approaching that quantity yields successively greater increases in Total Product. In Figure 1–2 we have identified the optimum proportion of workers to other productive resources at N'.

   NOTE: In fact, there may be a range of employment over which the proportion of labor to other resources is optimum. Over this range, Total Product may increase by a constant quantity for each unit increase in number of workers. Thus, the production function may rise with a constant slope over some range of employment. The production function in Figure 1–2 rises with a constant slope over a very short range of employment.

2. For any period of time in which all other economic variables are unchanged, an increase in workers beyond the optimum level at N' increases Total Product by smaller and smaller quantities. (The production function has a decreasing slope beyond N'.) Beyond N' the number of workers becomes excessive relative to available land and capital resources and the technology of production. Therefore, gains in Total Product are less as the labor force grows.

3. For any period of time in which all other economic variables are unchanged, an increase in workers beyond some level N'' causes Total Product to decline. (The production function has a negative, or downward, slope beyond N''.) The extreme disproportion of workers to other resources beyond N'' yields decreasing Total Product.

---

*We will define the optimum proportion of labor to other resources as that proportion at which the contribution of the last unit of labor employed yields the greatest increase in total production.

Marginal and Average Product

The implications of these results underlie all production theory. To illustrate, we will manipulate the production function in Figure 1–2 to show two additional economic relationships: **Marginal Product** and **Average Product**.

Marginal Product is the change in Total Product associated with a one-unit change in the independent variable, labor: Marginal Product = $MP = \Delta TP/\Delta N$, where Δ is read "change in." Marginal Product can be calculated by subtracting Total Product quantities at successive levels of employment. On a graph of Total Product, Marginal Product is the slope of the Total Product curve.

We have noted that Total Product tends to increase at an increasing rate at low levels of employment, a constant rate at some optimum level (or range) of employment, and a decreasing rate at high levels of employment. The behavior of Total Product over these ranges indicates, respectively, increasing, constant, and decreasing Marginal Product. At some very high level of employment, Total Product reaches a peak, and the employment of additional workers would cause Total Product to decrease. The behavior of Total Product over this range of employment indicates negative Marginal Product.

A Marginal Product curve is shown in Figure 1–3. The Marginal Product curve shows increasing growth in Total Product over the range of workers from zero to N', decreasing growth in production over the range N' to N'', and negative growth beyond N''. These results are consistent with statements 1, 2, and 3 above. A Marginal Product curve drawn for any production function of the form illustrated in Figure 1–2 will always have this distinctive shape.

Average Product is Total Product divided by units of workers: Average Product = $AP = TP/N$. An Average Product curve for the production function of Figure 1–2 will always have the distinctive shape shown in Figure 1–4. Because of the three characteristics of production outlined above, the Average Product of workers will tend to increase as the number of workers increases from zero to some number N''' and to decrease beyond that number. (N''' will always lie between N' and N''.) Average Product will never become negative unless Total Product should become negative.*

Note that Average Product is a measure of worker productivity:

$$\text{Average Product of Labor} = AP_L = \frac{\text{units of Total Product}}{\text{units of Labor}}.$$

Worker productivity increases over the range $N = 0$ to $N=N'''$ and decreases beyond that quantity. Note also that Average Product measures the average share of Total Product available for distribution to workers. Thus, it is a measure of **real per capita income** and average living standards.

We will have more to say about real per capita income later. For now we should note that measuring "real per capita income" tells us nothing about how

---

*This would imply that workers are employed for *destroying* goods and services.

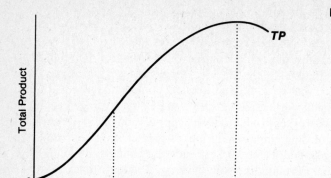

Figure 1–2

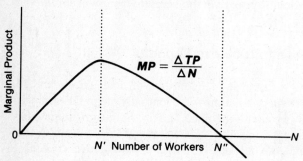

Figure 1–3

$$MP = \frac{\Delta TP}{\Delta N}$$

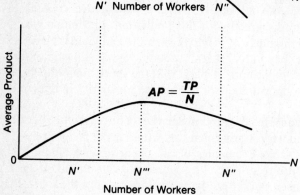

Figure 1–4

$$AP = \frac{TP}{N}$$

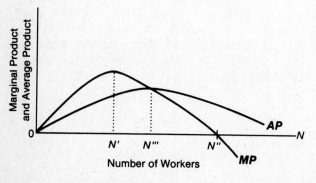

Figure 1–5

income is actually distributed within the community. If real income is distributed unequally, living standards may differ greatly.

The Marginal and Average Product curves are combined in Figure 1–5 to illustrate an important relationship. Note that as the working population increases from zero to N''' in Figure 1–5, the Marginal Product of workers is greater than their Average Product: that is, additional workers contribute more to Total Product than the average of all workers. The result is to pull the Average Product curve up, approaching peak worker productivity at a population of N'''. Over this range of employment, increasing employment means greater Average Product and higher per capita living standards for workers and their families. Beyond N''', additional workers' Marginal Product is below Average Product: that is, additional workers contribute less to Total Product than the average of all workers. This time the result is to pull the Average Product curve down and reduce per capita living standards.* Continuing growth in total employment will continue to worsen material conditions of life.

Increasing Productive Capacity

Figure 1–5 tells us that, with constant quantities of land and capital resources, increases in the working population will eventually mean falling Average Product and falling real per capita income. This is the reason some early economists referred to economics as the "dismal science." It seemed that population growth would condemn the society to ever declining levels of living. Needless to say, Adam Smith disagreed with this prediction. In Smith's view, rising Average Product over the range $N = 0$ to $N = N'''$ would yield the means for overcoming the tendencies beyond N'''. In this section, we will show how new developments in the economic environment might shift the short-run production function upward and create opportunities for continuing prosperity in the next period.

First, rising population would mean a growing market of buyers for the goods and services produced by industry. Larger markets would make possible mass production and economies of scale. **Economies of scale** occur when equipment is designed and factories are built to produce larger quantities of output. Large-scale production often increases worker productivity and prolongs the segment of the production function over which production grows at an increasing rate. Second, rising living standards for workers over the range zero to N''' would yield the personal savings that, through the financial system, make possible the purchase of new capital resources. For business firms, the expectation of profitable sales would provide incentives to increase productive capacity, so that the optimum proportion of workers to other resources would occur at a higher level of total employment.

---

*Students are familiar with the relationship illustrated in Figure 1–5 from computing Grade Point Average. Each quarter's GPA is the "Marginal Grade" that may raise or lower the student's "Average GPA."

These developments are shown in Figures 1–6, 1–7, and 1–8 by shifting the production function upward and extending the rising portions of the Marginal and Average Product curves. Continuing to increase productive capacity would yield continuing upward shifts in the curves so that real per capita income could continue to increase.

The reverse is also true, of course. Productive capital tends to wear out with use and must be replaced. New capital investment must be made regularly just to replace the equipment and buildings that depreciate each year, but replacement investment represents no increase in productive capacity. Failure to replace depreciated capital would change Total, Marginal, and Average Product curves in the opposite way. (Pencil the expected changes on Figures 1–6, 1–7, and 1–8.) The result would be a decline in worker productivity and a fall in real per capita income.

Technical progress and social and political changes can also affect the position and shape of *TP, MP,* and *AP.* New ways to use resources productively, incentives to work more efficiently, and improved organization of existing capacity can shift all the curves upward. On the other hand, repressive social and political regimes can destroy incentives for technological advance and bring on a downward shift in the curves. (Again, note the parallel between freedom and prosperity.)

PERFECT COMPETITION AND EFFICIENCY

The production function determines the maximum quantity of goods and services that can be produced with available resources and technology. Two questions now arise: What specific goods and services will actually be produced? and How can maximum production be ensured? The first question is the subject of *microeconomics* and the second of *macroeconomics.* Adam Smith and his followers in the nineteenth century developed the theory to explain the first and showed how certain conditions would guarantee the second as well.

A critical element of both bodies of theory is the existence of perfect competition. **Perfect competition** requires four market characteristics:

1. There must be many buyers and sellers, no one of which is large enough to affect price by deciding to increase or decrease the quantity bought or sold.
2. Each participant must have perfect information about products and prices available throughout the market, so that buyers can take advantage of the lowest price and sellers the highest.
3. There must be perfect ease of movement throughout the market, as well as to or from the market as a whole, so that participants can respond quickly to changes in conditions for buying and selling.
4. Goods and services traded in a particular market must be homogeneous: that is, they must be so similar that no buyer would pay a premium price for the product of a particular seller.

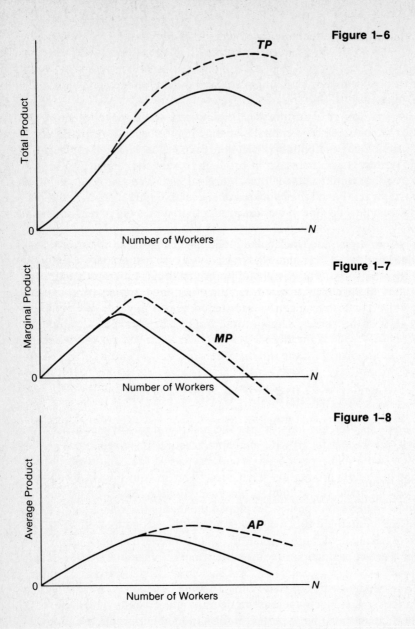

Figure 1-6

Total Product

TP

0

Number of Workers   N

Figure 1-7

Marginal Product

MP

0

Number of Workers   N

Figure 1-8

Average Product

AP

0

Number of Workers   N

Under these four conditions, microeconomic theory shows how competing firms strive to produce the goods and services most desired by consumers at the lowest possible cost. Competitive firms build plants large enough to enjoy economies of scale, and they operate their plants at the optimum rate for highest worker productivity.* They seek new technology for improving their products

---

*The observant reader will notice that a tendency toward large-scale production in some markets might lead to concentrations of market power that might threaten efficiency in production and equity in income distribution.

and improving productive techniques. The result of competition is a total combination of goods and services that comes closest to satisfying the material wants of the community (within the limits of existing resources and technology).

Perfect competition will yield other desirable results in terms of the distribution of total output. Under competition, payments to those who provide resources will reward each according to his or her own contribution to production. Thus, shares of total output will be distributed fairly according to the value of work.* Higher payments for more valuable contributions will provide incentives to improve worker skills, increase the stock of capital equipment, and increase the productivity of land. Moreover, differential payments will ensure that the most valuable resources are used only where they are most needed (and can command the highest payments), and the least valuable resources are used for production of lowest priority.

These were the expected microeconomic results of perfect competition that caused Adam Smith's optimism about markets in a free society. The expected macroeconomic results were equally favorable. Aside from the fact that competitive firms would strive to produce at lowest costs, competition among owners of resources would push resource prices down and encourage the fullest use of all available resources. Thus, production would always tend toward the maximum quantity shown on the production function. In terms of Figure 1–2, production would always be the greatest possible for the current level of employment (N); and real per capita income would be the highest, as shown in Figure 1–4. Without any sort of government control, with only the routine and innovative decisions of self-interested buyers and sellers, a system of free markets could achieve the material basis for the fullest possible development of human potential.

This ideal result is described as *efficient*. **Efficiency** refers to quantity of output relative to quantity of input: output/input. Maximum efficiency occurs when the maximum quantity of output is achieved with minimum cost in terms of productive resources: thus, the ratio output/input has the largest possible value. Because productive resources are scarce and have alternative uses, it is important to achieve efficiency, both in terms of the types of goods and services produced and in terms of their total quantity.

IMPERFECT COMPETITION AND INEFFICIENCY

The promise of the market system has been largely fulfilled in the prosperity of Western nations, and of the United States in particular. There are problems, of course, some of which were also foreseen by Adam Smith. Remember that Smith's optimistic predictions were based on the existence of perfect competition in product and resource markets. Competition is the "stick" that forces all market participants to strive harder for the "carrot" of material gain.

---

*Again, the observant reader will see that rewarding persons according to their ownership of productive resources may result in sharply unequal distribution of incomes, with possible social and political implications. We will consider both these possibilities later in this chapter.

Life would be easier without competition, so it is not surprising when buyers and sellers agree not to compete. Often in real life, business firms find ways to avoid competition: (1) they combine into larger units with power to raise prices by withholding goods and services from the market; (2) they withhold information about products and processes so as to (3) shut rival firms out of the market; and (4) they vary product design so that buyers are encouraged to pay premium prices.*

Occasionally resource owners avoid competition, too, by combining into unions or trade associations for limiting the supply of resources and keeping their prices higher than they would be in competition.

Unless competition is perfect, total production may be less than that shown on the production function. Production becomes inefficient when maximum possible output is not being produced with available resources. Imperfect competition also affects the distribution of goods and services, with disproportionate shares going to those buyers and sellers who have the greatest power to affect markets. Instead of rewards based on contributions to production, holders of market power receive rewards based on arbitrary or chance circumstances. The failure to reward on the basis of performance damages incentives, both among those who receive too little and among those who receive too much. Perhaps more important, it affects the allocation of resources, distorting their use away from their value in production.

Equity and Equality

A reward system based on market power is said to lack **equity**. Equity is not the same as equality. We have seen that a perfectly competitive economic system requires unequal rewards as incentives for greater productivity and to encourage efficient use of the most valuable resources. Equity is *fairness*—fairness in terms of the value system of the particular society. In general, our society believes that unequal rewards on the basis of market performance are *fair,* but unequal rewards on the basis of market power are *unfair.* Thus, the lack of perfect competition may reduce equity as well as efficiency.

Many economists believe it is fair to supplement the incomes of aged and disabled persons who are unable to contribute to production. Income supplements help bring the living standards of such people up to some minimum level generally regarded as equitable. We will have more to say about equity and equality later, particularly in chapter 8 when we examine the distribution of the nation's income.

GOALS OF NATIONAL ECONOMIC POLICY

Perfectly free markets would lead to efficiency in the use of the nation's productive resources. Free markets would also achieve equity in the distribution

---

*Compare these kinds of behavior with the four characteristics of competition described on page 11.

of goods and services—in the sense that distribution according to contributions to production is regarded as fair. The failure of free markets can bring on inefficiencies and inequities that call for remedies decided on by the community as a whole. This is the goal of much of government policy in the economic system: to influence the allocation of productive resources toward maximum efficiency and the distribution of income toward greater equity.*

New laws to preserve competition and improve economic efficiency followed the rise of market power in the latter part of the nineteenth century. Rapid industrial development in the midwestern and northeastern states called for expansion of steel-making and rail-transport facilities. Industrial magnates like Cornelius Vanderbilt and Andrew Carnegie spearheaded the drive to combine small firms into giant corporations with power to control prices and quantity of service. Often the result of market power was price discrimination, reduced service, and even corruption.

In 1887 Congress passed the Interstate Commerce Act regulating prices and routes of all the railroads, and in 1890 it passed the Sherman Antitrust Act forbidding all industrial combinations in restraint of free trade. In 1914 the Clayton Antitrust Act forbade certain kinds of unfair market behavior, and the Celler-Kefauver Amendment in 1954 limited mergers among business firms when the effect would be to reduce competition. The Federal Trade Commission was established in 1914 to receive complaints of unfair business practices and issue "cease and desist orders" against proven offenders. The Antitrust Division of the Department of Justice brings suit against firms found to be in violation of the **antitrust laws**.

Enforcement of the antitrust laws has varied in intensity according to the particular philosophy of the current national administration. An administration's belief that the inefficiencies from market power are outweighed by the advantages of economies of scale in large firms generally means lower funding for the enforcement agencies and a decline in antitrust activity. Still, the antitrust laws remain a deterrent to blatant acts in violation of competition.

New laws designed specifically to improve equity in the distribution of income are associated with the Great Depression of the 1930s. The Depression awakened Congress to the wide differences in market power and in the living standards of different groups of the working population. One law aimed at relieving unfair working conditions was the Fair Labor Standards Act of 1938. The law set wage and hour limits in industry and prohibited child labor. The Social Security Act of 1935 provided tax-financed benefits to retired and disabled workers and to the dependents of deceased workers. Its aim was to promote decent living standards for certain groups unable to provide for their own support.

Since the 1930s the federal and state governments have increased their financial obligations toward dependent groups through expanded public assistance programs. Income-support payments under Social Security, Aid to

---

*To say that our goals are efficiency and equity is not to say that economists are agreed on specific objectives and means toward those objectives. There is much disagreement on the precise definitions of efficiency and equity and on policies to achieve them.

Families with Dependent Children, Supplemental Security Income, Medicare and Medicaid, and unemployment insurance programs now amount to about sixty percent of total government outlays. These programs are described as **entitlement programs** because persons falling within certain classifications set forth in the law are "entitled" to receive benefits

Political pressure from interested groups has brought substantial increases in entitlement programs, and some voters have begun to question their efficiency and equity. Over the next decade, voters and their elected representatives will be asked to consider carefully the proper role of government in promoting efficiency and equity and decide on policies for achieving national goals.

CONFLICTS BETWEEN GOALS: EFFICIENCY AND EQUITY

Economists understand that attaining all the nation's economic goals may not be possible. Deciding on national economic policy requires trade-offs between goals based on priorities. Priorities are the result of the community's value system, which places more or less emphasis on such goals as *efficiency* and *equity*. A conflict arises when the goal of equity, or fairness, is misinterpreted to mean *equality*. A goal of equality may not be compatible with the goal of maximum efficiency.

Equality is not possible under a free market system. A free market system requires unequal rewards as incentives to maximum production and for allocating the community's most valuable resources toward the most productive purposes. Thus, unequal rewards are necessary for efficiency in the production of goods and services. Voters and elected representatives must decide on the appropriate level of equality (and inequality) for satisfying the goal of equity without seriously damaging the goal of efficiency.

Demand Management and Supply-Side Economics

In recent years other problems have arisen with respect to the fullest use of productive resources. Free market economies have experienced recurring periods of **recession**. *Recessions* are months or even years of declining total production, during which large numbers of workers and many factories are idle. Recessions reduce real per capita income and reduce the savings necessary for increasing productive capacity for the future.

Government policy has frequently been used to encourage the maximum use of productive resources. Two approaches have been attempted: **demand management** and **supply-side economics**.

Demand management is the guidance of consumer, business, and government purchases toward a level of total spending that requires the fullest use of the nation's productive resources. The expectation is that a high and rising level of total spending will encourage business firms to build additional factories and hire all available workers for increasing production. Demand-management policy involves changes in the level of taxes and government spending. It was the basis for much of the federal government's economic policies during the 1960s and promoted growth and rising real incomes for many U.S. citizens. However, during the 1970s fast growth in total spending, together with rising costs of food and fuel, led to rising price inflation. Policymakers looked for new kinds of economic policies to increase Total Product without causing inflation.

The 1980s began with a commitment to supply-side economics in government policies. *Supply-side economics* calls for a variety of incentives for business firms to increase total production. Some examples are reduced taxes on business profits, tax credits for business purchases of new capital resources, low-interest loans for growing firms, and government-sponsored research and development. In order that personal savings will increase to finance the purchase of new capital resources, some supply-side economists also recommend lower personal taxes and lower tax rates on interest income. The expectation is that increased saving and new capital equipment will provide the basis for increasing jobs and total production. Supply-side economics provided the basis for President Reagan's tax cuts in 1981 and 1982.

Positive and Negative Externalities

The economic model in this chapter illustrates the relationship between number of workers and total production. We have said that a model is a simplified view of reality that omits some of the complexities of the real world. One real-world complexity omitted from the production function in this chapter involves externalities.

Externalities are certain external effects of production that are not counted among the quantities of goods and services actually produced in business firms. Some of the external effects of production are favorable, in which case they are referred to as *positive externalities* or *external benefits*. Some of the external benefits from production are advances in culture, improved standards of nutrition and health, more leisure for creative expression, and a more healthy environment for personal growth. Unfavorable effects of production are *negative externalities* or *external costs*. Some of the external costs of production are all the various forms of pollution and environmental decay, worsened tensions in human relations, and perhaps a decline in appreciation of simple pleasures.

Omitting positive and negative externalities from the production function may distort the relationship between output and input. Figures 1–9, 1–10, and 1–11 include the possible occurrence of externalities. A net excess of external benefits over costs would shift *TP, MP,* and *AP* upward. A net excess of external costs over benefits would shift *TP, MP,* and *AP* downward.

The existence of externalities makes it impossible to draw a production function precisely. To locate with certainty the position of *TP, MP,* and *AP* would require precise measurement of all externalities, a truly impossible task. Externalities also make it difficult to achieve efficiency and equity. Unless externalities can be measured, we cannot be sure that the ratio of output to input has the largest possible value. Thus, changing output/input to: output plus external benefits/input plus external costs may reduce the value of the ratio below its maximum value. In this case, achieving efficient production would call for a shift

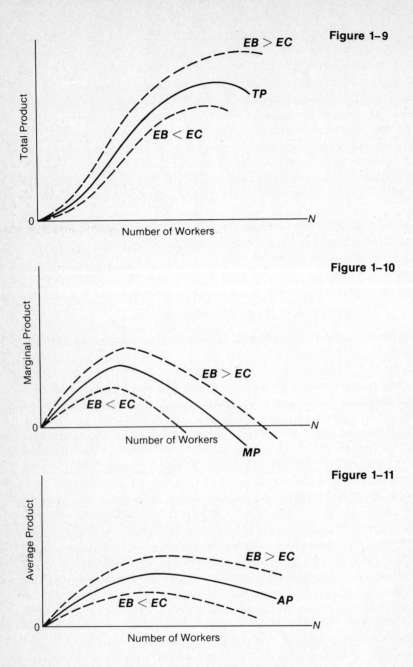

Figure 1–9

Figure 1–10

Figure 1–11

of resources away from production that yields external costs and into production that yields external benefits. Equity may be damaged also, if external benefits are enjoyed by some consumer groups and external costs are suffered by others.

It has been only fairly recently that voters and elected representatives have

Table 1-1 National Income and Capital Expenditures

	(1)	(2)	(3)	(4)	(5)	(6)
	Total Product*	Civilian Labor Force	Average Product (1)/(2)	Total Capital Expenditures*	Replacement Capital*	Net Additions to Capital Stock*
1940	$ 344.1	55,640	$ 6,184.40	44.5	16.86	27.64
1950	534.8	62,208	8,596.97	93.5	23.53	69.97
1960	737.2	69,628	10,587.69	104.7	39.01	65.69
1970	1,085.6	82,715	13,124.58	158.5	57.08	101.42
1980	1,480.7	104,719	14,139.75	204.0	93.45	110.55

*In billions of dollars, corrected for inflation, with 1972 as the base year. Correcting for inflation requires the use of a price index. Dividing current prices by a price index removes the inflation that has occurred since the year on which the price index is based. The appropriate price index for December 1980 was 177.4 (when 1972 is the base year). This means that an item that sold for $1.00 in 1972 cost on the average 1.77^{4/10}$ in December 1980. Or, stated differently, a consumer good that cost $1.00 in 1981 was worth $1.00/1.774=$0.56$^{4/10}$ in constant dollars of the base year.
Source: Economic Report of the President, February, 1982.

become concerned about externalities. During the 1970s, new government policies were established for dealing with externalities, but the results have not been very successful. One reason has been the problem of measurement discussed above; another is determining the proper incentives for encouraging production of external benefits and discouraging production of external costs. Since both are external to normal market processes, it has been difficult to agree on the kinds of policies that will promote efficient and equitable results.

PRODUCTIVITY GROWTH IN THE UNITED STATES

Figures 1-6, 1-7, and 1-8 showed how new capital equipment can increase worker productivity and raise real per capita income between one short-run period and the next. This kind of result has occurred in the United States. Look at Table 1–1. Column 1 gives the value of total production in the United States for selected years, measured in terms of **constant dollars:** that is, prices are adjusted for the effects of inflation. Column 2 gives the civilian labor force for the year. Average Product is Total Product divided by number of workers, as shown in column 3.

Increases in Average Product over the years shown indicate rising incomes for American workers. Since the values are stated in constant dollars, they represent real gains in terms of improved average living standards. A principal reason for the improvement is shown in columns 4, 5, and 6. Column 4 lists the value of new capital resources in the form of factories and equipment, inventories, and homes. Column 5 gives estimates of replacement capital required each year. The difference (column 4 minus column 5), shown in column 6, is the net increase in productive capacity for each year shown.

With only one exception, the data show increased productive capacity for the years in the table. The exception was probably the result of vigorous economic activity during the Korean War (1950) and slower economic growth in 1940 and 1960. A table including every year between 1940 and 1980 would reveal many more exceptions to continued growth in capital resources. However, the basic premise—that new capital resources increase the capacity for greater production and higher incomes — remains valid.

Special Case

Production Functions in the Third World

What can a nation do when its people begin to outgrow its land? How can a government ensure prosperity when there's not enough capital equipment for all the citizens who want to work? What happens when earnings from products sold abroad won't buy the things the people must have?

These are life-threatening questions for many of the world's people. Deciding policy is serious business when babies are starving and adults live their lives in hopeless drudgery.

To many analysts, the industrialized nations of the West and those of the Soviet bloc constitute the First and Second Worlds. Poor and underdeveloped nations constitute the Third World, so insignificant in the quantity of goods and services produced that they command scant attention from the rest. Third World nations are located chiefly in Latin America, Africa, and South Asia in areas where resources are poor or inaccessible to world markets.

As population of Third World countries grew over the centuries, production moved along the curve representing Total Product until Average Product began to fall. Some Third World countries may have even reached the range of declining Total Product. (Refer back to Figure 1–2 and locate the range of diminishing Total Product.)

Under such conditions, perhaps the only hope for poor countries is to increase capital resources—new tools and equipment—to shift the production function upward, raise the productivity of workers, and allow more workers to be employed. Then, greater productive capacity could provide the means for higher living standards with, ultimately, an increase in personal saving and still greater production of capital resources. Too poor to pay for new capital resources, many poor nations have turned to the First and Second Worlds for grants, loans, and advice. The last is probably hardest to give.

Two kinds of policies have been recommended for shifting upward a poor nation's production function; neither has enjoyed complete success. One approach has been to encourage the growth of a free market system. Governments have been advised to break up large plantations and return small plots of land to the peasants. Small landholders working their own land, it is said, would develop the incentives for more efficient production. Small farmers would gradually accumulate profits for purchasing tools and equipment. Government should help by providing low-interest loans to new business firms and other subsidies to encourage productivity growth. Then economic growth could proceed much as it did in the United States for the last two hundred years. El Salvador, Costa Rica, Uruguay, and (to a degree) Iran were encouraged to follow these policies.

Another approach was to aid the development of large-scale manufacturing by importing modern equipment and skilled technicians from developed countries and employing large domestic supplies of landless peasant workers. Under this plan, wide extremes of wealth and poverty would be allowed to continue, since only large concentrations of wealth would permit the high levels of saving necessary for financing industrial development. Taiwan, Chile, and (to a degree) Iran were helped to follow these policies.

Neither approach has produced prosperity. In the first approach, the extreme scarcity of capital resources has made development slow and painful. Governments have been pressured to increase their subsidies to farms and business firms at a time when scarce funds are sorely needed for purchasing new capital. Popular discontent has led to subversion and even revolution. In the second approach, large-scale manufacturing has frequently not created the expected large numbers of jobs. Moreover, in some nations, extreme income inequality has produced social instability and a movement of savings out of the country. In both cases, failures have led to the overthrow of governments and replacement by dictatorial rulers. Some nations have sought new approaches, priorities, and emphases in development plans. (The Western experience is not necessarily an appropriate guide for all poor nations.)

● How can the significant points in this special case be illustrated by our model of the production function? Contrast the experience of today's Third World nations with the past history of the United States and account for the difference. Include consideration of economic, cultural, and political characteristics.

● Consult recent issues of *The Wall Street Journal* and *Business Week* for articles describing economic development programs in Third World nations. Evaluate their major objectives.

Mathematical Supplement

Writing a Production Function

We have expressed the relationship between number of workers and Total Product in the form of an algebraic expression called a *production function*. Some examples of production functions are shown below, where *TP* represents Total Product and *N* represents Number of workers:

$$TP = f(N) = a + bN \qquad \text{(a linear production function)}$$
$$TP = f(N) = a + bN - cN^2 \qquad \text{(a quadratic production function)}$$
$$TP = f(N) = a + bN + cN^2 - dN^3 \quad \text{(a cubic production function)}$$
$$TP = f(N) = a + bN^g \qquad \text{(a power production function)}$$

Substituting the values of the unknowns in the appropriate production function yields an equation that can be used to estimate the value of the dependent variable *(TP)*.

The *a* term in each of the production functions above is called a *constant,* since its value does not change regardless of the number of workers (*N*) used in the equation. (In many production functions the value of a is zero, indicating zero production if the value of N is zero.) The *coefficients* b, c, and d measure the relationship between N and TP. They show the effect on TP of the use of various quantities of N, and their signs indicate a positive (+) or negative (−) effect. When a is zero, the *exponent* g in the last production function indicates an exponential relationship between N and TP. It shows the percentage change in TP associated with a percent change in N and may be greater than or less than one. An exponent greater than one indicates an increasing rate of growth in total production as N grows, and an exponent less than one indicates the reverse.

Taken together, the constant a, the coefficients b, c, and d, and the exponent g are the *parameters* of the equation. When estimating TP, the parameters of the equation are assumed to remain the same while the independent variable N takes on different values.

Most economists use the third production function above to describe production relationships:

$$TP = f(N) = a + bN + cN^2 - dN^3 \quad \text{(a cubic production function)}$$

Graphing a cubic production function yields a curve like the one in Figure 1–12. The horizontal axis in Figure 1–12 measures number of workers (N), and the vertical axis measures Total Product (TP) in physical units. Movement along the horizontal axis signifies the use of more workers and yields the observed quantity of Total Product.

In this mathematical supplement we will consider a production function in detail and show how it relates to current economic conditions. We will begin by substituting reasonable values for the parameters in the production function above. Thus, with $a = 0$, $b = 72$, $c = 6$, and $d = 0.5$:

$$TP = 0 + 72N + 6N^2 - 0.5N^3$$

This is the equation for the curve drawn on Figure 1–12. The Total Product curve increases at an increasing rate for values of N between $N = 0$ and $N = 4$, at a decreasing rate over the range $N = 4$ to $N = 12$, and at a negative rate beyond $N = 12$. Maximum total production at $N = 12$ is $TP = 72(12) + 6(12)^2 + 0.5(12)^3 = 864$ units of goods and services.

Marginal Product is shown in Figure 1–13. Marginal Product measures the change in Total Product associated with a change in number of workers and can be determined by calculating Total Product for successive levels of N and subtracting. An equation for Marginal Product can also be determined through the use of calculus.* Marginal Product reaches a peak when $N = 4$ and becomes negative when $N = 12$. Maximum Marginal Product at $N = 4$ is $MP = 72 + 12(4) - 1.5(4)^2 = 96$ units of goods and services.

Over the range $N = 0$ to $N = 4$, Marginal Product increases as the number of workers approaches the technically optimum proportion of workers to the constant quantity of land and capital. Beyond $N = 4$, increasing the number of workers worsens the proportion of labor to land and capital resources, so that Marginal Product declines.

Average Product is shown in Figure 1–14. The equation for Average Product is determined by dividing Total Product by number of workers:

$$AP = TP/N = \frac{72N + 6N^2 - 0.5N^3}{N} = 72 + 6N - 0.5N^2$$

---

*It is the first derivative of the Total Product function and is written $MP = \Delta TP/\Delta N = f'(TP) = 72 + 12N - 1.5N^2$.

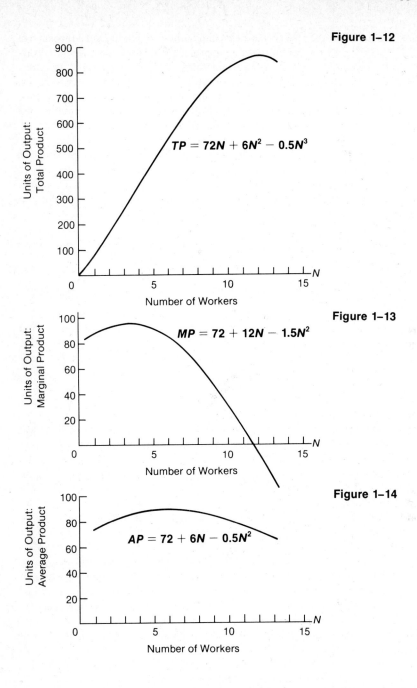

Figure 1–12

$$TP = 72N + 6N^2 - 0.5N^3$$

Figure 1–13

$$MP = 72 + 12N - 1.5N^2$$

Figure 1–14

$$AP = 72 + 6N - 0.5N^2$$

Average Product reaches a peak where $N = 6$ and $AP = 72 + 6(6) - 0.5(6)^2 = 90$ units of goods and services. Beyond $N = 6$ Marginal Product is below Average Product and pulls the Average Product curve down. This is the range over which the disproportionate number of workers relative to other resources reduces worker productivity and per capita living standards.

Let us suppose the labor force is actually $N = 5$. With $N = 5$, Average Product is AP $= 72 + 6(5) - 0.5(5)^2 = 89.5$ units of goods and services. Let us suppose also that the quantity of goods and services necessary to sustain life in the short run is only 85 units per worker. Rather than produce consumer goods and services beyond those necessary for life, suppose that some members of the community decide to produce new capital goods for increasing future productive capacity. The result of more capital equipment is to change the production function so that for the next period Total Product is determined by a new equation:

$$TP = 81N + 10.8N^2 - 0.6N^3.$$

Use graph paper to illustrate the new production function. Students who are familiar with calculus know that the first derivative of a cubic function is determined by $f'(TP) = b + 2cN - 3dN^2$ and should be able to calculate the equation for Marginal Product.* Those students should graph Marginal Product and point out the change in the optimum number of workers that results from the additional capital equipment. All students should be able to write an equation for Average Product and graph the Average Product curve.

- What does this exercise tell you about changes in worker productivity and living standards between one short-run period and the next?
- Would Adam Smith have agreed with the possibilities illustrated here?
- What circumstances might occur to interfere with the results we have shown?

QUESTIONS

1. "Democracy requires abundance." Discuss.
2. Now discuss "Abundance requires democracy."
3. The three levels of economic studies are: *describing* the problem, *analyzing* its causes, and *prescribing* corrective policies. Illustrate the three levels with respect to the problem of poverty in the United States.
4. Show how each of the following economic issues has both microeconomic and macroeconomic aspects: housing, public health, corporate taxes, military spending, vocational training.
5. Discuss the differences and similarities in the content of Adam Smith's two major works.
6. Explain three characteristics of the production function shown in Figure 1–2. How are Marginal Product and Average Product related to the Total Product function?
7. Discuss the characteristics of a perfectly free market economic system that would ensure that production reaches the value shown on the production function. What characteristics of a real-world economic system may hold actual production beneath that value?
8. Distinguish between equity and equality. Why is equality inconsistent with efficiency?
9. List the important pieces of national legislation mentioned in this chapter and explain how each is designed to improve efficiency and/or equity for the economy as a whole.
10. What specific government actions constitute the demand management and supply-side economic approaches to economic policy?

*With $MP = f'(TP)$, Marginal Product is $MP = 81 + 21.6N - 1.8N^2$.

DEFINITIONS

Antitrust laws are laws restricting business combinations that would tend to reduce competition and increase market power.

Average Product is Total Product divided by number of workers: $AP = TP/Q_L$. Average Product is a measure of worker productivity and a measure of the average quantity of goods and services available for distribution to workers and their families.

Capital is produced means of production, including buildings, equipment, tools, and inventories.

Constant dollars are dollars adjusted for the effect of inflation. To change a measure of current dollars into constant dollars requires division by a price index.

Demand-management policies involve guidance of purchases toward a level of total spending that fully employs the nation's productive resources.

An economic model is a system of algebraic equations that describes how elements of the economic system interact to yield economic effects.

Economic variables are the physical and financial elements that interact to yield economic results. Some examples of economic variables are number of workers, supply of money, and quantity of capital resources.

Economies of scale are the cost advantages that arise from producing in large volume. When goods and services are produced in large volume, equipment can be designed to use less labor, so that the Average Product of workers is greater and costs are lower.

Efficiency is maximum output per unit of input: output/input. When the ratio has the highest possible value, we say production is efficient.

Entitlement programs are government programs to distribute tax revenues to groups unable to maintain a decent standard of living without government assistance. Persons within designated groups are "entitled" to receive certain government benefits.

Entrepreneurship includes the organizational and managerial system for organizing other resources into a productive enterprise. An entrepreneur assumes the risks and makes the decisions that cause production to take place.

Equity means fairness. Equity is not necessarily equality. In general, Americans believe that inequality as a result of differences in contributions to production is fair, but inequality as a result of market power is unfair. Much of government policy is designed to improve equity in our economic system. Some of government policy is designed to promote greater equality of income distribution, particularly among groups who are unable to contribute enough to production to maintain a decent standard of living.

Externalities are the external effects of production that are not included in the measured quantity of new goods and services. Positive externalities are external benefits, and negative externalities are external costs.

A function is an algebraic expression of the relationship between economic variables.

Macroeconomics is the study of the economic system as a whole. Macroeconomic issues are those that affect the entire economic system.

Marginal Product is the change in Total Product that results from adding one unit of labor to some quantity of fixed resources: $MP = \Delta TP/\Delta Q_L$. As the number of workers increases from zero to the optimum proportion relative to other resources, Marginal Product tends to increase. If the number of workers becomes excessive relative to the constant quantity of other resources, Marginal Product may become negative.

The market system is a system whereby producing and consuming decisions are carried out in free markets. Adam Smith described the market system in his book *The Wealth of Nations*.

Microeconomics is the study of economic behavior relating to individual households and business firms. Microeconomic issues are those that affect individual economic units.

The optimum proportion of labor to other resources may be defined as the quantity of labor at which the last unit of labor added contributes the greatest amount to total production.

Perfect competition exists when there are many small buyers and sellers, each with perfect market information and ease of movement throughout the market, and all selling identical products.

A production function shows the relationship between productive resources and total production of goods and services.

Productive resources are the means of producing goods and services. They include land, labor, capital, and entrepreneurship.

Real income is the total quantity of goods and services produced during a period of time. Real income is the same as Total Product, written as *TP* in the production function.

Real per capita income is the average quantity of real goods and services relative to total population. Thus, real per capita income is a measure of average living standards.

A recession is a period of declining total production.

The short run is a period of time in which certain productive resources are in relatively constant supply. During the short run, other resources whose quantities are variable can be combined with available fixed resources for increasing total production.

Supply-side economics involves policies to increase the nation's capacity to produce goods and services.

SUGGESTED READINGS

Alexander, Tom. "The Right Remedy for R&D Lag." *Fortune,* January 25, 1982, p. 60.
Collins, Lora S. "The Odds on Better Times in the 1980s." *Across the Board,* January, 1983, p. 28.
Denison, Edward F. "The Puzzling Setback to Productivity Growth." *Challenge,* November/December, 1980, p. 3.
Feldstein, Martin, ed. *The American Economy in Transition.* Chicago: National Bureau of Economic Research, 1980, Chapter 8.
Galbraith, John Kenneth. *The Age of Uncertainty.* Boston: Houghton Mifflin Co., 1977.
Heilbroner, Robert L. "The Future of Capitalism." *Challenge,* November/December, 1982, p. 32.
"How to Get the Economy Growing Again: The Search for a New Policy." *Business Week,* November 8, 1982, p. 108.
"Industry Outlooks: 1983." *Business Week,* January 17, 1983, p. 57.
Johnson, Paul. "Has Capitalism a Future?" *Across the Board,* February, 1980, p. 27.
Lekachman, Robert. *A History of Economic Ideas.* New York: McGraw Hill, 1976.
"Survival in the Basic Industries." *Business Week,* April 26, 1982, p. 74.
"Technologies for the '80s." *Business Week,* July 6, 1981, p. 48.
Thurow, Lester C. *The Zero-Sum Society.* New York: Basic Books, 1980, Chapter 1.

CHAPTER TWO

Building Capital Stock Through Saving and Investment

Bread Today or Cake Tomorrow?

LEARNING OBJECTIVES

- To understand why savers are willing to sacrifice current consumption and why investors are led to purchase capital resources.
- To use a model of financial markets to illustrate lending and borrowing for new capital investment.
- To see the relationship between the level of saving and investment, on the one hand, and incomes and productive capacity, on the other.
- To note the effect of inflation, government policies, and uncertain consumer demand on the willingness to save and invest.
- To look at the recent behavior of saving and investment in the United States and the implications for the nation's productivity.
- To examine current proposals for policies to encourage saving and investment as well as prospects for the future.

If squirrels could think beyond the coming winter, they might do more than store acorns in hidden crevices. They might plant oaks (or even peanuts) in sunny climes to ensure future consumption in greater comfort. Of course, squirrels don't think at all and only instinctively do what human beings must

27

make a conscious effort to do. Fortunately for most squirrels, nature has decreed that oak trees produce enough acorns to sustain life over the summer and provide a surplus for the bleak days of winter.

The human population is not always so fortunate, in that our more advanced consumption needs cannot always be satisfied in the present, much less provided for in the future. Communities poor in productive resources may exist on the brink of starvation, so that saving for the sake of the future is simply not possible.

Primitive human societies probably endured millions of years at the edge of extinction until some lucky circumstance happened along to yield a small surplus of food over the community's current needs. Setting aside the surplus food for future consumption released some of the labor force from hand-to-mouth production and permitted the production of primitive tools. "Cutters," "scrapers," and primitive "plows" made from chipped stone were the first forms of capital investment. Capital equipment increased the productivity of labor and released still more workers for making tools. Today we set aside a part of a month's salary to buy new shares of stock so that General Motors can purchase robots to build automobiles.* The possibilities forthcoming in the *next* million years boggle the mind!

This chapter will examine the process of saving and investing. *Saving* is the sacrifice of current consumption, and *investing* is the purchase of new capital resources. Saving and investing are important for shifting a nation's production function upward, increasing real income, and raising average living standards for the people.

THE TIME VALUE OF MONEY

Why do we save? Why do we build tools for future production?

Saving requires the sacrifice of current consumption, a rational act only if, through saving, we expect to be able to consume more in the future. A feeling of uncertainty about the future encourages the attitude expressed in the old saying: "Eat, drink, and be merry, for tomorrow we may die!" Moreover, the expected future reward for current sacrifice must be great enough to overcome a natural preference to live for today alone. The shorter the period of certainty about the future, the stronger is the **time preference** and the greater is the necessary reward for saving. We experience time preference when we calculate the **time value of money.**

The concept of time preference is easily explained through the use of a little algebra. Let:

---

*Some of us invest less directly than this. We deposit our savings in financial institutions like commercial banks, savings and loan associations, mutual funds, credit unions, and insurance companies. Financial institutions pool the small savings of large numbers of people and lend the funds to business firms for purchasing capital equipment.

C signify a value in the current period,
F a value in the future, and
r the rate of time preference for current consumption and the rate of reward
   for saving.

A person with time preference r will sacrifice C today only if promised F in the future. The future reward (F) must be at least $(1 + r)$ times the current sacrifice (C). Or stated algebraically:

$$F = C(1 + r), \text{ or } F > C(1 + r),$$

where the symbol $>$ means "greater than."

The equation $F = C(1 + r)$ says that the values F and $C(1 + r)$ are equivalent in this person's preference system.

When we lend money, we are sacrificing C today in order to receive F in, say, a year's time. We will agree to make the sacrifice only if F is at least $C(1 + r)$, where r represents our time preference. Thus, a $500 loan for a year when time preference is $r = 10\%$ would require future compensation according to

$$F = C(1 + r)$$

so that

$$F = \$500 \, (1.10) = \$550.$$

The future reward for lending $500 must be at least $550, for an individual with time preference $r = 0.10$.

Compounding and Discounting

You will have noticed that time preference determines the interest rate at which loans will be made. In fact, the interest payment is the reward that is necessary to compensate a lender for sacrificing a normal preference for current consumption. If consumption is to be postponed for longer periods of time, the reward must be still greater. A sacrifice extending over two years, for example, must be rewarded according to

$$F = C(1 + r)(1 + r) \text{ or } F = C(1 + r)^2.$$

Multiplying $C(1 + r)$ by $(1 + r)$ is an example of *compound interest*. **Compounding interest** payments ensures that the second year's sacrifice yields additional reward according to the lender's time preference. Likewise, loans of five years require future compensation of $F = C(1 + r)^5$, loans of six months require compensation of $F = C(1 + r)^{1/2}$, and so forth.

Modern handheld calculators can perform the above mathematics quickly, and financial tables are also available for values of $(1 + r)$ and various exponents, so that today's savers are spared the tedious calculations necessary in the past.

The simple relationship above can be rearranged to provide even more valuable information. Changing $F = C(1 + r)^t$ to $C = F/(1 + r)^t$ tells us the maximum current sacrifice (C) that will be made if a certain amount (F) is promised in the future.* A bond that promises to pay \$500 after one year, for instance, would be worth no more today than

$$C = F/(1 + r)^t \text{ or } C = 500/(1.10)^1 = \$454.54$$

to a saver with time preference $r = 10\%$. Similarly, a bond that promises a "coupon" payment of \$10 after one year and \$500 after the second year would be worth no more than

$$C = 10/(1.10)^1 + 500/(1.10)^2 = \$9.09 + \$413.22 = \$422.31.$$

The longer period of sacrifice would reduce the current value of the promised \$500, and the bond itself would be worth less.

Reducing the value of an expected future payment is called **discounting**.† The discount rate r depends on the time preference of savers, and the exponent is the number of future periods over which the sacrifice is prolonged. Thus, multiplying an expected future receipt by $1/(1 + r)^t$ yields the maximum current sacrifice that will be made to receive it. Again, calculators perform the mathematics, and tables provide the values of $1/(1 + r)^t$ using various levels of r and t.

For example, with $r = 10\%$ and $t = 1$, tables provide the value $1/(1 + r)^t = 1/(1.10)^1 = 0.909$. Multiplying the \$10 "coupon" payment promised in the example above by $1/(1 + r)^1 = 0.909$ yields

$$\$10/(1.10)^1 = \$10(.909) = \$9.09.$$

With $r = 10\%$ and $t = 2$ the value of $1/(1.10)^2 = 0.8264$ so that

$$\$500/(1.10)^2 = \$500(0.8264) = \$413.22.$$

The value in parentheses is called a **discount factor.** It is the factor by which an expected future payment must be multiplied to yield the equivalent current sacrifice. Note that the discount factor is the reciprocal of the factor we used earlier to multiply a current loan and determine future compensation. The factor $(1 + r)^t$ is a **compound factor** by which interest payments are compounded over a certain period of time in the future.

The effects of compounding and discounting are shown in Figures 2–1 through 2–4. Figure 2–1 shows how a current loan of $C = \$1$ requires a larger future reward (F) the farther in the future payment is to be received. Figure 2–2 shows how the current value (C) of an expected future payment of $F = \$1$

---

*Where the exponent t expresses units of time over which the rate r applies.

†Discounting is the reverse of compounding. In the first example given, a saver with time preference $r = 0.10$ will pay no more than \$454.54 for the promise of \$500 after one year.

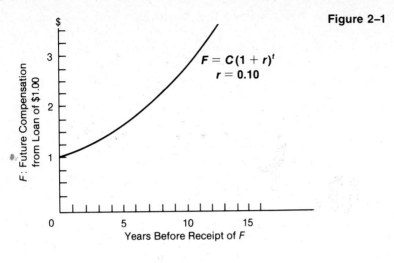

Figure 2–1

$$F = C(1 + r)^t$$
$$r = 0.10$$

F: Future Compensation from Loan of $1.00

Years Before Receipt of F

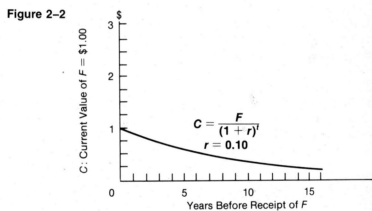

Figure 2–2

C: Current Value of F = $1.00

$$C = \frac{F}{(1 + r)^t}$$
$$r = 0.10$$

Years Before Receipt of F

diminishes with the time delay before receiving it. Both figures assume a time preference of $r = 10\%$. A greater preference for current consumption would require a greater reward for the sacrifice. With $r = 15\%$, for example, a $1 loan requires greater future compensation, as shown in Figure 2–3. Likewise, a stronger time preference diminishes the current value of a future receipt more sharply, as shown in Figure 2–4. Study Figures 2–1 through 2–4 carefully until you are certain you understand the relationship between C and F at various levels of r and t.

Return on Investment

The relationship between current sacrifice (C) and future reward (F) can be used also to determine the profitability of investment expenditures. Capital resources are purchased in the current period for the earnings they are expected to yield in the future. Investors compare the *current price* (C) of a particular capital resource with expected *future cash flows* (F) to determine whether the

Figure 2–3

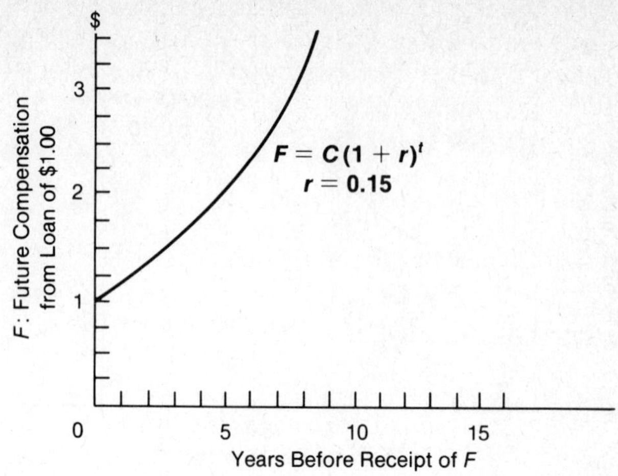

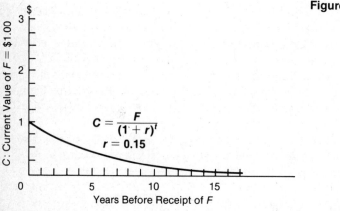

$F = C(1 + r)^t$
$r = 0.15$

F: Future Compensation from Loan of $1.00

Years Before Receipt of F

Figure 2–4

C: Current Value of F = $1.00

$$C = \frac{F}{(1 + r)^t}$$
$r = 0.15$

Years Before Receipt of F

purchase should be made. **Cash flow** is the net revenue from operating a capital resource after out-of-pocket expenses and taxes have been subtracted from total revenues. To illustrate, suppose operating a warehouse at dockside produces revenues for five years as follows:

Year 1	Year 2	Year 3	Year 4	Year 5
$180,000	$195,000	$200,000	$205,000	$200,000

Out-of-pocket expenses for utilities, maintenance, personnel, and taxes total $50,000 a year. Cash flows for each of the five years are the difference between revenues and expenses:

Year 1	Year 2	Year 3	Year 4	Year 5
$F_1 = \$130,000$	$F_2 = \$145,000$	$F_3 = \$150,000$	$F_4 = \$155,000$	$F_5 = \$150,000$

The current price of the warehouse is $C = \$700,000$, and it can be sold after five years for $200,000. An investor must decide whether future cash flows are high enough to justify the current price. Essentially, the problem is to solve the following equation for the value of r:

$$C = \Sigma \frac{F}{(1 + r)^t}$$

where Σ indicates the sum of all expected future payments. Thus,

$$700,000 = \frac{130,000}{(1 + r)^1} + \frac{145,000}{(1 + r)^2} + \frac{150,000}{(1 + r)^3} + \frac{155,000}{(1 + r)^4} + \frac{150,000 + 200,000}{(1 + r)^5}$$

Solving the equation for r yields the relationship between current sacrifice and future reward. It is the **rate of return** on investment in the warehouse. In the equation above the rate of return is $r = 9\%$. Its value was determined by trial and error, substituting alternative values of r until $\Sigma F/(1 + r)^t$ does indeed equal C. (Solving equations such as this for a value like r is done routinely by a computer.)

Most business firms have a variety of investment proposals that might be undertaken at any time. In addition to the warehouse, investments in office equipment, vehicles, and even patents might be under consideration. Each investment proposal would require an initial payment, with estimated cash flows expected over some future period. Solving the rate of return equation for each investment proposal determines its expected rate of return and provides information for making the investment decision.

The rate of return on investment proposals is called the **marginal efficiency of investment** (*MEI*). Taken together, the marginal efficiency of investment for all a firm's investment proposals constitutes a schedule like the one in Table 2–1. In a marginal efficiency of investment schedule, investments are arranged in descending order according to rate of return. Then, a firm chooses investments on the basis of the rate of return on the investment proposal and the cost of funds needed to acquire it. (A *MEI* curve for the economy as a whole can be derived by adding the investment schedules of all firms. This yields a step function that can be approximated by a smooth curve. We will have more to say about the *MEI* curve for the economy later.)

Table 2–1 A Firm's Marginal Efficiency of Investment Schedule

Investment Proposal	Rate of Return
Office machine	13.0%
Patent	10.5%
Warehouse	9.0%
Truck	7.3%

THE MARKET FOR INVESTMENT CAPITAL

Supply and Demand

The fundamental relationship $C = \Sigma\, F/(1 + r)^t$ is essentially a statement describing lending and borrowing for investment. It represents lending, since savers will lend C only if promised F in the future. And it represents borrowing for new capital investment, since investors will purchase a capital resource for C only if they expect to earn F by operating the resource.

Lending and borrowing for investment takes place in **financial markets.** A model of financial markets is shown in Figure 2–5. The horizontal axis in Figure 2–5 represents the quantity of savings available for use by investors. The vertical axis represents r; r is both the rate of return paid to savers for sacrificing current consumption and the expected rate of return on investors' purchases of new capital resources. The curves on the figure represent the supply of savings and the demand for investment funds.

The *supply of savings* is the upward sloping curve marked S. It represents the sum of all savings made available in the market by individuals, business firms, and governments. It is the quantities these groups are willing to sacrifice from their own current spending in return for various rates of return. The supply of savings curve slopes upward because higher values of r would normally persuade more savers to make their funds available for investment.*

The *demand for investment funds* is the downward sloping curve marked D. It represents the sum of all quantities that would be borrowed for investment by individuals, business firms, and governments: that is, the sum of all marginal efficiency of investment schedules. Quantities are expressed in relation to rates of return for each investment proposal. Investors will borrow only the quantity of funds for which the rate of return on the investment is at least as great as the necessary payment to savers. The demand curve for investment funds slopes downward so as to ensure that the more preferred investments (those with greater expected rates of return) are purchased before less preferred investments.

The intersection of supply with demand determines **equilibrium** in the market for financial capital. Equilibrium identifies the quantity of investment funds (I) which, when invested according to business firms' marginal efficiency of investment (r), yields an acceptable reward to savers for the use of their funds. Look at the demand curve in Figure 2–5. To the left of equilibrium at I, investment proposals are expected to earn a return greater than the cost of borrowing and therefore will be undertaken. Investment proposals to the right of I are expected to yield less than the cost of borrowing and therefore will not be

---

*The actual relationship between the quantity of new savings and the rate of return on savings may not be as shown here. Other factors influence saving, so that over any period of time the quantity saved may be unresponsive to interest rates. Thus, the supply of savings curve might be a vertical line drawn at that particular quantity. This possibility has been ignored here for the sake of simplicity.

Figure 2–5

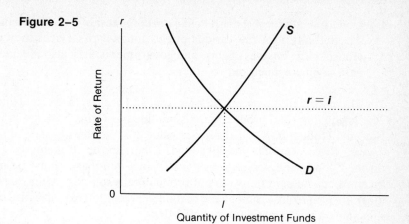

Quantity of Investment Funds

undertaken. At I, the last investment proposal undertaken is expected to yield an amount just equal to the cost of borrowing.

At the equilibrium level of borrowing and lending, the interest paid to lenders is equal to the expected rate of return on investment projects. The equality between the marginal efficiency of investment and the necessary reward to savers defines the market rate of interest: i. Look at the supply curve. The supply curve tells us that savers whose time preference is less than the market rate of interest lend freely in the market so that investments up to the equilibrium quantity are undertaken. Savers with time preference greater than the market rate of interest do not lend, so that investment proposals beyond I are not undertaken. Finally, the equilibrium quantity of investment funds (I) determines the increase in capital resources for the current period and the potential for increased production of goods and services in the future.

Deciding to Save and Invest

Unlike squirrels, human beings must make a conscious decision to save. The decision to save is a complicated one, including many aspects of the saver's personal and productive life. Probably the most significant factor in the decision is the saver's income. Income must be at least high enough to satisfy a person's immediate needs before saving becomes an option at all.

Income is a measure of a person's or group's contribution to production and sets a limit on what that person or group can draw out of production for its own use. Income is related to the kinds of resources provided in production. Income can be classified five ways:

1. Most households receive income in the form of *wages and salaries* for the use of their labor in production.
2. Business firms receive *rental income* for the use of their properties, and
3. *profit* for their ability to organize resources in a productive way.

4. Governments receive *tax revenues* to compensate (indirectly and unequally, but eternally!) for the various public goods and services they provide.
5. Households, business firms, and governments may also receive *interest* on past savings loaned out to others.

The sum of all wages and salaries, rent and profits, taxes* and interest for the year is equal to total production, also defined as **Gross National Product.** Gross National Product (GNP) is the dollar value of all goods and services produced in a year. Gross National Product is also the sum of all amounts spent for the finished goods and services produced, since purchases must be made before incomes can be paid to owners of productive resources. After sales and excise taxes are paid to government and certain depreciation expenses are set aside, the remaining value is national income (*NI*):

> Gross National Product
> less   Indirect Business Taxes
> less   *Depreciation Expense or Capital Consumption Allowances*
> National Income

Depreciation expense is often called Capital Consumption Allowance. Capital consumption allowance is an estimate of the portion of existing capital equipment, buildings, and inventories that have worn out, or depreciated, over the period. Subtracting an amount equal to the decline in productive capacity yields a measure that more truly reflects the net value of production for the year: **Net National Product,** or *NNP*. It is generally assumed that owners of capital resources set aside a capital consumption allowance for eventually replacing or compensating for fully depreciated capital. Thus, capital consumption allowance is a form of business saving.

Another kind of business saving is **retained earnings** or undistributed profits. Following a production period, a business firm normally pays out a portion of its after-tax profits to owners (or stockholders) and holds the remaining profits for use by the firm. After accumulating profits for several years, a firm may use its funds for expanding or modernizing its productive capacity. This is an example of saving and direct investment, where both actions are undertaken by a single unit.

Most saving and investment is done indirectly by many separate individuals and groups. Households set aside a portion of current income that they make available for investment by other units through financial institutions. Financial institutions such as commercial banks, savings and loan associations, investment companies, or insurance companies collect the savings of many households and make investment loans for large projects such as hotels, office parks, and manufacturing plants. State and local governments set aside a portion of their

---

*Indirect business taxes, including sales and excise taxes, as well as corporate and personal income taxes.

current tax revenues for investment loans through purchase of bonds, savings certificates, and other government securities. Business firms, too, use their current savings to purchase stocks, bonds, and commercial paper issued by other business firms. In all these examples, surplus income in some productive units is used by others to purchase capital resources.

Saving and Investing in Periods of Uncertainty

When the surplus income of all saving units is precisely equal to the borrowing needs of investing units, the economy as a whole is said to be in *equilibrium*. Financial markets are in equilibrium because the supply of savings is equal to the demand for investment funds. Equality of savings supply and investment demand establishes the market rate of interest (i) acceptable to lenders and borrowers and an equilibrium quantity of funds (I) for use in purchasing capital resources. Whether the equilibrium quantity permits rapid growth in productive capacity or causes economic stagnation and decline depends on the ability and willingness of economic units to save and invest.

We have seen that an important determinant of saving and investing is the expected rate of return. Savers must expect a future reward that compensates for normal time preference; investors must expect a rate of return that at least covers their cost of borrowing. When the future is uncertain, savers and investors may become fearful, reduce their flow of funds to financial markets, and increase the necessary return for their use. The result may be changes in the equilibrium level of investment (I) and changes in the interest rate (i).

Some reasons for uncertainty among savers and investors are *inflation, government policies,* and *fluctuations in consumer spending.* Let us look at each of these sources of uncertainty in turn.

Inflation.   Since the mid-1960s the United States has suffered serious **inflation.*** Inflation is an increase in the general price level. Normally some prices will be rising and others falling, so that the *general* level of prices remains roughly constant. When *all* prices (or almost all) are rising, we have inflation.

The Vietnam War has been blamed for setting off the nation's long struggle with inflation. During the war, government spending for military purposes raised incomes without at the same time increasing the quantity of civilian goods for sale. Military personnel and defense workers spent their rising incomes for a relatively constant quantity of consumer goods and services. The effect of higher spending was to push most prices up. The Great Society programs of President Lyndon Johnson added to inflationary pressures, since many government spending programs were expected to increase real production far in the future, if ever. Free breakfasts for preschool children, for example, might increase their learning ability so that they could become productive workers, say, twenty years later. In the meantime, additional government spending for food tended to push up prices and contributed to general price inflation.

---

*Until 1982, when the nation enjoyed a substantial drop in the rate of inflation.

Rising prices for consumer goods and services through the late 1960s gave rise to worker demands for wage increases. Higher wages pushed up production costs and made new price increases necessary. The strongest boost to prices and costs occurred in the 1970s. In 1973, oil-producing members of the Organization of Petroleum Exporting Countries (OPEC) set higher prices for their product. Since oil is a major component of many manufactured goods and since virtually all goods require energy in their manufacture or transport, the effects of higher oil prices spread to every sector of the nation's economy. Food prices also rose, due to poor growing conditions and climatic changes the world over. Price increases for these major components of household expenditures led to new wage demands and an accelerating cycle of rising prices.

One result of inflation was to increase the time preference of savers. Seeing prices rise on needed goods, households increased their current spending, hoping to avoid higher prices in the future. This was particularly true in the case of durable consumer goods like furniture, appliances, and vehicles. Many families rushed to purchase homes, believing that rising home prices would soon push prices above their capability to buy a home. Rising consumer spending had two consequences: It worsened the inflation that spenders were trying to avoid, and it reduced the available funds for saving—funds that might ultimately have been used to purchase new capital investment.

A second result of inflation was to upset investors' projections of future cash flows from new capital investments. Remember that cash flow is revenue from sales less the out-of-pocket expenses of operating the equipment. Unless revenues and expenses can be estimated fairly precisely, it is not possible to calculate the rate of return r on new investment proposals. In this event, firms are likely to underestimate the rate of return so as to avoid the losses that might come with a faulty investment decision.

The effect of inflation on investment can be shown using a model of financial markets. A lower level of total saving and higher time preference is shown as a leftward shift of the supply of savings curve to S_2, as shown in Figure 2–6. On S_2, smaller quantities of savings are available at higher interest rates. A lower rate of return on investment is shown as a leftward shift of demand for capital resources

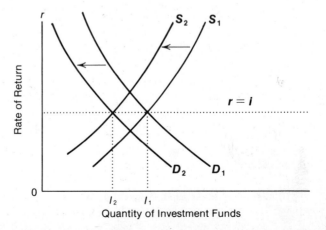

Figure 2–6

Rate of Return

S_2 S_1

$r = i$

D_2 D_1

0

I_2 I_1

Quantity of Investment Funds

to D_2. Proposed investments are expected to yield lower rates of return, so that the marginal efficiency of investment schedule is lower. With leftward shifts in both supply and demand, the equilibrium quantity of investment (I_2) will be smaller. Whether the market rate of interest (i) is higher or lower depends on the relative magnitude of the changes in saving and investment.

Government Policies.   If inflation increases the uncertainty of investment decisions, expected tax liability is also a major concern to business policymakers. Large corporations pay income taxes of up to 40% of profits. Then, when after-tax profits are distributed to stockholders as dividends, stockholders are subject to an additional personal income tax of up to 50% of the last dollars earned (depending upon their income tax bracket).*

Tax liabilities reduce savers' rewards and investors' rates of return. High taxes may reduce incentives and cause leftward shifts in savings supply and investment demand like those in Figure 2–6. In order to offset the possible disincentive effect of taxes, Congress taxes certain gains from investment at less than half an individual's personal tax rate through the **capital gains tax.** The capital gains tax is applied to gains from the sale of a profitable investment. Since the tax rate is less than the individual's ordinary income tax rate, savers may be encouraged to purchase new investments for a capital gain.

Government regulation of business firms produces other disincentives to investment. Beginning in the 1960s Congress became especially worried about the negative externalities or external costs of some industrial processes: chemical discharges into streams and rivers that damage wildlife and endanger human health; industrial pollutants in the atmosphere that cause disease and reduce worker productivity; destruction of landscapes that forever changes the ecology of a region. In order to reduce the external costs of industry, Congress passed laws and established agencies with the power to enforce health and environmental standards. New regulations have forced many business firms to change their operating procedures drastically and have even forced a few out of business. The threat of more regulations in the future adds to the uncertainty of cash flows and tends to reduce the expected rate of return on new investment proposals.†

Recognizing the disincentives that result from regulation, Congress has begun to focus on the costs of the regulations themselves: not only the cost of the enforcement agencies and the compliance costs of business firms, but also the long-range cost of lost production through the decline in capital investment and the drop in productivity. Regulatory agencies have been asked to examine their procedures to ensure efficiency and equity in enforcing health and environmental standards. Proposed regulations are being examined critically for their probable effect on capital investment. The hope is that a more relaxed regulatory

---

*Congress acted to reduce tax rates on certain business and personal incomes in 1981 as a part of its supply-side policies.

†Government regulations have positive effects as well as these negative ones. Later chapters in this text will discuss some of the benefits of government regulations.

policy will reduce some of the uncertainties of business planners and remove the disincentives for investment.

Consumer Spending.   No investment in capital equipment is profitable unless consumers are willing and able to buy the good or service it is used to produce. A high level of consumer spending is essential for guaranteeing a rate of return at least as great as borrowing costs. An uncertain business climate may produce uncertainty among consumers that aggravates uncertainties in business firms.

One source of consumers' uncertainty involves job security. Jobs in the United States depend on past investments in capital stock. On the average, almost $100,000 must have been invested in buildings, equipment, inventories, and homes for every American job. When the number of workers grows faster than capital stock, some workers will be unable to find jobs, and others will earn low pay. Consumer spending must fall. Even the fear of layoffs in the future could cause such a drop in consumer spending that new capital equipment could not be operated profitably.

The existence of inflation may be equally damaging to consumer spending. When the expectation of continually rising prices encourages a high level of current spending, future spending may actually fall below normal. Business firms may be misled by high sales in one period to expect high cash flows in the next, with the result that too much investment might be made to expand capacity. Having been burned once, investors may become too cautious and put off new investments that might have been profitable. Again, the effect is leftward shifts in supply of savings and demand for investment funds like those shown in Figure 2–6.

SOME DEFINITIONS

At this point we will pause to review some of the important language used in discussing economic issues. Economists are fairly precise about language, using words that have precise meanings in economic relationships. To use words carelessly might lead to seriously mistaken conclusions. This is especially true of common everyday words and is particularly true when talking about saving and investment. Some important definitions are listed here.

1. To save is to refrain from consumption. In a modern economy **saving** involves putting aside part of current income for consumption in the future. The ability to save depends first of all on a level of income sufficient to satisfy current needs.
2. To invest is to spend funds for purchase of capital resources such as goods, equipment, or buildings, not for current consumption but for providing goods or services over some future period. **Investment** may be direct (undertaken by the saver) or indirect (conducted through an intermediary by a third party).

3. **Capital resources** include the goods, equipment, or buildings that are expected to yield goods and services in the future. The use of capital is a "roundabout" method of production, since labor must be used first for producing capital before the capital can be used for producing goods and services.
4. *Financial capital* is money available for capital investment; it is the sum total of current savings of individuals, business firms, and governments.
5. *Financial markets* are the places where holders of financial capital make their funds available to investors, where lenders make their contacts with borrowers. We showed a model of financial markets in Figures 2–5 and 2–6. Equilibrium in financial markets determines the quantity of new investment spending (I) and the interest rate (i).
6. *Rate of return (r)* is a measure of an investment's expected profitability. It is based on the computation $C = \Sigma F/(1 + r)^t$. Rate of return determines a firm's marginal efficiency of investment and its demand for investment funds.
7. **Interest rates** (i) are the charges paid by borrowers to compensate lenders for the use of their savings. Borrowers demand investment funds only up to the point that the expected rate of return on capital resources is equal to the interest charged for borrowed funds.

INCORPORATING RISK IN INVESTMENT DECISIONS

Uncertainty about inflation, government policies, and consumer demand increases the risk of investment and raises the rate of return (r) necessary for accepting an investment proposal. Unknown events may have the effect of raising the rate of return on investment substantially above expectations during one period and pushing it below expectations in another period. Risk can be measured in terms of *probabilities*. A probability is a percentage value that expresses confidence in an event's occurrence. A 100% probability expresses absolute confidence that an event will occur, and a 0% probability expresses confidence that it will not. A 50% probability is associated with events that occur half the time or half of which occur all the time.

When used in investment decisions, probabilities can express the investor's confidence in the predicted rate of return. For example, under one set of assumptions about inflation, government policies, and consumer demand, the warehouse described on page 33 might be expected to yield a return of $r = 18\%$. Under less favorable assumptions, the rate of return might be only 8%. If the less favorable conditions are given a probability of 75% and the more favorable conditions 25%, the *expected value of return is the sum of the separate returns, weighted according to their probabilities. The computation is shown below:*

$$\text{Expected value of return} = \bar{r} = \Sigma\, r(p),$$

where $\bar{r}$ indicates expected value of return and p is the probability of occurrence of each event. (Note that the probabilities must add up to 1.00 because *something* must occur, but the rate of return associated with any given event may be zero.)

The expected value of return for the warehouse is

$$\bar{r} = \Sigma\ rp = 18\%(75\%) + 8\%(25\%) = 15.5\%.$$

This is not to say that the return will actually be 15.5%. We have seen that the rate of return may be as high as $r = 18\%$ or as low as $r = 8\%$. The value of $\bar{r}$ is useful only as a means of including risk in the investment decision.

The risk that comes from uncertainty has another effect on decisions to save and invest. Uncertainty about inflation, government policies, and consumer demand increases with the lapse of time between the current sacrifice and the expected future reward. One reason is the greater likelihood of cost or tax increases and the greater threat of new regulations and major changes in consumer spending patterns over a very long period of time. All these factors affect the rate of return on an investment that finally begins to earn positive cash flows only after years of incurring high costs.

To illustrate the effect of time, consider again the warehouse with a current price of $C = \$700,000$, and projected future cash flows of $F_1 = \$130,000$, $F_2 = \$145,000$, $F_3 = \$150,000$, $F_4 = \$155,000$, and $F_5 = \$150,000 + \$200,000$ for the next five years. On page 33 we calculated the rate of return at $r = 9\%$. Now suppose instead that a positive cash flow is not expected during the first year and that the stream of cash flows becomes positive only in the second year as shown below:

Year 1	Year 2	Year 3	Year 4	Year 5	Year 6
0	\$130,000	\$145,000	\$150,000	\$155,000	\$150,000 + 200,000

To compute the value of r we must solve the following equation:

$$700,000 = \frac{0}{(1+r)^1} + \frac{130,000}{(1+r)^2} + \frac{145,000}{(1+r)^3} + \frac{150,000}{(1+r)^4} + \frac{155,000}{(1+r)^5} + \frac{150,000 + 200,000}{(1+r)^6}$$

for which $r = 7\%$. A one-year delay in receipt of cash flows reduces the rate of return on this investment by two percentage points.

The example shows that cash flows farther in the future require a smaller discount factor:

$$1/(1+r)^6 < 1/(1+r)^5 < 1/(1+r)^4, \text{ and so forth.}^*$$

The effect of time is to reduce $\Sigma\ [\ 1/(1+r)^t\ ]$ and reduce the value of r for any long-range investment proposal.

It is understandable that business firms would prefer investments that yield cash flows soon and do not depend on long years of sacrifice for ultimate reward. Unfortunately, the capital investments that contribute most to the nation's productive capacity also require the longest sacrifice before earning substantial

---

*The symbol $<$ means "less than." It is the opposite of the symbol used before: $>$ or "greater than."

cash flows. Because they are costly, they require a large current expenditure; because they operate over the long term, cash flows occur in the distant future. For both these reasons, their rate of return r is likely to be less than the return on an investment that enjoys a brief period of productivity before becoming inoperable or obsolete.

Some quick-return investments are characterized as *speculative* because profitability depends on reselling the investment for more than its initial cost. Items like raw land, works of art, and precious metals are not investments according to the economist's definition, since nothing new has been produced. However, they are frequently the object of speculative purchases, using savings that might be used more productively to purchase buildings and equipment. The purchase of homes might also be classified as speculative if buyers bid up prices beyond the true value of housing services, expecting to resell later for a gain.

During periods of uncertainty, the use of financial capital for short-term or speculative investments may absorb so much of the available supply of savings that real, productive investment cannot be made. The level of investment (I) may fall below that necessary for maintaining the nation's total stock of capital. A deterioration of existing capital resources can mean falling productivity, rising costs with rising price inflation, and ultimately even greater uncertainty with continuing disincentives for investment.

RECENT FINANCIAL EXPERIENCE

Saving

Saving is the portion of current income that is not paid out for purchases or taxes. Gross saving in the United States includes private business saving, personal saving, and government saving: $S = S_b + S_p + S_g$.

1. Business saving is the sum of capital consumption allowances and undistributed business profits. Business saving rose fairly steadily from only 10 percent of Gross National Product in 1970 to 13 percent in 1980. (S_b = $333.4 billion).*
2. Personal saving in 1980 was S_p = $104.2 billion. This amounted to only 6 percent of disposable income, having fallen from 8 percent in 1970. The declining rate of personal saving reflects two circumstances: rising inflationary expectations among consumers and slow growth of income during the 1970s. Many consumers reduced their saving in order to maintain their living standards during a period of falling income.
3. Government saving is the difference between tax revenues collected (T) and government outlays (G) at all levels of government. It is the net **surplus** of all governments: $S_g = T - G$. For most of the 1970s, government outlays exceeded tax revenues so that government saving was negative. Only during

*Data are from *The Economic Report of the President*, 1981.

1973 and 1979 did government saving rise above zero, and in 1980 government dissaving was $S_g = -\$34.8$ billion. The "minus" sign indicates a **deficit** in the total budget of all governments.

Gross saving for 1980 was $S = S_b + S_p + S_g = \$334.4b + \$104.2b - \$34.8b = \$403.8$ billion. This total represents a decrease of $8 billion from 1979. The only period during the 1970s when savings failed to grow significantly was in 1974 and 1975 when the nation was experiencing its most severe postwar recession. The savings decline in 1980 reflected a decline in real production for the year and a reduced capacity for business and personal saving. Negative government saving reflected a decrease in tax collections and an increase in government outlays as the nation moved into recession. (Many government outlays increase automatically in recession. Unemployment compensation, welfare benefits, and food stamp allowances are examples. Because such payments help stabilize total spending in a recession, they are often called *automatic stabilizers*.)

Investment

Gross investment is the purchase of buildings, equipment, and inventories for use in production. Gross private domestic investment in 1980 was $I = \$395.1$ billion, a $20 billion drop from the previous year. The only decline in investment expenditures in the 1970s was during the recession of 1974–1975. **Net investment** is the actual addition to capital resources after capital consumption allowances have been subtracted. In 1980, after subtracting capital consumption allowances, net investment was $107.8 billion, having fluctuated over the preceding decade along with fluctuations in economic activity. The greatest total investment during the 1970s was in producers' durable equipment, which typically has risen fastest in years of general economic expansion. Business structures were the second largest investment expenditure, with new homes a close third.

The third component of total investment is **inventory investment** — investment in goods held for sale or for use in production in the future. Business firms try to hold inventories equal to about one and a half times their monthly sales; therefore, a certain amount of inventory investment is planned to accommodate expected sales for a coming period. Some inventory accumulation is *unplanned*, however, and results from unexpected changes in consumer purchases. Unplanned inventory investment tends to rise as the economy moves into recession and monthly sales fall. After a period of substantial unplanned inventory investment, actual inventory investment may turn negative, as business firms attempt to deplete inventories accumulated previously. Actual inventory investment was high and positive in the late 1970s and turned negative in 1980.

Financial Instruments

We have seen that much investment is *indirect*, using savings collected in financial institutions for use by a third party. Savings are made available for investment through acquisition of financial assets. For example, individual checking and savings deposits in commercial banks and thrift institutions enable these institutions to lend to individuals and business firms. Purchases of financial instruments like **corporate stock, bonds,** and commercial paper provide funds directly to business firms, and purchases of government securities provide funds directly to government. Life insurance and pension fund contributions are loaned to business firms for long-term construction projects, and other financial instruments are used for financing homes, durable consumer goods, and business investment.

Beginning in 1960, savers' purchases of stocks have declined relative to purchases of other assets. The result has been relatively slow growth (or decline) in stock prices and a reluctance on the part of corporations to sell new stock. The slow growth of stock ownership has serious implications for the level of capital investment. Shares of stock represent ownership shares in business and include the right to share in corporate profits. Unlike bonds, which require a regular payment of interest and principal, stocks pay dividends based on the firm's current profits. Declining profit expectations have reduced savers' willingness to purchase stocks; in turn, the scarcity of financial capital through issue of new stock has retarded the growth of capital investment.

Purchase of corporate bonds has fluctuated with inflation, falling when especially high inflation reduces the attractiveness of bonds issued at lower interest rates. For many firms, the high interest rates required for selling new bonds have made new issues impractical and have forced the cancellation of capital investment plans.

The greatest increase in holdings of financial assets has occurred in ownership of **money market fund** shares. Money market fund assets amounted to $200 billion in 1981. Money market funds purchase short-term government or corporate securities at current market rates. High interest earnings on these funds have attracted savings away from long-term capital investment. Since these securities have maturities of less than a year, borrowers must "roll over" their loans frequently at current interest rates. Rising market rates make short-term debt especially onerous and may cause business failures. The problem is especially difficult for firms that have borrowed short-term to finance large, long-term projects whose returns are expected far in the future. The risks associated with these kinds of projects have discouraged construction of long-term investment projects.

The Implications

Changing saving and investment patterns in the United States and abroad have contributed to a declining rate of growth of capital resources. Hardest hit over the decade have been plant and equipment investment in transportation, communication, and public utilities. In many cases, productive capacity has failed to grow at all. Capacity for producing durable goods increased only about 3 percent a year in constant dollars corrected for inflation. Investment in plant and equipment for the mining sector enjoyed the greatest gains, growing at about 12 percent a year.

New capital investment can have the effect of widening or deepening the supply of capital for use by each worker. **Capital widening** involves a rate of new investment equal to the growth rate of the labor force. Parallel growth of labor and capital ensures an adequate supply of tools for raising the productivity of each worker. **Capital deepening** involves a faster growth of capital resources than of the labor force, so that each worker has more tools and greater opportunities for productivity growth.

During the 1960s, the labor force grew about 1.8 percent a year and net business expenditures for plant and equipment (gross investment minus capital consumption allowances) grew about 3 percent. The annual increase in productivity of labor was almost 2.9 percent. Circumstances changed in the 1970s. Over the decade of the 1970s the labor force grew at an average rate of 2.4 percent. Real net investment rose on the average 2.7 percent annually, barely keeping pace with labor force growth. With slow growth of capital for enhancing labor's productivity, productivity growth has been slow. From a high of 3.5 percent in 1973, growth of labor productivity fell to negative values during recessions later in the decade.

SOME POLICY PROPOSALS

Increasing productive capacity is essential for raising our nation's Total Product curve, along with Marginal and Average Product. Increasing the supply of capital resources is important for employing our growing labor force in productive, well-paid jobs. Unless saving and investment occur at a steady rate, we will be unable to provide the living standards our people have come to expect.

In this chapter we have analyzed some of the economic conditions that encourage or discourage saving and investment. Explaining the cause of an economic event makes it possible to prescribe policies for bringing about desirable changes. In this case, the following kinds of policies have been proposed.

Policies to Ensure Ample Savings

Total savings should be great enough to supply needed investment funds but not so great as to reduce substantially the funds remaining for consumer spending. Savings will be used for investment only if investment is expected to be profitable. And the profitability of new buildings, equipment, and inventory depends on a high level of sales to consumers. Therefore, policy goals to increase total savings should also consider the possible negative effects on consumer spending.

Current savings depend fundamentally on the level of **disposable income** (personal income after taxes). Disposable income must be high enough to permit saving to take place. This suggests that high-income families will normally have a greater tendency to save, and that increasing the disposable incomes of high-income families would tend to increase total savings. A policy for producing this result would be a change in the schedule of tax rates to reduce the tax bills of high-income families. Shifting the income tax burden proportionally away from high-income groups would leave more disposable income in the hands of families most likely to save. Reducing estate and gift taxes would also have this result.

Conservative economists generally support a shift in the tax burden away from high-income families. They believe that temporary hardships among low- and middle-income families are necessary for increasing capital resources and real income in the long run. Liberal economists tend to disagree. Shifting the tax burden, they say, would cause the nation's disposable income (and total wealth) to rest even more heavily in high-income families. Greater inequality of income (and wealth) might also affect total spending, in that heavily taxed low- and middle-income families would have less income for spending on consumer goods and services. Thus, whatever additional savings would occur might also reduce total spending, so that existing capital resources would be underutilized and new capital investment would be unprofitable.

A second way to influence savings is through the level of interest income earned on financial assets. In the past, certain government policies have worked to reduce interest income and may have discouraged saving. Government regulations limit the interest that can be paid to savers by commercial banks, savings and loan associations, and savings banks. Reserve requirements in these and other financial institutions limit their own profits and reduce the interest available for paying savers. Interest rate regulations are now being phased out, and there is some discussion also of reducing reserve requirements. However, since both kinds of regulations have other economic objectives, removing them entirely may not be practical.*

Certain tax policies may also discourage saving. Our tax laws allow borrowers to deduct from taxable income interest paid on consumer loans; the incentive is to spend freely and borrow in excess of current income. Until 1981, tax laws required many savers to pay a higher tax rate on interest income than on ordinary income from work; again the incentive was to spend rather than save.

Reducing current tax advantages affecting interest charges might be difficult, since they originally were intended to encourage purchase of homes and durable consumer goods. Tax rates on interest income were reduced in 1981, but lower tax bills on interest income will probably require higher tax bills elsewhere. It is not clear which segment of the population should be taxed *more heavily* for the sake of higher savings!

Several nations with higher savings rates than the United States encourage saving by exempting a larger quantity of current saving from current income taxes. Germany rewards long-term savers with a bonus paid after several years of retained savings. The 1981 tax law in the United States allows workers to set aside a certain amount of income in tax-free savings accounts to accumulate interest until the worker reaches age 60. So-called **Individual Retirement Accounts (IRAs)** can be held in financial institutions until withdrawn at retirement, when tax rates are expected to be lower.

---

*Interest rate regulations were intended to hold down the interest cost of borrowing for new home building. Reserve requirements are one way of regulating the nation's supply of total credit.

Current tax policies on stock dividends have the effect of taxing savers twice. When an issue of new stock is used to finance purchase of new capital resources, corporate income taxes take a portion of added profits. Then, whatever portion of after-tax profit is returned to stockholders is taxed as a part of personal income. The result is a kind of *double taxation*. Many proposals have been suggested for reducing the double taxation of dividends: deducting dividend payments from corporate taxable income and allowing personal tax credits for corporate taxes paid are examples. Removing the double taxation of dividends might reverse the decline in new stock issues in the United States and encourage new savings. However, unless government spending needs decline also, the loss in revenues from these taxes would probably have to be made up by raising taxes elsewhere in the economy.

Policies to Encourage Investment

Recognizing the need for expanding and modernizing capital resources, our government has established certain investment incentives. Tax laws on depreciable capital permit business firms to deduct a portion of the purchase price of an investment from taxable income each year, thereby reducing their tax bills. **Accelerated** deductions for **depreciation** allow greater deductions and lower taxes in the early years of the life of capital, when cash flows are likely to be lower than in later years. In both cases, the effect is to increase the rate of return on investment proposals.

Congress has debated proposals to establish even more favorable tax treatment for depreciation, but there are certain disadvantages. Allowing tax deductions for investment in buildings and equipment may discourage investment in high technology research and development. A modern economy may require more "human" capital investment in the form of scientific education and training, and less "bricks and mortar" investment in the form of power plants, transportation systems, and so forth.

Another disadvantage is that depreciation expenses are based on the purchase price of an investment. In periods of inflation, the price of capital equipment may increase, such that current tax advantages may not be enough to ensure replacement. However, to raise the deduction for depreciation would aggravate the disadvantage mentioned earlier: that is, the emphasis on material investment rather than research and development of new technology.

Another tax advantage for investment is the provision for tax credits in the year an investment is purchased. A **tax credit** is a reduction in the taxpayer's tax bill. Beginning in the early 1960s, business firms were allowed to deduct 7 percent of the price of an investment from that year's tax bill. In 1979 the investment tax credit was made a permanent part of the tax code at 10 percent.

Finally, the capital gains tax applies to less than half an investor's gain from the sale of a capital resource. This means that a high-income earner might pay taxes on as little as 20 percent of the gain from the sale of productive capital.

There have been proposals to reduce the capital gains tax rate further and to reduce (or eliminate) the corporate income tax as well. The expected result would be an increase in incentives, with higher levels of total investment.

Other incentives for investment include low-interest loans from government-sponsored credit agencies. Lower interest charges increase the number of new investment proposals that will be undertaken. Some examples of government-sponsored loan programs are the following:

1. The Federal Housing Administration, Government National Mortgage Association, Federal Home Loan Banks, Federal Home Loan Mortgage Corporation, and Federal National Mortgage Association finance investment in residential construction.
2. The Federal Land Banks, Federal Intermediate Credit Banks, Farmers Home Administration, Banks for Cooperatives, and Farm Credit Banks finance agricultural investment.
3. The Export-Import Bank and U.S. Railway Association finance business investment.
4. The Tennessee Valley Authority and Rural Electrification Administration finance rural development.
5. The Student Loan Marketing Association finances investment in education, or "human capital."

Funds for these agencies come from tax revenues or from government borrowing, both of which reduce the savings available for other forms of investment. Thus, the effect of government-sponsored loan programs is to shift the allocation of financial capital away from private purposes and toward ends sought by particular government agencies. Whether the result is in the interests of the nation as a whole is a subject for debate.

Conservative economists generally oppose government loan programs, believing that financial markets allocate investment funds more efficiently when they are free of government intervention. Liberal economists tend to believe that market power shuts certain groups out of financial markets; therefore, government intervention may be necessary for the sake of improved equity. Other groups oppose or support government loan programs on the basis of their own economic interests: home builders favor construction loan programs, farmers favor agricultural lending, defense producers and other export industries favor export credit programs, rural citizens favor rural development loans, and students favor education loans. All these groups tend to oppose taxes paid to finance loan programs for *other* groups!

We have suggested that whatever tax or lending policies are established to favor saving and investment, there may be corresponding effects unfavorable to other sectors of the economy. This may not necessarily be true if investment expenditures bring such positive results to the economy as a whole that other sectors prosper as well. Of course, this is the ultimate expectation of those who propose such programs.

CONCLUSIONS AND PROSPECTS

We have described some long-range developments in the U.S. economy whose effects have been (1) to reduce the amount of savings for investment, (2) to reduce the level of investment and increase its risks, and (3) in general, to reduce the growth of capital resources for the nation as a whole. If present trends continue, the nation faces stagnating growth in productivity, with slow growth or decline in real per capita income and living standards. We have discussed some policy proposals for increasing savings and investment, along with their possible disadvantages.

Until now, we have neglected an aspect of savings and investment that may yield the greatest potential for new growth—**demographics.** Demographics is the study of population: in the current context, it is the study of the effect of population trends on savings and investment patterns.

The United States has experienced a major change in population. From historic population growth of around one percent annually through 1946, the nation experienced fifteen years of unprecedented population increase. Two percent annual population growth from 1946 through 1961 constitutes what has been called the postwar "baby boom." During those years rising prosperity encouraged family formation, and improved living conditions promoted family growth. Since 1961, population growth has returned to normal rates, and the children born in the 1950s and 1960s are becoming adults.

In general, the levels of savings and investment have been affected negatively by the "baby boom." Many families with young children are unable to save, and young adults must spend most of their incomes for housing and durable consumer goods. Funds that might otherwise have been loaned to business for capital investment have been invested in residential construction, providing fewer funds for increasing the stock of manufacturing capital. Whereas many young adults have invested heavily in education and vocational training, this kind of "human" investment is not normally included in the measured quantity of investment for the year.

As the "baby boom" grows older it creates a population bulge that will ultimately benefit savings and investment. First, older workers will be more productive and earn higher incomes, with greater opportunities for saving. Older workers have less need for new housing and consumer durables, releasing more funds for business capital investment. At the same time, an increasing participation of the population in the labor force will increase the need for capital resources and also increase family incomes for purchasing goods and services.

All these effects should stimulate savings and investment and help increase the nation's productive capacity. As the rate of saving and investment returns to levels experienced in the past, we might expect new tendencies for an upward shift in the nation's production function, with rising average living standards as well.

Special Case

Forced Saving

In certain economic systems, citizens can be forced to save so that resources that might otherwise have been used to produce consumer goods and services might be used instead for other purposes. Centrally controlled economies do this directly by allocating labor and capital resources toward production of such things as transportation systems, electric power networks, and steel mills. The objective may be industrial development of a backward society (as it is in the Soviet Union) or it may be conquest and exploitation of neighboring countries (as it was in the case of Nazi Germany). Throughout the process, sacrifices must be imposed on persons who may never live to experience the reward of increased future consumption.*

In a free market system, sacrifice is more commonly achieved through incentives. Free entrepreneurs are encouraged to save because they expect saving ultimately to improve their status in life. Moreover, the investment decisions made by free entrepreneurs may more correctly reflect popular demand than investment policies established by a central planning board. These kinds of saving and investment procedures have been largely responsible for the great technical progress our nation has achieved to date.

Certain of our incentive schemes have turned negative in recent years, as we have seen, and there is concern that saving and investment may not continue to grow fast enough to satisfy future needs. Even a free market has means to *force* additional saving, however, so that resources can be used for purposes other than current consumption. In general, **forced saving** involves government policies concerning taxation or inflation.

Tax policies can be a means of reducing consumer spending so that resources can be used for purposes decided by government. National defense and public works projects are typical uses of resources that are released from production of consumer goods and services through taxation. Tax revenues may also be used by government for investment in "human" capital. Programs to improve standards of health, nutrition, sanitation, and education, for instance, are a kind of investment in human beings. Such programs are expected to yield returns in the form of increased worker productivity (and ultimately in personal tax payments high enough to offset their initial cost).

Investments made by government have the disadvantage that they only indirectly add to the nation's capacity for producing goods and services. On the other hand, there is the advantage that government investment frequently fills needs that would not be undertaken by private investors.

Another use of tax revenues would directly enhance the investment opportunities of private investors. During prosperous years, government might use its tax revenues to retire a portion of the federal debt. This would leave savers with funds to purchase financial assets issued by private business firms. Greater purchases of corporate stocks and bonds would raise their prices and generally lower the cost of business borrowing. Lower borrowing costs would make additional investment proposals acceptable, and the capital stock might grow.

*Poland is an example of a nation whose people continue to experience this kind of forced saving.

All these results could also be accomplished through government economic policies that contribute to inflation. When consumer spending increases faster than real production, the tendency is for prices to rise. Government may aggravate inflation by continuing to spend more than tax revenues. If government finances its deficit through newly created money, total spending may increase even faster, and inflation may accelerate. Households can buy fewer consumer goods and services with their inflated dollars. Thus, even though consumers have not chosen to save, the actual result is a decline in purchases of consumer goods and an increase in saving for the nation. Then, new capital investment may be accomplished through government loans or direct government expenditures or through retiring government debt. In the first and second cases, the direction of new investment would be decided by government; in the third, the direction of new investment would depend on independent decisions in the private sector.

Both forms of forced saving are contrary to our system's primary emphasis on free market decision-making. There are other disadvantages. Because the effects of forced saving are not easily measured or predicted, it is not generally possible to ensure efficiency. Moreover, since government policies affect different groups differently, political pressure may be used to influence the direction of policy or to prolong policies beyond the point where they are useful.

Under certain circumstances, forced saving may be necessary. During periods of national emergency, coercion may be necessary to force the public to make the necessary sacrifices. Coercion may be necessary also to ensure that sacrifices are shared equitably among the population.

- Use a model of financial markets to illustrate the effect of the use of tax revenues to retire government debt.
- Show how additional savings may shift the supply curve in financial markets.
- Identify the equilibrium level of investment (*I*) and the market rate of interest (*i*).

QUESTIONS

1. Determine the value of a savings account on December 31 five years in the future after you have deposited $1,000 every January 1. Assume 8 percent interest compounded annually.
2. Refer again to Question 1 and suppose 4 percent interest is added to your account on June 30 and 4 percent again on December 31 every year. Explain the difference in your final value. How might the frequency of interest payments affect savings incentives?
3. Suppose you have time preference of 11 percent. What is the most you would pay for a bond that pays coupons of $25 at the end of the next three years and an additional $250 along with the last coupon payment?
4. Demonstrate the relationship between a compound factor and a discount factor and show how each is used.
5. What is the rate of return on investment in a donut machine with a purchase price of $4,000 that earns revenues of $5,000 annually for five years? The out-of-pocket cost of operating the machine plus taxes amounts to $4,000 a year, and the machine wears out completely after the fifth year.
6. Demonstrate the effects of expected inflation on computations of rate of return on investment. Show how inflation increases the uncertainty of investment.

7. Many local governments have placed legal ceilings on rental charges for apartments. Show how rental ceilings affect the marginal efficiency of investment and the quantity of investment expenditures. Use rate of return computations and the market model for investment capital.

8. A late nineteenth century three-cent nickel sold for $3,000 in 1980. How does this event affect the market for financial capital? What are the risks associated with this type of expenditure? What other expenditures might also be classified as "speculative"?

9. Federally-sponsored credit agencies ease the flow of savings to financial institutions that provide mortgage loans to home builders. Evaluate the consequences of this practice in terms of the level of savings and investment.

10. List five proposed policy acts for stimulating savings and investment and point out their disadvantages. How does this question illustrate the trade-offs necessary in all economic decisions?

11. Major banks establish a "prime" interest rate on short-term loans made to their best corporate customers. Other borrowers pay a percentage or so above the prime rate. When market interest rates change, interest rates on many existing loans change automatically. Discuss the possible effects on business investment.

12. What circumstances would induce a coal company to invest in a railroad? Would the fact that the owners of the coal company also own oil companies affect this decision? What other major noncoal investments are coal companies likely to make? What are the risks associated with all these investments? What government policies might work to stimulate these investments? Should such policies be established? Discuss.

DEFINITIONS

Accelerated depreciation is a tax advantage on capital investment. It is a means of reducing the tax bills of investors so as to encourage greater investment expenditures.

The Capital Gains Tax is a tax applied to the gain from reselling an asset. The capital gains tax rate is less than half the rate on a taxpayer's ordinary income.

Capital resources are produced means of production and include buildings, equipment and inventories.

Capital widening and deepening refer to increases in capital resources. Capital widening is an increase equal to the increase in the labor force. Capital deepening is an increase greater than the increase in the labor force, so that workers have increased capital resources with which to work.

Cash flow is the revenue earned from operating a capital resource minus out-of-pocket expenses and taxes.

A compound factor is equal to $(1 + r)^t$ for any value of r and t. Multiplying a current sacrifice by the appropriate compound factor yields the expected future reward.

Compound interest is the payment of interest on interest. When money is loaned for several interest periods, interest payments are usually compounded, so that the total interest paid to the lender is greater than the interest computed on the principal amount of the loan.

Corporate stocks and bonds are means of indirect investment. Corporate stocks convey a share of ownership to the holder and entitle the holder to share in business profits. Corporate bonds are a form of loan, with agreed interest and repayment provisions.

Demographics is the study of population trends.

Depreciation expense is sometimes called Capital Consumption Allowance. It is an estimate of the portion of capital resources that wears out during the production period, and is thus a cost of production. Capital Consumption Allowances constitute a portion of business savings set aside for eventual new investment.

A discount factor is equal to $1/(1 + r)^t$ for any value of r and t. Multiplying an expected future payment by the appropriate discount factor yields the equivalent current value.

Discounting is a process of reducing the value of an expected future payment according to the distance in the future the payment is to be received (t) and according to the time preference of the recipient (r).

Disposable income is the portion of personal income that remains after all taxes have been paid.

Equilibrium occurs in the financial market when the supply of savings is equal to the demand for investment funds. Equilibrium determines the market rate of interest and the quantity of funds that will be borrowed for investment.

Financial markets are places where savers supply their funds to borrowers for making new investment expenditures.

Forced saving is a means of compelling people to reduce their spending for current goods and services so that productive resources can be used for other purposes.

A government deficit is an excess of government outlays over current tax revenues.

A government surplus is an excess of government tax revenues over current outlays.

Gross investment is the total value of investment for the year.

Gross National Product (GNP) is the dollar value of all goods and services produced for sale during the year. Gross National Product is at the same time the total value of expenditures for current production and the total value of incomes received in business firms.

Individual Retirement Accounts or IRAs are portions of current income set aside in tax-free accounts to accumulate interest income until the owner's retirement.

Inflation is an increase in the general price level. Inflation has a variety of causes, to be discussed throughout this text.

Interest rates are percentage returns paid to lenders by borrowers.

Inventory investment is the purchase of materials, component parts, or finished goods for use in a future production period. Inventory investment may be planned — as assurance that needed goods will be on hand, or inventory investment may be unplanned — as when sales from current production fall short of expectations.

Investment is the use of funds to purchase capital resources. Investment may be done directly or indirectly through financial institutions. Investment may consist of material goods like buildings, equipment, and inventories. Or investment may be "human" capital in the form of improved education.

Marginal Efficiency of Investment is a schedule relating the current cost of investment proposals to their expected rate of return, ranked from highest to lowest.

Money market funds are financial institutions that receive savings of many households and purchase government securities, bank certificates of deposit, and commercial paper, thereby earning interest for their shareholders.

Net investment is the value of current investment minus the portion of investment that was required to replace fully depreciated capital resources.

Net National Product (NNP) is the dollar value of total production minus the portion of current production that replaces fully depreciated capital resources. Thus, *NNP* is a measure of the actual gain in goods and services for the year.

Rate of return is the percentage return expected on a current sacrifice. Rate of return is shown in the rate-of-return equations by the symbol r.

Retained earnings are also called *undistributed business profits*. They are the portion of business profits that are not paid out to owners of the business. Retained earnings constitute a portion of business savings set aside for eventual new investment.

Saving is the sacrifice of current consumption. Setting aside a portion of current income in savings provides a source of funds for lending.

Tax credits are deductions from a taxpayer's tax bill. Tax credits are given to purchasers of new capital investment as an incentive to make such investments.

Time preference involves a normal human desire to enjoy goods now rather than in the future. If people are to be persuaded to give up current use of their money for purchasing goods, they must be rewarded with a return high enough to make the sacrifice worthwhile. Time preference is shown in rate-of-return equations by the symbol r.

The time value of money refers to the difference in value between money held today relative to money to be received in the future. Time value is shown by the equations (1) $F = C(1 + r)^t$ and (2) $C = F/(1 + r)^t$. The equations express (1) the future compensation that is equivalent to a current sacrifice and (2) the current value of a payment to be received in the future.

SUGGESTED READINGS

"Behind the Market's Wild Ride." *Business Week*, October 25, 1982, p. 98.

"Investment Outlook: 1983." *Business Week*, December 27, 1982, p. 60.

Juster, F. Thomas. "Saving, Economic Growth and Economic Policy." *Economic Outlook USA*, Survey Research Center, University of Michigan, Summer, 1981, p. 54.

Loomis, Carol J. "The Fight for Financial Turf." *Fortune*, December 28, 1981, p. 54.

"The Perilous Hunt for Financing." *Business Week*, March 1, 1982, p. 44.

Sheffrin, Steven M. "What Have We Done to the Corporate Tax System?" *Challenge*, May/June, 1982, p. 46.

Smith, Winston. "The Myth of Declining Investment." *Challenge*, January/February, 1982, p. 50.

Thurow, Lester C. *The Zero-Sum Society*. New York: Basic Books, 1980, Chapter 4.

CHAPTER THREE

Energy, Productivity, and Income

Where Will We Get the Power?

LEARNING OBJECTIVES

- To examine the contribution of energy resources to the productivity of labor and capital and to understand the effects of a scarcity of energy.
- To develop a model of demand and supply in energy markets and show the effects of shifts in demand and supply curves.
- To understand and illustrate elasticity of demand and supply in energy markets and show how government policies affect elasticity.
- To learn how the resource-intensity of production affects productivity and incomes.
- To examine the efficiency, equity, and externalities of energy markets and the implications for government intervention.
- To use a "learning curve" to show falling production costs for energy supply in the very long run.

"R2-D2" would not recognize as a kindred soul any of the industrial robots that work in today's manufacturing firms. Unlike "R2-D2" modern robots cannot see or feel (although some are "learning" to). Still, they can receive information, act upon it, and report the results of their actions. A series of tiny

56

holes in a long tape can tell a drilling machine to pick up a certain tool, position it at a certain angle, and bore a precise hole in each of a hundred die castings before a skilled machinist is even ready to begin. Punched cards can tell a computer to figure wages due, write a hundred checks, and balance the checkbook before the payroll clerk has finished coffee. An automated textile mill can be programmed to knit Oriental design rugs while the technician reads the morning paper.

What do all these systems have in common? First, they perform work. And second, the source of their work is not so much human energy as the accumulated energy of the sun — thousands of years of sunlight, stored in coal, oil, natural gas, or water power and carried through various systems to the point where it is needed. In fact, much of our remarkable growth in production over the last century can be traced to the use of these energy sources to operate machines for doing work that once was man's alone.

The earliest example of the use of nonhuman energy involved work animals, and oxen and donkeys still serve primitive economies as they have for centuries past. Likewise, wind energy continues to be used in agriculture for irrigating fields and milling grain—and in transportation for fun and profit. Harnessing heat energy to propel the steam engine marked an important advance in man's ability to do work; and internal combustion moved the gasoline and jet propulsion engines. Although these examples involve using energy directly on the site where it is produced, other technology allowed energy to be transmitted from its source to farms and factories many miles away. Electromagnetic principles are used to convert energy into transmissible form and then back into energy for performing work.

Applying nonhuman energy to a machine allows us to produce greater output than would be possible with human labor alone. The result is an upward shift in the production function and a corresponding increase in Average Product per worker. More output per worker means higher real per capita income and improved living standards. Moreover, increased worker productivity releases more of the labor force from heavy and menial work and increases the capacity for investment in new capital resources.

THE RECORD

The greatest advance in productivity in recorded history occurred in the two decades following World War II. Between 1947 and 1967, average output per hour of work in the United States almost doubled, with gains of 3.2 percent annually. With roughly the same proportion of the population employed, disposable income per capita grew more than 2 percent a year in constant dollars.* The American people enjoyed unprecedented gains in material prosperity.

*That is, adjusted for inflation through use of a price index. The use of a price index was explained on page 19.

A major reason for the growth of worker productivity was the low price of energy. Prices of power, fuel, and related products rose by only 1.3 percent annually over this same period. Thirty years passed before fuel prices doubled, and manufacturers were able to substitute larger and larger quantities of cheap energy for costly human labor. Low energy prices helped hold the annual increase in consumer prices to an average of only 2 percent, in spite of wars and social upheaval.

Changes began to occur in the late 1960s, and between 1970 and 1980 energy prices rose almost 10 percent annually. They doubled in five years, tripled in eight, and quadrupled in ten! At the end of 1980, fuel and power prices were almost six times what they were in 1970.

More costly energy had two effects on industry. For many firms, rising energy costs reduced profits for investment in new and more modern capital equipment. For others, rising energy prices forced a return to the greater use of labor in production. The long-range shift from human to nonhuman energy for performing work slowed and, in some industries, began to be reversed. With less ''horsepower'' to boost human power, average output per worker grew by only about 1.6 percent annually during the 1970s.*

Slower productivity growth has meant slower real income growth for American workers. However, having grown accustomed to rising living standards, many workers have continued to increase their spending as if there were, in fact, increased quantities of goods. The result has been reduced saving for investment and a further negative influence on productivity growth, as well as added inflationary pressures throughout the economy.

THE MARKET FOR ENERGY: DEMAND

United States citizens use more energy than any other people in the world— the equivalent of 60 barrels of oil or 15 tons of coal per capita each year.† The single most important use of energy in the United States is transportation, which accounts for 25 percent of total energy consumption. We have more roads and more automobiles, and our automobiles are less fuel-efficient than those of any other country. Another 20 percent of our energy is used to heat, cool, and light our homes and to operate our household appliances. Home energy consumption has increased about three times as fast as the number of homes, in part because of the greater energy requirements of modern appliances.

About 15 percent of U.S. energy demand is accounted for by the business sector, a result of the widespread use of sealed glass windows and the high energy requirements of modern office equipment. Even agriculture uses large amounts of energy in the form of chemical fertilizers and pesticides and for operating farm

---

*There were other causes for slowed productivity growth, of course, many of which will be discussed in later chapters of this text.

†Henry Simmons, ''The Economics of America's Energy Future,'' 1975, U.S. Energy Research and Development Administration, Washington, D.C.

equipment. An estimated 10 energy calories are required to produce 1 food calorie. Our remarkable increase in farm productivity is largely a result of the increased use of energy in modern scientific farming.

The Demand Curve

The demand for energy is **derived demand:** that is, it is based on the demand for goods and services produced through the use of energy. Energy is used together with other resources: land, labor, capital, and entrepreneurship. Thus, energy is a "complement" to other resources for use in transportation, homes, businesses, and agriculture. A given stock of capital requires certain amounts of energy and human labor if it is to be operated at all. When any one resource is scarce, its **complementary resources** cannot operate as fully or efficiently.

Figure 3–1 shows graphs of the demand for two resources: (a) energy and (b) labor. The horizontal axes measure quantities of resources, and the vertical axes measure resource prices. **Resource demand curves** are drawn for the short run, during which time factors other than resource prices remain the same. This means that the supply and the nature of capital equipment are fixed for the period of time over which the demand curve applies.

In both graphs the demand curve shows the quantities of resources that will be employed at various resource prices, given the fixed supply of capital equipment. Thus, at a price of p_E, Q_E units of energy will be employed. Likewise, at a wage of w, Q_L units of labor will be employed. Both resource demand curves slope downward because larger quantities will generally be employed at lower prices. Changes in price will cause firms to move along their resource demand curves and employ different quantities.

The demand curves in Figures 3–1a and b are drawn with a relatively steep slope. The steep slope indicates little change in the requirements for labor and energy, regardless of price. This is because, in the short run, the existing capital resources require fairly fixed quantities of these other resources if they are to

Figure 3–1

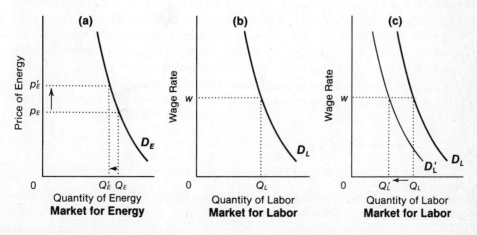

operate at all. Thus, resource employment is relatively insensitive to price changes in the short run.

When quantity demanded is insensitive to price change, we say that demand is relatively **inelastic**. **Price elasticity of demand** is defined as percent change in quantity demanded divided by percent change in price:*

$$\text{price elasticity of demand} = e_D = \frac{\%\text{ change in quantity demanded}}{\%\text{ change in price}} = \frac{\%\ \Delta\ Q_D}{\%\ \Delta\ p}$$

If percent change in quantity demanded is less than percent change in price, the value of the elasticity ratio is less than one, and we describe demand as inelastic. The demand curves in Figure 3–1 are drawn to show percent change in quantity demanded as less than percent change in price.

Now look closely at Figure 3–1a for the effect of an increase in the price of energy. An increase in the price of energy from p_E to p_E' would cause firms to move up their energy demand curves and purchase a smaller quantity (Q_E'). The lower level of energy use reduces the level of operation of capital resources and affects the firm's need for labor as well. In this case, we say that the *demand for labor falls*. A change in the demand for labor results from changes other than the price of labor and is shown as a shift in the labor demand curve.

Look at Figure 3–1c. The lower utilization of capital resources reduces the quantity of labor that will be demanded at every price level. A decrease in demand for labor is shown as a leftward shift of the labor demand curve to D_L'. With no change in the price of labor, a smaller quantity of labor will be employed. Thus, a leftward shift in D_L reduces employment from Q_L to Q_L' even though the wage rate remains at w. As employment falls, total output for the nation declines.

These results occurred in the United States during the recessions of 1975 and 1980. Sharp increases in the price of imported oil contributed to painful decreases in production and employment. During both recessions, real production dropped more than 9 percent (first quarter of 1975 and second quarter of 1980, annual rate) and worker unemployment rose to 8.9 and 7.6 percent in mid-1975 and mid-1980, respectively.†

Users of energy are slow to adapt their habits and attitudes to changing conditions in energy markets. The reason has to do with the long lifespan of buildings and equipment already in place. Homes and manufacturing plants designed for use with plentiful, cheap energy cannot quickly be replaced with energy-efficient buildings and equipment. Existing home appliances, office equipment, transportation systems, and scientific farming all require certain quantities of energy if they are to be operated at all. A considerable period of time is required for existing capital resources to wear out before a new capital stock

---

*The sign of demand elasticity will normally be negative, since *increases* in price generally produce *decreases* in quantity demanded (and vice versa). However, economists generally disregard the sign of the price elasticity ratio and concentrate on its magnitude: that is, whether the ratio is greater than or less than one.

†There were other causes for these recessions; however, the uniqueness of the energy price increase certainly contributed to their severity.

Figure 3–2

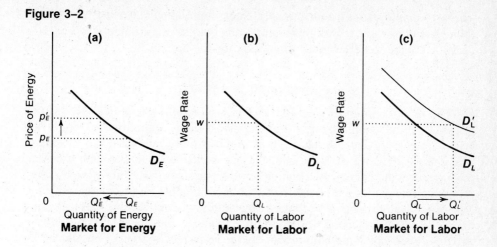

can be built. In the meantime, resource demand curves will remain fairly inelastic.

Taken as a whole, the nation's capital resources must eventually change in an important way. We have described energy as a complementary resource, used together with labor in a fairly fixed proportion for operating existing capital equipment. In an era of uncertain energy supplies, new capital resources must be developed so that labor and energy can be "substitutes": that is, used together with capital in variable proportions according to their relative prices. When such resources can be substituted for each other, quantity demanded will become more *elastic*.

To understand this, look at Figure 3–2. As before, the axes represent resource quantity and price. In Figures 3–2a and b greater ease of substitution makes both resource demand curves more sensitive to price changes. When quantity demanded is sensitive to price change, we say that demand is relatively elastic. Remember the definition of price elasticity:

$$\text{price elasticity of demand} = e_D = \frac{\%\text{ change in quantity demanded}}{\%\text{ change in price}} = \frac{\%\ \Delta\ Q_D}{\%\ \Delta\ p}$$

When percent change in quantity demanded is greater than percent change in price, the value of the elasticity ratio is greater than one, and we describe demand as elastic. The demand curves in Figure 3–2 are drawn to show percent change in quantity demanded greater than percent change in price.

With **elastic demand,** a rise in the price of energy causes firms to move up their energy demand curves for a greater drop in quantity demanded (Q_E'). But when resources can be substituted, higher energy prices can cause an increase in the demand for labor. An increase in the demand for labor is shown as a rightward shift in the labor demand curve. Look at Figure 3–2c. Substitution of labor for energy causes a rightward shift in labor demand to D_L'. At every wage level the quantity of labor demanded is greater than before. Thus, a rightward shift in D_L

increases employment from Q_L to Q_L'. Substituting a plentiful resource (labor) for a scarce resource (energy) is a more efficient use of available resources and permits a higher level of total production for the nation.

Resource Intensity

The mix of resources used together in production determines the **resource intensity.** Production that requires relatively large quantities of energy is energy-intensive, and production that requires more labor is labor-intensive. The energy-intensity of U.S. industry has contributed to the inelasticity of resource demand curves. As existing capital resources wear out, however, they may be replaced by capital resources with more flexible resource requirements. Sealed glass buildings may be replaced by buildings with windows. Fuel-guzzling autos may be replaced by energy-efficient autos and mass transit systems. Products requiring large amounts of energy in production may be replaced by other products, or their technologies may be replaced by less energy-intensive technologies. Scientific agriculture may come to depend less on scarce energy resources. Throughout the economy, business firms and individuals will learn to substitute more plentiful resources for scarce energy resources. By conserving our scarce energy resources, our nation can achieve greater efficiency in resource use.

All of this requires time. Remember we have been talking about the short run: a period of time in which certain resources and the technology for using them are fixed. Over the *long run* new capital resources can be built, and new technologies more appropriate to an era of costly energy can be developed. We will have more to say about long-run changes and their effects on the nation's productivity later in this chapter.

Productivity and Income

The mix of resources used in production determines the productivity of each. Remember that **resource productivity** is total output divided by the quantity of that resource: Thus, productivity of labor is TP/Q_L and of energy TP/Q_E, where TP represents total production and Q_L and Q_E represent quantities of labor and energy, respectively.

Reducing total output and resource employment by the same percentage has no effect on resource productivity, since numerator and denominator change by the same proportion. However, varying the quantities of labor and energy resources (*TP* remaining the same) will change their productivity in the opposite direction. Thus, more energy relative to labor reduces the productivity of energy, TP/Q_E, and increases the productivity of labor, TP/Q_L. In fact, the greater percentage increase in energy employment after World War II contributed greatly to the 3.2 percent annual increase in labor productivity over the period. On the other hand, the shift toward more labor relative to energy in recent years has contributed to the slowdown in the growth of labor productivity.

Lower worker productivity means lower real income. In the United States, workers experienced a decline in productivity in 1978 and 1979 and a decline in real per capita income in 1980. Factors other than energy contributed to the decline, of course. Likewise, other factors will play a part in increasing productivity and real incomes in the future. Energy users may develop more efficient equipment and procedures, so that a smaller quantity of energy resources can perform the same work. Workers may develop improved skills to increase labor productivity. Business policies may be designed so that firms can adapt more readily to changing market conditions. And finally, government policies may provide incentives for investments aimed at improving long-run production capabilities.

GOVERNMENT POLICY TOWARD THE DEMAND FOR ENERGY

Government policy in the United States has not always worked to promote the energy conservation and substitution effects we have indicated here. Our democratic system allows groups of citizens to defend their own economic interests against policies that might reduce their living standards. Frequently, interest group pressures to prevent declines in their own incomes actually result in greater losses for the economy as a whole. This may have been true in the case of energy.

The price of imported oil began to rise in the early 1970s. The United States at the time was experiencing wage-price controls, imposed by President Nixon. Domestic oil prices were controlled, and prices of natural gas sold across state lines had been controlled since the 1950s. Government controls to prevent price increases are called **price ceilings.** Ceilings on energy prices were intended to protect homeowners and other heavy users of oil and gas from loss of real income. When other price ceilings were finally removed in 1974, U.S. prices of these valuable resources remained under government control.

Price ceilings had the effect of holding energy prices at a particular level, p_E, as shown in Figure 3–1a. Price ceilings made it possible to postpone the change in habits and attitudes that would have made demand more elastic and reduced the energy-intensity of the U.S. economy. Foreign oil prices were outside the jurisdiction of the U.S. government, however. This meant that increases in import prices continued to be built into domestic prices. For the rest of the decade, average energy prices in the United States stayed at a level between the price ceiling and the rapidly rising price of foreign oil. Whereas other nations experienced the full force of oil price increases and began to adapt their technologies, the United States did not. Many Americans continued to purchase large, fuel-inefficient automobiles, to build energy-using homes and office buildings, and to increase their dependence on energy-intensive technologies.

Under these policies, energy demand curves remained relatively inelastic. Inelastic demand made American consumers and business firms even more vulnerable to future price increases and worsened the employment effects of cutoffs in energy supplies. In fact, import prices did rise and supplies fell again in 1979. At the same time, Congress began to phase out price ceilings on domestic oil and gas. Oil price ceilings were removed entirely by 1981, and gas price ceilings were to be completely eliminated by 1985. Prices of petroleum products rose sharply, increasing production costs throughout industry and slowing growth of production of goods and services.

Removal of price ceilings meant increased profits for energy producers. Profits rose 40 percent for producers of oil and coal and were twice as high per dollar of sales as the average for manufacturing firms. The substantial transfer of income from consumers to producers of energy raised a public outcry. Therefore, Congress passed a **windfall profits tax** to draw down oil industry profits. It was expected that tax revenues collected from oil producers would be used to help develop alternative energy sources and to pay benefits to low- and middle-income families especially harmed by high energy prices.

The goal of the new energy policy is to allow energy prices to rise to a level consistent with the true replacement cost of oil. Policymakers expect that a true market price will encourage energy conservation and substitution. In the meantime, government programs should help ease the process of adjustment for energy users.

THE MARKET FOR ENERGY: SUPPLY

It is customary to speak of energy in terms of British Thermal Units or BTUs. A BTU is the amount of heat required to raise the temperature of one pound of water one degree Fahrenheit. The United States uses about 75,000,000,000,000,000 or 75 quadrillion BTUs a year. A quadrillion BTUs is generally written 10^{15} BTU or 1 "quad."* The world's entire population uses 225 quads of energy per year; about one-third of this amount is used by the United States.

The United States relies most heavily for its energy on scarce resources and least heavily on plentiful resources. Most of our energy is provided by fluid hydrocarbons such as oil and natural gas, which supply about 75 percent of our total energy needs. Until only fifty years ago, our most important source of energy was coal, but today coal supplies only about 20 percent of our energy. Hydroelectric power and nuclear reactors each supply about 4 percent of our energy requirements.

The switch from relatively plentiful coal to oil and gas resulted in part from the great increase in automobile, air, and truck transportation, all of which require liquid fuels. Moreover, although our coal reserves are 15 to 25 times our reserves of natural gas and oil, coal is costly to extract and transport, and using it damages the environment. Persian Gulf oil fields produced oil as cheaply as 5 cents a barrel, with little damage to the landscape or environment. In the United States, Texas's Spindletop field and others produced oil cheaply until 1970, when production peaked at about 10 million barrels a day.

Natural gas was also plentiful and cheap. In fact, natural gas was once considered a nuisance to be burned off at the wellhead. Price controls held

---

*Multiplying by 10^{15} is a simple way to indicate a number with 15 zeroes.

interstate natural gas prices at 50 cents a thousand cubic feet until 1978, when price ceilings began to be removed.

Since 1970 the United States has been increasingly dependent on foreign sources to supply our energy needs. Almost 10 million barrels a day are imported from Venezuela, Canada, Mexico, and the Middle-Eastern states. In 1973 the Organization of Petroleum Exporting Countries (OPEC) cut off oil sales to the United States and increased the price from $3 to $12 a barrel. The Iranian revolution and the Iran-Iraq war brought on additional cutbacks in oil supplies, with a price increase to $35 a barrel in 1980. Although the United States has suffered from reduced oil supplies, the most severe effects have been felt in Japan, western Europe, and underdeveloped nations totally dependent on imported oil for industrial and agricultural development.

The Supply Curve

Figure 3–3 is a graph of the supply of energy. The horizontal axis measures quantities, and the vertical axis measures resource price. An energy supply curve shows the quantities of energy (Q_E) that will be supplied at various prices (p_E). The curve is drawn for the short run when factors other than resource price remain constant.

Remember that most supply curves slope upward. This is because higher prices generally encourage producers to supply larger quantities for sale. The supply curve in Figure 3–3 is drawn with a relatively steep slope. The steep slope indicates that quantities supplied are relatively insensitive to price changes.

The steep energy supply curve is a result of the characteristics of oil production. OPEC oil producers determine oil production on the basis of their need for export earnings. A higher oil price may not encourage greater OPEC production, since oil left in the ground will continue to be valuable for many years in the future. United States oil producers are already operating existing wells at maximum production. Without costly new procedures, existing wells cannot be made to produce much more oil. Prospects for new discoveries are not good, and proven reserves of oil and gas are dwindling. All these factors contribute to the relatively steep slope of the supply of energy curve.

We would describe the supply curve in Figure 3–3 as inelastic. **Price elasticity of supply** is defined as percent change in quantity supplied divided by percent change in price:*

$$\text{price elasticity of supply} = e_S = \frac{\% \text{ change in quantity supplied}}{\% \text{ change in price}} = \frac{\% \, \Delta \, Q_S}{\% \, \Delta \, p}$$

If percent change in quantity supplied is greater than percent change in price, the value of the elasticity ratio is greater than one, and supply is said to be **elastic.** If percent change in quantity supplied is less than percent change in price, the value of the elasticity ratio is less than one, and supply is **inelastic.**

*The sign of supply elasticity is generally positive. Can you explain why?

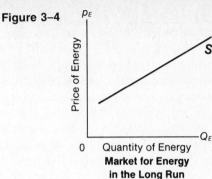

Figure 3-3

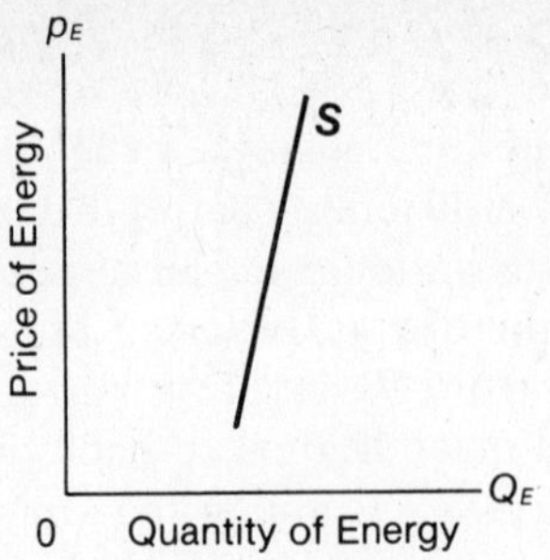

Price of Energy (p_E) vs. Quantity of Energy (Q_E), with curve S

0   Quantity of Energy

Market for Energy

Figure 3-4

Price of Energy (p_E) vs. Quantity of Energy (Q_E), with curve S

0   Quantity of Energy

Market for Energy in the Long Run

Inelasticity of energy supply has serious implications for the nation's economy. With inelastic supply in the short run, larger quantities of energy can be produced only at substantially higher prices. Then higher energy prices are built into all other U.S. prices. Rising prices for transportation services, manufactured goods, and agricultural products stimulate worker demands for cost-of-living wage increases. All of these factors aggravate price inflation.*

If we are to slow the pace of energy price inflation, we must take steps to increase the elasticity of energy supply. Over time, energy producers must be encouraged to seek new sources and new technologies for producing energy. The result could be a more elastic energy supply curve such as the one in Figure 3-4. New energy sources and new technologies can reduce the cost of producing additional energy, so that quantity supplied becomes more sensitive to price changes.

Alternative Energy Sources

If we are to resolve the crises associated with costly and scarce oil and natural gas, we must develop new energy sources that rely on our more plentiful and more dependable resources. This will require increased spending for research and development as well as substantial new investment in capital resources. Some possible sources of additional energy are described below.

Synthetic Fuels.   Coal can be used to produce fluid hydrocarbons—oil and gas — but the costs are high.† In addition to the heavy initial capital costs, handling, processing, scrubbing, and compression costs are high. Moreover, converting coal to fluid hydrocarbons involves substantial loss of energy into the environment. Finally, although coal reserves are plentiful, the increasing mining

---

*A rising short-run price for energy has positive results as well as these negative ones. In a free market system, high prices serve to discourage wasteful consumption of especially scarce resources.

†This is true of current technology and production levels. With increased production and advancing technology, the unit price of synthetic fuel may be brought down. We will have more to say about decreasing production costs later in this chapter.

and clean-up costs of coal might be expected to cause its price to rise along with the prices of oil and natural gas.

Oil from Shale.   Shale rock underlying Colorado, Wyoming, and Utah contains the equivalent of up to six times the most optimistic estimate of oil reserves in the United States. To obtain 10 to 25 gallons of oil, however, a ton of rock must be mined, crushed, and heated. Enormous amounts of water are required, as well as considerable expenditures for repairing environmental damage. Underground recovery techniques that would use less water and produce less waste rock are being tested, but not yet on a scale large enough for commercial use.

Nuclear Energy.   Light water reactors (LWRs) convert uranium energy to heat to produce steam for running turbines. However, reactors are grossly inefficient and require large amounts of increasingly costly uranium. Furthermore, LWRs also produce radioactive waste material that is difficult to dispose of. Recycling the plutonium that is produced in the nuclear reaction would save fuel and disposal costs. But plutonium can be used to make nuclear bombs, and storing it creates security problems. A "fast breeder" reactor would generate more fuel than it consumes, but none is presently operating and the lead time for building a "fast breeder" is long. Nuclear *fusion* is a new process now being developed in the Soviet Union, but it is not expected to be commercially practical any time soon.

Geothermal Power.   In Geysers Field near San Francisco, hot springs produce up to 100 tons of steam an hour at 400°F. and at pressures of 140 pounds per square foot. The steam is used to run turbines for generating electricity. Production costs are low, but there are few sites appropriate for this kind of power generation.* Moreover, underground steam contains impurities that could damage power generating equipment.

Solar Power.   Solar energy is plentiful and nonpolluting, but equipment to collect and convert it to electricity is costly. Since the sun's rays are intermittent, solar energy would have to be stored until needed. Still, there are ways to use solar energy for heating and cooling buildings, for changing wind energy to electric power, for changing urban wastes and agricultural products to fuels and fertilizers, and for using heat differentials at various ocean depths for running turbines.

Hydrogen Power.   Hydrogen is plentiful and clean, but its density is so low that enormous quantities would be required for producing energy. Moreover, specially designed containers for storing hydrogen would be costly to build.

---

*Iceland is interested in converting the steam from its geysers into a form of energy that can be beamed to satellites, transported, and beamed down as energy somewhere else where it is needed in the world.

Prospects

Robert Stobaugh and Daniel Yergin of Harvard conducted an extensive research effort into the potential of alternative energy sources for resolving the problem of scarce and costly energy.* Their conclusions can be summarized as follows:

1. Coal production involves human and environmental costs that limit its potential as a solution to the energy problem.
2. Nuclear energy production has encountered severe problems involving uranium supplies and waste disposal, in addition to health and safety hazards.
3. Few additional reserves of domestic oil and natural gas will be discovered, and their extraction costs will be high.
4. All these conventional energy sources can be enhanced, however, by government policies to lease offshore properties for oil exploration, to remove price ceilings on oil and natural gas, and to focus attention on solving the problems associated with nuclear energy.
5. Finally, a variety of government policies could help achieve a more balanced system of energy use. In particular, Stobaugh and Yergin recommend policies to encourage energy conservation in homes and factories. Conservation could be encouraged through tax credits and depreciation advantages for investments in energy-saving equipment. Solar energy production could be subsidized and policies designed to enable individuals or firms to sell solar power to local utility companies.

GOVERNMENT POLICY TOWARD THE SUPPLY OF ENERGY

In fact, government policy has generally had a negative effect on domestic production of energy. Price ceilings held the price of oil and natural gas below costs of production and discouraged investment in new exploration and development. A complicated "entitlements" program protected small, high-cost oil refiners from competition with more efficient, lower-cost producers. Artificially low energy prices discouraged exploration and development of alternative energy sources. Without domestic energy substitutes, energy supplies were limited to imported oil and oil from existing domestic sources. As as result, energy supply curves remained relatively inelastic.

For the future, some analysts have proposed more active government programs to promote development of new energy technologies. Still, there is disagreement regarding the scope and direction of government intervention in the market for energy.

*Robert Stobaugh and Daniel Yergin, *Energy Future*. New York: Random House, 1979.

Some of the disagreement over energy policy comes from disagreements about the proper role of government in the private economy. Our economic system depends primarily on decisions of individual consumers and producers who are expected to respond efficiently to market signals. Conservatives argue that government intervention in free markets distorts signals and may worsen efficiency of resource allocation. On the other hand, liberals argue that private industry in the United States has been slow to develop energy substitutes. One reason has to do with the **bottom line syndrome** of American business firms. United States corporations are required to balance their accounts regularly and report current earnings to their stockholders and creditors. This means that many business policymakers focus their attention on increasing current profits and postpone changes in fundamental technologies. They know that many stockholders want positive profits on the "bottom line" and may not tolerate large expenditures for risky, innovative energy systems. The result of the bottom line syndrome has been a lack of commitment and a shortage of private funds for investment in energy research and development.

Most of the alternative energy sources described in this chapter require heavy initial capital costs. Cash flows tend to be low or negative for many years until new plants reach full production. The long wait for profits reduces the rate of return on investment and increases the risks. Some new energy technologies face the likelihood of future shortages of engineers, technicians, and skilled labor, as well as shortages of materials and equipment. Furthermore, the threat of new environmental regulation discourages investment in new energy technologies. Finally, the U.S. patent system provides poor protection to developers of processes that may only become profitable after the developer's patent rights have expired.

Another problem has to do with the expected selling price of the finished product. Remember that the world price of oil is determined not in free markets, but largely by OPEC. At any time OPEC could allow the price to fall, making alternative energy processes unprofitable. All these considerations act to slow the response of U.S. industry to changing resource supplies.

Measuring the Costs

If government is to help develop alternative energy sources, it is important that government act efficiently. Unless government programs increase the efficiency of resource allocation, the nation may fall farther behind in reaching its energy goals. Efficient planning is especially difficult with new and untried technologies that have long time horizons.

Many energy-producing technologies are extremely costly, particularly in terms of the energy consumed in the production of energy itself. William Baumol of Princeton and New York Universities has divided the energy costs of producing alternative energy sources into three categories:*

*William J. Baumol and Sue Ann Batey Blackman, "Unprofitable Energy Is Squandered Energy," *Challenge,* July/August, 1980.

1. **Direct energy costs** of producing the energy itself; direct energy costs may constitute only about half the total energy costs of producing any of the alternative energy sources we have described.
2. **Indirect energy costs** of producing the material and component parts of the energy-producing equipment; indirect energy costs are included in the purchase price of materials and equipment used in any of the processes described in this chapter.
3. **Opportunity costs** of using available resources for producing one kind of energy apparatus instead of another; using a more energy-intensive procedure than necessary for accomplishing a production goal involves an opportunity cost.

Private business firms must evaluate all the direct, indirect, and opportunity costs before making any production decision. This is done through free market pricing. Market price is a measure of the value of all resources—including energy resources—used in production. Unless a new energy technology produces more energy than it consumes, private industry cannot be expected to undertake it. For government to undertake a project judged unprofitable by private industry may be inefficient and may weaken our nation's capacity for dealing with future energy crises.

Efficiency, Externalities, and Equity

Government intervention in free markets may be necessary if private markets are themselves inefficient, whether because of externalities or because of market power and inequities in the results of market decisions.

We have defined *externalities* as the benefits and costs of production that extend beyond an individual firm to the society at large. Some of the negative externalities associated with the energy shortage are: the threat of international political pressure, a tendency toward economic crisis with high unemployment and price inflation, and a slower pace of technological development. On the other hand, a positive externality from government intervention might be a general increase in information about energy technologies. Professors Stobaugh and Yergin point out that "information generated by an installation that does not work is often of less value to the innovator who failed than it is to society." Government intervention can provide helpful information to private business firms through programs supporting alternative energy production.

Inequities are the effects of market power that the nation as a whole regards as unfair. Some of the inequities often associated with the energy shortage are: disproportionate profits and losses among producers and users of energy, regional conflicts over allocation of available energy supplies, and wide income inequality among domestic consumers. These are the concerns that have prompted government intervention in energy markets and are likely to lead to further intervention in the future.

Government policy toward the energy sector might take the form of taxes and subsidies. Taxes and subsidies can help reduce the inequities of market decisions and offset their positive and negative externalities. They have the disadvantage of imprecision. Since inequities and externalities cannot be measured precisely, taxes collected and subsidies paid may not compensate correctly for the benefits expected. The result might be artificial incentives to carry on high-cost production, even when lower-cost processes are available.

Taxes and subsidies to promote energy development have another disadvantage. The **incidence of a tax or subsidy** may differ from what is intended. Incidence refers to the person who actually pays the tax or receives the subsidy. If the actual cost of a tax or the gain from a subsidy falls on someone other than for whom it was intended, incentives and disincentives may also be different from those intended. In general, we might expect taxes and subsidies to interfere with market efficiency: by imposing a government mandate on private decision-making, they endanger the complex system of resource allocation through free markets.

The problems associated with market power are equally complex. Market power is the result of the structure of the energy sector of the economy. Energy production requires large investments in capital equipment, with fairly continuous operation for lowest costs. The result is a high level of **industrial concentration:** a few large firms produce a significant portion of total energy output. Industrial concentration reduces competition and strengthens market power. With market power, prices may be higher than otherwise and incentives to improve productivity may be lower.

Many of the nation's energy companies have extended their holdings beyond a single energy source. Oil companies have purchased coal fields and uranium deposits so as to guarantee profits in an uncertain future. Varied holdings of energy sources increase industrial concentration and strengthen a firm's power to affect markets.

Under the nation's antitrust laws, legal action against energy producers might break up large firms into a number of competing firms. Increased competition would have both desirable and undesirable results:

- A desirable result would be to force prices down to the level of minimum production costs.
- An undesirable result would be the possibility that small firms might have higher costs because of their small scale.
- A desirable result might be elimination of monopoly profits through separation of energy production from processing and distribution.
- An undesirable result would be a loss of coordination of operations that might reduce efficiency and raise costs.

Measuring the strength of all desirable and undesirable results is impossible. For this reason, there has been no real effort to break up large energy companies. Instead, there has been greater pressure to monitor their operations and use other means to influence their production decisions.

Some form of government regulation is likely to continue in the energy sector. The loss of efficiency that results from government intervention may be compensated by a gain in equity and an increase in positive externalities. The willingness to trade off efficiency for equity and positive externalities should determine the level of government intervention in the energy sector.

Supply Curves Again

We have suggested that over time advances in technology can change the inelastic supply curve of Figure 3-3. In fact, investments in new capital resources help increase productive capacity, so that the **long-run supply curve** can become more elastic, as shown in Figure 3-4. With more elastic supply, larger quantities of energy can be produced with smaller percentage increases in price.

There are other possibilities for the *very* long run. More fundamental advances in technology in the *very* long run might enable firms to produce larger quantities at *lower* costs. Look at Figure 3-5, showing a possible energy supply curve in the very long run. The downward sloping supply curve in Figure 3-5 differs from typical supply curves in that larger and larger quantities can be produced and sold at *lower* prices. Under these circumstances, we would say that there is **negative elasticity of supply** in the very long run.

Remember the definition of supply elasticity:

$$\text{price elasticity of supply} = e_S = \frac{\%\ \text{change in quantity supplied}}{\%\ \text{change in price}} = \frac{\%\ \Delta\ Q_S}{\%\ \Delta\ _p}$$

When a percentage *increase* in quantity supplied is accompanied by a percentage *decrease* in price, the sign of supply elasticity is negative.

Negative elasticity of supply would enable industrial users of energy to increase the energy-intensity of production, raising labor productivity and real incomes. Lower energy costs would reduce production costs throughout industry and hold down the prices of most consumer goods and services. As fewer of our nation's resources are required for producing the necessities of life, more can be allocated toward improvements in the quality of life—education, health care, recreation, and cultural events. Achieving these kinds of results should be the objective of national economic policy.

Figure 3-5

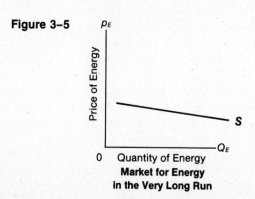

Market for Energy
in the Very Long Run

EQUILIBRIUM IN ENERGY MARKETS

When energy demand and supply curves are combined on a single graph, the result is a model of the market for energy. Figure 3–6a combines inelastic energy demand and supply curves. The intersection of demand and supply identifies the price that "clears the market" for energy. Thus, at price p_e in Figure 3–6a consumers are willing to purchase precisely the quantity of energy offered for sale.

Price p_e and quantity Q_e are the equilibrium price and quantity in energy markets. If price were higher, say, p'_e, consumers would move up their demand curves and purchase less energy. Producers would move up their supply curves and produce more energy. With quantity demanded lower than quantity

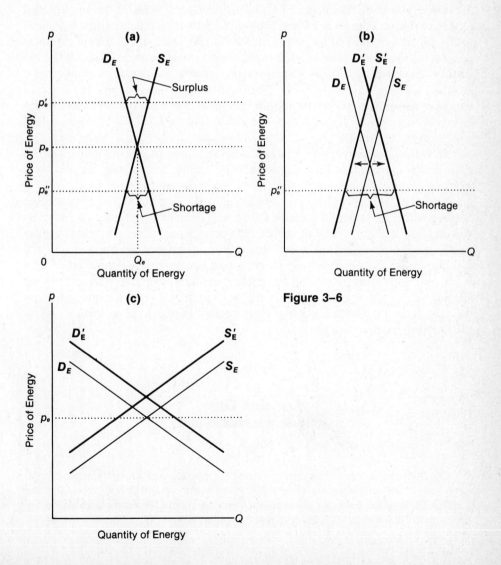

Figure 3–6

supplied, there would be a surplus in the market for energy. On the other hand, if price were lower than equilibrium, say, p''_e, consumers would move down their demand curves and attempt to use more energy. Producers would move down their supply curves and produce less. With quantity demanded greater than quantity supplied, there would be a shortage in the market for energy.

In free markets the actions of individual consumers and producers work to push price and quantity toward their equilibrium levels. When a high price yields a **surplus,** producers attempt to sell the surplus by reducing price. When a low price creates a **shortage,** consumers attempt to acquire the product by offering a higher price. In both cases, the tendency is toward equilibrium, with quantity demanded equal to quantity supplied at the equilibrium price.

When government imposes a price ceiling, the effect is to hold price below equilibrium and create a shortage. The artificially low price encourages wasteful use of energy and discourages additional production. Over time, energy demand tends to increase, shown in Figure 3–6b as a rightward shift in the demand curve to D'_E. Moreover, as existing energy sources are depleted, energy supply tends to decrease, shown as a leftward shift in the supply curve to S'_E. The result is even greater shortages, shown by the difference between quantity demanded and quantity supplied in Figure 3–6b. Shortages tend to persist until the price of energy is allowed to rise to the equilibrium level. Pencil in the new equilibrium level of energy prices after the curves have shifted on Figure 3–6b. How would you interpret this result?

The effects of more elastic demand and supply are shown in Figure 3–6c. In Figure 3–6c consumers have adjusted their habits, and business firms have modified their capital equipment so that energy demand is more responsive to price changes. Energy producers have developed new equipment and processes for responding more readily to price changes. If demand increases over time, the demand curve shifts to D'_E as before. If energy sources are depleted, supply shifts again to S'_E. Pencil in the new equilibrium price and compare with the equilibrium price in Figure 3–6b. How would you interpret this result?

There is another possibility in energy markets. We have suggested that alternative energy sources might in the very long run yield an energy supply curve with negative price elasticity. How would negative supply elasticity affect the market shown in Figure 3–6c?

Special Case

Producing Gasohol

One possible new source of energy is gasohol: a mixture of 90 parts gasoline for 10 parts alcohol. Gasohol is sold at about 8,500 filling stations in the United States and has received $800 million in federal government loan guarantees. The raw materials necessary for producing alcohol include corn, grain sorghum, wheat, cull potatoes, sugar beets, .

Figure 3–7

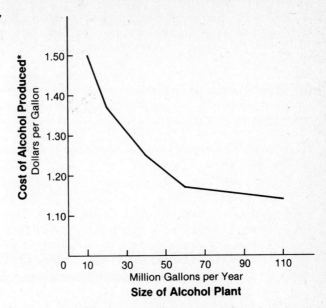

*Assumes a corn price of $2.50 per bushel and includes credit for the value of the by-product.

sugar cane, and molasses. These materials are plentiful on many farms, making small-scale production on the farm an efficient possibility. After producing alcohol, the waste material can be fed to livestock, for additional cost savings for farmers.

The use of gasohol was encouraged early in this century. Plentiful crops had pushed food prices down, and farmers needed a new use for farm products. Some years later, high gasoline prices gave another boost to alcohol fuel. Poor performance in automobiles, however, eventually turned drivers away from gasohol. Then in the Great Depression, low farm prices again caused an increase in production of gasohol. During World War II much of the German airforce flew on gasohol. Today Brazil uses excess sugar cane to produce alcohol for use in automobiles.

On-the-farm production of gasohol has certain advantages. There is a readily available source of raw materials and a need for fuel to operate farm machinery. However, small-scale production sometimes involves higher average cost than would be true for large enterprises. Cost per gallon of alcohol is high for plants designed to produce less than 60 million gallons a year. For larger plants, cost per gallon is much lower. See Figure 3–7; the horizontal axis measures the annual capacity of the plant, and the vertical axis measures cost per gallon. With corn priced at $2.50 a bushel, average cost per gallon falls to $1.15 for plants built to produce as much as 60 gallons.* This price would make gasohol competitive with gasoline except for the fact that users of gasohol need about half again as much gasohol to provide the energy equivalent of gasoline or diesel fuel.

The high cost of capital equipment is another problem for small-scale producers. High capital costs make it necessary to operate capital equipment continuously. But when food prices rise, farmers will stop producing alcohol and sell their crops in food markets. This

*SOURCE: Jennifer D. Miles, "Small-scale Production of Alcohol Fuel: Not Feasible for the Farmer," *Federal Reserve Bank of Dallas Voice*, October, 1980, pp. 12–17.

problem might be solved through cooperative enterprises that include several farms. Some advantages of cooperatives would be improved continuity in the operation of equipment, a steady supply of raw materials, and more efficient use of by-products for livestock feed.

Like other alternative energy sources, alcohol production creates some pollution. Carbon dioxide can cause suffocation, and production of gasohol can ignite fires or explosions. Moreover, the enormous amounts of water used in production can pose problems in areas of scarce water.

- What are the externalities (positive and negative) associated with the production and use of gasohol?

Mathematical Supplement

Producing Alternative Fuels

A major reason for the failure to develop alternative energy sources is the high cost of new equipment and the uncertainty of operating costs once the equipment is in place. Most new technologies follow a predictable cost pattern, often described as a **learning curve.** Costs are high in the beginning; but as the accumulated total volume of output increases, unit costs fall sharply. The reason is that every time a job is performed, workers and technicians learn to use resources more efficiently for producing greater output.

Average costs of production can be stated as a function of the accumulated volume of Total Product:

$$\text{Average Costs} = \text{function (Total Product)}$$
$$AC = f\,(TP),$$

where AC represents average unit costs and TP represents accumulated volume. The average cost equation for a learning curve is

$$AC = aTP^{-b}.$$

The coefficient a represents the theoretical cost of the first unit produced, and the exponent b represents the percent rate of change in average cost as volume increases. The sign of b is negative because a learning curve implies that average cost will decline.* A negative b can be shown as in the equation above, or the expression can be rewritten

$$AC = a/TP^{b}.$$

---

*The value of b depends strongly on the labor-intensity of the technology, since only labor can "learn" by doing. For highly capital-intensive technologies, learning depends on improved design, more efficient machines, improvements in tooling, attention to cost accounting, and reductions in waste or losses.

Figure 3–8

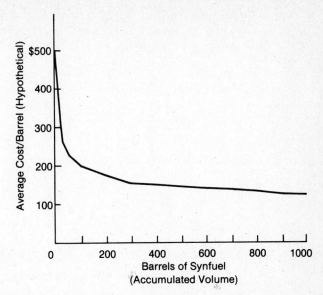

The theory behind the learning curve is that each percentage increase in volume of output reduces resource inputs by the fraction b. Lower resource inputs mean lower unit costs and higher profits for producing firms. Higher profits increase the rate of return on investment and encourage new capital investment. The ultimate result is that supply curves become more elastic, and larger quantities can be sold for lower prices than before.

Figure 3–8 is a learning curve for which the theoretical cost of producing the first barrel of synthetic fuel is $a = \$500$. The process of learning includes improvements in tooling and automation, increases in production runs, and improved skills of technicians and skilled labor, as well as technological progress in synfuel production. These improvements cause a 20 percent reduction in resource inputs for each percentage increase in accumulated volume.

The result is that $b = -0.20$. Thus, the equation for the curve on Figure 3–8 is $AC = 500(TP)^{-0.20}$.

The curve in Figure 3–8 begins with output $TP = 1$ barrel at a unit cost of $a = \$500$ and slopes downward according to $b = -0.20$. For the one hundredth barrel produced, average cost is $AC = \$500(100)^{-0.20} = \$199.05$. For the one millionth barrel, average cost falls to only $AC = \$500(1,000,000)^{-0.20} = \$31.55$. Average cost per barrel continues to fall as accumulated volume increases, although the dollar change in average cost is not as great as that associated with the first increase in volume. At some level of total production, average cost per barrel would reach the lowest possible level and become almost constant, regardless of further increases in accumulated volume. At this level, average cost would reflect the true costs of production with existing synfuel technology.

Figure 3–9 shows learning curves for $b = -0.10$ and $b = -0.30$. The relative steepness of the curve for $b = -0.30$ reflects the greater cost savings when resource inputs are reduced as much as 30 percent. The greater capacity for "learning" means that larger quantities can eventually be produced for substantially lower average cost. With $b = -0.30$, average cost levels off at about \$75 per barrel. What is the "true cost" of production if $b = -0.10$?

Until production actually begins, it is impossible to know for certain the "true cost" of producing synfuel. Engineers may estimate the value of b, however, and determine the

Figure 3–9

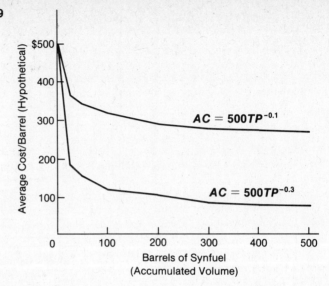

accumulated volume of synfuel production at which the average cost of production becomes competitive with the world price of oil. To illustrate, suppose engineers estimate initial average costs of $a = \$500$ with a "learning" factor of $b = -0.25$. The current world price of oil is $\$40$ a barrel. What volume of synfuel production would be necessary before average cost per barrel is reduced to $\$40$?

With $AC = aTP^{-b}$, the equation is

$$40 = 500TP^{-0.25} \text{ or } 40 = \frac{500}{TP^{0.25}}$$

Rearranging terms: $TP^{0.25} = 12.5$. To solve for TP, it is necessary to raise both sides of the equation to a power of $1/0.25$ so that

$$(TP^{0.25})^{1/0.25} = 12.5^{1/0.25}$$
$$\text{or} \quad TP^1 = 12.5^4$$
$$\text{Solving:} \quad TP = 12.5^4 = 24,414$$

According to the estimated values of a and b, the 24,415th barrel of synfuel can be produced and sold for a price that is competitive with world oil prices. Beyond this volume of output investment in alternative energy sources would become profitable.

If government-sponsored research and development can be used to increase the (negative) value of b, the rate of return on private investment could become high enough to encourage investment by the private sector. When the learning curve flattens out, average cost becomes practically constant, and producers can sell additional quantities profitably at relatively constant prices.

• Nuway Synfuel Corporation estimates that production of 50,000 barrels of synfuel will be necessary before the product will be competitive with oil at $\$40$ a barrel. Unit costs are expected to fall by 5 percent for each percentage increase in production. What is the theoretical cost of Nuway's first barrel of synfuel?

QUESTIONS

1. In what sense are labor and energy complements? Substitutes? Give examples of processes in which labor and energy are complements and substitutes.
2. Explain why increasing employment of labor is often expected to yield decreasing per capita real income. Under what conditions would this not be so?
3. Legally enforced auto fuel-economy standards have the objective of reducing energy demand and ultimately price inflation resulting from high energy prices. Under what circumstances would market forces alone impose fuel-economy standards, and when might government regulations be appropriate? Discuss.
4. To what extent should the external costs of alternative energy sources be a consideration in encouraging their production?
5. Distinguish between the direct, indirect, and opportunity costs of alternative energy sources. Which costs are most likely to be considered by private energy firms? Least likely?
6. What circumstances contribute to negative supply elasticity over the very long run? Illustrate algebraically and graphically. What are the implications of negative supply elasticity?
7. List as many examples as you can of circumstances in which popular opinion and political pressure have worked to reduce efficiency in the production and consumption of energy. What have been the effects of such pressures on equity?

DEFINITIONS

The bottom-line syndrome is concern with profits reported on the bottom line of financial statements. The bottom-line syndrome may discourage major technological changes in favor of policies that maintain an acceptable level of current profits.

Complementary resources are resources that must be used together in production.

A derived demand is demand for a resource to be used to produce a good or service desired by consumers. The demand for energy and the demand for labor are derived demands.

Direct energy costs are the energy costs involved directly in production of a good or service — in this context, in production of alternative energy sources.

Elastic demand reflects a substantial response of quantity demanded to price changes. With elastic demand, percent change in quantity demanded is greater than percent change in price, so that the elasticity ratio is greater than one.

Elastic supply reflects a substantial response of quantity supplied to price changes. With elastic supply, percent change in quantity supplied is greater than percent change in price, so that the elasticity ratio is greater than one.

Equilibrium in energy markets occurs at the price and quantity at which all buyers are satisfied and all sellers can sell their output.

Incidence of a tax or subsidy refers to who actually sacrifices to pay the tax and who actually gains from the subsidy. Depending on the incidence of the tax or subsidy, a tax may discourage certain activities and a subsidy may encourage certain activities.

Indirect energy costs are the energy costs involved in production of the materials and equipment used in producing a good or service — in this context, in production of alternative energy sources.

Industrial concentration involves the combination of several business firms into a firm large enough to enjoy a degree of market power.

Inelastic demand reflects a low response of quantity demanded to price changes. With inelastic demand, percent change in quantity demanded is less than percent change in price, so that the elasticity ratio is less than one.

Inelastic supply reflects a low response of quantity supplied to price changes. With inelastic supply, percent change in quantity supplied is less than percent change in price, so that the elasticity ratio is less than one.

A learning curve is a mathematical device for describing falling unit costs of production as the accumulated volume of output increases.

A long-run supply curve shows the quantities that will be supplied at various prices over a period long enough to allow for construction of new capital resources and development of new technologies. In the long run, additional quantities of a good or service may be supplied at lower costs.

Negative elasticity of supply occurs when increases in quantity supplied can be provided at lower prices. Under such circumstances, the terms of the elasticity ratio have different signs and the value of the elasticity ratio is negative.

Opportunity costs are the sacrifices of one kind of production for the sake of another. In this context, the opportunity cost of producing one type of alternative energy source is the other type that might have been produced.

Price ceilings are legal prohibitions against price increases. Price ceilings were a part of President Nixon's wage-price controls.

Price elasticity of demand is a measure of the responsiveness of quantity demanded to changes in price. Price elasticity of demand is calculated according to:

$$e_D = \frac{\% \text{ change in quantity demanded}}{\% \text{ change in price}} = \frac{\% \ \Delta Q_D}{\% \ \Delta p}$$

Price elasticity of supply is a measure of the responsiveness of quantity supplied to changes in price. Price elasticity of supply is calculated according to:

$$e_S = \frac{\% \text{ change in quantity supplied}}{\% \text{ change in price}} = \frac{\% \ \Delta Q_S}{\% \ \Delta p}$$

A resource demand curve indicates the quantities of that resource that will be purchased at various prices. Resource demand curves typically slope downward from left to right, since larger quantities will normally be purchased at lower prices.

Resource intensity refers to the proportions of resources used together in production. A high proportion of energy is associated with energy-intensive production and a high proportion of labor is associated with labor-intensive production.

Resource productivity is Total Product divided by the quantity of the resource. Thus, the productivity of labor is TP/Q_L and the productivity of energy is TP/Q_E.

A shortage of a commodity occurs when price is held below equilibrium, so that quantity demanded is greater than quantity supplied.

Substitute resources are resources whose quantities may vary in production according to relative prices.

A surplus of a commodity occurs when price is held above equilibrium, so that quantity supplied is greater than quantity demanded.

A windfall-profits tax is a tax on gains achieved through higher prices, rather than through improvements in production methods and reductions in costs.

SUGGESTED READINGS

Anderson, Alan, Jr. "Energy in Transition." *Across the Board,* August, 1980, p. 53.

Baumol, William J., and Sue Anne Batey Blackman. "Unprofitable Energy Is Squandered Energy." *Challenge*, July/August, 1980, p. 28.

Davidson, Paul. "The Economics of Natural Resources." *Challenge,* March/April, 1979, p. 40.

"Energy Growth Fuels Problems for a Conglomerate." *Business Week,* November 23, 1981, p. 80.

"Gas Pipeliners." *Business Week,* July 2, 1982, p. 44.

"The Great Arctic Energy Rush." *Business Week,* January 24, 1983, p. 52.

Hill, David H. "The Impact of Natural Gas Deregulation on the American Family." *Economic Outlook USA,* Survey Research Center, University of Michigan, Autumn, 1981, p. 84.

Jorgenson, Dale W. "The Answer is Energy." *Challenge,* November/December, 1980, p. 16.

"The Leverage of Lower Oil Prices." *Business Week,* March 22, 1982, p. 66.

Levy, Walter, J. "Oil and the Decline of the West." *Across the Board,* September, 1980, p. 5.

Millenson, Michael L. "Industry's Own Search for Energy." *Across the Board,* May, 1978, p. 11.

"Oil-field Suppliers: The Crash After a Boom." *Business Week,* September 27, 1982, p. 66.

Rogers, James T. "Synfuels." *Across the Board,* June, 1981, p. 41.

Rowen, Henry S., and John P. Weyant. "Will Oil Prices Collapse?" *Challenge,* November/December, 1981, p. 11.

Stobaugh, Robert, and Daniel Yergin. *Energy Future.* New York: Random House, 1979.

Thurow, Lester. *The Zero-Sum Society.* New York: Basic Books, 1980, Chapter 2.

CHAPTER FOUR

Providing for the Nation's Defense

How Much Can We Afford?

LEARNING OBJECTIVES

- To examine the allocation of resources for production of civilian or military goods and the opportunity costs of the allocative decision.
- To use a model of production possibilities to illustrate the marginal rate of substitution in production associated with decisions to provide civilian and military goods.
- To show how the existence of fixed resources causes increases in marginal costs and in the marginal rate of substitution in production.
- To illustrate consumer preference for goods through indifference curves representing various levels of total utility.
- To explain the shape of indifference curves in terms of decreasing marginal utility or a declining marginal rate of substitution in consumption.
- To show the most efficient allocation of resources where $MRS_P = MRS_C$, or where the additional cost associated with acquiring the current combination of civilian and military goods is equal to the additional utility.
- To apply the model of production possibilities to recent and prospective military programs in the United States and abroad.

There is a primitive Indian tribe in the Aleutian Islands that follows a unique tradition. The tradition is called the "Potlatch" and involves weeks of planning, ending with a feast and ceremonial bonfire. What do the islanders burn? They burn the products of weeks of careful work! Handwoven baskets and blankets, carved chests and prized bronze plaques, furs, and household furnishings. Whatever is precious to them — whatever has consumed their careful attention and energy — is destroyed.

A society must be rather rich if it is to observe traditions like the Potlatch. If there is to be a surplus for ceremonial destruction, workers must be able to produce more than enough material wealth to satisfy the people's needs. Such wasteful behavior contradicts the usual assumption underlying the study of economics. Economic theory is based on the assumption of scarce resources and unlimited wants. With an inevitable gap between wants and the capacity to satisfy wants, the goal of economic policy is to use resources efficiently for producing the largest possible quantity of desired goods and services. To destroy goods and the resources for producing goods is not efficient in the usual economic sense. Therefore, we must look outside conventional economic theory for an explanation.

Karl Marx had an explanation for the kind of behavior carried on in the Potlatch. Marx was a German philosopher whose analysis of the market system falls within the realm of **political economy.** Political economy is the study of conflicting interests of various groups in the economy, particularly with respect to the distribution of the nation's wealth. Thus, political economy involves considerations other than strictly economic considerations.

According to Marx, all economic systems throughout world history have carried within themselves the "seeds of their own destruction." Each has generated internal conflicts that finally caused its downfall and its replacement by another. The result has been a series of imperfect systems, progressing to what Marx believed would be the perfect economic system: **communism.** Under communism, productive wealth is owned "in common" by all the people of the society, and income is paid to all the people on the basis of need.

Marx called the market system **capitalism** because it depends on private ownership of capital resources. Owners of factories and equipment are called **capitalists.** Capitalists employ workers to operate capital equipment. Income from operations is paid to workers in the form of wages and to capitalists in the form of profit.

Capitalism's internal conflict, according to Marx, results from the mismatch between its tremendous ability to produce goods and services and an unequal pattern of income distribution, such that much of its output cannot be sold. Over time, he said, advances in technology tend to increase the capital-intensity of production, increasing worker productivity and stimulating economic growth. But as workers are replaced by machines, a larger share of total income is paid to the owners of capital. This leaves less buying power in the hands of workers. At the same time, increasing profits for the capitalists mean increasing funds for new investment. More workers are replaced by machines, income distribution becomes still more unequal, and sales grind to a halt.

Unless goods can be sold, said Marx,. the capitalist system will suffer worsening recessions and, finally, revolution. To avoid this violent end, capitalist nations would arrange to destroy surplus production through war. Producing goods for war and employing resources for military production would maintain the capitalists' profits and preserve the capitalist system, despite its internal conflict.*

Marx would explain the Potlatch in the same way he explained wars: that is, as a way of eliminating surplus production. Eliminating surplus goods and services ensures that there will be new demands and new job opportunities for workers. Additionally, maintaining a scarcity of goods helps to maintain the existing social order.

Eliminating the surplus has other effects, however. In this text we have been considering the use of resources for producing some quantity of goods and services. We have shown how new capital investment and improvements in technology can shift upward a nation's production function and increase real income. New investment depends on producing a surplus of goods and services over and above the current needs of the people. Then releasing other resources for construction of new capital resources and development of new technologies yields advances in material standards of living.

On the other hand, when surplus production is destroyed, the community sacrifices the additional capital resources that might otherwise have been produced. Production for war has a similar effect. It reduces the quantity of resources available for satisfying the current and future needs of the people.

True, some level of military production is necessary for ensuring the nation's security. And military production may yield positive externalities in terms of new products and new industrial processes. Wars bring profits to firms that produce military equipment. Not only do capitalist owners prosper, but many workers also enjoy rising incomes as a result of military production. Moreover, the stimulus to technological development from a military emergency is often extended to the production of consumer goods and services, promoting economic growth and development throughout the economy.

The important issue is the same as that faced by the Aleutian Indians: *using scarce resources efficiently to produce goods and services the people want.* The informed judgment of the people is necessary for deciding the appropriate allocation of resources: for production of consumer goods and capital resources, on the one hand, or production of military goods, on the other.

This chapter will explore the process by which any nation—whether primitive or advanced—decides on the allocation of its productive resources. When resources are allocated according to the wants of the people, we say that

---

*Marx's insights are of value today more for their sweeping perspective than for their consistency with reality. The wars of the twentieth century have been as much a struggle to *acquire* goods and services as to *destroy* them. It is more often the aspiring, developing industrial nation that has fought to extend its control over such resources as coal and iron deposits, fertile farmlands, cheap labor, seaports, and rail lines. Although the motives may have been acquisition, however, the results have generally been destruction.

production is *allocatively efficient:* that is, resources are being used to produce as much as possible of the things people want. We will begin with an analysis of a nation's possible production and continue with an analysis of the people's preferences. Then we will combine production possibilities with preferences to determine equilibrium production for a nation. Finally, we will discuss policy issues of the United States over recent decades and some possible issues of national security for the future.

THE THEORY OF RESOURCE ALLOCATION

Deciding to allocate productive resources toward military purposes implies a corresponding decision to reduce resources for civilian production. The sacrifice associated with choosing one alternative over another is called an **opportunity cost.** The opportunity cost of tanks, bombers, and submarines is things like automobiles, schools, and vacation homes.

Production Possibilities

Opportunity costs can be illustrated through use of a model of **production possibilities.** Production possibilities are shown in Figure 4–1, with civilian production measured on the vertical axis and military production on the horizontal axis. The curve in Figure 4–1 defines maximum production possibilities of both types of goods when all resources are used efficiently and the best available technology is applied. The maximum quantity of goods such as tanks, bombers, and submarines is shown at point X, where production of goods such as automobiles, schools, and vacation homes is zero. The maximum quantity of civilian goods is shown at point Y with zero production of military goods. Points along the curve define all possible combinations of both types of goods.

Figure 4–1

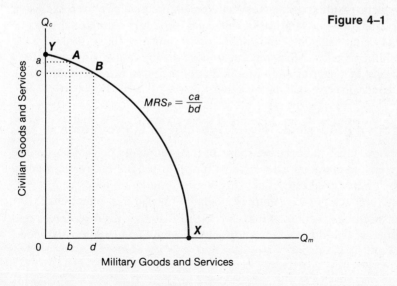

$$MRS_P = \frac{ca}{bd}$$

Movement along the production possibilities curve reflects decisions to reallocate productive resources from one combination of civilian and military production to another. The slope of the curve measures opportunity cost, in terms of quantities along the vertical axis associated with a one-unit gain along the horizontal axis: slope $= -\Delta Q_c/\Delta Q_m$. The necessary sacrifice of one type of good for producing another type is called the **marginal rate of substitution in production.** The marginal rate of substitution in production in Figure 4–1 is the quantity of civilian goods given up for each additional unit of military goods produced: $MRS_P = -\Delta Q_c/\Delta Q_m$. Thus the marginal rate of substitution in production is also the slope of the production possibilities curve.

The production possibilities curve is concave to the origin. The concave shape is a result of the increasing marginal rate of substitution in production as more resources are allocated to one type of production or the other.

To understand this, begin at point Y where production includes OY units of civilian goods and zero military goods. Move along the curve to point A for production of one unit of military goods and note the sacrifice of civilian goods necessary for increasing military production. The necessary sacrifice for producing the first unit of military equipment is aY of civilian goods. Stated differently, the marginal rate of substitution in production is $MRS_P = -\Delta Q_c/\Delta Q_m = aY/Ob$, which is the slope of the production possibilities curve between Y and A. Now move along the curve to point B for production of a second unit of military equipment. The sacrifice of civilian goods is shown by $-\Delta Q_c = ca$. The marginal rate of substitution in production is $MRS_P = ca/bd$, which is the slope of the production possibilities curve between A and B. Compare the slope of this segment with that between Y and A. The steeper slope indicates a higher marginal rate of substitution in production for the second unit of military production.

All along the curve, additional units of military production require higher opportunity costs and, therefore, a higher marginal rate of substitution in production. The same result accompanies a movement up the curve from exclusive production of military goods at X. In this case, producing additional units of civilian goods requires higher and higher opportunity costs in terms of the sacrifice of military goods. Along any segment of the curve, the slope measures the marginal rate of substitution in production of the good measured along one axis for the good measured along the other.

Increasing Marginal Rate of Substitution in Production

We have noted that the concave shape of the production possibilities curve indicates increasing marginal rate of substitution in production for producing either good. The marginal rate of substitution in production tends to increase because of differences in the resources available for use in production.

Economists divide resources into two classifications: **fixed resources** and **variable resources.** Fixed resources are things like land and capital equipment, which are in relatively constant supply in the short run.* Variable resource things like labor, electric power, and raw materials, the supply of which may be varied according to the desired quantity of output.

Technical characteristics of fixed resources limit the kinds and quantities of output they can produce. Still, within these limitations, fixed resources can be used more or less intensively by varying the quantities of other resources used with them. Thus, labor, electric power, and raw materials can be used in greater or lesser amounts for increasing or decreasing the quantity of output from a given quantity of fixed resources.

Increasing the quantity of variable resources for use with some constant quantity of fixed resources ultimately yields smaller gains in total output. When additional units of variable resources yield fewer additional units of output, the opportunity cost of those additional units is greater. We say that marginal costs increase. Higher costs for producing more of one type of good mean greater sacrifice of the other. The result is an increasing marginal rate of substitution and a steeper production possibilities curve.

To summarize, the production possibilities curve defines the maximum quantities of goods that may be produced with current resources and technology. The concave shape of the curve reflects increasing marginal rate of substitution in production: that is, the increasing sacrifice of one type of good necessary for producing an additional unit of the other. As more of one type of good is produced, its marginal cost increases; this is because of the limitations associated with using existing supplies of fixed resources.

Consumer Preferences

A production possibilities curve shows the necessary trade-offs for producing various quantities of goods, in particular, civilian and military goods. A nation's willingness to sacrifice one good for another is shown on curves like those in Figure 4–2. Thus, Figure 4–1 is drawn from the standpoint of production; Figure 4–2 is drawn from the standpoint of consumption. Again, we have used the vertical axis to measure civilian goods and the horizontal axis to measure military goods. People's willingness to sacrifice one good for another is based on the relative usefulness of the two goods. Individuals normally prefer a combination of goods that provides the greatest total usefulness or **utility**. The curves in Figure 4–2 define various combinations of military and civilian goods that provide equal utility. The curve labeled U_1 provides total utility equal to some quantity 1. Curves drawn to the right of U_1 contain larger quantities of one or both goods and, therefore, greater total utility. The curve to the left of U_1 contains smaller quantities and less total utility. Along a single curve all combinations of goods yield equal utility, so that persons are "indifferent" about the choices on a single curve. Therefore, the curves in Figure 4–2 are called **indifference curves.**

*We have defined the short run as a period of time in which quantities of one or more of the four kinds of productive resources are unchanged.

Figure 4-2

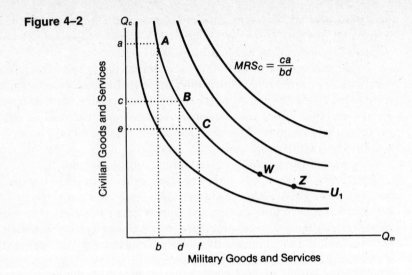

Military Goods and Services

Indifference curves are drawn convex to the origin.* The reason has to do with changes in preferences as persons acquire more or less of certain goods included in the available combinations. To understand this, select a point A on the curve U_1 representing $Q_c = Oa$ of civilian goods and $Q_m = Ob$ of military goods. Then move along the curve to point B and note the large quantity of civilian goods $(-\Delta Q_c = ca)$ that would willingly be sacrificed to acquire one additional unit of military goods $(+\Delta Q_m = bd)$. The amount of the sacrifice is reflected in the steep slope of the indifference curve between A and B.

Now move along the curve to point C for a combination that includes one more unit of military goods and note the quantity of civilian goods that would willingly be sacrificed to acquire an additional unit of military goods. For an additional unit $(+\Delta Q_m = df)$ persons are willing to sacrifice the smaller quantity $(-\Delta Q_c = ec)$ of civilian goods. The smaller sacrifice is reflected in the flatter slope of the indifference curve. In fact, continuing to move down the indifference curve involves still smaller holdings of civilian goods and less willingness to sacrifice civilian goods for the sake of military production. As the willingness to sacrifice civilian goods declines, the indifference curve becomes flatter.

The decreasing slope of an indifference curve reflects the smaller added usefulness or utility associated with additional quantities of the good on the horizontal axis. We say that **marginal utility** decreases. Decreasing marginal utility is a result of the proportions of the two goods held in the various combinations along the curve. In general, when combinations include relatively large amounts of one good, the usefulness or utility associated with additional units of that good is low.† Large quantities of that good may willingly be sacrificed for the good held in relatively smaller quantities. On the other hand, as combinations

---

*Note the contrast with the concave shape of the production possibilities curve.

†This is true of civilian goods at point A.

come to include smaller quantities of a good, its marginal utility will be higher, and smaller quantities will be willingly sacrificed.*

Note that decreasing marginal utility occurs also when moving from a point Z low on the indifference curve to W. In this case, the flat slope indicates a willingness to sacrifice relatively large quantities of military equipment for smaller quantities of civilian goods. The reason is the low marginal utility of military goods at point Z. However, as combinations come to include less military equipment, the marginal utility of military goods increases. As a result, the willingness to sacrifice military equipment for additional civilian goods decreases and the curve itself becomes steeper.

The willingness to sacrifice one type of good for another is called the **marginal rate of substitution in consumption.** In Figure 4–2 the marginal rate of substitution in consumption is the willingness to sacrifice civilian goods for an additional unit of military goods: $MRS_C = -\Delta Q_c/\Delta Q_m$. This is also the slope of the indifference curve. Thus, the decreasing slope of the indifference curve reflects a decreasing marginal rate of substitution in consumption of civilian and military goods. Stated differently, the slope of an indifference curve reflects a reduced willingness to sacrifice one kind of good as holdings of that good decrease.

The Equilibrium Quantity of Production

Figures 4–1 and 4–2 illustrate two fundamental characteristics of an economic system:

1. Figure 4–1 illustrates *trade-offs in production* — the opportunity costs associated with a decision to allocate resources in a certain way. The quantity of one good that must be given up to produce the other is the marginal rate of substitution in production. Thus the marginal rate of substitution in production of civilian and military goods is $-\Delta Q_c/\Delta Q_m = MRS_P$. This is the sacrifice that *must be made* for some additional quantity of military production. Using fixed resources and technology to produce more of a good ultimately leads to increasing marginal costs and a rising marginal rate of substitution in production. The concave shape of the production possibilities curve reflects increasing marginal costs as larger quantities of either good are produced.
2. Figure 4–2 illustrates *trade-offs in consumer preferences* — the characteristics of particular goods that fulfill the needs of people. The marginal rate of substitution in consumption ($MRS_C = -\Delta Q_c/\Delta Q_m$) is the sacrifice that *will be made* for some additional quantity of military production. The marginal rate of substitution in consumption depends on the usefulness or utility associated with additional units of goods. The convex shape of the indifference curve reflects decreasing marginal utility associated with larger holdings of either good.

---

*This is true of civilian goods at point Z.

Figure 4-3

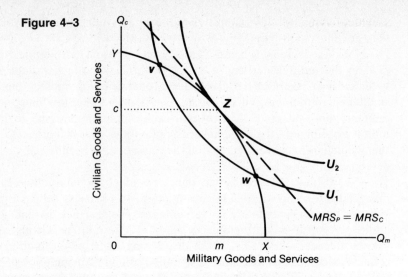

We may assume that a nation will attempt to allocate its resources so as to achieve the level of total production that yields maximum total utility for its people. In terms of our economic model, the best combination of civilian and military goods would be defined at the point on the production possibilities curve in Figure 4-1 that touches the highest possible indifference curve on Figure 4-2. We have drawn a production possibilities curve together with a group of indifference curves in Figure 4-3 and identified the appropriate choice at Z, with Oc production of civilian goods and Om of military goods. The total utility of the nation at Z is defined by U_2, the level of utility for which the indifference curve was drawn.

Where the production possibilities curve touches an indifference curve, their slopes are equal. Thus, the marginal rate of substitution in production is equal to the marginal rate of substitution in consumption: $MRS_P = MRS_C$. The dashed line in Figure 4-3 is drawn where the curves touch. It has a slope of $-\Delta Q_c/\Delta Q_m$ at the point of tangency. The slope of the dashed line represents the nation's ultimate trade-off, both in terms of production possibilities and in terms of the preferences of the people. At Z, the combination of military and civilian goods is such that the added cost of military production is equal to the added usefulness of military goods. (Likewise, the added cost of civilian production is equal to the added usefulness of civilian goods.) Stated differently, production of both goods is carried to the point at which the gain in utility associated with additional production of both goods is equal to their added cost.

Equality between the marginal rates of substitution in production and consumption represents the *most efficient allocation of resources* for the nation: it is the maximum output possible with given resources and technology to achieve maximum satisfaction in terms of the preferences of the people. Inequality between MRS_P and MRS_C would indicate inefficient resource allocation and call for a reallocation toward a combination more consistent with preferences. For instance, $MRS_C > MRS_P$ at point V would indicate a greater willingness to sacrifice civilian goods than is required at the existing level of military and civilian production. Moving down the production possibilities curve would yield military goods providing greater utility than the cost, in terms of civilian goods given up. At point W, on the other hand, $MRS_P > MRS_C$ indicates greater current sacrifices of civilian goods than consumers are willing to make. Moving up the production possibilities curve would avoid the excessive sacrifice associated with military production and achieve greater total utility for the nation's people.

At both V and W, resources are misallocated, such that total utility is less than the maximum utility that would be possible at Z. We would call the combination at Z **equilibrium production** for the nation. It represents the most efficient allocation of available resources, consistent with the preferences of the people.

Changes in Equilibrium Production

The position and shape of production possibilities depend on the quantity and quality of available resources and technology in the short run. In the long run, both resource supplies and productivity tend to increase. We have seen that a major reason for rising productivity in the long run is an increase in capital resources — both *material* capital in the form of buildings and equipment and *human* capital in the form of improved health and education of workers. Long-range growth in production possibilities would be shown by a shift to the right of the production possibilities curve. Changes in resources or technology that affect different kinds of production differently would be shown by shifting the production possibilities curve farther along the axis of the favored good.

Changes in production technology also cause changes in the shape of the production possibilities curve. An increase in the production costs of military goods, for example, would increase the necessary sacrifice of consumer goods for each additional unit of military goods. This would mean a higher marginal rate of substitution in production and a steeper production possibilities curve along its entire length. A steeper production possibilities curve would touch an indifference curve along a steeper segment. The result would be reduced production of military goods and increased production of civilian goods at the point where the higher MRS_P is equal to MRS_C. Falling production costs of military goods would yield the reverse changes.

The position and shape of indifference curves depend on the public's preferences for civilian and military goods. Changes in preferences change the position and shape of the curves. A sense of national danger, for instance, would increase the usefulness of military equipment and increase the willingness to sacrifice civilian goods for the sake of military production. The marginal rate of substitution in consumption would increase, and indifference curves would become steeper along their entire length. Steeper indifference curves would touch the production possibilities curve along a steeper segment. The result would be increased production of military goods and reduced production of civilian goods. Equilibrium production would occur where the higher MRS_C is equal to MRS_P.

On the other hand, a sense of world peace would reduce the public's desire for military production and reduce the willingness to sacrifice civilian goods for the sake of national defense. Or critical domestic problems might change the preferences of the people toward civilian production of consumer goods and services, capital resources, and government expenditures for social programs. MRS_C would fall, and indifference curves would become flatter. Changes in the shape of indifference curves would be accompanied by a movement along the production possibilities curve and a corresponding change in resource allocation. A change in the ultimate trade-off in terms of production possibilities and preferences would be shown by a shift in the dashed line drawn at the point of tangency.

Changing circumstances are shown in Figures 4–4a and b. Explain the possible basis for each change shown. Then suggest other possible changes in one or both curves and discuss their effects on resource allocation.

Over time a nation's production possibilities curve may be expected to shift to the right. Greater production possibilities enable a nation to achieve higher levels of total utility with larger quantities of *both* goods. Equilibrium points for successive years would lie higher and to the right. Connecting the points associated with successive years produces a curve representing the proportion of military production relative to total production for the nation. A curve rising straight from the origin, as in Figure 4–4c, indicates a constant share of resources allocated to military production. A bend toward the axis representing military production indicates an increasing share, and a bend away from the axis indicates a decreasing share.

MILITARY PRODUCTION IN THE UNITED STATES

In the United States, annual expenditures for national defense have varied from 2.2 percent of Gross National Product (GNP) in the year prior to World War II to more than 41 percent of GNP toward the end of that war. Defense expenditures rose again to more than 13 percent of GNP during the Korean War and 9 percent during the war in Viet Nam. Throughout the 1970s defense expenditures declined relative to GNP and constituted only 6 percent of GNP in 1981. Expenditures associated with war continue for many years after the war has ended because of the continuing cost of veterans' benefits, interest charges on debt, and war reparations.

The opportunity cost of defense expenditures (in terms of the sacrifice of civilian goods and services) is difficult to measure. One reason is the time lag required for defense expenditures to affect civilian production. Initially, increased defense production may take place through the use of unemployed resources so that both kinds of production can increase. Some time may elapse before the scarcity of resources begins to affect civilian production. Another reason involves the technology of production. Expanded research and development efforts, undertaken for military production, may at the same time increase the capacity for producing civilian goods and services. And the expanded level of economic activity in general might stimulate growth of production throughout the civilian sector.

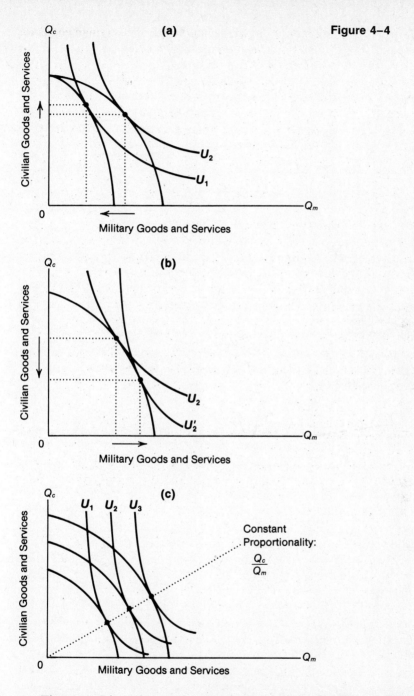

Figure 4–4

Figure 4–5 is a time series graph showing the fraction of GNP spent for military purposes since 1940. Compare Figure 4–5 with the following figures showing rates of change in the civilian sector. Figure 4–6 is a time-series graph showing percentage changes in real per capita income since 1940. Although the pattern of income change is similar to the pattern of military production, correla-

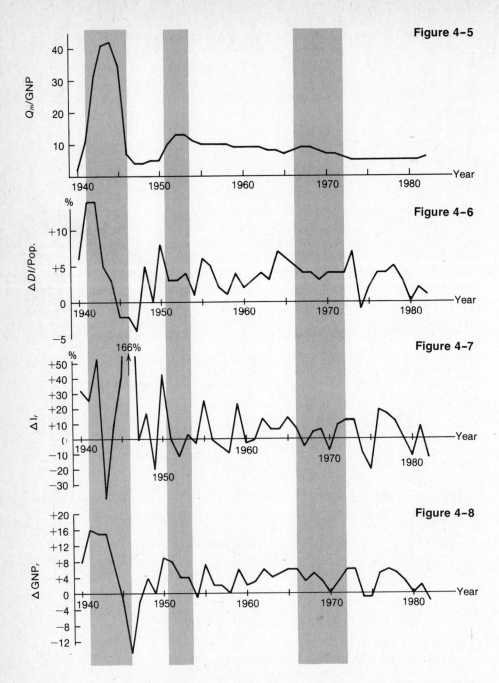

Figure 4-5

Figure 4-6

Figure 4-7

Figure 4-8

tion between the two series is weak. The same is true of Figure 4–7, which shows percentage changes in real investment spending annually. Investment spending fluctuates widely in response to changing profit expectations in business firms. Profit expectations depend strongly on expected sales of military and civilian goods and services, but also on the rate of operation and the age of existing capital equipment. The series of real per capita income and investment expenditures (Figures 4–6 and 4–7) correspond more closely with cycles in total production, shown as Figure 4–8. In Figure 4–8, six postwar recessions are identified with negative growth in real GNP. Recessions are also associated with negative growth in per capita income and real investment, as shown by the corresponding dips in the series in Figures 4–6 and 4–7.

Analysts are divided on the question of the relationship between spending for military purposes and cycles in total production. The leader of the Russian revolution, V.I. Lenin, was a follower of Karl Marx. However, Lenin modified and extended Marx's view of capitalist wars to conform to what he believed to be true of modern industrial nations. Instead of using wars to destroy surplus production, he said, capitalist nations use war to acquire the resources and exploit the markets of less developed nations. Thus, wars bring on prosperous upswings in economic activity, followed by recessions during peacetime.

A more contemporary economist, N. Kondratieff (also a Russian but not a Marxist), confirmed a relationship between wars and economic activity but raised questions about the direction of causality: Do wars bring prosperity? he asked, or does prosperity lead to war? In the first case, wars might be expected to stimulate production and raise incomes. In the second, increased production might stimulate warlike behavior to secure materials and markets. There is probably an element of truth in each of these explanations.

Whatever the cause of the urge toward military activity, the immediate effect is an increase in the marginal utility of military goods and a movement along the nation's production possibilities curve. Equilibrium will occur along a steeper segment, where the marginal rates of substitution in production and consumption are equal. If the nation has unemployed resources, the shift to military production can be accomplished without sacrificing civilian production, and there will be economic growth. Rising prosperity will encourage new investment spending and increase production possibilities for the future. The long-range effect might be a rightward shift in production possibilities and a higher level of total utility. Once all resources are fully employed, however, a shift toward military production requires a sacrifice of other goods and services. Then, the long-range effect might be reduced production possibilities and slower growth in living standards for the people.

EVALUATING DEFENSE POLICY

The most efficient allocation of the nation's resources occurs where $MRS_P = MRS_C$. At this level of production, the usefulness or utility gained from additional production is equal to the additional costs, in terms of other goods not produced. Unless $MRS_P = MRS_C$ the nation is not achieving maximum total utility from its available resources and technology.

Needless to say, measuring the utility and cost associated with these kinds of allocative decisions is difficult. The marginal utility associated with military expenditures, for instance, includes such vague and immeasurable benefits as the following:

- deterrence of physical attack and preservation of trillions of dollars of productive capital and millions of human lives;
- defense of national interests abroad, including resource and product markets as well as vital transport lanes;
- protection of our way of life and that of allied nations.

Marginal costs are equally vague and immeasurable. Costs include not only the immediate sacrifice of civilian goods associated with production of tanks and planes and the salaries of military personnel, but other opportunity costs as well:

- the civilian technology that is not developed or exploited because of war;
- the human capital that is destroyed or not developed;
- the irreversible social, economic, and environmental changes that may accompany military production.

The utility and cost of civilian production are equally difficult to define and measure.

The 1960s.   The first systematic attempt to measure the utility and cost of military expenditures occurred under Secretary of Defense Robert S. McNamara during the 1960s. Until the 1960s, the U.S. military establishment had grown rather haphazardly. There was little relationship between *planning* for achieving defense goals and *budgeting* to finance the plans. Typically, the Administration and Congress would allocate a certain level of defense expenditures for the year, and the military services would compete among themselves for funds to finance their separate programs. The frequent result was duplication and waste.

McNamara initiated a system of planning-programming-budgeting (PPB). Under PPB, the first step was to define national security objectives and plan a long-range strategy consistent with these objectives. Then planners would decide on the military forces and equipment required for carrying out the strategy. Finally, the cost of the strategy would be evaluated, coordinating current costs with cost projections at least five years in the future. Programs were to be under continuous review for efficiency, especially in relation to other possible strategies and to the separate parts of the prevailing strategy. Weapons systems would be evaluated in terms of their contribution to the strategy as a whole — their destructive potential, reliability, accuracy, and cost.

The diversity of military systems and the wide range of contingencies in their use made PPB uncertain. Furthermore, new research and development continued to make old strategies obsolete and to present new strategic opportunities to the nation's policymakers.

The 1970s.   The strategy of the 1970s was to build the capacity to fight one and a half wars simultaneously: a major war with the Soviet Union and a "brushfire" war in a less developed part of the world. Capacity to fight two different types of war required two different types of military equipment: heavy, long-range nuclear equipment on the one hand and smaller, more mobile weapons for use by conventional military forces on the other.

The fundamental focus of U.S. policy, however, became *deterrence:* that is, a collection of defense equipment sufficient to deter a nation from attacking. The United States has relied on a three-sided defense system, the "triad," to deter the Soviet Union from attacking. The sides of the triad are:

1. 1,054 land-based missile launchers armed with Minutemen missiles carrying multiple nuclear warheads;
2. 419 B-52 and FB-111 bombers to penetrate enemy territory with nuclear or conventional weapons;
3. 41 Polaris and Poseidon submarines positioned around the world, each carrying 16 missiles and ready to respond to attack (the Trident submarine is expected eventually to replace the Polaris and will carry 24 missiles with ranges up to 4,500 miles).

Each part of the triad has particular strengths and weaknesses, making coordination between them essential. Furthermore, better Soviet defenses and improved guidance systems on their own missiles require continuous reassessment and improvement of U.S. deterrence to ensure maximum efficiency.

The 1980s.   By 1980 many analysts feared that declining U.S. defense expenditures during the 1970s had allowed the Soviet Union to achieve equality in heavy military equipment and superiority in conventional military forces. Policymakers revised U.S. defense strategy to prepare for *two* and a half wars. The new strategy reflects policymakers' belief that future wars will not necessarily end in a brief, decisive nuclear explosion. It assumes that the United States may have to fight a long war with the Soviet Union in Europe, another in the Middle East, and a third "brushfire" action in another disputed part of the world.

Building such capability is considerably more costly than is concentrating on nuclear equipment alone. It requires heavy investment in transport facilities to move forces and equipment around the world; and it requires investments in defense and support facilities in allied nations, some of which may be unwilling to pay the price.

Special Case

The B-1 Bomber or the Cruise Missile?

Changing technology and changes in world politics require continuous changes in defense strategy. In 1977 the U.S. government decided on a fundamental change in one part of the defense triad: the decision was to shift from long-range bombers to pilotless aircraft.

The B-52 bomber was designed and built early in the 1950s. Although it has been highly dependable and serviceable, by 1970 it began to be viewed as obsolete. Accordingly, the Air Force and Rockwell International developed the B-1 bomber. Development costs for the first three test models came to more than $2.4 billion, and the cost of a fleet of 244 bombers was estimated at more than $40 billion, as much as $250 million per aircraft.

The B-1 is smaller than the B-52 but has much greater bomb-carrying capacity. It can fly at supersonic speeds at high altitudes and near sonic speeds at treetop altitude. Low flight enables the plane to avoid detection by enemy radar and escape ground-to-air missiles. The B-1 carries 24 Short Range Attack Missiles with a range of 100 miles at supersonic speeds. Since the bomber's range is only 6,000 miles, it would have to be refueled in flight before dipping into enemy territory and firing its missiles.

Economists estimated that including the B-1 in the nation's defense triad would have created 70,000 jobs directly and 120,000 indirectly across 48 states.* Supporters of the B-1 believed that building it would have conveyed to the Soviet Union a sense of U.S. commitment to a strong defense and that it would probably have helped forge agreements in the Strategic Arms Limitation Talks (SALT). In general, having an effective bomber force in the United States would require that an attacking nation simultaneously destroy missile launchers and bomber bases. The risk that accurately targeted U.S. missiles and manned bombers would survive a first strike and retaliate inside enemy territory would tend to deter an attack.

Although the costs of the B-1 would be substantial, supporters in Congress and in the defense sector recommended that it be built. Nevertheless, Secretary of Defense James Schlesinger ordered evaluation of other possible strategies before making the decision to go ahead.

One alternative strategy would achieve many of the same benefits as the B-1 at significantly lower costs. It called for a "stand-off" bomber to fire carefully targeted cruise missiles from outside enemy territory. B-52 bombers or modified Boeing 747 jumbo jets could be used as "stand-off" bombers at considerably lower production and operating costs than the B-1. They could carry 50 or more cruise missiles at only $1 million each. Cruise missiles are nearly 100 percent accurate, able to hit a target from more than a thousand miles away. They are actually small pilotless aircraft with conventional jet engines. Cruise missiles would be so numerous and fly so low that radar defenses would be useless against them. This would require the Soviet Union to make additional defense expenditures to protect their territory.

All these considerations influenced President Carter's decision to postpone further development efforts on the B-1 and place greater emphasis on the cruise missile. The decision may have signalled a fundamental revision of our defense strategy: that is, a movement away from heavy use of military personnel to greater reliance on the United States' technical advantage. (The mix between labor and machines for fighting wars is the subject of the next section.)

● List the benefits associated with the various weapons systems discussed in this case. What are the opportunity costs of each?
● One additional factor in the decision about the B-1 was the prediction that the planes would not be available in force until the 1990s. How would this information have affected the measurement of its benefits?

*This does not mean that these economists actually supported the B-1 as an efficient weapons system.

SOURCE: John W. Finney, "Who Needs the B-1?" *New York Times Magazine,* June 25, 1976.

THE MARKET FOR MILITARY PERSONNEL

Part of the nation's defense strategy involves choosing the correct combination of labor and machines for carrying out military objectives: that is, the labor-intensity or capital-intensity of our defense strategy. Because the United States enjoys a high level of technology and because we place special value on human life and freedom, we have tended to emphasize machines in our military strategy. We rely on a relatively small regular army of trained technicians to operate the various weapons systems, and since 1972 we have not drafted additional personnel into the military.

Figure 4–9a is a graph of the market for military personnel when there is no draft. Quantities of military personnel are measured on the horizontal axis, and military pay is measured on the vertical axis. The supply curve in Figure 4–9a slopes upward to show that more civilian workers would volunteer for military

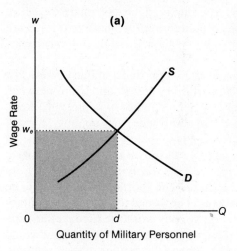

Figure 4–9a
In free markets for labor, the demand for military personnel reflects the value of the contribution of additional workers. Supply reflects workers' opportunity costs in terms of their value in civilian enterprise. Equilibrium determines the number of military workers and their wage. The wage rate is that at which workers' value to the military is equal to their value in civilian enterprise.

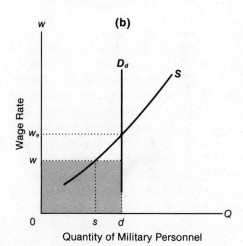

Figure 4–9b
With the draft, the required quantity of military workers are acquired through voluntary enlistments and the draft at less than the market wage. Some workers are employed in military jobs in which their value to the military is less than their value in civilian enterprise.

service at higher wages. The lowest acceptable wage for each volunteer depends on his or her opportunity cost—the value of his or her work in alternative jobs outside the military.

Without the draft, the demand for military personnel is shown by a typical downward-sloping demand curve. Wages shown on the demand curve reflect the value of each additional worker's expected contribution to the military service. Additional workers will be hired up to the level at which the value of an additional worker's contribution is equal to the wage rate. Equilibrium between supply and demand identifies the number of military personnel to be hired and their wages.

Free labor markets for military personnel have certain advantages. Costs determined in free markets reflect the true opportunity cost of resources and encourage their efficient use. At market wage rates, there is no incentive to overuse labor relative to machines, and workers are used in jobs where they are most productive. Persons whose value outside the military exceeds their value to the military are not hired; thus the economy as a whole gains from the most efficient allocation of human resources. And finally, decisions made freely are less likely to be soon reversed; persons volunteering for military service are more likely to remain, contributing the value of their training and experience toward a stronger defense.

For these reasons, economists have generally opposed a military draft. The draft disrupts labor markets and establishes arbitrary cost relationships between men and machines. Figure 4–9b calls for a specific number of military workers, shown by a vertical demand curve (D_d) drawn at the necessary quantity. Since a draft does not require a market wage, the wage is set below equilibrium at w. At this wage, Os soldiers would enlist voluntarily, as shown on the supply curve. The difference between the quantity supplied voluntarily and the quantity demanded is the shortage of military personnel, sd. The shortage would have to be made up through the draft. Many draftees would be forced to serve in the military at wages lower than their value to the economy. They would be used inefficiently in activities that might be performed efficiently by machines. And they would leave the military at the first opportunity, depriving the service of their accumulated expertise.

The draft has one advantage: it is cheap—at least in terms of *direct* military expenditures. Compare the direct cost of the army in Figure 4–9a with that in Figure 4–9b. The direct cost of military personnel is the quantity of recruits times their wage. In both figures, quantity is shown along the horizontal axis and the wage rate along the vertical axis. A rectangle with base Od = quantity and height Ow = wage has for its area base times height, or quantity times wage. Thus, the area of the shaded rectangle is the direct cost of the army, without (4–9a) and with (4–9b) the draft. The difference in cost is even greater in the case of a national emergency when demand for personnel may increase faster than supply.

The lower cost of the draft shown in Figure 4–9b reflects only the **direct cost of military personnel,** however. It does not reflect their opportunity cost to the economy as a whole, nor the fact that artificially low personnel costs may result in inefficient resource allocation.

Since 1972, the United States has had an all-volunteer army. There have been both positive and negative results:

- Rather than pay the high wages necessary to attract a larger supply of qualified personnel, the military services have tended to substitute more "hardware" for human labor.
- Persons with attractive employment opportunities outside the military have left the market; as a result, the supply of labor for the military has come to include workers with lower skills and capabilities.
- Whereas draftees tend to leave the military after their required period of service, volunteers tend to remain for longer enlistments; the result has been substantial savings in training costs.
- In an effort to attract better qualified personnel, the military services have increased the use of incentives such as bonuses and educational programs for volunteers.

Some economists have suggested a way to use volunteer personnel even more efficiently. The current practice is to pay the same wage to all military workers with a given rank and seniority. There may be wide differences in skill levels and job assignments, however, contributing to worker dissatisfaction and frequent job turnover. Changing the pay schedule to reward workers according to the job performed would increase incentives and improve efficiency.*

Relying on an all-volunteer army has raised military wages and pushed manpower costs to almost 60 percent of annual military expenditures. In prosperous years when civilian jobs are plentiful, recruiting costs may be expected to rise even higher. Moreover, in a national emergency the greatly increased need for military personnel would become extremely costly — costly, that is, unless the draft were to be reintroduced.

Policymakers in Congress worry about the rising cost and deteriorating quality of our military personnel. Some recommend a return to the draft. One proposal would establish a kind of universal national service, with all young men and women required to spend a certain period of time in the service of their country. Draftees could choose military or civilian service: in environmental, urban rehabilitation, or rural service jobs. Universal service might be expected to encourage feelings of patriotism as well as to provide valuable training during a young adult's formative years. The program might be less costly than payment of unemployment compensation, job subsidies, or other benefits to youths who might otherwise be unemployed.

A return to the draft might provide other noneconomic advantages. A draft would bring into the service persons from a wider range of social and economic backgrounds, thus relieving what may have been a tendency to enlist persons from the lowest income levels. The result might be more equitable in terms of the sacrifice borne by the nation's young people.

*Martin Binkin and Irene Kyriakopoulos, *Paying the Modern Military,* Brookings, 1981.

Financing Defense Expenditures

Once the appropriate defense strategy is decided, the next consideration is paying the costs. Using funds to purchase things like tanks and planes is a way of transferring resources from production of things like autos and homes. The U.S. Treasury can acquire the funds for defense expenditures in three ways:

1. *Taxation.* Taxing the public withdraws funds from civilian markets and releases resources for military production.
2. *Borrowing.* Sale of government securities to the public withdraws savings that might otherwise be spent for civilian goods and services.
3. *Creating Money.* The Federal Reserve Bank may create new money for lending to the Treasury.

All three methods are used to some extent, each having particular advantages and disadvantages. Taxing and borrowing are more difficult to accomplish, since they depend on full public support of defense objectives. Creating money may be simpler, but it is likely to cause inflation. The reason is that money creation does not withdraw funds from the civilian sector. Consumers and business firms are left with the same amount of purchasing power for spending. Their continuing purchase of civilian goods and services — along with the Treasury's purchase of military equipment — tends to drive prices up. Unless there are unemployed resources to move into production, expanding both civilian and military production may be impossible. General price inflation will reduce the buying power of incomes, however, so that the quantities of civilian goods actually purchased will fall. The final result is that productive resources are, indeed, transferred from the civilian to the defense sector.* The result is not necessarily efficient, however. Price inflation disrupts markets and distorts market decisions. In general, policymakers agree that money creation is an inefficient method of acquiring funds for defense. They prefer to persuade the public of the correctness of the defense strategy: that the nation's defense requires a sacrifice of civilian goods and services. In terms of our model, the public must be persuaded that the marginal utility of military goods is greater than the marginal utility of civilian goods.

An Issue for the Future

The North Atlantic Treaty Organization

An important part of the nation's defense is our relationship with allied nations. Agreements to contribute toward a mutual defense strategy are included in the North Atlantic Treaty Organization (NATO), created in 1949. European members of NATO spend about one-half as much per capita on defense as the United States. They depend for their

*The alert student will recognize this as a form of "forced saving" described in chapter 2.

defense on the 19 U.S. divisions stationed in Europe, which cost about one-half the U.S. military budget.

Some analysts have questioned the wisdom of such a large U.S. commitment to NATO. The presence of troops in Europe, they say, worsens the division of the world into two armed camps and encourages heavier military expenditures by Warsaw Pact nations, under the leadership of the Soviet Union. Moreover, our willingness to subsidize Europe's defense may have reduced Europe's own defense effort and made possible a greater allocation of European resources to new civilian technologies superior to ours. One result has been to diminish capital investment in the United States and to worsen U.S. inflation.

Support for the present arrangement comes from U.S. military personnel, who welcome career opportunities in NATO forces, and defense producers, who profit from sales of military equipment. President Eisenhower referred to this coalition as the **military-industrial complex,** which, he said, would attempt to influence U.S. policies toward excessive emphasis on military expenditures.

Concerned about our faltering commitment to NATO, some European governments have moved to establish more peaceful relationships with the Soviet Union, at the same time resisting U.S. proposals to deploy medium-range missiles on their territory. Their fear is that in a real attack on European cities, the United States would back off rather than risk an attack on American cities.

● Describe European nations' preferences in terms of the model in Figure 4–3. What circumstances in Europe account for differences in their approach to defense expenditures?

An Issue for the Future

Producing Arms for Export

Defense-related industries in the United States employ about 5 percent of our total labor force. A healthy armament industry is essential for equipping our own forces; and selling additional equipment abroad gains economies of scale for lower unit costs of production. Moreover, exporting arms helps U.S. firms earn foreign exchange for importing needed goods and materials. Still, production of arms for export uses resources that might otherwise be used to produce civilian goods and services.

The United States accounts for more than one-half the arms sold internationally. The Soviet Union is in second place, and Western European nations also export arms. Several small nations have special military products for which they are noted. Many producing nations produce for export in order to spread their research and development costs over a larger volume and to earn funds to finance their oil imports.

The leading customers for U.S. arms are Israel, Saudi Arabia, and, until 1979, Iran. Sales amounted to more than $20 billion in 1980. Only about one-third of arms sales involves military equipment (fighter and cargo planes, helicopters, tanks, submarines, destroyers, and missiles); another one-third goes for military training, construction, and administration; and another one-third for spare parts and support equipment. Officials of the armament industry estimate that for every $1 billion of sales abroad, 31,000 Americans are employed directly and 60,000 additional jobs are created in support industries.

Toward the end of the 1960s Congress became concerned about weapons proliferation abroad and placed some restrictions on U.S. arms sales. Eventually, Congress came to believe that refusing to sell arms would only drive foreign buyers to producers in other nations and not really solve the problem of proliferation. Also, the expectation that allied nations would assume responsibility for their own defense required that the United States remain a dependable source of arms. Finally, many of the restrictions on arms sales were relaxed.

President Carter initiated a new policy for gradually reducing the dollar value of arms sales, for prohibiting resale of U.S. arms to a third country, and for prohibiting development of advanced weapons specifically for export markets. In addition, the Carter policy would ensure that the United States would not be the first to supply advanced weapons to a region. There were additional restrictions on arms sales to nations that engaged in human rights violations, and there were attempts to persuade the allies and the Soviet Union to cooperate in reducing arms sales. President Reagan relaxed many of these restrictions but stressed his administration's opposition to the offensive use of U.S. arms.

The appropriate question for world policymakers continues to be: Does the current level of armament production and sales bring about an equivalent level of international security? Stated differently: Is the additional utility of military production equal to the added costs? The question is particularly relevant for developing nations, whose expenditures for arms reduce their capacity for investment in capital resources and new technology. In recent years, almost a fourth of U.S. armament exports have gone to non-oil developing countries. Regrettably, arms expenditures in one nation may increase tensions among neighboring nations and create a chain reaction of military expenditures. Other objections to sales of sophisticated military equipment involve the fear that examples of our most advanced military technology may fall into unfriendly hands.

- How is the model of the "learning curve" (described in the preceding chapter) relevant to the discussion of producing arms for export?
- How might arms production affect the shape and position of the nation's production possibilities curve? What is the effect on the marginal cost of military production?

A FINAL QUESTION

Our discussion in this chapter has focused on military expenditures as the principal way a nation achieves long-range security. However, to look upon arms production as essential to national security may no longer be correct. In fact, the enormous destructive power of modern weapons may have finally made general war obsolete. And the growing importance of economic and political factors for a nation's security may have opened new grounds for international competition.

Critics of U.S. defense policy contend that excessive military production weakens our nation's capacity to correct domestic problems and increases our vulnerability to economic crisis. They argue that the allocation of resources to defense purposes reduces investment in new productive facilities, research and development, and educational programs for improving workers' skills. The long-range effect may be to reduce our ability to produce goods and services, with an accompanying decline in real incomes, lower tax collections, accelerating inflation, and deteriorating quality of life. Expenditures for defense may also aggravate differences in regional output and income and interfere with programs to correct urban financial problems. All these circumstances may ultimately reduce efficiency and equity in the use of productive resources.

The issue before U.S. voters and policymakers is the relative importance of the economic and military threats facing the nation. A judgment of real military danger would justify almost any sacrifice to protect and preserve our values. If the grounds for international conflict have shifted to economic competition, however, to waste our productive capacity in military pursuits would be dangerous. There is an old saying: Generals always prepare to fight the last war. Is that saying still relevant today?

QUESTIONS

1. Explain how the ceremony of the Potlatch may contradict or confirm the fundamental assumption of economics.
2. Illustrate graphically the basis for the statement that there has been a "hardening of the U.S. defense posture" relative to the Soviet Union.
3. What is the significance of the slope of the dashed line in Figure 4–3? State your answer algebraically and verbally.
4. Discuss the relationship between military expenditures and indicators of the nation's economic health. How does your discussion illustrate the important difference between a social science and a physical science?
5. Explain the difficulty of measuring the cost of military operations.
6. Debate the arguments for and against the military draft.
7. In what sense is *money creation* preferable to *taxation* to finance a war? How is it less preferable? How does a citizen's purchase of a "Defense Bond" differ from purchase of a corporate bond? How is it similar?
8. Discuss the factors that might influence perceptions of marginal utility and the shape of a nation's indifference curves: the median age of the population, historical experiences regarding war, the character of media information about foreign affairs, knowledge of foreign peoples, and so forth.
9. By what means can U.S. policymakers determine the strength of the military danger facing the nation? Discuss the debate over this question. Discuss this issue in terms of the model of resource allocation developed early in this chapter.
10. Use a production possibilities curve to illustrate the opportunity costs of producing agricultural products and manufactured goods. Explain how changes in technology might affect the shape of the production possibilities curve. What is the definition of the marginal rate of substitution in production in terms of your model?
11. Use indifference curves to illustrate relative preferences for agricultural products and manufactured goods. What circumstances would affect the shape of indifference curves? Explain the marginal rate of substitution in consumption in terms of your model.
12. Combine the production possibilities curve from question 10 with the indifference curves in question 11 and locate the equilibrium level of output. What are the

characteristics of production at the equilibrium level? Show how technological change influences the trend of production over time and the relative proportion of agricultural products and manufactured goods.

13. Try to think of a way to use a production possibilities curve and indifference curves to illustrate the process of making a personal decision: for example, a decision as to personal expenditures for food and clothing or a decision as to allocation of study time between two subjects in school. Explain the usefulness of the model in these kinds of decisions.

DEFINITIONS

Capitalism is an economic system in which productive resources are owned by capitalists and income is distributed according to contributions to production.

Communism is an economic system in which productive resources are owned "in common" by all members of the society and income is distributed according to need.

The direct cost of military personnel is the product of quantity of personnel times the wage. Direct cost can be shown on a market model by a rectangle drawn beneath the demand curve at market equilibrium.

Equilibrium production for the nation occurs where the nation's production possibilities curve touches the highest possible indifference curve. At equilibrium, resources are allocated most efficiently to produce what the people want.

Fixed resources are resources whose quantity and function are constant over a certain period of time.

Indifference curves show combinations of particular goods or services that provide equal amounts of total utility; thus, consumers are "indifferent" among the various combinations on a single indifference curve.

Marginal cost is the cost associated with increasing some kind of production by one unit.

The Marginal Rate of Substitution in Consumption (MRS_C) is the quantity of one kind of good that people will willingly give up in order to acquire another. The MRS_C is also the slope of an indifference curve.

The Marginal Rate of Substitution in Production (MRS_P) is the sacrifice of one kind of good as resources are allocated to produce another. The MRS_P is also the slope of a production possibilities curve.

Marginal utility is the change in total utility that results from acquiring one additional unit of a good or service.

The military-industrial complex involves the combined interests of military personnel and equipment manufacturers to maintain a high level of military activity.

An opportunity cost is the sacrifice of one type of good for the sake of acquiring another. In this context, opportunity costs refer to the sacrifice of civilian goods necessary for acquiring military goods.

Political economy is the study of conflicting interests of different groups within an economy, particularly with respect to the ownership of wealth and distribution of income.

Production possibilities are the maximum combinations of goods that can be produced, given a nation's available resources and technology. Production possibilities can be shown on a graph.

Utility is the usefulness associated with a particular good or service.
Variable resources are resources that can be used in greater or lesser amounts along with the existing quantity of fixed resources.

SUGGESTED READINGS

Aspin, Les. "The Three-Percent Solution: NATO and the U.S. Defense Budget." *Challenge,* May/June, 1979, p. 22.

Barnet, Richard J. *The Economy of Death.* New York: Atheneum, 1969.

Cohen, S. T. "The Logic of the N-Bomb." *Across the Board,* November, 1981, p. 27.

"General Dynamics: Striking it Rich on Defense." *Business Week,* May 3, 1982, p. 102.

"Guns vs. Butter." *Business Week,* November 29, 1982, p. 68.

Holzman, Franklyn D. "Is There a Soviet–US Military Spending Gap?" *Challenge,* September/October, 1980, p. 3.

Kennan, George F. "Kennan's Fifty-Percent Solution." *Across the Board,* September, 1981, p. 8.

"Killer Electronic Weaponry." *Business Week,* September 20, 1982, p. 74.

La Rocque, Gene. "The Defense Budget Controversy." *Challenge,* May/June, 1980, p. 3.

Palme, Olof, et al. "Military Spending: The Economic and Social Consequences." *Challenge,* September/October, 1982, p. 4.

Schultze, Charles L. "Do More Dollars Mean Better Defense?" *Challenge,* January/February, 1982, p. 30.

Weidenbaum, Murry L. "Let's Examine National Defense Spending." *Challenge,* January/February, 1983, p. 50.

CHAPTER FIVE

Intergovernmental Fiscal Relations

What Should Governments Do?

LEARNING OBJECTIVES

- To learn how governmental responsibilities have evolved with the changing needs of our economic system, particularly with respect to the need for efficiency, equity, and positive externalities.
- To distinguish between regressive, progressive, and proportional taxes and the tendencies of governments to levy them.
- To describe the basis for tax sharing among levels of government and the effects of intergovernmental grants on efficiency, equity, and externalities.
- To understand the importance of elasticities in deciding tax policy.
- To examine the concept of tax equity and the goal of horizontal and vertical equity.
- To consider proposals for changing the nation's tax structure.
- To understand the procedures of government borrowing and the implications for savers and investors.
- To look closely at the special problems of city governments and at national policies for dealing with them.

108

Like lots of people the world over, we Americans want to "eat our cake and have it, too." We want to enjoy all kinds of benefits, even some benefits that may be inconsistent with others. We often forget that there are trade-offs: Acquiring certain good things requires that we sacrifice other good things. We must balance off the things we want against the other things we cannot have. If we achieve the greatest quantity of total "cake" with the least sacrifice, we call the result *efficient*.

One of our contradictory attitudes has to do with the way we want to be governed. We want a small accessible government responsive to our needs and too weak to dominate our personal lives. At the same time, we want a strong central government capable of ensuring national security and promoting rising living standards nationwide. To achieve either objective completely would require some sacrifice of the other. So we have developed a combination of governments, some of which respond to local needs while others attend to broad national goals. The precise arrangement of powers and responsibilities among levels of government has evolved over time. And it continues to change today as voters reevaluate the relative strengths of their contradictory objectives.

The founders of our nation were also divided about the kinds of benefits they expected from various forms of government. Many of the colonists had come to America to escape what they regarded as dictatorial governments in Europe. Naturally, they wanted to make sure that control of their new government would reside with the people. Toward this objective, the Articles of Confederation, drawn up in 1776, gave the federal government no power over the states or their citizens. The national government was not even allowed the power to collect taxes or to regulate trade.

By 1788, the weaknesses of the Articles of Confederation were beginning to be apparent, and the United States Constitution was drawn up to strengthen the central government and balance its power against that of the states. Under the Constitution, Congress was given power to collect taxes, establish a money system, regulate trade, and conduct wars. Individual states were allowed to carry on all powers not prohibited by the Constitution. They were specifically forbidden to create money or to interfere with the free flow of trade.

Subject to these limitations, the states drew up their own constitutions and established rules for chartering local governments. In general, state constitutions allowed the greatest taxing power for the state government and permitted local jurisdiction within carefully defined local areas.

Some of the restrictions on state governments were meant to ensure freedom of trade across state lines. Free trade would encourage regional specialization, and regional specialization would permit economies of scale and lower production costs. Differing money systems and barriers to trade between the states would have kept production small-scale and inefficient. With no barriers to trade, resources could move to areas where they were most needed and could earn the greatest return. Goods could move to markets of greatest demand and highest prices.

Indeed, these expected results did come to pass. Ease of mobility among the states helped achieve the benefits of competition and ensured economic growth.

Along with efficiency, the free flow of goods and resources promoted development of positive externalities such as exchange of technologies among regions and the growth of workers' skills and industrial enterprise. And finally, the influence of the national government helped ensure fairness or equity in the distribution of the nation's considerable wealth. By moderating some of the inequalities in resource endowments among regions, the national government promoted greater equality in the living standards of citizens nationwide.

Citizens continue to be concerned about achieving the proper balance of power between state and local governments, on the one hand, and the federal government, on the other. In general, we want to preserve the efficiency that has come with an integrated national economy. And we want to enjoy the externalities that come from the diversity of resources and opportunities among regions. Occasionally we are divided, however, about the question of equity — the distribution of goods and services that is, in fact, fair — and the scope of governmental policies to achieve more equal distribution.

THE GROWTH OF GOVERNMENT

Each of the three levels of government in the United States performs particular roles financed by particular kinds of taxes. There are some services and some taxes in which the roles of governments overlap, making for occasional tension among them. In general, *local* governments are concerned primarily with activities that closely affect the health and safety of local citizens, such as public education and fire and police protection. *State* governments are concerned with broader services whose effects are felt more widely over a larger area, such as higher education, highways, and natural resource development. The *national* government carries on functions that could not be conducted efficiently by state governments, such as defense and international trade. The choice of tax sources at each level of government depends on the ease with which citizens can *avoid paying,* a subject we will discuss later in detail.

Throughout this century, the influence of government on the nation's economy has grown. In 1980, all levels of government purchased goods and services equal to 20 percent of GNP, as contrasted with only 6 percent in 1900. Expenditures of the national government grew fastest, with defense expenditures the greatest reason for growth. When defense expenditures are excluded, local government expenditures are the highest, equal to the sum of all state and nondefense federal expenditures taken together.

Along with growth in all government has come a gradual shift of many responsibilities to higher levels of government: from local to state governments and from the states to the federal government. Whereas highways and public welfare were once exclusively local responsibilities, these services are now shared between the federal and state governments. Public health and natural resource management are growing responsibilities of the federal government. Only public education is still primarily the responsibility of local government.

Payments made to other governments make up a growing portion of total governmental outlays. In 1980, almost one-fourth of state expenditures were paid for with funds received from the federal government. Of local government expenditures, almost one-third came from the state or federal government. Intergovernmental grants help equalize the ability of rich and poor governments to provide an acceptable level of services to local citizens and business firms.

Total tax revenues have grown, too. From only about 6 percent of GNP in 1900, total tax revenues grew to almost 32 percent of GNP in 1980. Again, federal taxes showed the fastest growth, led by Social Security taxes and personal income taxes. State tax revenues once came primarily from property taxes, but now the most important state tax sources are sales taxes, gasoline taxes, and motor vehicle licenses. Property taxes are still the most important local taxes, although their significance has declined. Many local governments have levied sales taxes, and a few have levied income taxes. In 1980, state and local taxes averaged about $1,330 per capita, up from only $540 in 1970. State and local tax bills varied state-to-state, being highest in Alaska and lowest in Arkansas. Federal taxes averaged $2,370 per capita in 1980, up from $950 per capita in 1970. See Table 5–1 for a comparison of state taxes per capita.

As the nation's economy continues to grow and change, there will continue to be new demands for public services. Some levels of government may reach the limits of their taxing ability from existing sources. New ways must be found to coordinate federal, state, and local responsibilities: for improving efficiency, developing positive externalities, and ensuring equity.

Figures 5–1 and 5–2 are time-series graphs showing the growth of federal and state and local government purchases and taxes over recent decades. Notice the substantial increase in state and local spending over the most recent decade.

Table 5–1 Per Capita State Taxes in 1980

State	Tax	State	Tax	State	Tax
Alabama	$ 934	Louisiana	$1,140	Ohio	$ 762
Alaska	7,529	Maine	1,048	Oklahoma	1,036
Arizona	944	Maryland	1,146	Oregon	1,170
Arkansas	920	Massachusetts	1,176	Pennsylvania	950
California	1,251	Michigan	1,110	Rhode Island	1,253
Colorado	966	Minnesota	1,288	South Carolina	932
Connecticut	1,001	Mississippi	985	South Dakota	1,019
Delaware	1,500	Missouri	746	Tennessee	778
Florida	750	Montana	1,202	Texas	838
Georgia	839	Nebraska	904	Utah	1,066
Hawaii	1,696	Nevada	1,038	Vermont	1,233
Idaho	972	New Hampshire	730	Virginia	942
Illinois	967	New Jersey	971	Washington	1,170
Indiana	787	New Mexico	1,526	West Virginia	1,117
Iowa	1,015	New York	1,256	Wisconsin	1,189
Kansas	915	North Carolina	914	Wyoming	1,702
Kentucky	1,023	North Dakota	1,389		

Source: *Statistical Abstract of the United States,* 1981.

Figure 5–1

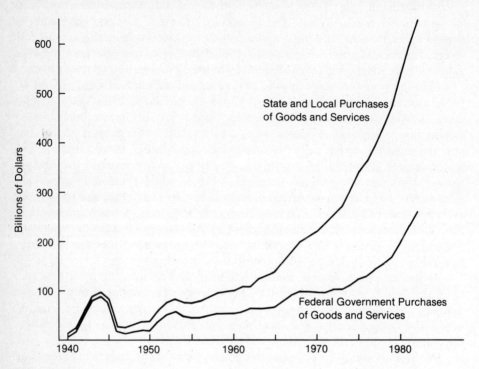

State and Local Purchases
of Goods and Services

Federal Government Purchases
of Goods and Services

Billions of Dollars

Figure 5–2

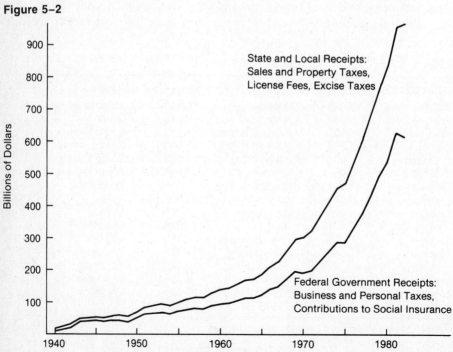

State and Local Receipts:
Sales and Property Taxes,
License Fees, Excise Taxes

Federal Government Receipts:
Business and Personal Taxes,
Contributions to Social Insurance

Billions of Dollars

SOME CHARACTERISTICS OF TAX POLICY

The single most important factor in tax policy is tax **jurisdiction.** Jurisdiction defines a government's **tax base:** that is, the geographical area or the economic activity over which a tax may be applied. Since any government's jurisdiction is limited, it will impose a tax that earns the greatest revenue at the lowest administrative expense. In general, this means that the heaviest taxes will be imposed on activities that cannot leave the jurisdiction to avoid paying and the lightest taxes on those that can.

A government may go so far as to levy zero or **negative taxes** on certain activities. Negative taxes are tax credits or low interest loans that may be offered to especially desirable activities. Thus, negative taxes are a form of subsidy used by governments to encourage new industry to move into that jurisdiction. It is expected that the new industry will bring new local jobs and increase local incomes. The result will be enough additional tax revenues from other sources to offset the cost of paying the subsidies.

Regressive and Progressive Taxes

The effect of jurisdictional limits is a kind of *competition* among governments to reduce taxes on desired activities and raise taxes on activities that cannot leave the jurisdiction. This is particularly true of state and local governments. Accordingly, state sales taxes, gasoline and license taxes, and city property taxes are designed to fall heaviest on local residents who have no choice but to pay. This is why state and local taxes tend to be *regressive.* **Regressive taxes** take a larger fraction of personal income from low-income earners than from high-income earners.

The federal government is not forced to engage in tax competition, since its jurisdiction extends nationwide, and few U.S. citizens are inclined to leave the country to avoid paying U.S. taxes.* This fact enables the federal government to levy **progressive taxes.** Progressive taxes take a larger fraction of income from high-income earners than low-income earners. Personal and corporate income taxes do this. Furthermore, the federal government can influence state and local tax policies by allowing taxpayers to deduct other taxes from their taxable income or from their tax bill itself. Allowing federal taxpayers to deduct their state income taxes encourages some states to use this tax and increase the progressivity of taxes in general. The result is believed to be a more reliable and more equitable source of funds for state governments.

Tax Sharing

Another determinant of tax policy involves tax *administration,* which aims for efficiency in collecting revenues with lowest possible administrative costs.

---

*This is not to deny that some wealthy movie stars leave the country to avoid paying income taxes and that some corporations move plants abroad for the same reason.

Preparing tax returns is costly for the taxpayer, and evaluating them is costly for the receiving government. Centralizing tax policy with the federal government may reduce administrative costs. Then the federal government can share its tax revenues with state and local governments. Through most of the 1970s federal government payments to state and local governments grew by more than 15 percent a year (9 percent after correcting for inflation). A conservative trend toward the end of the decade had the effect of reducing growth in government outlays, so that federal grants leveled off at about 17 percent of the federal budget. Total grants were $87 billion in 1980, about a fourth of state and local budgets and their largest single source of revenue.

The federal government shares tax revenues with state and local governments in either of three ways: *categorical grants, block grants,* and *general revenue sharing.* Categorical grants must be spent for a particular project, and block grants must be spent for a broader public purpose. General revenue sharing can be spent any way the receiving government wishes. In every case, tax revenues are collected at the federal level, and programs are designed and/or carried out at the state or local level. Let us look at each of the three kinds of tax sharing in detail.

Categorical Grants. The philosophy behind **categorical grants** is that certain programs create positive externalities in cities and states. Therefore, these programs should be paid for by a higher level of government. Since members of a free society move frequently, many of the benefits of local programs spill outside the local area and raise living standards in others. Local taxpayers are likely to overlook these external benefits and provide programs only to the level of expected benefits within the community itself. The result is a level of expenditures too low for maximum efficiency.

There are between 500 and 1,000 different kinds of categorical grants. Categorical grants pay for educational programs, highway construction, and aid to low-income groups.

During the 1960s, the federal government began categorical programs for higher education, vocational education, agricultural research, and mental retardation. Improved education is expected to provide these positive externalities:

a. educated people make better citizens and voters,
b. widespread education promotes technical progress and economic growth,
c. a trained and literate work force is likely to be more productive,
d. more productive workers earn higher incomes and pay higher taxes,
e. an educated population requires lower expenditures for police and fire protection and for health and welfare services.

Highway construction may also provide positive externalities through lower transportation costs for consumer goods, increased opportunities for social relations, and ease of mobility for national defense. Highways can be financed by user charges, or tolls. However, to the extent that highway costs cannot be paid from user charges or built into the market price of goods, highways must be financed by taxation. Ninety to ninety-five percent of the interstate highway system is financed by the federal government from taxes levied on sales of gasoline, tires and tubes, and other transportation products.*

Categorical grants for low-income groups provide positive externalities in the form of human resource development. Along with education and health programs, aid to low-income families is expected to improve skills and work incentives and permit recipients to participate more fully in the U.S. economy.

Block Grants. The philosophy behind **block grants** is that state and local governments are better able than the federal government to plan public projects suited to local needs. Most block grants are "matching" grants: the giving and receiving governments share the cost of the programs. The share of each is based on the expected distribution of external and internal benefits. In general, 90 percent of highways and mass transit funds are paid by the federal government and 10 percent by state and local governments; 50 percent of food stamps and medical assistance programs are paid by each; and 25 percent of water treatment plants are paid by the federal government. Many block grants are described as "open ended" in that there is no limit to the level of grant support as long as a need exists. (To set a limit might encourage state and local governments to design programs precisely to absorb the maximum grant.) And finally, block grants must include controls to ensure that the intended benefits are indeed produced.

During the late 1970s, a portion of federal block grants was paid directly to cities. Urban Development Action Grants (UDAGs) provided federal funds for constructing convention centers, low-income housing, and other projects designed to attract private investment to urban areas.

General Revenue Sharing. The purpose of **general revenue sharing** is to supplement the tax revenues of low-income areas that are unable to pay for an acceptable level of public services. General revenue sharing can help maintain public services in the period before expected benefits from block grants could begin to occur.

Since World War II, the growth and movement of industry across the United States have helped reduce income differences between regions. Still, there are wide differences in the taxing ability of state and local governments across the nation. Revenue-sharing funds are paid to state or local governments on the basis of formulas that take into consideration per capita income, population density and age, state taxing ability, and service needs. General revenue sharing amounted to $8.6 billion in 1980, only 1.5 percent of total federal outlays. Revenue sharing outlays are expected to decline in the early 1980s.

---

*The availability of earmarked funds for highways may have had the effect of expanding this form of expenditure beyond the level of maximum efficiency.

An Evaluation

Federal tax sharing has come under various kinds of criticism:

1. *Categorical grants are intended to create positive externalities.* But measuring externalities is impossible, especially from as far away as the federal government. This makes it difficult (if not impossible) to determine the proper level of support for various programs. Paying general revenues to states and allowing states to distribute the funds has the advantage that state governments have greater understanding of local needs. On the other hand, in the past many state governments have paid more attention to the needs of rural and suburban voters and have neglected the increasingly serious problems of cities. Whatever the form of aid, results may be more efficient if grant programs are flexible enough to accommodate differences in service needs, if programs are coordinated throughout broad areas, and if related governmental functions are integrated for more efficient administration.

2. *Federal revenue sharing is intended to increase efficiency of tax administration.* But many critics contend that the "round trip" of taxes to the federal government and back is wasteful and inefficient. Instead of paying grants, they say, the federal government should reduce federal tax rates and enable state and local governments to raise theirs. This would permit state and local governments to provide public services according to the wishes of their citizens. We have seen that this is not generally a good idea, since competition between state and local governments tends primarily to *reduce* taxes. If any state or local taxes are raised, they are likely to be property and sales taxes, so that the nation's total tax structure becomes more regressive and (in the eyes of some) less equitable.

3. *Federal grants are intended to promote equity in the distribution of income and wealth.* But some critics object to any sort of government interference in free markets. If certain regions experience lower than average income growth, they say, there are probably fundamental economic causes. The solution might be to encourage out-migration, reducing local population to a level that can be supported by the resources available in the area. Out-migration might not solve the problem of low-income growth, however. In fact, out-migration could perpetuate a worsening cycle of poverty. And out-migration might worsen the problem of crowding in other nearby areas. In such cases, cooperation among federal, state, and local governments could yield programs to develop local resources and begin technological progress. Better employment opportunities could help reduce income inequality between regions.

4. *Finally, we have emphasized concerns about maintaining the proper balance between the federal and state and local governments.* Some critics worry that the availability of federal tax revenues encourages state and local governments to reduce their own tax effort and neglect improvements in needed services. The result could be a decrease of the powers and responsibilities of state and local governments and an increase in the powers and responsibilities of the federal government.

TAXES AND ELASTICITY

The significance of elasticity to government has to do with the effect on economic activity when a tax is added to the price of a good or service. Consumers' sensitivity to higher prices determines government's revenue from a tax. Producers' sensitivity to a tax determines business decisions to locate or expand operations. Business decisions affect local job opportunities, incomes, and, again, tax revenue within that particular tax jurisdiction.

Consumer and producer sensitivity to prices is measured by elasticity. Remember that elasticity measures percent change in quantity relative to percent change in price:

$$\text{price elasticity} = e = \frac{\% \text{ change in quantity}}{\% \text{ change in price}} = \frac{\% \, \Delta \, Q}{\% \, \Delta \, p}.$$

1. *Price elasticity of demand* measures the sensitivity of *consumers* to changes in the price of a good or service. Consumers may be expected to change quantity demanded in the opposite direction from a change in price. If quantity demanded changes by a greater percentage than the change in price, we say demand is price *elastic*. If quantity demanded changes by a smaller percentage than price, demand is *inelastic*.
2. *Price elasticity of supply* measures the sensitivity of *producers* to changes in price. Producers may be expected to change quantity supplied in the same direction as a change in price. If quantity supplied changes by a greater percentage than the change in price, we say supply is price *elastic*. If quantity supplied changes by a smaller percentage than price, supply is *inelastic*.

Price elasticity of demand may differ at different price levels. Figure 5–3a shows a **linear demand curve** along which price elasticity varies from elastic at high prices to inelastic at low prices. The reason is that percentage change in quantity is great when the base quantity is low. This is true for points high on the demand curve where price is high. A large percent change in quantity means a large numerator for the elasticity ratio and a large value for demand elasticity. On the other hand, percentage change in quantity is small where the base quantity is high. This is true for points low on the demand curve where price is low. A small percent change in quantity means a small value for the numerator and a small value for demand elasticity. On any linear demand curve like the one in Figure 5–3a, the elasticity ratio changes from greater than one for small quantities (high prices) to less than one for large quantities (low prices). At some midpoint on a linear demand curve, the demand elasticity ratio will be precisely equal to one.

The steeper demand curve in Figure 5–3b shows inelastic demand over a wider range of prices. This is because changes in quantity are small over more of the demand curve. The flatter curve in Figure 5–3c is elastic over a wider range, since changes in quantity are quite large. A precisely vertical demand curve has **zero elasticity,** since percent change in quantity is zero. A horizontal demand curve has **infinitely great elasticity,** since change in price is zero.

Figure 5–3

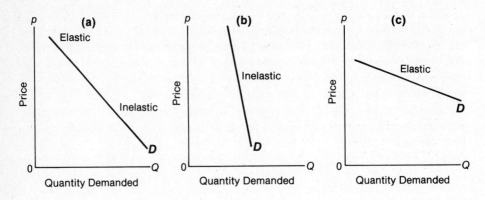

A **linear supply curve** has the same elasticity for every price: that is, a percent change in price will always bring the same percent change in quantity. The steep supply curve in Figure 5–4a is inelastic over its entire range, and the flat curve in Figure 5–4b is elastic. A vertical supply curve has zero elasticity, and a horizontal curve, infinitely great elasticity.

Figure 5–5 combines typical demand and supply curves and identifies the equilibrium quantity and market price at Q_e and p_e, respectively. Adding a tax to the price of a good is shown in Figure 5–6 by shifting the supply curve upward by the amount of the tax. Thus, the selling price of quantity OQ' is the sum of market price Op' plus tax $p't$. With the tax, the equilibrium quantity falls to OQ'' and price rises to p''.

Most taxes do have the effect of reducing quantity sold and raising price. The extent of the change depends on the sensitivity of consumers and producers to the addition of a tax. The demand curve in Figure 5–7 is inelastic over a wide range of prices shown, and the supply curve is relatively elastic. In practical terms this means that: (1) consumers will reduce their purchases by a smaller percent than the increase in price and (2) producers can supply a wide range of quantities with little change in price. In this case, the addition of a tax has little effect on quantity sold, even though price rises by almost the full amount of the tax.

Now look at Figure 5–8. The tax added to the supply curve is the same as in Figure 5–7, but this time the more elastic demand curve indicates that consumers will respond to a price increase by significantly reducing purchases. The inelastic supply curve means that producers will not supply significantly different quantities whatever the price. Adding a tax increases equilibrium price very little and reduces quantity hardly at all.

The results in these cases depend on the responsiveness of buyers and sellers. If consumers have little choice but to buy (as in Figure 5–7), adding a tax has little effect on total production. State and local governments can collect substantial revenue without seriously disrupting economic activity in the area.

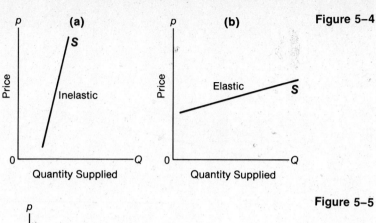

Figure 5–4

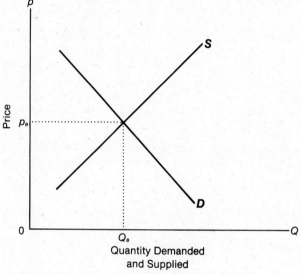

Figure 5–5

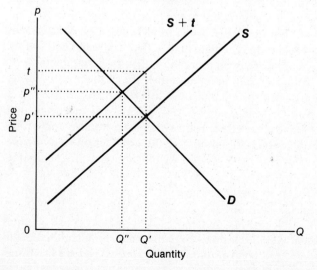

Figure 5–6

Figure 5–7

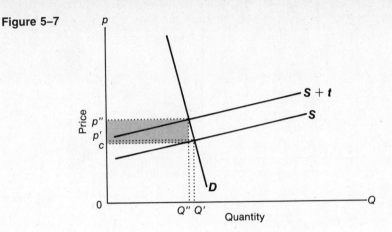

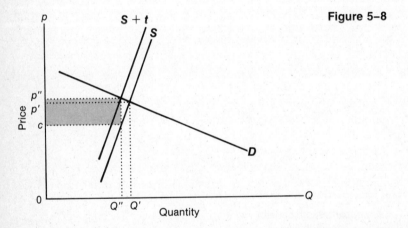

Figure 5–8

Total tax revenue is shown on Figure 5–7 as the shaded rectangle with base equal to equilibrium quantity OQ'' and height equal to the tax. Likewise, if producers have little choice but to sell (as in Figure 5–8), total production will remain roughly constant, and tax revenues may remain high. (If both demand and supply are relatively inelastic, the results are even more favorable for tax collections.)

When goods or services are unique to an area or if they are essential to its citizens, demand and supply tend to be inelastic. Governments can freely tax such activities, knowing that citizens cannot avoid paying. This is the reason cities and states tax liquor and cigarettes, rooms in resort hotels, and office buildings in busy population centers. To go outside the jurisdiction to purchase these kinds of goods and services is usually not possible or practical, and people continue to pay the tax.

They continue to pay, that is, until the passage of time opens up more choices to buyers and sellers. High taxes in one tax jurisdiction may eventually force consumers to seek other resort locations, and may cause producers to seek other locations for office buildings. High liquor and cigarette taxes may lead to development of outside markets (or to illegal activity). With time to respond to price

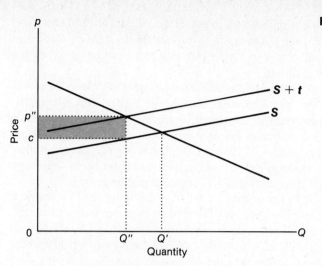

Figure 5-9

change, consumers and producers can find ways to avoid paying the tax. State and local governments soon discover that high tax rates in one year can mean low tax revenues in a future year.

In Figure 5-9 the passage of time has made buyers and sellers more sensitive to price change. Supply and demand curves have become more elastic. A tax added to the supply curve substantially reduces quantity produced and sold so that jobs are lost, incomes are reduced, and tax revenues are smaller. This problem is particularly severe for state and local governments, since other cities and states offer choices that enable buyers and sellers to avoid paying a tax. This is why cities and states compete to levy the *lowest* tax rates in their area. Each wants to encourage consumers and producers to move in, stimulating economic activity and increasing jobs, income, and (it is hoped) tax revenues. (The unhappy result for state and local governments may be increased demand for public services while tax revenues are too low to pay for them.)

The federal government is not so concerned about elasticities. Most U.S. consumers and producers want to remain in the country, which makes their demand and supply curves relatively inelastic. The federal government can levy taxes without worrying about consumers or producers moving outside its jurisdiction. Nevertheless, the passage of time may create problems even for the federal government. Very high tax rates might finally discourage certain kinds of consumer spending and discourage production as well. The ultimate result of very high federal taxes could be a lower level of economic activity for the nation as a whole.

The Incidence of a Tax

Tax incidence refers to the persons who sacrifice in order to pay a tax. The person who actually pays the tax is not necessarily the one who bears the sacrifice. For example, property taxes are paid by owners of buildings, but part of the sacrifice is borne by renters of apartments, offices, and retail establishments in the form of higher rents. Renters, in turn, pass on part of the sacrifice to consumers in the form of higher prices for their services—insurance protection, health care, consumer goods, and so forth. Defining the true incidence of the property tax is especially difficult.

The precise incidence of business taxes is also difficult to define. Taxes on business profits are paid by the owners or managers of a firm. But part of the sacrifice is borne by consumers in the form of higher prices for the firm's product, by employees in the form of lower wages and salaries, and by stock-holders in the form of lower dividends. To pass on the burden of a tax to another is called "tax shifting." A tax may be shifted backward—to workers—through reduced wages or forward—to consumers—through higher prices.

Defining the incidence of a tax is important because it determines whether a tax is regressive, proportional, or progressive. If low-income groups bear the greatest sacrifice relative to income, a tax is said to be *regressive*. If high-income groups bear the greatest sacrifice, it is *progressive*. If the sacrifice is shared in equal proportion to incomes, it is *proportional*.

We have seen that competition between state and local governments tends to keep their taxes regressive. The federal government's greater freedom in taxing allows it to levy progressive income taxes. Over a wide range of income groups in the United States, the combination of regressive state and local taxes and progressive federal income taxes makes the tax structure as a whole roughly proportional.*

The incidence of a tax is easy to see on market models like the ones in Figure 5–10. For a consumer, the sacrifice as a result of a tax is the difference between the amount paid for a good or service before the tax and the amount paid after. For a producer, the sacrifice is the difference between the amounts *received* before and after the tax. A consumer's sacrifice is shown in Figure 5–10 as the difference between p' and p''. A producer's sacrifice is the difference between p' and c, where c is the part of the purchase price remaining for the producer after paying the tax t. The shaded rectangles represent total tax payments, and the dashed lines indicate the relative sacrifices made by consumers and producers.

Note the differences in tax incidence when demand and supply are relatively inelastic or elastic. When consumers have little choice but to buy, as in Figure 5–10a, they bear the greater sacrifice. The burden of the tax has been shifted forward. When producers have little choice but to sell, as in Figure 5–10b, they bear the greater sacrifice. The burden of the tax has been shifted backward. Similar circumstances for both consumers and producers, as in Figures 5–10c and d, mean similar sacrifices.

Tax Equity

State and local government officials are concerned with tax incidence primarily insofar as it affects their own political futures. This explains their tendency toward regressive taxes: the tendency to levy taxes on low-income

*Joseph A. Pechman and Benjamin A. Okner, "Who Bears the Tax Burden?" The Brookings Institution, Washington, D.C., 1974.

Figure 5–10

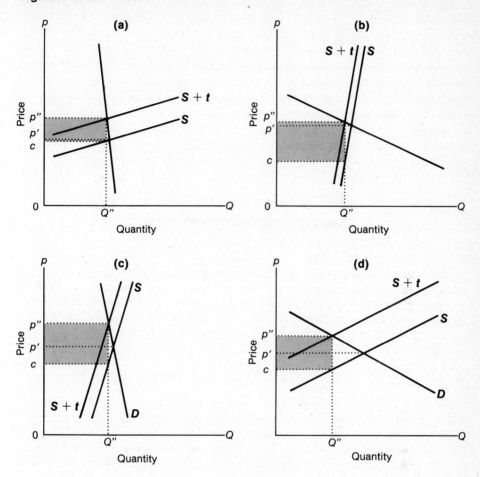

groups that cannot avoid paying. We have seen that the federal government has greater freedom in setting taxes. This allows the writers of federal tax law to consider tax incidence and its effect on equity.

Equity in taxation can be described two ways:

1. **Horizontal equity** refers to taxpayers with similar economic circumstances. Horizontal equity would require that taxpayers with similar economic circumstances bear similar tax burdens. Artificial devices for avoiding taxes affect the tax bills of similar taxpayers differently and violate the principle of horizontal equity. Differences in tax policies between tax jurisdictions have the same effect.

2. **Vertical equity** refers to persons of high and low economic circumstances. Vertical equity would require that taxpayers bear greater or lesser tax burdens according to their ability to pay. How much greater the tax burden should be for high-income persons cannot be defined precisely. This depends

on voters' perceptions of what is fair and healthy in our political and economic system.

One objective of taxation by the federal government might be to reduce some of the horizontal and vertical inequities that may result from state and local tax policies—to offset the effect of artificial devices that reduce some tax bills and to offset the differences in taxes that result from a variety of different tax jurisdictions. The federal government may also be more able than state and local governments to interpret voters' perceptions of fairness and establish taxes that satisfy the nation's concerns regarding equity.

Tax Policies for the Future

A General Sales Tax

As a nation grows and develops, the needs for government programs and the capacity to tax change. Governments must continually evaluate their tax and spending policies and seek new ways to achieve new objectives. The United States has been undergoing major changes: social and political, economic and strategic. These kinds of changes may call for reforms in the ways governments pay for government programs.

By far the greatest source of tax revenues is the personal income tax. The personal income tax is progressive: that is, it collects a larger fraction of income from high-income earners than from low-income earners. Our progressive income tax has several *advantages:*

1. Placing a greater tax burden on high-income earners is believed by many to be more equitable than other forms of taxation.
2. The smaller tax burden on low-income earners leaves those families with more spendable income than otherwise and encourages a higher level of total spending for the economy as a whole.
3. Progressive income taxes smooth out the effects of the business cycle by collecting higher taxes when incomes rise and lower taxes when incomes fall. The effect is to moderate tendencies toward inflation or unemployment.*

Progressive income taxes have these *disadvantages:*

1. Higher tax rates for high-income earners may discourage work effort and stifle productivity.
2. Rising incomes cause a greater tax drain from taxpayers to government, reducing private savings and reducing funds for investment in new capital resources.
3. Income taxes are buried in the costs of everything we produce, raising prices and reducing our competitiveness in world markets.

*This feature of progressive income taxes has come under attack in recent years as inflation has pushed income earners into higher and higher tax brackets even though their real income has not increased. This is what the tax system is supposed to do, but it may also have the effect of limiting consumer spending and stalling economic growth.

The advantages of progressive income taxes were especially valuable to our nation when our capacity to produce was growing rapidly. Particularly in the decades after World War II, new technologies, improved worker skills, and vigorous capital investment made for regular growth in productive capacity. The progressive income tax helped equalize spending power, increased spending among low- and middle-income groups, and encouraged still greater capital investment.

Beginning in the 1970s, circumstances changed, so that some policymakers are recommending a change toward less progressive forms of taxation. Slower productivity growth, obsolete technologies, a decaying capital stock, and persistent inflation seem to call for new policies to discourage spending and encourage saving for investment. One way to accomplish this would be to change from a tax on income to a tax on spending: that is, a **nationwide sales tax.** A nationwide sales tax would require taxpayers to pay taxes only on the portion of income *not saved.** Since low-income families tend to spend a larger portion of income, they would pay a larger fraction of income in tax. High-income families would be left with more income to save and invest.

Exempting savings from taxation might have either of two effects: (1) The greater after-tax rate of return on *not spending* might encourage families to save *more*. Or (2) the greater after-tax rate of return on saving might enable families to enjoy a given level of total savings through smaller amounts of current saving, thus, causing them to save *less*. Analysts have studied available data on the relationship between saving and after-tax return and arrived at no clearcut predictions as to the effect of exempting savings from taxation. Moreover, they recognize that even if saving were to increase, there is no guarantee that funds would actually be invested in the U.S. economy. (The accompanying decline in consumer spending might reduce the rate of return on domestic investment, so that a greater amount of savings might be invested abroad.)

There is also a question as to the total revenue government could collect from a nationwide sales tax. Exempting savings from taxation would necessarily reduce total tax revenues unless tax rates were set fairly high or unless other taxes were to be raised. It is not clear which of these changes would be most efficient or equitable. Another disadvantage of a nationwide sales tax is the possibility that a sales tax would indeed encourage high-income families to save more and that the result would be a greater concentration of the nation's wealth.†

A Taxpayers' Revolt

When the U.S. Constitution reserved certain powers for state governments, the aim was to give all citizens close contact with governments responsive to their immediate needs. In 1978, California voters used that close contact to

*Most European nations now rely on sales taxes for a portion of tax revenues.

†The regressivity of a nationwide sales tax could be modified by varying the tax rate at successive levels of expenditure, by exempting essential purchases from the tax, or by allowing sales tax deductions from other taxes.

proclaim what many citizens around the country had come to feel about their own local governments.

California cities depend heavily for revenue on property taxes. During the 1970s, inflation and speculation in housing drove property taxes in some cities up by as much as 20 percent a year. In the meantime, the state treasury began to accumulate an embarrassing surplus that many Californians felt should be used for local tax relief. Citizens Harold Jarvis and Paul Gann (both of whom are large property owners) proposed a citizens' initiative, Proposition 13, that would cut local property taxes by 60 percent and put a ceiling on future property tax increases. Put to a vote in a statewide referendum, Proposition 13 gained a landslide victory.

The result of Proposition 13 was to add an amendment to California's state constitution slashing tax revenues of local governments an average of 22 percent and as much as 70 percent. Faced with a sharp reduction in property tax revenues, many local governments acted immediately to cut services: summer schools, parks and recreation programs, and fire protection. Many cities began looking for new revenue devices — garbage collection fees, dog licensing fees, and ambulance charges. Other states and the federal government listened to the message from California voters and began cutting back their own spending programs in anticipation of a spread of the taxpayers' revolt to their voters.

What are the likely results of the taxpayers' revolt? One result is expected to be favorable: that is, the imposition of user fees for some services formerly provided free of charge. Payment of a user fee is a more market-oriented approach to provision of service. It ensures that only services regarded as valuable by consumers will actually be performed, increasing the efficiency of government. On the other hand, to assess a user fee reduces the positive externalities that would otherwise be available to all citizens. There are equity considerations in user fees, too, since needy families may be unable to purchase certain desired services.

Other results may be even less favorable. The hope was that lower property taxes on homes and businesses would stimulate such great increases in economic activity that persons who lost their jobs in local government would quickly find jobs in the private sector. Such stimulus has been slow in coming, in part because of substantial cuts in spending among unemployed government workers. Declining consumer spending has meant declining job opportunities throughout the state's economy. Business firms, which formerly paid two-thirds of local property taxes, were expected to benefit; but the state's inventory tax was raised, reducing businesses' tax advantage. Under the amendment, property can be reassessed for tax purposes only when it changes hands. Since residential property changes hands more often than other property, the result has been relatively higher taxes for homeowners.

A more serious result concerns long-range consequences in terms of the balance among various levels of government. To deprive local governments of major revenues forces them to appeal to the state and federal governments for the means to carry on needed programs. Dependence on higher levels of government removes certain decision-making powers from local citizens and weakens local control. Moreover, the loss of local funds needed to "match" federal block grants will reduce revenues from this source. And finally, since local property taxes are deducted from federal taxable income, federal tax payments will increase.

GOVERNMENT BORROWING

Of the three levels of government, the federal government has the greatest capacity for borrowing. Its greater taxing power ensures that the debts of the federal government will be paid. Some state constitutions prohibit any borrowing at all by the state government, and local governments are limited in their borrowing by the respective states.

Federal Government Debt

A century and a half ago the federal government collected so much revenue from customs duties that it was able to pay off all its borrowing and distribute funds to states for return to taxpayers. Such a fortunate circumstance has been rare in the intervening years. In fact, for twenty of the last twenty-one years the federal government has paid out more than it has collected in taxes and has been required to borrow.

At the beginning of 1983, the debt of the federal government was $1,150 billion, the accumulation of years of deficits in the federal budget. Much of the borrowing was done to finance wars. The debt grew by almost $200 billion during World War II (1942–1946) and by $87 billion while U.S. forces were stationed in Viet Nam (1966–1973). Other federal government borrowing has been associated with business cycles. During recessions, income tax revenues tend to grow more slowly than government outlays for unemployment compensation and social welfare programs. Borrowing during recession may be paid back when taxpayers grow more prosperous, or it may remain a part of the national debt, continuing to be "re-funded" each time old debts mature.

The federal government borrows by issuing short- and long-term securities. Short-term **bills** mature in 90, 180, or 360 days and pay whatever market rate of interest prevailed at the time of issue. Their selling price reflects a discount below **face value** equal to the interest rate: thus, a security paying $100 in 360 days at 10 percent would sell for about $90, at 12 percent about $88, and at 5 percent about $95. At maturity, the bill can be exchanged for its "face value": $100. Short-term Treasury securities are considered to be risk-free, since the federal government will not default on its obligations. Short-term bills may be exchanged before maturity at prices that reflect the discount over the remaining time to maturity.

United States Treasury **notes** have maturities up to 7 years, and **bonds** can have longer maturities. Congress limits the Treasury's issue of bonds above minimum interest rates (4½ percent). Notes pay a **coupon payment** at regular intervals and face value at maturity. Thus, a four-year, $100 note at 10 percent would sell for about $100, pay a $10 coupon each year, and pay $100 at maturity. Some bonds accumulate interest over their life and pay the total of interest and face value at maturity. A five-year U.S. savings bond purchased in 1982 for $100 would be worth $150.37 at maturity, an implied interest rate of 8½ percent annually.

Most long-term Treasury securities can be resold to other investors before maturity, but there are risks. The risk is not associated with default but with the possibility of changes in market rates of interest. Suppose the four-year note described above is to be resold shortly after its purchase. If interest rates have risen to 15 percent, the note will be worth only about $95 in resale markets; representing a $5 **loss of capital** to the original buyer. Of course, the reverse is also true. A 5 percent drop in interest rates would mean a selling price of about $105, for a $5 **capital gain.**

The relative safety of government securities makes them an important part of the investment holdings of individuals, business firms, financial institutions, other governments, and educational institutions. However, their safety also means a relatively low interest return, making it generally desirable to hold other higher-yielding securities as well.

State Borrowing

The federal government exempts interest earnings on state and local government securities from federal income taxes.* This makes it possible for state and local governments to borrow at lower interest rates than other borrowers. A 5 percent interest return to a bondholder in the 50 percent income tax bracket, for instance, would be equal in value to 10 percent on a taxed security.

State borrowing was heavy in the 1800s to finance "internal improvements": canals, railroads, highways, and so forth. This kind of borrowing continues to make much of state debt long-term. Most state debt includes provision for repaying part of the principal along with regular interest payments. Or state governments may make regular contributions to a sinking fund for eventual repayment of long-term debt. The result of the repayment provision is to limit state budgetary freedoms for as long in the future as the debt remains unpaid.

Some state constitutions prohibit state borrowing except as authorized by a constitutional amendment; some permit borrowing only after approved by popular vote; and some allow the state legislature to make the borrowing decision. Most states also limit the borrowing capacity of local governments, generally in terms of the city's property tax base.

Local Government Borrowing

City borrowing was heavy early in this century for financing city streets, water and sewage systems, urban development, and so forth. Lately, the rise in income tax rates with inflation has made local tax-exempt securities especially attractive to investors and stimulated this kind of government borrowing.

*The reason for the exemption is the Supreme Court decision that the "power to tax is the power to destroy." Unlimited power of the federal government to tax state and local governments could destroy them.

Cities and states issue **revenue bonds** and **general obligation bonds.** Revenue bonds are issued to finance a particular project — toll road, stadium, or urban renewal project—the earnings of which are used to pay interest and principal on the bonds. General obligation bonds are issued to pay ordinary operating expenses only until tax revenues are to be received, so they are generally short-term.

The risk of local government securities varies with the credit-worthiness of the issuing government. Two investors' services, Standard and Poor's and Moody's, rate securities according to the credit reputation and financial health of the issuer. Triple-A securities are considered practically risk-free, B are risky, and C are "not investment quality." Sometimes the rating services make mistakes, as when New York City and Cleveland retained their "A" ratings almost up to the time they were unable to pay maturing debt.

Legal limits on state and local government borrowing have had the effect of encouraging a search for other methods of borrowing. One method is to establish an "authority" to finance, design, and operate a needed public project. An authority may extend over several separate tax jurisdictions. Bonds issued by an authority are exempt from federal taxes and may be used to finance such things as area-wide rapid transit, port facilities, or water resource management. They have the disadvantage that they are not guaranteed by the "full faith and credit" of any single government. Thus they cannot draw on tax revenues to make debt payments.

Another type of borrowing involves state or local government sale of **industrial development bonds.** Funds acquired this way are loaned to private business firms for establishing new industry in the area. Since most industrial development bonds are tax exempt,* the interest charged new business borrowers can be lower than market rates. Thus, there is an added incentive to move business into the area. There is a disadvantage, too, in that the low interest charge may promote inefficiency in the allocation of resources.

Some General Conclusions About Government Borrowing

The total of federal, state, and local borrowing for the year constitutes new government debt. Governments with tax surpluses use their surpluses to purchase the debt of governments with deficits. In this way, they earn interest on their funds until needed. For the last two decades, the federal budget has tended to be in deficit, and state and local budgets in surplus. The result of these offsetting tendencies is a level of total government borrowing that remains roughly constant. Figure 5–11 shows current borrowings at federal, state, and local levels of government and net additions to government debt over recent years.

The pattern of borrowing at various levels of government suggests something important about our governmental system. We want state and local governments to take on the responsibility for local service needs, and we want the federal government to ensure a healthy economic environment for the nation.

*Since 1968, *tax exemption* refers only to projects costing less than $5 million.

Figure 5–11

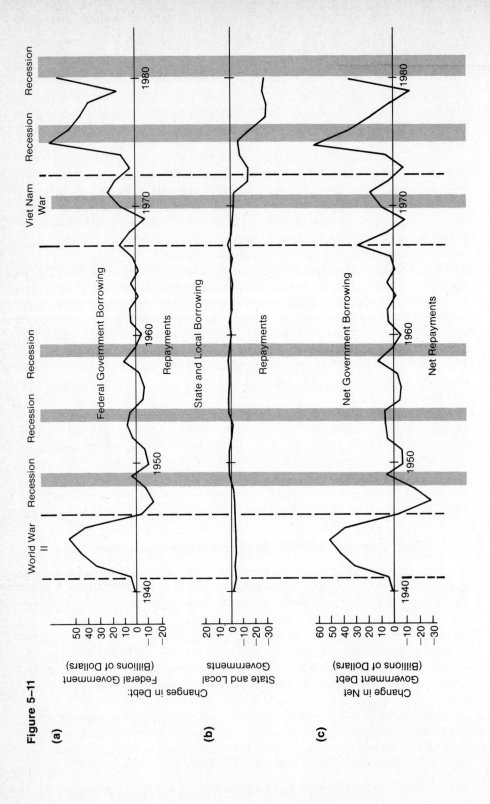

Toward that objective, we expect state and local governments to spend during prosperity, and we depend on the federal government to borrow and spend during recession. The spending of one complements the other and helps ensure the efficient use of resources and allocation of responsibilities.

METROPOLITAN FISCAL PROBLEMS

The most serious financial problems facing governments today are those of the cities. City governments are more limited in their jurisdictions than others and, therefore, more limited in their taxing powers. The natural tendency for most cities is to grow, spilling the population out into the suburbs and beyond. The central city tends to lose its most vigorous, skilled, and productive citizens —those whose tax payments are essential for financing city services. Frequently the city is left with low-income or unemployable persons—those who have never fully adapted to modern industrial life and who, alas, require substantial city services just to survive.

City governments face a terrible dilemma, but the problem and its possible solutions affect more than city residents. The combination of a central city and related suburbs is called a **metropolitan area.** In 1981, three-fourths of the U.S. population lived in metropolitan areas. Citizens of a metropolitan area derive their livelihood from the economy of the whole. They repair the teeth, rent the apartments, drive the buses, and provide the entertainment for persons throughout the area. Whether or not they live inside the central city's tax jurisdiction, they enjoy the external benefits of city fire and police protection, public education and transportation, and even welfare payments to the city's poor (who might otherwise be forced into crime or even starvation).

Cities around the nation have been affected differently by the problems of growth. Economic growth has made some metropolitan areas more attractive than others, easing their financial dilemma. Still, these more fortunate cities must face the possibility that, eventually, desperation in poorer regions will cause a new movement of poor people into their own jurisdictions and a movement of middle-income taxpayers out. Table 5–2 provides information about the nation's fastest and slowest growing cities.

Some Characteristics of Metropolitan Fiscal Policy

Because metropolitan areas include a hodgepodge of small, independent jurisdictions, they also experience a variety of externalities—both positive and negative. The problem of measuring externalities and paying for programs that yield positive externalities suggests either of two approaches for local government: (1) the creation of a broad **metropolitan government** in which tax revenues flow together to pay for needed services throughout the entire area, or (2) the use of **intergovernmental grants** in which tax revenues from high-income jurisdictions in the metropolitan area flow into low-income jurisdictions. The advantages of these and other approaches should be evaluated critically.

Table 5-2 Population Changes in Major Cities

	Population Gain 1970 to 1980 (in percent)	Federal Aid as Percentage of City's Total Revenue (1978–1979)
FASTEST GROWING CITIES		
San Jose	+36.1	12.5
Phoenix	+33.7	22.5
El Paso	+31.7	36.7
Houston	+26.1	12.2
San Diego	+24.7	18.1
San Antonio	+19.7	13.0
Jacksonville, Florida	+ 7.3	6.7
Dallas	+ 6.8	12.7
Los Angeles	+ 4.9	12.2
Columbus, Ohio	+ 4.1	22.2
Memphis	+ 3.3	6.5
Nashville-Davidson, Tenn.	+ 3.2	8.3
SHRINKING CITIES		
St. Louis	−27.9	17.4
Cleveland	−23.8	26.7
Detroit	−21.3	18.8
Pittsburgh	−18.5	15.5
Washington, D.C.	−16.0	38.8
Atlanta	−14.7	15.2
Philadelphia	−13.8	10.0
Baltimore	−13.5	19.1
Boston	−12.3	14.2
Kansas City, Mo.	−12.0	20.4
Chicago	−11.9	21.7
Milwaukee	−11.8	11.6
New York City	−11.1	6.7
Seattle	− 7.3	12.5
New Orleans	− 6.2	33.0
San Francisco	− 5.8	17.8
Denver	− 5.0	15.4
Indianapolis	− 4.8	23.2

Source: *The New York Times*, Sunday, March 15, 1981.

One advantage of centralizing the collection of taxes and the administration of spending programs is the possibility of *economies of scale*. We have defined economies of scale as the cost reductions that often come with production of a large volume of a good or service. Some government services may enjoy significant scale economies: public schools, transportation, health and hospitals, water and sewage are examples. (Others, like welfare, fire and police, parks and recreation, and garbage collection are more suitable for small-scale administrations.) Large jurisdictions may be better able to hire skilled professionals, such that the quality of public service is higher. Another advantage of centralized metropolitan government is the ability to compare benefits and costs of a wider range of programs for more efficient selection.

Many of the disadvantages of metropolitan government stem from the loss of citizen choice and participation when government becomes larger. A variety of small neighborhood jurisdictions with a variety of tax and spending policies may enlarge individual options. (The option to flee a high-tax area for a low-tax area is a source of the metropolitan government's dilemma, as we have seen.) And citizens are better able to participate in governmental decisions made close to home. On the other hand, variations in property tax assessments and exemptions among neighborhoods have the effect of reducing tax equity across the metropolitan area.

Some metropolitan areas have designed plans for achieving the advantages of greater centralization while avoiding some of the disadvantages. In some areas, individual governments have joined together to provide a particular service; in others, planning commissions have surveyed metropolitan needs and tried to coordinate local government programs; and special districts have been created to provide fire protection, water and sewage, or resource development programs for the entire area. Intergovernmental cooperation in taxing can help also by reducing tax competition and changing the sources of tax revenues toward greater progressivity.

Efficiency, Externalities, and Equity in the Evolution of American Cities

American cities grew because they were efficient. They provided a healthy environment for the development of commerce and manufacturing. The ease of transportation and communication in a city encouraged the growth of firms supplying specialized services and component parts to producers of finished goods. As improved agricultural technology released labor from the production of life's basic necessities, farm workers found new opportunities in cities. The prosperity of the American economy was closely tied to the prosperity of its cities.

Cities produced positive externalities that flowed out to other areas. They provided a kind of laboratory for innovation, dispersing risk and reducing the probability of catastrophic failure. They provided an outlet for savings and a source of investment capital for new enterprises. They permitted economies of scale in higher education and cultural activities. And finally, the ease of mobility in cities increased incentives, and the variety of job opportunities stimulated productivity, both of which benefited the nation as a whole.

Some of the circumstances that favored city growth in the past have reversed in recent decades. One change has been the improved technology of transportation and communication. Improved transportation facilities have reduced the advantage of locating in urban areas. Moreover, modern manufacturing requires costly materials and skilled labor, so that transportation is a smaller part of total production cost. Nowadays, coast-to-coast communication is simpler than intra-city communication was years ago. Today's cities have become centers of specialized *functions* — like finance, government, or wholesale trade — rather than centers of manufacturing — like autos, apparel, or furniture.

Along with these changes has come the separation of the location of work from the location of residence. Whereas years ago displaced farm workers moved to the city for economic opportunity, today's affluent urban workers choose to live outside the city. Through modern communications, suburban dwellers can enjoy the kinds of cultural opportunities that were formerly available only in cities. And they are removed from urban problems of congestion, crime, and social blight.

Certain federal government policies had the effect of encouraging the trend toward "suburbanization." Since World War II, loan guarantees under the Federal Housing Administration and the Veterans' Administration have enabled many families to purchase new homes. Deductibility of mortgage interest payments from taxable income has made home ownership cheaper for middle- and upper-income earners. One of the goals of these policies was to stimulate the construction industry. But new construction was most attractive in the suburbs where land was plentiful and cheap — thus encouraging movement out of the cities to suburbs, small towns, and rural areas.

A similar result followed the federal government's policy toward subsidized highways. The interstate highway system enabled suburban dwellers to commute longer distances to work and enlarged their options for residential choice. At the same time, construction of new highways broke apart urban neighborhoods and took valuable land out of the urban tax base. The result was to weaken cities' ability to cope with worsening city problems.

Other social policies of the federal government contributed to urban decay. The emphasis on civil rights protected suspected criminals and probably aggravated urban crime. And finally, policies to speed city-wide school desegregation drove many middle- and upper-income families out of the city.

All these policies originated with the federal government, whose policy goals do not necessarily coincide with the goals of the nation's cities. Where broad national goals conflict with the goals of urban health and prosperity, it is not difficult to predict the outcome. In general, the policies described above were aimed at improving equity among population groups, particularly members of minority groups frequently accused of crimes and frequently subjected to educational and job discrimination. Ironically, policies intended to aid the disadvantaged may also have aggravated other trends that have had the effect of worsening their living standards and reducing equity.

National Policy Toward the Cities

President Lyndon Johnson was the first to establish a comprehensive national plan for dealing with the problems of American cities. Under his administration, a Model Cities Program was set up to provide federal funds directly to cities. The Model Cities Program provided coordinated services within a single distressed area: job counseling and training for unemployed workers, day care centers for single parents, improved transportation facilities for urban workers, and low-interest loans for neighborhood rehabilitation. The hope was that an improved urban environment would encourage private business firms to return to the cities and stimulate economic growth. Regrettably, the available funds were spread so thinly over so many areas that the results failed to live up to expectations.

Urban problems worsened in the 1970s, and President Carter's administration tried to target funds more precisely and plan more effectively toward solution of these problems. Programs were designed for restoring downtown areas and for moderating certain federal policies that may have encouraged the abandonment of urban properties. Concern about inflation and a rising federal deficit, however, meant that the level of federal financial support was lower than city governments had hoped.

President Reagan's urban policy centered around a plan for Urban Enterprise Zones. Under this plan, new business and industry established within a zone would be given tax credits and relief from certain kinds of government regulation. Some of the nation's major corporations joined in the effort to revitalize distressed areas, building plants in depressed areas and providing on-the-job training for urban workers.

In 1980, a Presidential Commission on the problems of the cities recommended a new arrangement for federal and local cooperation. Since much of city expenditures go for welfare and health, the Commission proposed centralizing all welfare and subsidized health programs (Medicaid and Medicare). Other proposals would remove the responsibility for education from local governments and pass it on to the states.

Special Case
New York City

The trends that now affect many of the nation's cities appeared first in New York. For decades New York City experienced an inflow of poor and unskilled immigrants, increasing the need for costly city services and raising the wage demands of city workers. The city moved desperately to tax all sorts of city services. Then in the early 1970s New York added an especially dangerous element to its financial crisis. When the cost of city services began to rise above its tax revenues, the city borrowed the necessary funds.

Typically, cities borrow for capital construction, with the expectation that interest and loan payments can be made from fees earned by the capital project. For a government to borrow to meet day-to-day expenses is risky. Elected officials may not hesitate to borrow excessively, knowing that the loans will have to be paid off by their successors! Much of New York's borrowing was short-term and subject to rising interest charges each time loans had to be refinanced. By 1975 interest and loan payments amounted to almost $2 billion, nearly one-sixth of New York City's annual budget.

Many large bank holders of city bonds began to worry that New York would never be able to pay its debts, and they refused to lend more. Unable to borrow to pay old debts, the city faced default. In fact, some observers recommended default, believing that a serious financial crisis would force the city to cut costs and force the banks to resume lending (so as to avoid further loss). Others, including New York State's governor, believed that default would cause such a drop in the value of city securities that many holders would go bankrupt as well. Default might also make it impossible for other state and local governments to sell their own securities.

To avoid default, the city's major lenders set up a Municipal Assistance Corporation (MAC) to borrow for the city and receive city tax revenues directly. New York was required to:

1. Lay off many city workers and freeze the wages of remaining city employees;
2. Eliminate certain free services and raise user fees for others; and
3. Finally, gain control over the city budget.

The Municipal Assistance Corporation sought federal loan guarantees for additional borrowing. Congress resisted, fearing that loan guarantees would open the door to similar requests from other city governments. On the other hand, many members of Congress believed that failing to help New York might set off a chain reaction of crises among other city governments and financial institutions.

Finally, the federal, state, and local governments agreed to cooperate on a long-term plan for correcting New York's problems. New York city and state pension systems were asked to purchase MAC bonds, and banks and other financial institutions agreed to make further loans. The federal government agreed to guarantee $1.65 billion in loans to help MAC sell its bonds.

- What positive and negative externalities would be associated with a city's default? With "rescue" by federal loan guarantees?
- What are the arguments for and against letting New York City continue on its course without federal government assistance?
- What policies would you recommend for the future?

An Issue for the Future

Regional Growth and Decay

Intergovernmental financial relations become especially critical when different regions of the country experience different growth rates. Different growth rates mean changing tax bases and changes in governments' ability to pay for public services. Differences in the quality of public service can aggravate tendencies toward growth or decline and worsen inequalities between regions.

Differential growth rates result in part from fundamental economic causes: differences in labor and resource costs, differences in tax policies toward business, and differences in environmental regulations. Differential growth may result also from policies of the federal government. In years past, federal defense spending and social welfare payments have tended to favor the South and the far West. The industrial Northeast and the Great Lakes region have suffered from industrial decline, with slowed growth of incomes and tax revenues. Whereas some southern and western states receive more than

$1.25 of federal money for each $1.00 of federal taxes they pay, many of the older industrial states receive less than $.75 for each $1.00 paid.

These differences have led to conflicts between governments and to demands for changes to equalize public services nationwide. One proposal would make the federal government responsible for all public welfare programs. Since poverty is a national problem, proponents say, it should be paid for through the taxes of all the people. More centralized administration of welfare programs would reduce inequality of benefits across the nation and reduce the incentive for poor families to move to the major population centers of the Northeast.

A second proposal would remove the advantage federal tax policies now allow for home ownership. Deducting mortgage interest payments and property tax payments from taxable income has benefited the suburbs and the West and South, where home ownership is more common than in Northeastern metropolitan areas. Federal tax policies toward depreciation have given special advantages to new construction and discouraged rehabilitation of existing buildings. One result has been to encourage "urban sprawl": spreading development over the countryside, requiring new roads, water and sewage facilities, and increased use of the private automobile.

In the past, our governments have been flexible enough to solve conflicts like these. Regional cooperation in solving problems has made our nation stronger — politically, economically, and strategically. In the future, elected representatives at all levels of government will be asked to decide on proposals for dealing with these kinds of intergovernmental issues.

QUESTIONS

1. Illustrate graphically how low taxes might over time increase a city's total tax revenue. What circumstances might interfere with this result?
2. Georgia taxpayers subsidize scientific and technical education at Georgia Tech for about 5,500 Georgia residents and 5,500 residents of other states. Only 30 percent of Georgia Tech's graduates remain in the state. Is this an efficient allocation of the state's resources? Explain your answer.
3. What are some arguments for and against centralizing responsibility for welfare programs with the federal government? Should welfare payments be equalized across the nation? Discuss.
4. What characteristics of our governmental structure may be described as efficient? Inefficient?
5. Explain why taxes on property, gasoline, and liquor are generally described as regressive. What circumstances contribute to regressivity in local taxes?
6. Under what circumstances are negative taxes efficient and equitable?
7. Under what circumstances are user charges efficient and equitable?
8. Describe a process by which state tax revenues might be used to help equalize the quality of public services across the state. Is this process efficient and equitable?
9. New York City levies a "transfer tax" on exchange of securities. What would be the expected short- and long-term effects of the transfer tax on New York's employment, personal income, and tax revenues?
10. How would you explain the existence of a "departure tax" levied on persons leaving certain Caribbean islands? How would you explain the fact that many Caribbean islands have no income tax? Contrast their situation with that of the United States government.

11. Define horizontal and vertical equity and explain why they are difficult to achieve. Which of the two do you think is *more* difficult to achieve and why?
12. Explain the significance of "jurisdiction" for intergovernmental fiscal relations. Where are jurisdictional problems most serious?
13. What circumstances have contributed to efficiency in urban growth and decline? What circumstances have contributed to inefficiency?
14. Evaluate the advantages and disadvantages of income taxes versus a general sales tax.
15. What are the short- and long-range consequences of a government's failure to meet local service needs?
16. Explain the basis for risk associated with U.S. government securities.
17. What circumstances make state and local government securities more or less attractive to investors?

DEFINITIONS

Bills are short-term debt instruments of the federal government.

Block grants are payments from the federal government to state or local governments to finance a broad public program. Block grants are usually "matching grants": matched in some proportion by state or local funds.

A capital gain occurs when the resale value of a debt instrument rises above its purchase price.

Categorical grants are payments from the federal government to state or local governments to finance particular public projects.

A coupon payment is an amount paid regularly during the life of a debt instrument. The amount of the coupon payment is determined by the interest rate on the instrument and its face value.

Equity in taxation refers to the fairness of the tax structure.

The face value of a debt instrument is the amount that is to be paid the holder at maturity.

Federal government debt is the accumulation of federal government borrowing during years when federal outlays exceeded revenues from taxation.

General obligation bonds are debt instruments sold to finance ordinary government expenses. It is expected that tax collections will be sufficient to pay interest and principal on the debt.

General revenue sharing involves payments from the federal government to state or local governments to use in any way they see fit.

Horizontal equity refers to taxes paid by persons in the same economic circumstances. Horizontal equity would require that persons in the same economic circumstances bear the same tax burden.

Industrial development bonds are sold to obtain funds for subsidizing new industrial development. It is expected that industrial development will create jobs and generate income and tax revenues for paying interest and principal on the debt.

Infinitely great elasticity describes markets in which percent change in price is zero for any change in quantity. Infinitely great elasticity is shown by horizontal demand or supply curves.

Intergovernmental grants are payments from one government to another.

A jurisdiction is an area over which a particular government may exercise authority.

A linear demand curve is a straight line curve, having high elasticity at high prices and low elasticity at low prices.

A linear supply curve is a straight line curve, having the same elasticity along the entire curve.

Loss of capital occurs when the resale value of a debt instrument falls below its purchase price.

A metropolitan area is the combination of a city and its related suburbs.

Metropolitan government is a combination of local governments into a broad metropolitan jurisdiction.

A nationwide sales tax would collect a certain percentage (or percentages) of the purchase price of goods and services sold nationwide.

Negative taxes are subsidies paid to desirable activities to encourage them to move into a particular government's jurisdiction.

Notes and bonds are long-term debt instruments of the federal government.

Progressive taxes are taxes that take a larger fraction of income from high-income families than from low-income families; for example, income taxes.

Regressive taxes are taxes that take a larger fraction of income from low-income families than from high-income families; for example, sales taxes.

Revenue bonds are debt instruments sold to finance a particular public project. It is expected that earnings from the project will enable the issuing government to pay interest and principal on the debt.

The tax base is the geographical area or economic activity over which a particular government may exercise its taxing powers.

Vertical equity refers to taxes paid by persons at the high and the low end of the income scale. Vertical equity would require that persons at the high end bear a greater tax burden than those at the low end. The difference in the tax burden would be based on the voters' sense of what is fair or equitable.

Zero elasticity describes markets in which percent change in quantity is zero for any change in price. Zero elasticity is shown by vertical demand or supply curves.

SUGGESTED READINGS

Alcaly, Roger E., and David Mermelstein. *The Fiscal Crisis of American Cities.* New York: Vintage Books, 1977.

Beek, David C. "Rethinking Tax-Exempt Financing for State and Local Governments." *Federal Reserve Bank of New York Quarterly Review,* Autumn, 1982, p. 30.

Berman, Lewis. "Reaganizing the Inner Cities." *Fortune,* December 14, 1981, p. 98.

Bradford, David F. "The Case for a Personal Consumption Tax." In Joseph A. Pechman, ed., *What Should Be Taxed: Income or Expenditure?* Washington, D.C.: Brookings, 1980.

Collins, Lora S. "Do Deficits Matter?" *Across the Board,* April, 1982, p. 27.

Feldstein, Martin, ed. *The American Economy in Transition.* Chicago: National Bureau of Economic Research, 1980, Chapter 9.

_____. "Budget Deficits and Political Choices." *Challenge,* January/February, 1983, p. 53.

Goode, Richard. "The Superiority of the Income Tax." In Joseph A. Pechman, ed., *What Should Be Taxed: Income or Expenditure?* Washington, D.C.: Brookings, 1980.

Hale, David. "Simple: Tax Every Income at the Same Rate." *Across the Board,* January, 1983, p. 51.

Kirkland, Richard I., Jr. "The Flatter-Tax Movement Picks Up Steam." *Fortune,* July 26, 1982, p. 33.

Levy, Frank. "The Biography of Proposition 13." *Across the Board,* January, 1980, p. 26.

Maxwell, James A. *Financing State and Local Governments.* Washington, D.C.: Brookings, 1971.

Minarik, Joseph J. "What's in Store for the Income Tax?" *Challenge,* November/December, 1982, p. 14.

Rasmussen, David W. *Urban Economics.* New York: Harper and Row, 1973, Chapters 5, 8–10.

Seidman, Laurence S. "The Personal Consumption Tax and Social Welfare." *Challenge,* September/October, 1980, p. 10.

Sommers, Albert T. "The Federal Budget Should Be Rebuilt from the Ground Up." *Across the Board,* May, 1982, p. 18.

"State and Local Government in Trouble." *Business Week,* October 26, 1981, p. 135.

Weinstein, Bernard L. "New Federalism—or New Feudalism?" *Challenge,* May/June, 1982, p. 38.

CHAPTER SIX

Growth and the Quality of Life

Is More Always Better?

LEARNING OBJECTIVES

- To understand the importance of economic growth for increasing real per capita income and living standards.
- To describe the course of economic growth in the United States, the role of government in promoting growth, and the current concern with growth problems.
- To apply a short-run production function to illustrate long-range growth in productive capacity.
- To include Marginal Social Product and Marginal Social Cost in a benefit/cost ratio for making growth decisions.
- To examine governmental policies for encouraging efficient production decisions.
- To assess global limitations to growth, along with international policies to avert catastrophe and ensure equity in an era of limitations.

"It isn't possible to do *just one* thing."

Think about that. That is the way a famous ecologist explained our dilemma over economic growth and the quality of life. The statement reminds us that our total ecosystem is like a pond: disturbing the surface in even a small way sends ripples across it. Ripples bump into the edge and rebound to bump against each other until finally no part of the pond is unaffected.

The thought can be either very comforting or terrifying, depending on how confident we are that the disturbances we create in the pond are the right ones in terms of benefiting the world's people. Making the right decisions about economic growth can be especially critical for the quality of life, now and for the future.

In this text we have described our economic goal as *efficiency*: the use of resources for producing the greatest benefits at the lowest cost. And we have described the distribution of benefits and costs in terms of fairness, or *equity*. We have shown how the existence of *externalities* complicates the measurement and distribution of benefits and costs and makes achieving our goal more difficult. The concepts of efficiency, equity, and externalities are especially useful for analyzing the dilemma of growth and the quality of life.

This chapter considers growth and the consequences of growth for the quality of life. We will begin with a look at the sources and processes of growth. Then we will discuss some ways for determining growth policies. We will want to choose growth policies that are efficient and equitable. Finally, we will explore certain limits to growth and some modern growth problems.

SOURCES OF GROWTH

To begin, let us distinguish between growth and development. Growth refers to an increase in productive capacity more or less as it was before. *Development* refers to fundamental changes in methods of production. Growth may be regarded as a *quantitative* change, and development as a *qualitative* change. For a complex industrialized economy, it is difficult to separate the effects of growth from those of development. Therefore, in the discussion that follows we will use the terms interchangeably.

Growth and/or development can be shown graphically through the use of two economic models described in this text:

1. *The Production Possibilities Curve.* More and better resources, along with improved technology, cause the production possibilities curve to shift to the

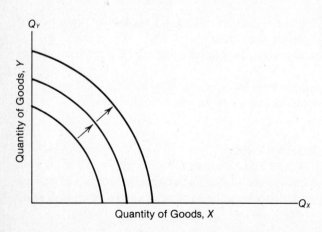

Figure 6-1
Economic growth increases production possibilities.

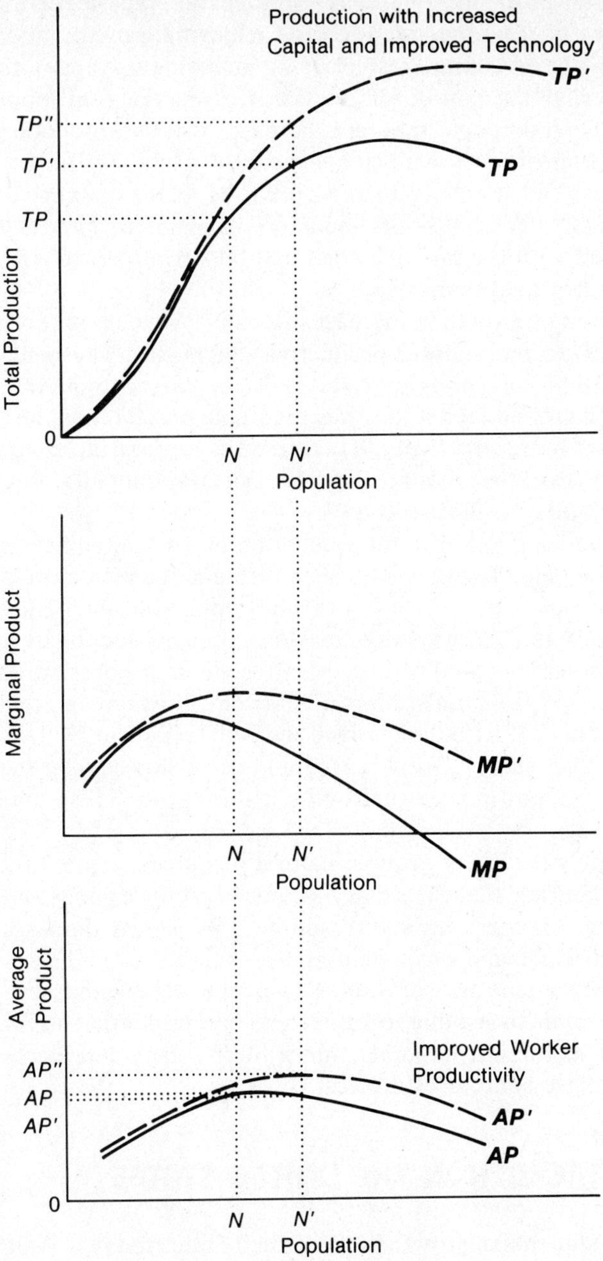

Figure 6-2
Economic growth shifts the production function upward.

right. As production possibilities increase, more of all kinds of goods and services can be enjoyed. See Figure 6–1.

2. *The Production Function.* Improved productive capacity shifts the production function upward, increasing Marginal and Average Product and raising real income. See Figure 6–2.

Whether growth of total production actually improves average levels of living depends on the types of resources required for achieving growth: labor resources, on the one hand, or capital resources — including advances in technology — on the other. If the source of growth is an increase in labor resources alone, real per capita income may not increase. Unless production possibilities increase more than proportionally to the increase in labor resources, average living standards may fall. Look again at Figure 6–2. As the quantity of labor increases from N to N', Total Product increases from TP to TP'. But Average Product associated with the larger labor force falls from AP to AP'. People live poorer, on the average, than before.

A more favorable source of growth is increases in capital resources (both human and material capital) so that worker productivity increases. The result can be either larger quantities of goods and services per capita or greater opportunities for leisure. Improved technology has favorable possibilities, too, allowing resources to be used more effectively. If increased capital and improved technology accompany growth of the labor force so that Total Product increases from TP to TP'', Average Product will rise to AP''.

Figure 6–3a is a time-series graph of total production in the United States (adjusted for inflation) since 1940. The dashed lines indicate percentage rate of growth over successive decades. Figure 6–3b shows total population, and Figure 6–3c shows production per capita. The growth of real per capita production over the period suggests that increased capital resources and technology contributed to growth in production. In fact, economist Martin Feldstein has estimated real net nonresidential investment of $21.5 billion in 1948 and $48.7 billion in 1979, an increase of almost 3 percent annually.* Growth in capital stock slowed near the end of the series, however, suggesting a reduced potential for growth from this source in the future.

Consider another possible source of growth: natural resources so plentiful that using them is costless; land and materials that continue to produce goods and services in a limitless stream. Are there any such resources? We used to think so. We used to regard air and water and unspoiled land as limitless — endlessly exploitable for producing new goods and services. Few people believe that way any more. In fact, we have come to see that using such resources inefficiently — not to mention others such as forests, minerals, and wildlife — may deprive us and future generations of these sources of growth.

STAGES OF GROWTH IN THE UNITED STATES

One of the best known students of growth in the United States today is Walt W. Rostow.† Professor Rostow studied the growth of nations and regions for

*Martin Feldstein, "Has the Rate of Investment Fallen?" Working Paper No. 670, National Bureau of Economic Research, Inc.

†Walt W. Rostow, *The Stages of Economic Growth* and *Politics and the Stages of Growth,* Cambridge University Press, 1964 and 1971. Rostow's five growth stages have been compressed into three stages here for simplicity.

Figure 6–3

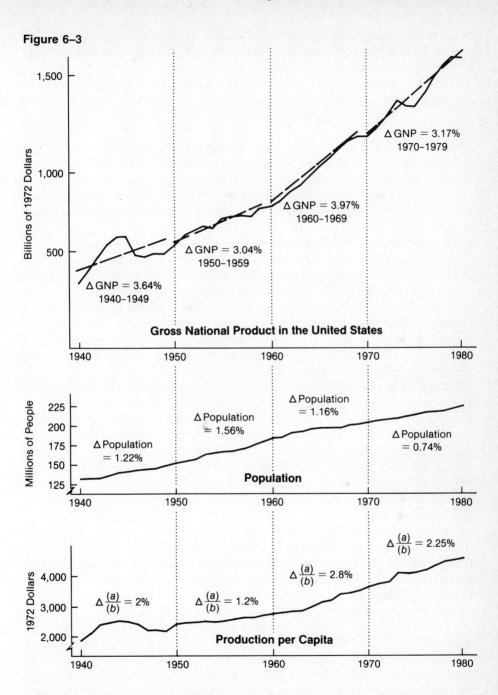

information about their similarities and differences. He concluded that each nation experienced well-defined stages of economic growth; during each stage circumstances changed to prepare the society for the next stage.

1. During Stage 1, certain necessary social and economic **preconditions** are laid down before a *take-off* into sustained economic growth can occur.

2. After the **take-off to growth,** the society moves into Stage 2. Stage 2 includes the **drive to maturity,** over which scientific and technical knowledge spreads through more and more sectors of the economy.
3. Stage 3 is characterized by **high mass consumption.** Increasing prosperity during Stage 3 enables the society to shift its attention away from increasing Total Product toward achieving a more equitable distribution of output.

Each growth stage requires fundamental changes, not only in economic· arrangements but also in social and political conditions. Some of the changes are painful. They require destruction of old ways,* and they sometimes cause resistance and conflict between various groups in the society. Differences in resolving conflicts make for differences in the pace of movement through the growth stages.

In the United States, certain preconditions for take-off were, in a sense, "inherited" from Britain. One essential precondition was the freedom that allowed enterprising people to seek improvements in their living standards. The vast richness of the North American continent provided natural resources for expanding production and called for construction of roads, bridges, and port facilities. Such investments are called **social overhead capital**, since they are necessary capital resources for the use of society as a whole. Construction of social overhead capital is a precondition for integrating markets and encouraging regional specialization and large-scale production.

During the preconditions period, conflict with an outside power can help unify a nation. For the United States, external conflicts with the British, French, and Spanish helped break down local attitudes and led to creation of a single central government. The central government helped draw together regional interests with common national goals. External conflicts also contributed in the United States to feelings of national uniqueness. Early citizens felt a special moral duty to exploit our magnificent resources and achieve a truly democratic society. The United States Constitution established the central means for pursuing these national goals.

Through the mid-1800s, technological change spread across the United States. The agricultural and manufacturing sectors led the drive to maturity, and their profits provided the funds for investment in new capital resources. Technical progress and new forms of organizations created ties of interdependency, so that growth spread to still other sectors. New financial institutions sprang up to smooth the flow of savings into their most productive uses.

During the drive to maturity, government policy helped promote growth and helped to relieve some of the problems of growth by providing education and political opportunities to more citizens, providing funds for social welfare to offset some of the harsh effects of industrialization, and legalizing labor unions to improve labor's bargaining power. The Civil War helped to establish the dominance of manufacturing over agriculture and also led to wider political participa-

---

*Economist Joseph Schumpeter described this process as "creative destruction."

tion. Progressive politics called for new laws regulating conc
power and relieving some of the abuses of power.

The U.S. economy reached maturity toward the
century. New industries were developed that exporte
foreign currencies to use for importing new capital equip..
the railroad network led to growth in coal, iron, heavy engineei..._
and machine tools. The workforce changed to include more urban w__
skilled technicians, and professionals. Finally, new consumer goods industries
were born, and people came to expect ever-rising standards of living.

The era of high mass consumption in the United States was dominated by the
automobile. The automobile required new investments in roads, service
facilities, homes, community centers, and so forth. Suburban living made personal services scarce and expensive and called for the development of new kinds
of home appliances, recreational equipment, communications, and processed
foods. The health of the economy came to depend on extending prosperity to
more and more segments of the society — in particular, the great American
middle class. The progressive income tax, begun in 1913, had the effect of
reducing income inequality. And the extension of voting rights to women in 1919
contributed to passage of welfare legislation and laws regulating business practices. Following the Great Depression of the 1930s, Keynesian economic policy
called for increases in government spending programs to stimulate and stabilize
growth in total production.

Rising levels of living in the mid-twentieth century allowed the nation to shift
attention toward alternative uses of resources: expanded public services, improvements in the quality of life, and protection of national security. Expanded
public education was seen as an investment in increased worker productivity.
Social insurance and welfare payments were considered to be the means toward
high consumption and stable production. New public investments were seen as
necessary complements to prosperity in the private sector. Farm legislation,
banking regulation, and subsidies to home ownership helped reduce the economy's vulnerability to business cycles. Social welfare programs helped reduce
social conflict, increase individual freedoms, and expand economic opportunity.

In the 1960s, some citizen groups began to worry about the side-effects of
industrial growth: in particular, the costs associated with air pollution, damaged
landscapes, and urban decay. Beginning to correct such problems required
tremendous increases in private and public investment, investment that continues to absorb a substantial portion of private savings in the 1980s. The growing
emphasis on national security in the 1960s and 1970s called for closer ties between
government and private industry in chemicals, electronics, and transportation
and communications equipment. Government-supported research and development has become increasingly important, not only for military purposes but
for maintaining our technical edge in manufacturing for world markets. And
finally, the spread of growth problems to other nations has made international
consultation and cooperation essential for achieving efficient and equitable
growth policies.

A MODEL OF GROWTH

In Figure 6–2 we showed a typical production function with the following characteristics:

1. When various quantities of labor are combined with a constant quantity of land and capital resources, the resulting *Total Product* increases first at an increasing rate, then at a decreasing rate, and finally at a negative rate.
2. The change in Total Product associated with a one-unit increase in labor is called labor's *Marginal Product*. Marginal Product increases as labor approaches the optimum quantity for use with existing fixed resources and decreases beyond the optimum quantity. If variable resources become excessive relative to fixed resources, Marginal Product may ultimately become negative.
3. The *Average Product* of labor increases to a peak, at which labor's Marginal Product is equal to its Average Product. Beyond this point, Average Product declines but does not become negative. Average Product measures, on the one hand, labor's productivity and, on the other hand, real per capita income of workers. This makes growth in Average Product an important goal of an economic system.

The production function in Figure 6–2 is essentially *static*. It is drawn for the short run, in which the quantity of certain resources and the level of technology are constant. Changes in the quantity of labor in the short run enable the nation to move along its production function. Changes in capital resources or technology shift the production function up or down, with corresponding shifts in Marginal Product and Average Product.

With a few changes, we can use the production function of Figure 6–2 to illustrate *dynamic* processes: that is, more fundamental growth in production capacity over longer periods of time. A long-range growth function will have the same form as the production function, with increasing, decreasing, and negative rates of growth in Total Product. But for the long-range growth function, we will use the horizontal axis to measure quantities of *all* resources: new lands, labor, and capital resources, as well as advances in organization and management procedures for combining these resources. We will assume that increasing *all* resources together will yield first increasing, then decreasing, and finally negative changes in Total Product.

How are we able to assume this? The reason is the existence of global limits to total production: limited supplies of minerals for producing material goods, of energy for running machines, of farmland for growing food, and even a limited supply of air for absorbing the pollution caused by industry. Over time, the world's people will be forced to use lower-quality minerals, harder-to-produce sources of energy, less-fertile farmlands, and less-polluting industrial processes. The use of lower-quality resources will mean smaller and smaller gains in Total Product.

Look again at Figure 6–2. Instead of thinking of the horizontal axis as numbers of workers, think of total resources. Then note the behavior of *TP, MP,* and *AP* as all these sources of growth increase. Dynamic processes affect Marginal and Average Product (and the productivity and real per capita income of workers) in much the same way we found to be true of the short-run production function. Likewise, new technical progress (or restraints on technology) may shift upward or downward the long-range growth function.

Consciously or unconsciously, members of an economic society make the decisions that influence long-range growth prospects. They allocate resources toward new capital investment, or they spend for current consumption. They decide to increase family size or to postpone family formation. They allocate more or less resources toward "human" capital investment in education or health care. These choices affect the society's position on the horizontal axis on Figure 6–2 and the shape of the production function. Thus, they affect the productivity of resources and the level of real per capita income for the people.

Some of the decisions described above are made haphazardly. Some are based on market considerations: in particular, the expected benefits and costs to the person or group making the decision. Increasingly, decisions that affect long-range growth prospects are made by the society as a whole. In this way, decisions may be sure to reflect the external benefits and costs that growth may impose on the nation and the world.

The Benefits of Growth

We can summarize the sources of growth under three categories: increases in the quantity of resources, improvements in the quality of resources, and advances in the technology of resource use. We have seen that changes in any of these variables may yield increasing, decreasing, or negative growth in Total Product. A typical Marginal Product curve is shown in Figure 6–4, showing increasing, decreasing, and negative Marginal Product. The horizontal axis measures growth in all resources, and the vertical axis measures the additional production associated with additional units of resource employment.

Figure 6–4

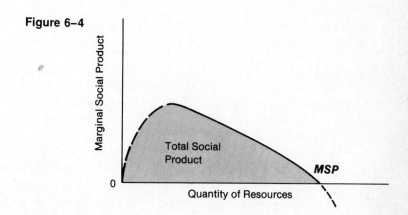

In general, a society will decide to employ a quantity and quality of all resources in the range of decreasing Marginal Product. The range of increasing Marginal Product is not a permanent objective, since further growth would increase production by greater and greater amounts. Neither would the range of negative Marginal Product be an objective, for rather obvious reasons! Figure 6–4 shows the range of decreasing Marginal Product as a solid line. The most efficient growth choice will lie within this range.

For the society as a whole, measures of Marginal Product should consider also the positive externalities that result from growth: such things as opportunities for improved health and longer life, for recreation and cultural enrichment, and for creative participation in social and political activities. The Marginal Product curve shown in Figure 6–4 is drawn to include these positive externalities as well as the goods and services intentionally produced by farmers, manufacturers and professionals. Including positive externalities yields a measure of the **Marginal Social Product** associated with growth: Marginal Social Product = Marginal Product + positive externalities. We will use *MSP* to stand for Marginal Social Product.

Remember that a Marginal Social Product curve measures the additional production associated with employing additional units of productive resources. This means that the total area under the *MSP* curve up to any static level of resource employment represents Total Social Product associated with that particular stage of growth.

The Costs of Growth

The other side of the growth decision focuses on costs. Increasing resource quantity and quality and the technology of resource use involves certain *opportunity costs*:

1. The increasing quantity of labor resources involves costs in terms of land for homes and for growing food.
2. Increasing capital investment involves the sacrifice of current consumer goods and services as well as the material costs of constructing buildings and equipment.
3. Increasing resource quality and the technology of resource use may require sacrifice of leisure and possibly even of personal freedoms.

The additional costs associated with each additional unit of resource use are the Marginal Costs of growth. We would assume that any society would choose first the least costly source of growth, so that the Marginal Cost of growth curve would begin low on the vertical axis and rise over its entire length. A typical Marginal Cost curve is shown in Figure 6–5.

For the society as a whole, the Marginal Costs of growth involve more than the material resources and goods given up for the sake of growth. In fact, growth includes external costs like air and water pollution, urban congestion and blight, depletion of wilderness areas and of natural species, climate changes that affect patterns of living and resource use. We have called these external costs of growth

Figure 6–5

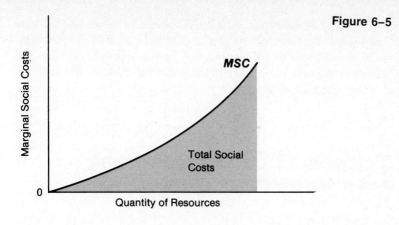

Figure 6–6

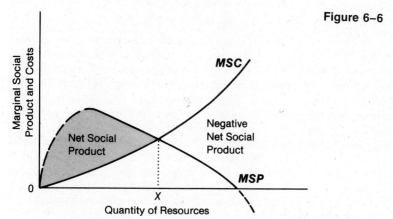

negative externalities. Including negative externalities along with the material costs of growth yields a measure we will call **Marginal Social Cost.** Thus, Marginal Social Costs = Marginal Costs + negative externalities. We will use *MSC* to stand for Marginal Social Costs. Since the *MSC* curve measures the additional costs associated with growth, the area under the curve represents Total Social Costs up to that level of resource employment and technology.

When all the benefits and costs of growth are considered, it is theoretically possible to compare Total Social Product with Total Social Costs for choosing the optimum level of resource use and technology for the nation. Figure 6–6 combines the Marginal Social Product curve with the Marginal Social Costs of growth. Areas under the curves represent Total Social Product and Total Social Costs, respectively. The area between the curves represents **Net Social Product:** Total Social Product − Total Social Costs = Net Social Product. To the left of the intersection at *X*, Total Social Product is greater than Total Social Costs. Therefore, over this range, increments of growth yield positive Net Social Product. To the right of the intersection at *X*, Total Social Product is less than Total Social Costs. Over this range, increments of growth have the effect of reducing Net Social Product.

Maximum Net Social Product occurs at X. We would say that X represents the most efficient growth choice for this nation. Given current technology, employing X units of resources yields maximum living standards for the people. Actual living standards depend on the size of the population and on the distribution of claims to the nation's wealth.

Mathematical Supplement

Using a Benefit-Cost Ratio

Individuals and groups are constantly making choices regarding resource employment and technology. Each increase in productive capacity may be thought of as occupying a space along the horizontal scale of Figure 6–6. Growth programs to the left of X yield positive Net Social Product and should be undertaken; growth programs to the right yield negative Net Social Product and should not be undertaken.

Achieving positive Net Social Product can be expressed in terms of the relationship between Marginal Social Product and Marginal Social Costs. If Marginal Social Product is greater than Marginal Social Costs, the ratio of the two values is greater than one: $MSP/MSC > 1$. A ratio greater than one means that the addition to total production is greater than the value of resources used and production is efficient. A ratio less than one means that the addition to total production is less than the value of resources used and production is inefficient. The ratio MSP/MSC is called a **benefit-cost ratio.** A benefit-cost ratio is useful for evaluating proposals to expand productive capacity.

Calculating the values for the benefit-cost ratio is difficult and imprecise. Moreover, since many benefits and costs are expected to extend into the future, the amounts must be discounted to determine their present value. Remember that a discount factor reflects two circumstances: the distance in the future when an event is expected to occur and the value the nation places on experiences in the present relative to those in the future. (Discounting was explained in chapter 2.) An event far in the future in a society that strongly prefers the present would require a large discount factor. A more imminent event would require a small discount factor. In the first case, the value of an event (whether a benefit or a cost) would be reduced sharply. In the second, the value of the event would be reduced hardly at all.

Benefits and costs that are expected to occur in the future can be shown as MSP_t and MSC_t, where the subscript t indicates the time period in which an individual event occurs. Thus, MSP_1 would indicate a benefit expected to occur in period "1" in the future and MSC_2 would indicate a cost expected to occur in period "2." The sums of all MSP_t and MSC_t are the total expected benefits and costs associated with a growth decision.

When expected future benefits and costs are discounted, the result is the following ratio:

$$\frac{MSP}{MSC} = \frac{\Sigma\ MSP_t/(1 + r)^t}{\Sigma\ MSC_t/(1 + r)^t} \geq 1,$$

where r represents the time preference of the people and t represents distance in the future. A decision to develop synfuel technology, for example, would include all the expected benefits in personal and commercial transportation, industrial use of energy, political independence from international energy sources, related technologies that may evolve from synfuel development, and so forth. All the expected costs would include the costs of coal production and transportation, the health and environmental costs of coal extraction and synfuel production, the opportunity costs of developing synfuel technology instead of other technologies, and so forth. Then, benefits and costs would be discounted according to when in the future they are expected to occur (t) and the community's time preference (r). The ratio of discounted benefits and costs should equal at least *one* if the project is to be efficient.

There is another necessary element in benefit-cost analysis. Predictions of future benefits and costs are uncertain, so probabilities must be attached. Extracting coal for synfuel production, for example, may be expected to cause as many as 100 coal miner deaths a year or as few as 10. Suppose historical experience has shown a 50 percent probability of both events. Under these circumstances, the *expected value* of coal miner deaths annually is the weighted sum of all events, where the weights are the probabilities associated with each event:*

$$\text{expected value of coal miner deaths} = (\text{number of deaths}) \times (\text{probability}) =$$
$$(100)\ (0.50) + (10)\ (0.50) = 55.$$

If the value of a coal miner's life can be evaluated at, say, $1 million, the appropriate cost figure to include in *MSC* would be $55 million.

Including probabilities in benefit-cost analysis yields:

$$\frac{MSP}{MSC} = \frac{\Sigma\ (MSP_t)\ (p_t)/(1 + r)^t}{\Sigma\ (MSC_t)\ (p_t)/(1 + r)^t} \geq 1,$$

where p_t refers to the probability associated with each event.

Needless to say, assigning probabilities to expected future events is especially difficult (as is calculating the value of a human life, time preference, and distance in the future, along with all the other values in the benefit-cost ratio). This makes efficient decision-making uncertain and subject to the judgment of the analyst. Moreover, the complexity of environmental circumstances means that new information can completely change the results and call for changes in policy decisions. Regrettably, most decisions to add resource capabilities or advance technology are not easily reversed: strip mined areas cannot easily be restored, extinct species cannot be recreated, technical knowledge cannot be erased, human lives cannot be relived. All of this makes correct growth decisions especially critical.

- What are some of the benefits and costs that should be included in a decision to build a dam? A superhighway? A mass transit system?
- What are the circumstances that would require the use of probabilities in the decision ratio?

---

*Again, the student may refer to chapter 2 for a discussion of expected value.

DECIDING GROWTH POLICY

Most of us think of environmental pollution as a modern problem. We associate air pollution with electric power plants and steel mills, noise with traffic jams, water pollution with chemical manufacture, and industrial accidents with sawmills and heavy machinery. We tend to blame such problems on economic growth and suggest that halting growth would eliminate them. It is wise occasionally to stop and think back through history to decide whether these judgments are correct.

In the Middle Ages, for example, people crowded into walled cities, tossed garbage and sewage into alleys, hawked their wares by shouting through the streets, and battled constantly with lice and rats. Disease spread quickly, and early death from cholera or typhoid was common. Colonial America suffered from similar environmental problems. Travel by horse and buggy was probably just as polluting as travel by automobile! It has only been recently that our nation has become wealthy enough to consider environmental pollution when making routine production decisions.

Growth in production of life's necessities has made it possible to consider the negative externalities associated with growth when determining growth policy. However, measuring the negative externalities of alternative choices is difficult. For example, how can we measure such social costs as:

a. The cost to New Jersey of the highest cancer rate in the nation versus the cost associated with losing New Jersey's profitable chemical industry;
b. The loss of income to fishermen and property owners along Chesapeake Bay versus the loss of income from shutting down Virginia's Kepone factory;
c. The cost of birth defects to residents of Love Canal versus the cost of proper disposal of chemicals once produced there;
d. The cost of brown lung disease among textile workers versus the loss of the entire textile industry to competing firms in other nations;
e. The cost to consumers of spoiled foods versus the increased risk of cancer associated with food additives;
f. The political cost of dependence on imported oil versus the loss of woods and wildlife to strip mining for coal.

You can probably add many more items to the list.

Federal laws passed in the 1960s and 1970s require changes in production to correct some of the most obvious external costs of growth. Over the next decade, private industry, government, and consumers will spend hundreds of billions of dollars to install and operate equipment to purify air and water, safely dispose of toxic chemicals, and improve the safety of the workplace and of consumer products. Some jobs will be destroyed and others created, as industry adapts to these new circumstances. Costs of production will rise, and prices will rise, too. As consumers, we will find ourselves enjoying fewer additional material goods associated with economic growth and paying more of the costs of protecting environmental quality.

Efficiency and Equity in Growth Policies

Increasing prosperity has made it possible to focus national attention on the negative externalities associated with growth and to change the course of growth to reduce negative externalities. In this discussion we have defined our objective as one of achieving a level of resource employment and technology at X, where $MSP/MSC = 1$. Total production at X is efficient in terms of total resource employment. Actual levels of living depend on total population and on distribution of the benefits and costs of production.

Achieving efficient production and equitable distribution depends on the kinds of growth policies actually adopted. In general, there are four kinds of policies for influencing growth.

1. *No-growth policies.* Activities that generate negative externalities can be prohibited. The result might be to shut down air-polluting steel mills, water-polluting chemical plants, land-destroying strip mines. Such policies would be inefficient, since to eliminate these activities entirely would eliminate their benefits along with their costs. Such policies might also be inequitable, since regions that depend on these activities would suffer relative to regions that depend on other industries. Moreover, the necessary decline in total production would reduce real per capita income and living standards nationwide. For this reason, the chances of conflict among regions and income groups might be expected to increase.

2. *Taxes and fines.* Activities that generate negative externalities can be taxed or required to pay fines based on the magnitude of their offense. Revenue collected in this way could be used to correct the environmental damage resulting from the activity. Setting taxes and fines to measure the damage done would be difficult, so that these policies might be inefficient. Also, the methods used to correct the problems would have to be designed by government policymakers, who may lack the necessary skills. To the extent that fines and corrective methods are decided incorrectly, the result may also be inequitable.

3. *Mandated pollution-control devices.* Similar disadvantages are associated with policies to require specific clean-up devices and procedures. The complexity of industrial processes makes it unlikely that procedures dictated by government will actually be the most efficient or equitable ones.

4. *Market-oriented policies.* Many economists favor policies that would rely on market forces to reduce negative externalities. Under one proposal, government would call on scientists to measure the level of pollutants a particular ecosystem could sustain over a period of time: the industrial discharge that would be neutralized by a river's own natural processes; the particles that would be harmlessly dissipated through the atmosphere over populated areas; the chemicals that could be buried in a region without harm to underground water supplies. Then certificates would be offered for sale entitling business firms to commit some portion of the maximum permitted level of pollution. Many firms would find low-cost ways to eliminate pollution entirely and avoid purchasing the certificates. Some would install cor-

rective devices up to the point where further antipollution efforts would be more costly than purchasing the required certificates. Others would find installing any corrective procedures at all so costly that they would have to pay heavily for the privilege to pollute.

Most economists believe the fourth approach is the most efficient. Market-oriented policies would require private business firms to compare the costs of eliminating pollution with the cost that pollution imposes on the community. Then firms would design the lowest-cost procedures for correcting pollution problems. A market-oriented approach is also equitable because the costs of pollution control would fall heaviest on the most serious offenders and, through higher prices, on consumers of offending products. Consumers might be expected to compare the private benefits they expect to enjoy from the product with its total costs to the community as a whole. They would purchase the product only to the point that benefits received are at least as great as total costs paid.

Actual policy toward pollution has tended to follow approaches 2 and 3. Governments have imposed daily fines in the thousands of dollars, with the result that some firms have gone out of business and jobs have been destroyed. Governments have required investments in pollution control equipment at costs beyond the capacity of many small firms. Inefficient policy may have worsened some growth problems. And, in fact, enforcement agencies are now looking for market-oriented solutions to the problem of negative externalities.

Some policy-makers have set aside benefit-cost ratios entirely and employed the **cost-effectiveness approach** to environmental pollution. Because measuring benefits is so difficult, the cost-effectiveness approach accepts as given a particular environmental objective: so many micrograms of particulate material per cubic-foot of air, so many decibels of industrial equipment noise, so many parts of toxic and nontoxic waste in water supplies. Then studies are made to determine the lowest-cost method for achieving the given objective. Cost-effectiveness is generally acceptable to business firms because it encourages a search for efficient antipollution procedures.

THE LIMITS TO GROWTH

More than a century ago, Thomas Malthus was the first economist to focus public attention on the potential problem of excessive growth. Population, he said, tends to grow exponentially while the capacity for producing goods and services grows linearly. Under these circumstances, total production will tend to fall farther and farther below the needs of the population.

Linear production growth is expressed algebraically as $Y = a \left[1 + r(t) \right]$, where Y represents total production after t years, a represents production at some initial period, and r represents annual growth in production. With initial production of 100 and growth of 5 percent, total production (Y) ten years in the future is $Y = 100 \left[1 + (0.05)(10) \right] = 150$. **Linear growth** means that production

Figure 6–7

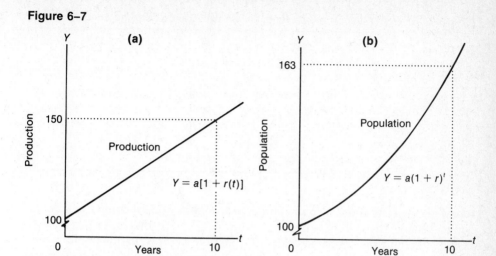

grows by the same amount each year. Hence, the curve of total production has a constant slope, as shown in Figure 6–7a.

Exponential population growth is expressed algebraically as $Y = a\left[(1 + r)^t\right]$, where Y represents total population after t years, a represents population at some initial period, and r represents annual growth in population. With beginning population of 100 and a growth rate of 5 percent, total population (Y) ten years in the future is determined by $Y = 100\left[(1.05)^{10}\right] = 163$. **Exponential growth** means that population grows by more than the total of 5 percent for each year, so that the curve representing population slopes more steeply upward, as shown in Figure 6–7b.

Table 6–1 shows the long-range effects of linear growth of production and exponential growth of population. Column 2 gives annual production in each of the years shown, and Column 3 lists population. Column 4 shows real production per capita in each of the years. If people require at least 0.50 units of output to survive, population will reach its maximum level soon after the thirtieth year with population somewhat greater than 432.

Exponential population growth places increasing demands on limited global resources such as forests and farmlands, energy and mineral resources, air and water. Malthus believed that resources would become scarcer and crises more severe. During prosperous times, fewer deaths relative to births would cause population to deplete available resource supplies until finally conflict and starvation would reduce population to a level that could be supported by existing resources.

Malthus' predictions have not come to pass, at least on the scale that he imagined. One reason has been advances in technology that have increased agricultural productivity (raised the value of r in the linear equation above). Another reason has been more widespread family planning that has reduced population growth (reduced the value of r in the exponential equation). This is not to say that the problem has been resolved. In fact, the 1970s experienced

Table 6–1. Effects of Linear and Exponential Growth Trends Over the Long Term

(1) Year	(2) Annual Production	(3) Total Population	(4) Annual Production per Capita: (2)/(3)
0	100	100	1.00
10	150	163	0.92
20	200	265	0.75
30	250	432	0.58
40	300	704	0.43
50	350	1,147	0.31

renewed concerns about resource limits to growth.* Modern computer technology has enabled researchers to *simulate* growth trends: that is, to project past experience onto the future and identify possible crisis situations before they develop. Some analysts have concluded that exponential population growth and global resource limits call for drastic changes in world behavior, if we are to avert catastrophe.

Critics of the "doomsday" philosophy contend that, like Malthus, modern researchers have ignored the potential effects of technological advances. Why not assume that *technology* will grow exponentially, they ask, and that behavior will change to slow the use of available resources? When scarcities do appear, prices will rise, discouraging resource use and encouraging development of alternative processes. Free markets help make such adjustments gradually, and international cooperation can help guide government policy toward more efficient growth decisions.

A more serious criticism involves the precise nature of the growth crisis. The crisis is not *physical* some critics say—not the result of material limitations, but *economic*—the result of faulty economic policies. In particular, critics claim that what appears to be physical scarcity is often the result of unequal market power. Poverty and starvation in certain areas result from inadequate command over world resources and are offset by lavish living standards elsewhere. Growth problems could be resolved by more equitable distribution of claims to the world's wealth.

Special Case

...And Not a Drop to Drink!

Over the decade of the 1970s, while America's attention was focused on the problem of depletion of energy supplies, an even more serious growth problem was developing: the problem of ensuring adequate water for America's homes, farms, and factories. Unless

*D. H. Meadows, D. L. Meadows, J. Ramders, W. W. Behrens III, *Limits to Growth*, Universe Books, New York, 1972.

solutions are found to the impending water shortage, citizens may face a future of mandated "bath holidays" and "shaveless Saturdays," with fines or even jail sentences for person who violate the rules!

One reason for the problem has been the weather. For most of this century, moist winds from the Pacific have spread abundant rainfall over the continental United States. Recently, however, high atmospheric pressure in western Canada has diverted these winds farther to the north where they have been stripped of their moisture. Meanwhile, storms from the Gulf of Mexico have been forced offshore into the Atlantic, depriving the Eastern Seaboard of adequate rainfall. Meteorologists disagree over the cause of the weather change, but many fear it may be permanent.

Another reason for the impending water shortage involves economic growth. Population growth has encouraged residential development on cheap land outside the cities. Farmers have been obliged to grow more food on less land, frequently on land that is ill-suited for agriculture. Increased crop production has required the use of irrigation, chemical fertilizers, herbicides, and pesticides. Irrigation depletes ground water and leaves harmful mineral deposits on the land; agricultural chemicals drain from the land and pollute streams.

Most of the nation's rainfall is not captured for use. More than half evaporates and another one-fourth runs off to Canada, Mexico, or the oceans. Only about 60 billion gallons a day sinks into underground water and remains available for use. Since the United States uses about 80 billion gallons daily, we must continually withdraw more water from underground sources than is replaced by rainfall.

Underground water reservoirs are called *aquifers*. Aquifers were laid down during prehistoric times by rivers flowing down the mountains and carrying sand and gravel to low plains. Layers of shale trapped the water from below, and layers of accumulated rock prevented evaporation from above. Even today, billions of acre-feet of water remain trapped underground.* In recent years, however, too little rain and heavy use of water have depleted aquifers in parts of the American West, causing the surface of the land to drop by as much as 30 feet. Near the oceans, depletion of aquifers has sucked salt water into the underground reservoirs, spoiling the water and damaging plant life in affected areas.

Certain government policies may have aggravated the water shortage. With the goal of encouraging settlement of the West, the federal government helped provide cheap water to otherwise arid regions. Subsidized water supplies may have had the effect of distorting resource allocation toward inefficient uses.

Figure 6–8a is a model of the market for water in an area of adequate rainfall. The demand curve shows the quantities that will be demanded at various prices. The supply curve shows the quantities that will be supplied. At equilibrium, farmers and local residents purchase OQ gallons at a price of p per gallon. Figure 6–8b is a model of the market for water in an area of inadequate rainfall. The demand for water is similar to Figure 6–8a, but because of inadequate rainfall the supply curve of water has been shifted upward to indicate higher costs of production and higher prices to farmers and consumers. The equilibrium price of water rises to p', and the quantity of water used falls to OQ'. Free market pricing would increase living costs in areas of inadequate rainfall. High costs would discourage farmers and consumers from locating in areas unsuitable for agriculture or residential development, and the result would be more efficient use of scarce water resources.

Now suppose government subsidizes the transport of water to the area described in Figure 6–8b. Government subsidies would reduce unit costs and increase the supply of

*An acre-foot is the amount of water required to cover an acre of land to a depth of one foot and is equal to 325,851 gallons.

Figure 6–8
The market for water.

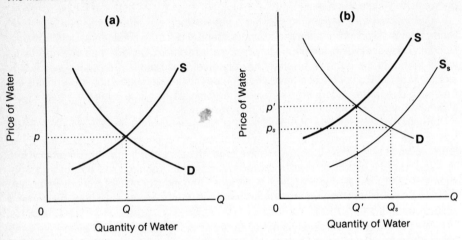

water to the area. This would shift the supply of water curve rightward to S_s. The artificially low price, p_s, would encourage farmers and consumers to use more water, with the result that resources would be used inefficiently. Furthermore, investment in agricultural capital would make farmers increasingly immobile and dependent on further subsidies for survival. (To add insult to injury, subsidized transport of water would use substantial quantities of energy, worsening the energy shortage as well.)

Like most growth problems, the potential water shortage does not confine itself to a single jurisdiction. In fact, single jurisdictions left to compete for scarce water would tend to use the water faster than otherwise and aggravate the problem. Existing facilities for delivering water are so diverse and fragmented that a surplus in one area often cannot be shared with a neighboring area. Solutions to the water shortage will be long-range and costly, and they will require cooperation between governments.

The developing water shortage in California is already pitting community against community. Inyo County north of Los Angeles has fought Los Angeles' encroachments on area water supplies for 60 years. Mexico complains that Colorado River water is rendered too salty through irrigation runoff before it crosses into Mexico. In the Northeast, cities and states are battling over scarce water supplies. In New York, Boston, Pittsburgh, Philadelphia, and Baltimore faulty water systems are blamed for wasting up to one-fifth of total usage through leaks.

- Demonstrate the use of benefit-cost ratios in decisions regarding:
  providing subsidized water to residential areas in arid regions;
  applying chemical fertilizers to farmland;
  repairing water systems in congested areas.
- Show the effects of including external benefits and costs and of discounting all values to the present.

When Growth Ends . . .

In this chapter we have stressed efficiency in growth decisions and have referred occasionally to the resulting effects on equity. *Equity* refers to the distribution of benefits and the distribution of costs: who receives the scarce water and who pays the subsidy; who enjoys the chemical products and who suffers black lung disease; or whose longer life depends on another's early death. As resource use continues to grow and technology to advance, these kinds of questions will become more critical and more complex.

Questions of equity involve more than purely economic considerations or purely mathematical calculations. Equitable distribution must be based on broad social, political, and strategic circumstances and objectives.

Equitable distribution of benefits and costs becomes especially difficult when economic growth begins to encounter ceilings and bottlenecks. In the past, economic growth has been the way nations have improved the living standards of the poor without reducing those of the rich. Growth helps reduce the sources of conflict between income groups within the society. All this changes when a nation reaches the most efficient growth stage. When a nation reaches maximum efficiency (at X in Figure 6–6), further growth would have the effect of reducing Net Social Product. Beyond this point, improved living standards for some would mean reduced living standards for others.

Increasing conflict over the fruits of growth could have destructive results, using energy for settling claims that might otherwise be used for improving growth potential and solving environmental problems. Democratic processes have helped the United States settle distributional questions in the past, but there are no similar assurances for the future.

Similar conflicts may arise over the distribution of the costs of growth. Affected groups are increasingly able to mobilize opposition to technologies that impose external costs. The result may be to halt entirely the use of technologies that may yield positive net benefits to the society at large. Voters and policymakers must constantly seek new information for deciding growth questions efficiently and equitably.

Special Case

Toxic Materials in the Food Chain

Certain metals are essential to life: iron, manganese, copper, cobalt, and zinc. Living creatures absorb quantities of essential minerals through air, water, and food. Excessive quantities are harmful, of course, and some minerals, such as cadmium, mercury, and lead, are lethal in even small amounts. Improper dumping of such hazardous materials can cause contamination of streams and ground water. Small organisms absorb the metallic pollutants, fish feed on the organisms, and the toxic materials are taken into the food chain.

In 1956, Japan experienced an outbreak of Minamata disease resulting from mercury-contaminated fish. Victims suffered severe neurological defects and learning disabilities. Persons living near contaminated streams in the United States have been found to experience greater than normal rates of heart disease and certain forms of cancer. Workers exposed to cadmium have been found to experience abnormal levels of prostate cancer. Until controls were established in the 1960s, many children in the United States were afflicted with lead encephalopathy, involving dullness, irritability, and headaches, and often leading to delirium, coma, and death.

Environmental groups have organized to inform the public of dangers like these and to work toward correcting the agricultural and industrial practices that cause them. In the 1970s, a campaign was begun to restore Lake Erie from the industrial pollutants that kill fish and create evil-smelling slime. Billions of dollars were spent by cities and business firms along the lake and the rivers that feed it to protect against abuse of this valuable resource. Although progress has been made in controlling the pollutants that enter Lake Erie, the existing materials continue to contaminate the water.

Clean-up campaigns sometimes stir up public opposition. When environmental standards discourage industrial location, local workers may lose jobs. Business firms lose profits, and governments lose tax revenues. Deciding to suffer short-range costs for the sake of long-range benefits is difficult, particularly when regions or groups are already below national income averages.

- Discuss the difficulties of designing market-oriented approaches to the problem of toxic materials.
- How are strong pollution control policies damaging to economic growth?

Source: Linda Garmon, "To Fish in Troubled Waters," *Science News*, March 8, 1980.

Special Case

Nuclear Power

Before the nuclear accident at Three Mile Island, proponents of nuclear energy enthusiastically promoted their industry as a safe, clean, and cheap solution to the negative externalities associated with the use of oil and coal. At the time of the accident, 70 nuclear reactors in the United States had the capacity to generate 13 percent of the nation's electricity. A year later only 67 were operating, with capacity of only 10.6 percent. Among western nations, only France remains fully committed to nuclear energy.

The Nuclear Regulatory Commission is responsible for overseeing the operation of nuclear utilities in the United States. Before Three Mile Island, the N.R.C. believed that accidents were practically impossible, but afterward the Commission proposed a list of more than 100 safety improvements, costing each currently operating reactor about $30 million.

Repairing the reactor at Three Mile Island and buying replacement electricity in the meantime are expected to cost almost $2 billion. This is far more than the reactor's original cost. Furthermore, health experts estimate that radiation following the accident may cause 1 to 3 more cancer deaths than might otherwise have occurred in the area. The cost of the clean-up will be paid from higher insurance premiums, increases in consumers' power bills around the country, and higher federal taxes. Once restored, the plant can produce $900,000 worth of electric power daily.

If the costs of restoring the Three Mile Island plant are judged to be too great, the plant could be decommissioned. Decommissioning would involve either removal of the radioactive uranium core and dismantling the plant or filling the entire containment building with concrete. Either choice would require protection against release of considerable radioactivity into the air and water and onto surfaces inside the plant. Workers on the clean-up team would have to be rotated frequently to avoid absorbing unhealthy quantities of radioactivity.

The issue of nuclear power production concerns not only the technical aspects of generating electricity but also the nation's productive capacity as a whole. Industry analysts have estimated that increasing per capita GNP will require at least a doubling of · electrical generating capacity by the year 2000. They contend that increasing alternative energy sources, greater use of coal, and increased energy conservation cannot significantly alter this requirement. And they claim that the kilowatt-hour cost of nuclear power is substantially less than the cost of other energy sources.

- Discuss the benefit-cost considerations involved in a decision to promote nuclear power for generating electricity.
- Why do analysts have so much trouble agreeing on the kilowatt-hour cost of electricity from coal, hydroelectric power, and nuclear energy?

QUESTIONS

1. Discuss the relationship between efficiency and equity as they relate to growth decisions. Are there stages of growth when equity should be of greater or lesser concern to policy makers? How might limits to growth affect equity?
2. Select a currently developing nation and study its growth experience. What social or political circumstances have influenced growth? What industrial or agricultural sectors have led growth, and what technologies have been critical to growth? What are the nation's prospects for the future?
3. Consider each of the following situations and describe the process by which a benefit-cost ratio might be calculated. Explain the difficulties associated with your answer.
   a. Nitrogen fertilizers add billions of dollars to U.S. crop yields annually, but they also indirectly weaken the ozone layer and allow more cancer-causing ultraviolet rays from the sun to filter through.
   b. Burning coal releases substantial amounts of carbon dioxide, which collects in the earth's atmosphere, traps the sun's heat, and causes earth temperatures to rise.
   c. Biomass technology involves crops grown specifically for conversion to energy. Burning biomass produces carbon dioxide, but the plants themselves absorb carbon dioxide as they grow.
   d. Clear-cutting forests endangers the topsoil, reduces moisture in the air, and aggravates accumulation of carbon dioxide. Destruction of their forest homes causes wildlife to leave, opening the way for pests and parasites to move in. But many non-oil nations need the wood for fuel.
   e. The industrial chemical PCB floats invisibly in air and water and is absorbed by fish and other foods. It has been found to cause cancer in laboratory animals. According to the World Health Organization, exposure to such substances accounts for 70 to 90 percent of all human cancers, but 20 to 40 years may elapse before the cancer appears.

    f.   Strip mining regulations place particularly heavy costs on small mineral firms, reducing their profits and making them vulnerable to takeover by giant enterprises. Enforcing strip mining regulations is normally the responsibility of individual states.

    g.   Fluorocarbons used in aerosols, air conditioners, and foam cushions and insulation rise to the stratosphere and destroy the ozone layer. Ozone is a form of oxygen that protects the earth's surface from ultraviolet light; its destruction can mean greater risk of cancer as well as changes in climate and agriculture.

4. Consult news magazines for information about the effects of environmental regulations on business. Evaluate the effects in terms of efficiency and equity.

5. More Advanced Problem. The hypothetical equations below describe a certain nation's population and capacity for production of goods and services. Identify the values in the equations. Then determine the year, t, when population will exceed available resource capacity. (Each unit of production will sustain one person.)

$$\text{Population} = 150(1.08)^t \qquad \text{Production} = 200(1 + 0.04t)$$

6. Discuss the use of mandatory insurance coverage against environmental dangers as a replacement for current regulatory standards.

7. Suppose you were offered a set of tires that are guaranteed never to blow out and would thus ensure you against death in this kind of auto crash. How much would you be willing to pay for the tires? What factors would influence your answer? How is this question related to the subject of this chapter?

8. Select one of the following regulatory agencies and conduct research into its major functions, special characteristics, and recent activities: Corps of Engineers, Environmental Protection Agency, Nuclear Regulatory Commission, Consumer Product Safety Commission, Food and Drug Administration, Occupational Safety and Health Administration, National Highway Transportation Safety Administration, Mining Enforcement and Safety Administration.

9. Growing worldwide demand for food has encouraged U.S. farmers to plow for cultivation even land subject to excessive erosion. New chemical fertilizers and herbicides have removed the need for crop rotation and have eliminated ground cover. Terraces designed for small machinery are not practical for today's massive farm equipment, and many have been obliterated. Fertile farmlands in the heart of U.S. agricultural regions annually lose 5 to 10 tons of topsoil per acre of cropland to wind and water erosion. Silt flowing into streams reduces municipal water supplies and increases the danger of flooding. Discuss this problem in terms of efficiency and equity.

10. How does the discussion of the nation's water shortage illustrate the saying that began this chapter? What is the significance of governmental *jurisdictions* in the water problem? Can you identify other circumstances where government action to relieve one problem has worsened another?

11. In December, 1979, the Environmental Protection Agency adopted a revolutionary new approach to air quality control. The new concept treats an industrial plant as if it were an enormous bubble with a single smokestack. The agency calculates the total allowable emissions from the "bubble" as a whole and allows the firm to determine which of its own sources of emission to correct. The results are expected to be an acceptable level of air quality at minimum cost for the offending firm. Evaluate this policy in terms of efficiency and equity.

DEFINITIONS

A benefit-cost ratio is a ratio of the total benefits expected from a growth decision to the total costs (total benefits/total costs). The value of the ratio should be at least *one* if the growth decision is to be carried out.

The cost-effectiveness approach to growth decisions involves selection of the lowest-cost approach to achieving a particular growth objective.

The drive to maturity is a growth stage in which economic development extends over a broad range of activity.

Exponential growth is growth of larger and larger amounts in successive time periods. Population tends to grow exponentially.

Growth and development refers to changes in productive capacity. Growth involves an increase in productive capacity: development involves a change in the kind of productive capacity.

High mass consumption is a growth stage in which basic material needs are easily satisfied and the economy begins to enjoy a wider variety of consumer goods and services.

Linear growth is growth of the same amount in successive time periods. Agricultural production tends to grow linearly.

Marginal Social Cost (MSC) is the change in total costs and negative externalities that results from an increment of growth. Combining all the cost changes from growth yields a measure of Total Social Cost.

Marginal Social Product (MSP) is the change in total goods and services and positive externalities that results from an increment of growth. Combining all the positive changes from growth yields a measure of Total Social Product.

Net Social Product is the difference between Total Social Product and Total Social Cost. Net Social Product is greatest where Marginal Social Product is equal to Marginal Social Cost.

Preconditions for growth include changes in social attitudes and skills as well as construction of roads, bridges, and so forth.

Social overhead capital is construction of such facilities as roads, bridges, and ports for use by the society as a whole.

The take-off to growth is a period of time in which conditions are appropriate for the beginning of sustained economic growth.

SUGGESTED READINGS

Anderson, Alan, Jr. "There Is No Such Thing as Free Water." *Across the Board*, October, 1981, p. 40.

Collins, Lora S. "Grow We Must." *Across the Board*, March, 1981, p. 16.

Commoner, Barry. *The Closing Circle*. New York: Alfred A. Knopf, 1972.

Dolan, Edwin G. *TANSTAAFL: The Economic Strategy for Environmental Crisis*. New York: Holt Rinehart and Winston, Inc., 1971.

Etzioni, Amitai. "Choose America Must —" *Across the Board*, October, 1980, p. 42.

Georgescu-Rogen, Nicholas. "The Crisis of Natural Resources." *Challenge*, March/April, 1981, p. 50.

Lipset, Seymour Martin. "Futurology." *Across the Board*, April, 1980, p. 28.

Mason, Edward S. "Natural Resources and Environmental Restrictions to Growth." *Challenge*, January/February, 1978, p. 14.

Meadows, Donella H., et al. *The Limits to Growth*. New York: Universe Books, 1972.

Thurow, Lester. *The Zero-Sum Society*. New York: Basic Books, 1980, Chapter 5.

Tucker, William. "The Chemistry Is Getting Better at the EPA." *Fortune*, September 20, 1982, p. 57.

Wallich, Henry C. "Can Growth Go On Indefinitely?" *Across the Board*, November, 1982, p. 30.

—— "'The Limits to Growth' Revisited." *Challenge*, September/October, 1982, p. 30.

Weinberg, Alvin M., and John O. Blomeke. "How to Dispose of the Garbage of the Atomic Age." *Across the Board*, September, 1982, p. 26 and October, 1982, p. 36.

CHAPTER SEVEN

Work, Wages, and Price Inflation

Can We Learn to Work Better?

LEARNING OBJECTIVES

- To describe the changing character of the job market and the implications for employment.
- To use a model of labor markets to illustrate the level of employment and the wage rate and show how free markets promote efficiency and incentives.
- To use the Phillips curve to describe the behavior of employment and price inflation over recent years.
- To evaluate government policies toward inflation and employment, particularly with respect to the implications for efficiency and incentives.
- To consider the effect of worker psychology on productivity and employment stability.

I know an island where living is so easy that work is hardly necessary. A few hours of pleasant work a day can yield all the fish and fruit necessary to sustain life. The islanders seldom need fuel oil for heat, and ocean breezes cool their homes without air conditioning. The scarcest resource is (strangely) water, which is captured on rooftops or purchased from other islands when the rains fail. Whatever few outside items are required—cloth, shoes, radios—may be financed through a day's charter excursion with tourist fishermen.*

The life seems ideal, yet there are problems. Living in such pleasant surroundings makes many of the natives dull and listless. The absence of challenge and the limited range of experience mean that there is little stimulus to personal growth and development, little incentive to innovate and improve. Although the islanders are descendants of vigorous European stock, recent generations have produced no serious poets, artists, builders, scientists, or strivers of any kind.

This story suggests that we should be grateful for an environment that *forces* us to work! As we work to produce the things we need, we enhance our own personal worth. We develop skills, experience challenges, and come to know more of the complex world in which we live.

This chapter will explore the world of work. We will discuss major issues important to producers and consumers in the U.S. economy. First, we will look at job markets—at the changing characteristics of work and the work force and the opportunities that await persons soon to enter the job market. Second, we will discuss current problems relating to average wage rates and the level of employment—in particular, the relationship between total employment and the rate of price inflation. We will consider a wide range of government policies toward work. Federal job programs, the minimum wage law, and unemployment compensation are examples of government programs that significantly affect the supply of labor and, ultimately, total production of goods and services. Finally, we will explore the question of the quality of work life, including the psychology of work and the effect of job quality on the productivity of labor.

In each of these major topics there are issues that divide workers from employers, from consumers, and from other workers. Resolving these issues efficiently and equitably will yield increased productivity and improved living standards.

EMPLOYMENT TRENDS IN THE UNITED STATES

What we *have* depends on what we *produce*. And production depends in large part on the size of the **labor force** relative to the population as a whole. Over the last half century, total population in the United States has increased slightly more than 1 percent a year; the labor force has increased faster, as more and more people have chosen to work.†

1. New home appliances and child-care facilities have enabled more wives and mothers to seek paying jobs outside the home. More than half of adult women are now employed, versus about a fourth fifty years ago.

*A tourist once asked a local shopkeeper for an item not found on the shelf. The reply: "Oh, I don't stock that anymore. Every time I'd get in a shipment, people would buy it so fast I just quit ordering it."

†The growth rates were about 1.5 and 1.75 percent, respectively.

2. A larger percentage of teenagers are seeking job opportunities to supplement their family incomes or to finance higher education. A rising minimum wage along with price inflation have encouraged more teenagers to seek employment. Many teenagers benefit from a variety of job experiences, thus developing skills that can be used later.
3. The only significant decline in labor force participation has occurred among black men, particularly those aged 16 to 19. Lingering job discrimination and a lack of industrial skills may be partly to blame. The minimum wage law has probably *reduced* the labor force participation of black men, some of whose low skills make them ineligible for even the lowest paying jobs.
4. A smaller decline in labor force participation has occurred among white males. Sharing financial responsibility with wives has enabled many men to take early retirement or to pursue avocations outside the labor force.

The net result of these and other factors during the 1970s was annual growth in new entrants to the labor force at twice the rate of the 1950s and early 1960s. Remarkably, job opportunities increased almost as fast, with almost 2 million additional jobs created each year. Labor force growth is expected to slow in the 1980s, creating scarcities in certain labor markets. Immigrants or retired workers may be needed to fill vacant job slots.

Job Characteristics

Along with demographic changes in the composition of the labor force has come a change in the type of work people perform. Fifty years ago almost 25 percent of the labor force was employed in agriculture; today, the percentage is only about 3 percent.

Table 7–1 shows the distribution of jobs in the nonagricultural labor force today versus 50 years ago.*

Table 7–1

Job Description	1930	1980	Percent Change
Manufacturing	27%	22%	− 5%
Mining	3	1	− 2
Construction	4	5	+ 1
Transportation and Public Utilities	10	6	− 4
Wholesale and Retail Trade	15	22	+ 7
Finance, Insurance, and Real Estate	4	6	+ 2
Services	9	19	+10
Federal Government	1	3	+ 2
State and Local Government	6	14	+ 8

*Totals do not sum to 100 percent because of rounding.

The occupations that have gained the most job opportunities are described as *service occupations*. Services are performed on or for people and include: selling and brokering, health care and education, recreation and travel accommodations, legal and government services. Performing certain service jobs requires particular skills, often acquired through specialized education. Thus, the capital required for service jobs tends to be more *human* than *material*. Many service workers are described as technicians or professionals and think of their roles as "careers" rather than jobs. The relative growth of service occupations has implications for the quality of work life. Whereas work in manufacturing may involve numbing routine or back-breaking drudgery, some service jobs may provide creative stimulus and the enjoyment associated with working with people.

Other conditions of work life have been changing as well. Fifty years ago the average work week was between 40 and 45 hours; today it is 35. At the same time, real hourly earnings have doubled. Rising real incomes reflect increasing worker productivity, particularly in agriculture, where output per hour of work has risen an average of 5 percent annually over the last half century. (Although farm employment was cut by 80 percent, the use of farm machinery and agricultural chemicals increased by a factor of 18.)

Jobs for the Future

Tomorrow's workers are today's students, who are learning skills they hope will increase their job opportunities in the future. When making their vocational plans, students should be aware of certain fundamental changes that are occurring in labor markets:

1. The excess supply of labor during the 1970s and early 1980s will begin to give way to labor scarcity late in the decade, accelerating the drive to increase worker productivity in many occupations.
2. New technologies will eliminate many low-skilled jobs and call for workers with the skills to design, operate, and repair sophisticated new equipment.
3. Demand for more and better business and consumer services will call for a range of new skills that require advanced education.
4. Continuing scarcities of energy and materials will provide job opportunities for researchers and scientists of all kinds, as well as technically trained managers for managing scientific enterprises.

The United States Department of Labor estimates that during the 1980s total employment will increase by roughly 1.7 million workers annually. Matching up almost 2 million additional workers each year with the available jobs will be difficult and imprecise. Unlike the Soviet Union, where young people are classified early and specifically trained to occupy certain jobs, the United States depends on individual choice and job counseling to determine the labor force mix.

Most new job openings in the 1980s will occur in occupations classified as white-collar jobs: in particular, professional, managerial, sales, and clerical jobs that already account for more than half of total employment. Workers in these occupations will profit from the growth of professional services, government, and environmental regulation. Jobs with the most openings annually (more than 25,000 and as many as 305,000) are:

secretaries and stenographers	cashiers
retail and wholesale sales workers	bookkeepers
licensed practical nurses	registered nurses
kindergarten and elementary teachers	accountants
bank clerks, bank officers and financial	typists
managers	engineers
real estate agents and brokers	computer programmers

Blue-collar jobs will grow more slowly; these are craft, operative and labor jobs that account for about a third of total employment. Advances in technology will displace unskilled and many semiskilled workers, as well as other workers who are unable to adapt their skills to new job requirements. Jobs with the most openings in this classification (more than 37,000 and as many as 180,000) are:

building custodians	dishwashers
industrial machine repairers	assemblers
construction laborers	guards
dining room attendants	carpenters
worker supervisors	local truck drivers

Personal service occupations are expected to grow fastest of all; these include cleaning, food preparation, health, and personal care occupations, which now absorb only a small fraction of the labor force.* Rising prosperity and the movement of many services from the home to the market will fuel growth in these occupations. Jobs with the most openings annually (more than 11,000 and as many as 94,000) will be:

nursing aides and orderlies	cooks and chefs
waiters and waitresses	teacher aides
home health aides	

Farm employment is expected to continue to decline, as more advanced equipment and improved efficiency reduce the labor intensity of farming.

LABOR MARKETS

The level of employment and the wage rate in particular markets depend on labor supply and demand. Figure 7–1a is a graph of the market for a particular kind of labor. The **demand for labor** curve shows the quantities that will be

---

*Personal service jobs listed here differ from white-collar professional services in that the latter require some sort of formal training.

employed at various wage rates. Points on the curve reflect the dollar **value of Marginal Product**. Remember that Marginal Product is the additional output associated with employing an additional unit of labor. The labor demand curve slopes downward because adding units of labor to a fixed quantity of capital equipment normally causes workers' Marginal Product to decline. Then selling workers' Marginal Product yields smaller and smaller gains in sales revenue for the producing firm.

The **supply of labor** curve indicates hours of work that will be supplied at various wage rates; stated differently, the supply curve indicates the necessary wage for employing various quantities of labor. The labor supply curve slopes upward because workers will supply additional hours of work only if the wage rate is increased.

The rule of employment is: *Continue to employ additional units of a resource up to the point where the value of its Marginal Product is equal to the cost of hiring it.* Following this rule of employment ensures that each increase in employment of a particular resource adds enough to a firm's sales revenue to offset what it adds to the firm's costs. In Figure 7–1a, the value of labor's Marginal Product is equal to the wage rate at the intersection of the demand and supply curves. This is the equilibrium level of employment, where total employment is Q_1 and the wage rate is w.

In actual labor markets, measuring the value of workers' Marginal Product is very difficult. This means that actual wage rates depend to some extent on the relative market power of workers and employers. Labor unions help increase the market power of various labor groups, often pushing wage rates above the equilibrium wage. On the other hand, **trade associations** help increase the market power of employers, tending to hold some wages below the equilibrium rate.

Efficiency and Incentive Effects in Labor Markets

Different kinds of labor are affected by different demand and supply circumstances, so that the levels of employment and wage rates differ among markets. In free markets, differences in wage rates cause labor resources to be allocated efficiently and provide incentives to increase productivity. However, when market power influences resource markets, the result may be reduced efficiency and reduced incentives. To understand this, consider the efficiency effects and incentive effects in resource pricing.

Efficiency effects involve the allocation of resources for maximum output at minimum costs. Employing and rewarding resources according to the value of their Marginal Product ensures that resources will be used efficiently: relatively plentiful resources will be cheap and large quantities will be employed, while relatively scarce resources will be costly and used sparingly. These circumstances are shown in Figures 7–1b and c. The plentiful resource shown in Figure 7–1b is employed in large quantities to the level that the value of its Marginal Product is just enough to offset a low wage. In Figure 7–1c the high wage paid to the relatively scarce resource encourages employers to conserve; the resource is used only to the point that the value of its Marginal Product offsets its high wage.

Figure 7–1

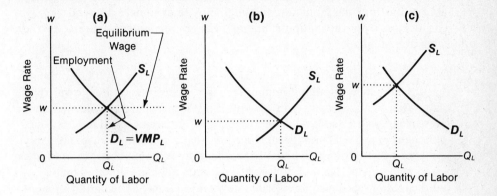

When differences in market power create arbitrary differences in resource prices, resources may be used inefficiently: plentiful resources may be over-priced and underused, while relatively scarce resources are underpriced and overused. An example of the first is the auto industry, where high union wages have caused many workers to be replaced by industrial robots. An example of the second is the apparel industry, where "sweat shops" with cheap labor have retarded the introduction of labor-saving new machines. Pencil in artificially high and low wages on Figures 7–1b and c and explain your findings.

Incentive effects involve encouragement to do certain things. When pay is based on the value of their Marginal Product, workers are encouraged to increase their productivity. The result is a tendency for total product to grow. On the other hand, tying pay to market power increases incentives to achieve power and may interfere with productivity growth.

Special Case

Immigrant Workers

We often call ourselves a "nation of immigrants." For the first hundred years, our borders were freely open to the world's "tired...poor...huddled masses." The first laws limiting immigration came in 1875 and applied only to prostitutes and convicts. In 1921, quotas were established for immigrants from various nations or regions, on the basis of the ethnic background of the current population. Quotas favored immigrants from England, Germany, Italy, and Ireland.

During the late 1960s, immigrant quotas were relaxed. Immigration into the United States increased substantially, largely in response to the promise of job opportunities and high wages. Throughout the 1970s, it was estimated that more than a million immigrants crossed the border annually, more than half illegally.* Most came from Central American countries, the Caribbean, or Mexico, where probably a fourth of the labor force is unemployed or underemployed.

The debate over the nation's liberal immigration policy centers on the following arguments:

1. *Immigrants take jobs away from native-born Americans.* Critics complain that the presence of willing immigrant labor keeps wage rates lower than many American workers will accept. This is particularly true in labor-intensive industries such as women's apparel, auto repair, and food service. Although some illegal immigrants take jobs that Americans refuse, probably half earn wages at least as high as the minimum wage in jobs that would be acceptable to Americans. Economist Ray Marshall has estimated that without the millions of illegal immigrants now in the country, the nation's unemployment rate might be less than four percent. On the other hand, supporters of a liberal immigration policy argue that without a source of low-cost labor, many service industries would probably disappear, and other manufacturing industries would become more fully mechanized. Also, cheap labor in certain industries helps keep U.S. exports competitive with foreign products, thus helping the U.S. balance of payments.

2. *Immigrants (particularly illegal immigrants) are subject to abuse and exploitation by employers, landlords, and alien smugglers.* Critics complain that illegal immigrants form a lawless class whose exclusion from power leads them to reject United States laws and customs. The growth of ethnic neighborhoods has produced social and political conflicts that are costly to state and local governments and damaging to industrial productivity. Supporters of a liberal immigration policy suggest that these problems could be resolved by granting amnesty to immigrants now in the country illegally and by encouraging a more complete integration of immigrants into the social and economic fabric of the nation.

3. *Immigrants place especially heavy burdens on our already strained public services.* Critics claim that immigrants receive welfare and social security benefits at substantial cost to taxpayers. Furthermore, immigrants often require special expenditures for bilingual education, health care, and low-income housing. In fact, many immigrants fail to take advantage of available public services while paying the same state and federal taxes as other workers. After becoming accustomed to American life, immigrants frequently become more prosperous than native-born citizens.† Apparently, greater ability or motivation of immigrants in general is passed on to their immediate descendants. As immigrant families become familiar with the nation's culture and language, their incomes tend to grow. Highest wage gains have been noted among immigrants from Italy, Russia, and Poland.

---

*Estimates of illegal immigrants currently living in the United States range up to about 3 million.

†Barry R. Chiswick, "The Earnings of Immigrants and their Sons," *Challenge*, May/June 1978, pp. 55–61.

The Economics of Immigration

Immigrant workers are responding to very definite market forces. Surplus labor and low wages in one country call for a movement of labor into other countries where workers are scarce. An outflow of labor provides a kind of "safety valve," relieving social and economic pressures in the home country, and reducing the tendency toward political revolution.* In the host country, the inflow of foreign labor helps relieve labor scarcity and provides a pool of labor willing to take the lowest-paid jobs.

A flexible source of labor may become especially desirable in future years when the excess labor associated with the "baby boom" gives way to labor scarcity associated with the "baby bust" of the 1960s and 1970s. Beginning in 1982, fewer U.S. workers will enter the labor market each year. Unless immigrants are allowed to supplement the native-born labor force, wage rates will tend to rise. Furthermore, a decrease in labor supply will mean fewer workers contributing to the Social Security benefits of retired workers.

Resource mobility is one of the necessary characteristics of a free, competitive economic system. With free mobility we would expect a tendency toward greater efficiency in resource allocation. As resource supplies adjust to demand in markets around the world, the pay of similar workers would adjust to reflect the value of their Marginal Product. The result would be increased incentives toward higher productivity and growth of real incomes.

- Use a market model to illustrate the theoretical explanation of immigration. Show how immigration can improve efficiency and incentives in labor markets. Point out the bases for opposition to a liberal immigration policy and the bases for support.
- Are there noneconomic (i.e., foreign policy) considerations involved in deciding on an immigration policy for the United States? To what extent should other considerations influence immigration policy? Discuss.

EMPLOYMENT AND PRICE INFLATION

Look again at Figure 7–1a, showing a free market for labor. The figure shows that all workers willing to work at the equilibrium wage are employed. In perfectly free labor markets there is no (involuntary) unemployment; qualified workers willing to work at the equilibrium wage will be hired, and others will leave the labor force. Changes in the value of Marginal Product will cause *shifts in demand*; changes in the number of qualified workers will cause *shifts in supply*. In either case, wage rates will change to reflect the value of Marginal Product at the **equilibrium level of employment**.

These results are shown in Figures 7–2a and b. Note that whereas the *quantity of employment* changes, (involuntary) *unemployment* is zero. If wages adjust as shown, all willing workers will be hired. We know that this does not happen in the real world. In the real world the existence of (involuntary) unemployment suggests that labor markets are not pefectly free to adjust to changes in demand and supply.

*Can you suggest other not-so-favorable consequences for the home country?

Figure 7–2

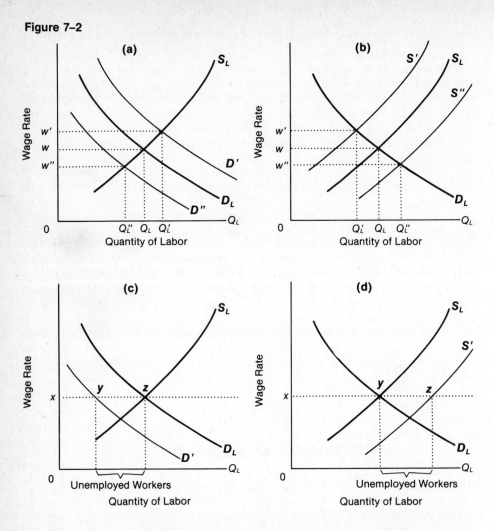

Figures 7–2c and d illustrate two market circumstances in which (c) a drop in the value of Marginal Product and (d) an increase in the supply of labor would call for a decrease in wage rates. In both cases, market power or tradition combine to hold the wage rate stable, as shown by the horizontal line marked *xyz*. If wage rates are not permitted to fall, the labor market cannot reach equilibrium. Firms will hire the number of workers indicated on their labor demand curve at the artificially high wage (*xy*). The difference between the number of workers hired and the number willing to work at that wage (*yz*) constitutes *unemployed* workers.

Much of national economic policy in the two decades following World War II was based on the fundamental assumption that labor markets are free. In free labor markets, government tax and spending could influence total spending in the nation and, through spending, the level of total *employment*. High total spending would increase the value of labor's Maginal Product, shift labor demand curves to the right, increase wage rates, and increase total employment. Or low total spending would reduce the demand for labor, create slack in labor markets, and force wages down until all willing workers would be hired. Thus, there would be a direct relationship between the level of total employment and the level of wage inflation. (Stated differently, there would be an indirect relationship between the level of *unemployment* and wage inflation.) Government tax and spending policies to increase employment (reduce unemployment) would increase wage inflation. Policies to reduce wage inflation would reduce employment (increase unemployment).

The Phillips Curve

The free labor market theory and the policy conclusions that followed it are illustrated in a curve called the **Phillips curve**, developed by British economist A. W. Phillips in the 1950s (Figure 7–3). The annual rate of wage inflation is measured along the vertical axis, and the rate of unemployment along the horizontal axis. Point *A* on the Phillips curve indicates low employment (high unemployment) with low wage inflation. Government policies to increase total spending would increase the demand for labor and move the economy up the Phillips curve toward higher employment (lower unemployment). At the same time, wage inflation would rise.

The reverse is true at Point *B*. High inflation and low unemployment at point *B* would require government policies to reduce total spending in the nation and reduce the demand for labor. Then falling wage inflation would be accompanied by lower employment (higher unemployment).

If the fundamental assumptions underlying the Phillips curve are valid, there is a simple trade-off between inflation and unemployment. In this case, deciding on tax and spending policy for correcting either problem would be straightforward. Unfortunately, in recent years wage and employment behavior has not

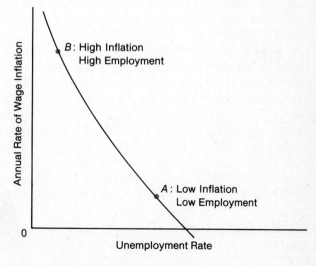

Figure 7–3

B: High Inflation
High Employment

A: Low Inflation
Low Employment

Annual Rate of Wage Inflation

0

Unemployment Rate

followed the traditional pattern, and conventional economic policies have been unable to correct either high unemployment or high wage inflation. Figure 7–4 includes points representing actual rates of inflation and unemployment for the last 14 years. The figure shows a tendency for *both* variables to increase, whatever the spending policies of government.

Changes in the Phillips Curve

Certain changes in labor markets have been blamed for the change in the inflation/employment relationship. One labor market change has been a more rigid structuring of the labor force. Instead of large labor pools of easily substitutable workers, there are now a variety of specialized job categories. Wage rates for each job category depend on supply and demand in separate labor markets. Furthermore, each individual wage rate bears a particular relationship to wage rates in other job categories. Under these circumstances, a supply or demand shift that increases wages in one job classification will disturb the entire wage structure and set in motion pressures to increase other wages proportionally. The ultimate result is general wage inflation without a significant increase in employment. In fact, as employers move up their labor demand curves to the higher wage rate, total employment may fall.

Other changes in the labor force have affected the Phillips curve. Changes in the level of total spending affect high- and low-skilled workers differently. Broad increases in spending may have little effect on demand for low-skilled workers. As a result, government policies to increase employment tend to increase wage inflation in skilled occupations while leaving many low-skilled workers without jobs.

Unemployment of low-skilled workers is a kind of **structural unemployment**. Structural unemployment is caused by a mismatch between the structure of the job market and the structure of job skills of workers. Many economists regard 6 percent unemployment (94 percent employment) as the limit beyond which policies to increase total spending have no effect on total employment.* Workers in this 6 percent must acquire the skills needed in modern industry if they are to avoid unemployment.

Some liberal economists cite another possible reason for a change in the inflation/employment relationship: an increase in *market power.* In labor markets, the existence of market power can force wage rates up and at the same time reduce the number of workers hired. In product markets, market power can increase consumer prices and increase workers' cost-of-living wage demands. Higher wages cause employers to move back up their labor demand curves and employ less labor.

The most obvious recent example of the use of market power has been the actions of OPEC to increase the price of oil. Rising energy prices have indeed contributed to wage inflation and reduced the growth of employment opportuni-

---

*For simplicity, the 6 percent structural employment here includes also **frictional unemployment**: workers temporarily unemployed as they move from job to job.

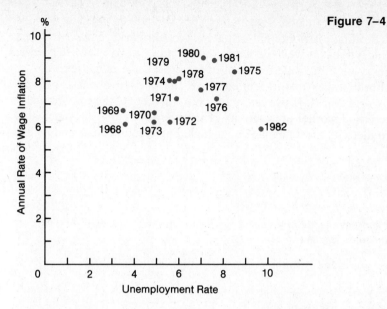

Figure 7–4

ties. Rising prices for certain other commodities—food and lumber—have been less a result of market power, however, than of rising world demand and faltering supply. Market power is doubtless responsible for some portion of wage inflation in the last thirteen years. However, there is no conclusive evidence that market power has increased in the United States over the years represented in Figure 7–4.

POLICIES FOR EFFICIENCY AND INCENTIVES

Changes in the inflation/employment relationship over the last decade have implications for national economic policy. In this section we will look at specific government policies designed to correct rising wage inflation or rising unemployment. As you read, keep in mind the efficiency and incentive effects of free labor markets. Then ask yourself to what extent government policies help or harm efficiency and incentives.

Policy Toward Inflation

Increased efficiency and improved incentives can have the effect of increasing resource productivity. Increased productivity means larger Total Product and greater income shares for the resources used in production. In fact, a 3 percent increase in productivity means that a contributing resource can receive a 3 percent increase in pay without causing production costs to rise.

Inflation interferes with the distribution of gains from productivity growth. When there is inflation, it becomes more difficult to distribute pay increases according to the value of Marginal Product. Moreover, inflation creates uncertainty about the equity of income distribution and strengthens the drive toward market power. Settling distributional disputes through market power reduces efficiency and incentives, as we have seen. Furthermore, a drive toward market power uses energy that might better be used for productive purposes.

Nonagricultural wages in the United States have risen about 6 percent annually since World War II. However, only about 2 percent of the gains actually represented increased worker productivity. The difference between wage gains and gains in productivity must be made up in higher production costs and higher prices:

average annual money wage increases since World War II	*6 percent*
average annual increase in productivity	*−2 percent*
average annual increase in labor costs of production since World War II	*4 percent*

Real wages are money wages minus the effects of inflation:

annual money wage increase since World War II	*6.0*
annual pecentage increase in prices	*−4.0*
annual real wage increase since World War II	*2.0*

In a few of the years since World War II, general price inflation rose faster than wage rates so that **real wages** actually fell. Real wages fell by an average of 3.4 percent annually during the recession of 1974–1975 and again by 3 percent a year during the long recession of 1979–1981.

To protect real wages against inflation, many workers have insisted on **Cost-of-Living Adjustments** (or COLAs) in job contracts. Under a COLA, workers receive wage gains equal to increases in productivity *plus* automatic increases to help compensate for general price inflation. Almost half of the U.S. population receives cost-of-living protection against inflation, through Social Security and Civil Service retirement pay, as well as wages. Only in 1949, when the consumer price index fell 1.8 percentage points, did COLAs cause wage rates to fall.

Cost-of-living adjustments have probably contributed to greater employment stability. Guaranteed protection against inflation enables workers to sign long-term contracts at lower initial wage rates. There is a disadvantage, of course. Inflation-adjusted wages combine with other cost increases to raise total production costs; then higher production costs are passed on to consumers in the form of higher prices. In this way, COLAs may worsen the problem they are designed to correct. In the meantime, persons without COLA protection are harmed, and the nation's resolve to fight inflation is weakened.

During the administration of President Nixon, wage-price controls were instituted to reduce the pace of wage and price increases. Some liberal economists welcomed controls as a way of limiting the inflationary effects of market power. Other economists pointed out that controls interfere with the market signals that help employers allocate resources efficiently. Moreover, artificially low wages and prices reduce incentives to increase productivity. Conservative economists objected to wage-price controls as unwarranted government intervention in free markets.

General wage-price controls were allowed to lapse in 1974, and inflation worsened. In 1977 President Carter recommended the approach of **tax-based income policies** (TIPS) to help reduce inflation while maintaining equitable distribution of the gains from increased productivity. Under one proposal, a large company and its union would agree to hold annual wage and price increases below a certain percent. In return, workers and the firm would receive income tax rebates. Under another proposal, firms that granted higher wages than an agreed-on ceiling would suffer tax increases. Under a third proposal, workers accepting low ceilings on wage increases would receive tax rebates if actual inflation rose higher than the ceiling.

Congress feared that either proposal would be too costly (in terms of lost tax revenue) and refused to go along. Unit labor costs rose 9 percent in 1978 and 10 percent in 1979. The 1980s began with fears of worsening inflation and further increases in labor costs. President Reagan's approach to inflation was to use government policies to reduce total spending: cuts in government programs and cuts in taxes for groups that are likely to save and invest their added incomes. The result of the President's program was a relative decline in the demand for labor, decreases in real wages, and a lower level of total employment. Inflation did slow down, but the costs in terms of reduced output and employment were high.

Policy Toward Unemployment

Achieving economic efficiency requires the fullest possible use of all available resources. Maximum use of labor resources is especially desirable since the output of labor not used is lost forever. Moreover, failure to use labor resources may lead to a decline of labor skills, as well as to a variety of social problems associated with idleness. Promoting efficient use of the nation's labor resources has come to be a major responsibility of the federal government.

The first United States president who was willing to commit the federal government to full employment was Franklin Roosevelt. When Roosevelt took office during the Great Depression, unemployment amounted to 12 million workers, one quarter of the labor force. Under Roosevelt's administration, the Works Progress Administration (WPA) was created to provide jobs for hundreds of thousands of unemployed workers. The WPA built post offices, dams, and other public projects across the country. Still, unemployment remained high until the nation began gearing up for war at the end of the decade.

Fears that peace would again bring widespread joblessness prompted Congress to pass the Employment Act of 1946. The new law gave the federal government responsibility for designing policies toward maximum total employment, but it gave few specifics for doing so.

The problem of high and prolonged unemployment did not arise again for several decades.* (The recession beginning in 1958 left unemployment above 5 percent until 1963.) In general, policymakers worried more about inflation, which was thought to be aggravated by government-financed job programs. By the mid-1970s, however, severe unemployment aroused new concerns in Congress, culminating in passage of the Full Employment Act of 1978 (the Humphrey-Hawkins Act).

The 1978 law included specific employment goals: an overall unemployment rate of no more than 4 percent by 1983, with unemployment of only 3 percent for workers over age 20. Each year, the president is required to present to Congress the employment and production goals for the year and outline the administration's programs and appropriations for achieving them.

Accomplishing the goals of the Full Employment Act has proved to be more difficult than stating them. Measuring needed jobs and targeting programs to create them is imprecise. Moreover, even small improvements in the job market tend to encourage more workers to enter the labor force, erasing any progress that might have been made.

The primary emphasis of federal employment policy continues to be government tax and spending policies for stimulating hiring in the private sector. But if tax and spending policies provide too few private jobs, the President must establish specific job programs to absorb the remaining unemployed workers. The federal government uses three means for directly affecting employment: **public service jobs, public works programs,** and **job training**. Let us look at each of these kinds of programs in detail. Then we will look at a government program for directly affecting employment in the private sector. Finally, we will examine government policies for ensuring a minimum level of purchasing power for workers and their families: **unemployment compensation** and **the minimum wage law**.

The efficiency and incentive effects of all these programs are complex. Thus, the net result in terms of employment and wage inflation is uncertain. This is particularly true when we consider the long-range effects of such programs on workers' skills and attitudes and on business firms' drive to compete.

Public Service Jobs.   Public service jobs are jobs in state and local government, financed at least in part by the federal government. Public service jobs are probably the most efficient way of creating jobs because substantially all of the money goes directly into workers' paychecks.

Under the Comprehensive Employment and Training Act (CETA) of 1973, Congress appropriated billions of dollars annually to finance public service jobs in 460 state and local governments. Public service employees worked as clerk-typists, recreation aides, park rangers, general repair persons, fire fighters, building inspectors, librarians, truck drivers, police cadets, and maintenance

---

*One concern during the 1950s and 1960s was "technological unemployment"—unemployment that results from increased automation in industry.

persons. The hope was that workers in CETA job programs would eventually move into permanent jobs in government or private business.

In general, CETA jobs were awarded in areas with substantial unemployment to persons currently unemployed or underemployed. Veterans and welfare recipients were given special consideration for employment through CETA. All CETA jobs paid the "prevailing wage" to avoid organized labor's complaint that job programs create low-wage jobs that compete with union jobs. Including fringe benefits, each public service job was estimated to cost the federal government about $9,200 (in 1979).

The results of CETA job programs were mixed. Since most public service jobs require particular skills, few CETA jobs actually went to the hard-core unemployed. Although CETA funds financed major new state and local government programs, most of the hiring probably just replaced what would otherwise have been lay-offs. There were some reports of fraud and abuse, including the use of CETA money to pay workers already on government payrolls. For CETA workers, there was little incentive to leave high-paying public service jobs to seek employment in the private sector. President Reagan cut CETA programs substantially as part of a major effort to reduce government spending.

Public Works Programs.   Public works programs involve construction of social overhead capital for use by governments and citizens. Since construction projects require large expenditures for materials and equipment, only a relatively small fraction of public works money goes for wages.

In the late 1970s, President Carter proposed significant increases in federal public works programs. The goal was to employ some of the nation's nearly 8 million unemployed for building schools, municipal buildings, and parks. The Congressional Budget Office estimated that each $1 billion spent for public works would create between 16,000 and 46,000 jobs immediately and 56,000 to 70,000 additional jobs within a year.

Well-planned public works projects create valuable social overhead capital that can increase productivity in the private sector. Still, construction of public works draws resources from use in private business and may worsen inflation and retard growth. This is especially true when public works projects begun in a recession continue into a period of economic expansion, when productive resources are scarce.* Many public works programs were also cut by the Reagan administration.

Job Training Programs.   Critics of federal employment policy contend that public service and public works programs have only temporary effects. Instead, they recommend training workers to perform needed skills in the private sector. Most federal job programs do include training. For example, under CETA some business firms were given wage subsidies for hiring and training the hard-core unemployed. Teenagers were provided job counseling, training, and summer

---

*One possible solution to this problem is to plan a number of short-range projects that can be completed before the economic situation changes substantially.

work experience. Labor Department officials estimated that at least half of the youths involved in these programs eventually either found jobs in the private sector, joined the military, returned to school, or otherwise became productive workers.

The most effective job training programs are generally those involving on-the-job training, with some assurance that the trainee will be retained in the same position at the end of the training program. Without such assurance, there is the danger that workers will be trained for jobs that no longer exist.

The Reagan administration cut federally-sponsored job training programs substantially and encouraged private business firms to take the responsibility for training unskilled workers.

Government Support for Private Sector Jobs. In 1980, the federal government became involved directly in guaranteeing jobs in the private sector. The occasion was the imminent bankruptcy of the Chrysler Corporation, the nation's third largest manufacturer of automobiles. Analysts had concluded that a Chrysler failure would have destroyed the jobs of 100,000 production workers directly and nearly three times as many jobs indirectly among suppliers, dealers, and freight carriers to the automotive industry.

Job losses would have been particularly painful for certain communities where auto-related industries are concentrated. Severe economic distress in particular regions could quickly snowball into a national economic crisis, with falling property values, collapse of tax revenues and public services, and a rise in radical political protest. To avoid this possibility, Congress agreed to guarantee $1 billion in Chrysler loans. In return, Chrysler's management, union, and creditors agreed to accept financial sacrifices in order to help the corporation return to profitability.

By 1981, Congress was considering bills outlining various approaches to the problem of layoffs in the private sector: payment of moving costs and retraining costs for laid-off workers; advance notice of plant closings to aid job mobility; mandated job transfers within a single firm to avoid lay-offs; severance pay along with supplemental unemployment benefits. One bill would require firms to compensate local governments for tax revenues lost as a result of plant closings. There is pressure also for industry-wide hiring and transfer rights, especially for the airlines and railroads.

Unemployment Compensation. The Social Security Act of 1935 provides temporary compensation for laid-off workers under its unemployment insurance program. The program is financed by federal and state taxes paid by employers: a total of 3.4 percent of the first $6,000 of a worker's earnings. Tax rates depend on each employer's record for lay-offs. State unemployment programs normally pay 26 weeks of unemployment benefits, and an additional 13 weeks of benefits during recession may be partially supported by the Federal government. Benefits differ between states, but they average about half an unemployed worker's gross wage. Workers who quit their jobs without cause are not eligible for benefits.

Unemployment compensation may have the effect of reducing the supply of labor and worsening unemployment and wage inflation. Recipients of unemployment benefits may have little incentive to seek work. An employed worker who pays income and social security taxes on income from work may not be much better off than an unemployed worker (whose unemployment benefits are not taxed). Some recipients of unemployment compensation also receive other income, further reducing their financial need and prolonging the search for a new job. To deal with this problem, Congress has made unemployment benefits subject to income taxes for recipients with substantial additional income.

The Minimum Wage.   Government policy toward the minimum wage may also have had the effect of reducing employment in the private sector and forcing low-skilled workers into public service jobs or onto welfare.

In 1912, Massachusetts was the first state to pass a minimum wage law. By 1932, sixteen other states had passed minimum wage laws, often applicable only to women and children. A minimum wage law for the nation was passed in 1938 as a part of the Fair Labor Standards Act. The federal law established a minimum hourly wage of $.25 for workers involved in interstate commerce. The minimum wage was only about 40 percent of average wages in manufacturing and covered less than half of the labor force.

The largest increase in the minimum wage took place in 1967 when the first "baby boom" workers began replacing older workers at wages below the prevailing minimum. Since 1967, the minimum wage has been adjusted upward frequently until today it is more than 50 percent of average wages in manufacturing and applies to about 85 percent of the workforce. Only farm workers and some small business employees are exempt from the minimum wage.*

Critics argue that a rising minimum wage worsens unemployment, eliminates jobs in low-profit industries, distorts other wage relationships, and contributes to inflation. They cite these specific problems:

1. The minimum wage makes low-skilled workers especially vulnerable to boom-and-bust cycles in economic activity. When business expands, low-skilled workers are hired; when sales fall, they are the first to be fired.
2. A rise in the wages of the least productive workers frequently requires increases in other wages so as to maintain traditional wage differentials.
3. When laid-off workers seek employment in jobs not covered by the minimum wage, they increase the supply of labor in other markets and push those wages down.
4. The minimum wage raises labor costs of production; then high wage costs in labor-intensive industries raise the prices of finished goods and reduce quantities sold. The effect is to worsen job prospects for low-skilled workers in general.

*In January 1981, the minimum wage was raised to $3.35. Fewer than 5 million workers were affected directly by the increase, but other wages experienced a ripple effect as employers adjusted other wages to restore traditional relationships.

5. The minimum wage hits teenagers especially hard.* There have been proposals to set a separate, lower minimum for teenagers, but unions worry that the difference would cause some firms to hire teenagers instead of adult workers.

In spite of these objections, supporters of the minimum wage maintain that placing the major burden of fighting inflation on low-skilled workers is unfair. Major labor unions support the minimum wage law and favor tying minimum wage increases to increases in the cost of living. Unions maintain that the minimum wage ensures an adequate level of total spending for the nation, and that it helps ensure equity in an economy strongly affected by market power, differences in access to education and training, and discrimination.

THE QUALITY OF WORK LIFE

For most of human history, the quality of work life was of little concern. All people knew that work — sometimes grueling, never-ending — was absolutely necessary for life. Survival depended on the work of the entire family. Fathers worked in the fields, forests, mines, or factories; mothers frequently worked alongside fathers; and even young children worked in the most pitiable conditions of all. Until advances in technology and increases in capital resources brought tremendous gains in productivity, every person's work was necessary to sustain that person's life.

The Industrial Revolution brought machines, with new opportunities for mass production, to raise worker productivity and real income. Frederick W. Taylor, the "Father of Modern Management," showed how dividing production jobs into simple routine tasks could yield greater total output. The assembly-line method of work organization meant a sacrifice of worker pride in creation, but the higher incomes it produced seemed worth the sacrifice.

Little attention was paid to the *psychology* of work until the 1930s, when researchers at Western Electric's Hawthorne Works in Chicago set out to measure the relationship between lighting in the workplace and worker productivity. What the researchers found had very little to do with lighting. More important, they found that workers were eager to discuss their work, to suggest ways to improve work, and to cooperate toward increasing total output. The Hawthorne experiments became the basis for a totally new way of thinking about the quality of work life.

New ways of thinking were badly needed in the 1950s. Boredom on the assembly line had created a new malady called "blue collar blues," with increased absenteeism, alcoholism, and even vandalism on the job. **Behavioral**

---

*Economist Ray Marshall (President Carter's Secretary of Labor) points out that forcing teenagers to remain in school longer before taking a job may increase their productivity and enlarge their job options in the long run.

scientists explored the problem and described new styles of management for correcting it:

1. Abraham Maslow described a hierarchy of needs beginning with the primary needs of food and shelter and progressing to emotional needs such as self-esteem and self-actualization. According to Maslow, high and rising worker productivity would depend on satisfying workers' higher needs for involvement and self-fulfillment.
2. Douglas McGregor described two theories of management. Theory X was old-style and autocratic and depended on *forcing* workers to perform jobs they probably would not like. McGregor's Theory Y assumed that workers would *enjoy* work that involved mutual trust and cooperation toward shared goals.
3. Elton Mayo pointed out that treating workers as adversaries interested only in collecting their pay caused a loss of group loyalty and a decrease in productivity. He believed that if workers saw themselves as part of a specific *group*, they would strive harder to achieve group goals.
4. Amitai Etzioni participated in studies that confirmed workers' desires to work better and to be rewarded according to their productivity.
5. William Ouchi described Japanese management and successful management in the United States as conforming to Theory Z. Under Theory Z, managers work to develop a long-term bond between workers and the firm—in fact, they develop an entire corporate culture in which the firm exhibits a sense of responsibility toward employees, and employees reciprocate with a sense of loyalty to the firm.
6. Michael Maccoby contends that changes in the social fabric have changed the habits and attitudes of workers away from exclusive emphasis on material rewards. In his view, jobs and job incentives must change to provide workers a greater sense of personal fulfillment.

Fortunately, many of today's managers understand the importance of worker psychology in job performance. They are developing the mechanisms for increasing worker participation in work decisions, with the expectation that both labor and management can gain from the results. **Work improvement councils** have been formed in some firms to look at job characteristics and conduct quality-of-life seminars, instructing managers on the new psychology of work. Some jobs have been redesigned for performance by *teams* of workers who set their own pace, divide responsibilities, and are rewarded according to team output. Some firms have established **quality circles**, committees of workers that analyze and solve problems involving product quality. A few firms have allowed worker representatives to sit on their **boards of directors** and contribute directly to corporate decision-making. Many firms invite employee suggestions for changes to improve production, rewarding workers whose suggestions are adopted.

The quality of work life has important implications for our willingness to perform work. Along with wage rates, the psychology of work determines the level of employment and production and, ultimately, our standards of living.

Special Case

Wage and Employment Practices in the United States and Abroad

During the 1960s, many U.S. firms built manufacturing plants in other countries to take advantage of lower wage rates abroad. United States labor unions complained that tax advantages on foreign earnings were depriving Americans of jobs. By the mid-1970s, the situation seemed to be reversing. Relatively faster wage inflation in many other industrial countries was making the United States an attractive location for foreign-owned business firms. Currently, Sweden, Norway, Denmark, and Canada have higher pay scales than the United States. Belgium, the Netherlands, and West Germany have pay scales almost as high.*

The cost of labor constitutes from 50 to 75 percent of **value added** in manufacturing processes. Value added is the difference between the dollar value of a firm's sales and the dollar cost of materials and component parts purchased by the firm. Industries with a high labor component are said to be labor-intensive. For such industries, international differences in wages can make substantial differences in profitability. Labor-intensive industries tend to have low pay scales and relatively large differences in wage rates between nations. Textiles, apparel, and footwear are examples. Because labor costs are a large part of total costs, there is substantial incentive to move these kinds of industries. This is less true of capital-intensive industries like chemicals, electrical equipment, and motor vehicles. Capital-intensive industries tend to have high wages and small differences in wage rates between nations.

Layoff rates in European and Japanese firms tend to be lower than layoff rates in the United States. In those nations, greater stability of work and a reluctance to fire and rehire workers make for generally lower unemployment rates. Another reason for fewer layoffs is national policy concerning layoffs. For instance:

1. In some countries, prenotification is required before workers may be laid off. The length of the prenotification period varies with the job experience of the worker.
2. Many governments require employers to consult with workers' councils and to consider suggested alternatives to layoffs.
3. Some governments require that employers make substantial payments to laid-off workers.
4. The British government pays employers a subsidy for avoiding layoffs of unnecessary workers.
5. French employers must receive permission from the Minister of Labor for layoffs associated with economic causes.
6. In some countries, work-sharing is encouraged, and overtime work during layoffs is discouraged.

The only comparable deterrents to layoffs in the United States are seniority agreements and severance benefits in unionized industries and the fact that an employer's unemployment insurance costs go up when layoffs increase.

The inability to dismiss workers in Europe and Japan means that labor becomes more nearly a **fixed cost** of production. A fixed cost is a cost that must be paid regardless of the level of production and sales. One result is that when demand for finished goods falls, firms

*At the bottom of the pay scale for major industrialized countries are the workers of Japan.

are more likely to react by reducing prices than by cutting production. By maintaining production and selling its product at prices at least as high as its labor and material costs, a firm can continue to supply its market. Any revenue greater than labor and material costs can be used to pay the firm's other fixed obligations. Under these circumstances, a decline in consumer demand is felt as a drop in profits. The threat to profits ensures that employers will use workers efficiently, shifting them among tasks according to production needs.

Guaranteed Lifetime Employment

Japan is said to have a policy of lifetime employment. A Japanese worker makes a total commitment to one employer for his or her entire working life. The employer assumes that workers will be loyal to the firm and, in turn, accepts an obligation to provide jobs and to consider workers' interests when making business decisions.*

Some labor and industry analysts in the United States have looked enviously at lifetime employment policies in Japan and recommended that they be adopted here. Guaranteed lifetime employment, they say, improves worker motivation, increases productivity, and creates a more harmonious work environment. Some unions in the United States are moving toward lifetime job security for their members. Steel workers with more than 20 years service, for example, are guaranteed double supplemental unemployment benefits, opportunities for early retirement, and 32 paid hours a week and 90 percent of pay if transferred to a lower-paying job.

Lifetime job security has the effect of tying a worker's fortunes more directly to those of his or her employer rather than to a union. Perhaps job security has enhanced job loyalty and increased productivity among Japanese workers. Nevertheless, U.S. workers may react differently to guaranteed employment. In contrast to Japan, the United States is composed of a variety of worker groups, with different notions of what is equitable and what work habits and attitudes should be rewarded. Moreover, the United States tends to be more concerned about equal opportunity and equal pay for equal work. These concerns may conflict with plans for guaranteed incomes and job protection.

- Discuss the pros and cons of guaranteed lifetime employment in terms of: productivity, union organization, economic growth.
- Explain how guaranteed lifetime employment may conflict with the goal of equality of opportunity.
- What forces other than those described here help reduce the layoff rate in the United States? What are the implications?

LIFE AFTER WORK: PENSIONS

As this century began, life expectancy at birth was about 47 years. The average worker remained at work 30 years and, sometimes literally, died on the job. Under such circumstances, there was little need to plan for retirement.

The fastest-growing segment of the U.S. population today is the group aged 65 years and over. Twenty-three million Americans now live in retirement, and millions more will be added over the next decades. Better health care is helping

---

*The Japanese employer gains some flexibility in hiring by designating a large portion of the workforce as "temporary," subject to layoff when economic activity slows.

us live longer and raising questions about how to spend those additional years comfortably and productively.

Age 65 was the customary retirement age until the late 1970s, when Congress amended the 1967 Age Discrimination in Employment Act to prohibit mandatory retirement before age 70. Whereas today most elderly workers look forward to retirement, a few want the option to remain in the labor force beyond the traditional retirement age. Their participation may be sorely needed in the late 1980s and 1990s when "baby boom" workers will be middle-aged, and slower population growth will have reduced the number of younger workers entering the labor force.

A major concern for retired workers is their pension income. Ninety-seven percent of retired persons receive at least part of their incomes from public or private pension plans. Private pension plans became a major part of employment contracts following World War II; but until 1974, pension benefits depended rather loosely on the policies of individual business firms. Quality varied widely in terms of financing, administration, and vesting:

- *Financing* refers to the regular contributions from payroll by workers and employers and payments of benefits to retirees;
- *Administration* refers to procedures for investing accumulated pension funds;
- *Vesting* refers to the necessary time on the job before a worker is guaranteed a share in pension benefits.

Without controls, small firms often provided too little financing for pension plans, and many went out of business, leaving employees with nothing. Pension plans administered by certain labor unions were found to be corrupt, and others were invested unwisely. Vesting rules frequently excluded certain workers without proper disclosure.

To help remedy abuses and promote more secure retirement, in 1974 Congress passed the Employee Retirement Income Security Act (ERISA). Under ERISA, pension plans must be adequately financed and administered, and most participants in private pension plans are guaranteed some benefits after 10 years. (Still, workers who move from job to job before they are vested cannot carry their pension benefits with them.) In addition, Congress established the Pension Benefit Guarantee Corporation, an insurance fund for paying workers if their company should go out of business or if their pension fund should fail.

Close to $1 trillion is now held by public and private pension plans, the largest single source of investment capital in the nation. Employers contribute 8 to 10 percent of an average worker's salary to the firm's pension fund. Some pension plans are described as **funded**: worker and employer contributions are invested, and investment income is used to pay retirement benefits. Other pension plans are **unfunded**: contributions from currently employed workers and employers are used directly to pay retired workers. Unfunded pension plans run into problems when current contributions grow more slowly than the number of retirees. The largest unfunded pension plan is the Social Security fund. Contributions to Social Security are 6.7 percent of wages up to $32,400 (from employer and employee). Roughly 25 million retired persons are currently receiving Social Security retirement benefits averaging about $300 per month.

Benefits of private pension plans average about 40 percent of the last year's salary for workers who retire after 30 years. Government pension plans are more generous. State and local government pension plans pay about 50 percent of salary, but because benefits depend on tax revenues, they may be uncertain. Federal government pension plans pay even more, and military plans pay highest of all.

Benefit plans vary in terms of their advantages to workers and employers. *Defined-benefit plans* guarantee a specific retirement income regardless of contributions. *Target-benefit plans* set goals but make no commitment to pay out fully. *Profit-sharing plans* gear pension benefits to the fortunes of the firm. Firms without pension plans may sponsor **Individual Retirement Accounts** (IRAs) to which workers and employers may make tax-free contributions. Individual Retirement Accounts enable workers to escape taxes on specified amounts saved each year. After retirement, when income and income tax rates are lower, workers may withdraw funds and pay taxes at lower rates.

Whatever the structure of pension plans, they are all subject to deterioration through inflation. A sustained 5 percent annual rate of inflation will reduce each pension dollar to 33¢ after 25 years of retirement; inflation of 10 percent would reduce each dollar to 9¢. Few private pension plans are adjusted upward for inflation, since to do so would drastically increase costs. Pension fund investments tend to reflect profitability in the economy as a whole, and investments have generally not been profitable in recent years (when adjusted for inflation).

In 1981, a Presidential Commission on Pension Policy recommended establishing a minimum universal pension system, to be phased in over three years and to cover virtually all working people, whatever their job history. It would be financed through an annual 3 percent payroll tax on employers.

Special Case
Labor's Changing Strengths

From a high of 25 percent in the early 1950s, labor unions now represent only 20 percent of wage earners in the United States. Today's more highly skilled service workers are not impressed by union organizing tactics, while more enlightened management offers acceptable alternatives to union membership. Moreover, since wage gains won through union action are passed on to all workers, many workers find joining the union unnecessary. The heart of union membership in the industrial Northeast and Midwest is rapidly losing jobs to the Sunbelt, where workers are particularly resistant to union organizers. It is estimated that 60 percent of the U.S. workforce is employed by firms with fewer than 100 employees. Organizing workers in small businesses is difficult, expensive, and time consuming.

There are divisions within the labor unions themselves. The difficulty of organizing new workers has made many unions especially protective of their traditional jurisdictions. The craft unions of the old American Federation of Labor (AFL) and the industrial unions of the Congress of Industrial Organizations (CIO) tend to raid each other's membership, sometimes ignoring the mutual interests that might otherwise hold them together. In addition, when unemployment averages more than 7 percent, workers tend to desert the union and cooperate with management in an effort to save their jobs.

Past successes of the labor movement have pushed most workers into the middle class. With wages of $10 or more an hour and attractive fringe benefits, workers have grown more conservative and often vote against government programs for aiding other workers. There has developed a kind of two-tier arrangement, with powerful unions in autos, steel, and coal achieving major wage gains while textile and garment workers, hospital employees, and farm laborers scarcely earn the minimum wage.

In 1979, the AFL-CIO signed an accord with President Carter strengthening what has become a more cooperative relationship with government toward the solution of inflation and unemployment problems. Together with big business, unions have shown increased willingness to press for wage-price restraint. (This has been particularly true for employees of New York City, Chrysler Corporation, and the Ford Motor Company.)

In the 1980s, labor discovered a new tool for enforcing demands and gaining new bargaining power with management—union-controlled pension funds. An estimated $560 billion of union money is held by major banks and insurance companies for lending to business firms. When unions have conflicts with major employers, they sometimes threaten to withdraw their funds from lending institutions. Threats to withdraw pension accounts helped gain powerful bank support for labor in its confrontation with J. P. Stevens and Company.*

In another significant change of strategy, labor unions have been influential in helping workers buy out their own companies. Money-losing firms whose collapse would mean job losses for many workers have been rescued by employee stock purchase, followed by greater employee representation in management. Under such arrangements, workers have been willing to take pay cuts and have become more concerned about the firm's long-range good health. Not all such efforts have been successful, since under employee ownership many of the problems that initially created losses for a firm remain.

Many workers share in company ownership through **Employee Stock Ownership Trusts** (ESOTs). These were first proposed by Louis O. Kelso, a specialist in corporate finance. Allowing workers to participate in ownership, says Kelso, helps bridge the separation between income from work and income from capital. It awards labor a share of prosperity that results from advances in technology and increases in productive capital. Forming an ESOT involves borrowing from a bank, using the general credit or assets of the firm as collateral. Borrowed funds are used to buy the firm's stock, which is to be held by the ESOT and sold to employees. Earnings from the stock are used to repay the bank loan, so that ultimately ownership will be largely in the hands of workers.

- How would you assess the future prospects of labor organizations in the United States? What organizing strategies are likely to be most successful?
- What are some of the disadvantages of recent changes in workers' strategy toward relations with employers?

*The union's long conflict with J.P. Stevens and Company was the subject of the popular motion picture, *Norma Rae*.

Mathematical Supplement

Monopsony and the Minimum Wage

Some economists defend the minimum wage as a means of offsetting the effects of market power: not the power of unions to maintain *high* wages but the power of certain employers to maintain *low* wages. When a business firm is the only employer of a certain type of labor, it becomes a monopolist on the demand side of the labor market. A monopoly buyer is called a **monopsonist**.

Figure 7–5 illustrates the market for a certain type of labor employed by one firm only. The firm may be the only employer of blue-collar labor in a small town, the only employer of females in a particular job classification, or the only employer of workers without specialized job skills. The firm's labor demand curve is determined in the usual way. It represents the dollar value of Marginal Product associated with employing additional units of the labor resource. The supply of labor curve slopes upward, indicating that larger quantities of this particular type of labor will be offered at higher wages.

In a perfectly free market, the equilibrium wage and level of employment would be determined by the intersection of demand and supply: hence, $Q_L = 6$ and $w = \$3.50$. Because total wages are quantity (Q_L) times wage (w), the total wage bill would be shown as the rectangle formed by the equilibrium wage and the quantity of labor employed.

The ordinary supply of labor curve is not the one used by the monopsony firm for making its hiring decision. This is because the firm is the only employer of this type of labor. In effect, the single firm "makes the market" for labor, buying a certain total quantity at a single market price.

Remember the rule of employment: Continue to employ a resource up to the point where the value of its Marginal Product is equal to the cost of hiring it. For a monopsony firm, the cost of hiring an additional worker is *not* the worker's wage. To understand this, look at the supply curve in Figure 7–5. If the firm employs one unit of labor at $1 an hour, its total wage bill is $Q_L \times w = 1 \times \$1 = \$1.00$. Employing two units requires a $.50 increase

Figure 7–5

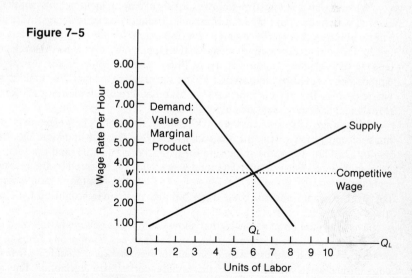

Figure 7-6

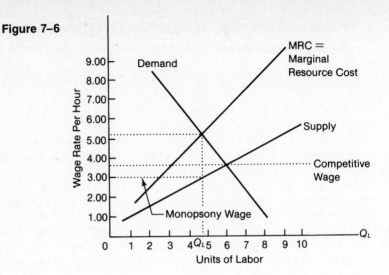

in the wage rate and a total wage bill of $Q_L \times w = 2 \times \$1.50 = \$3.00$. One additional unit of labor increases the firm's wage bill *not* by the wage paid the added unit but by the wage of the additional unit *plus* a \$.50 higher wage for the first unit. In this case, the change in the firm's wage bill is $\$3.00 - \$1.00 = \$2.00$.

The change in total resource cost associated with a one-unit change in employment is called **Marginal Resource Cost**. Marginal Resource Cost is the significant cost consideration for a monopsony firm employing a certain type of labor. The Marginal Resource Cost associated with increments of labor shown in Figure 7–5 has been calculated and shown as Table 7–2. Marginal Resource Cost (MRC) is shown between the lines in the table to indicate that the cost increase occurs with a change from one level of employment to another. An *MRC* curve has been drawn in Figure 7–6. This is the curve to be used in the monopsony firm's hiring decision.

When the monopsony firm follows the rule of employment, it looks for the quantity of labor at which the dollar value of Marginal Product is equal to Marginal Resource Cost. The resulting level of employment, shown in Figure 7–6, is $Q_L = 5$ units of labor. Note that the equilibrium level of employment for the monopsony firm is less than the equilibrium level in a free labor market. If many firms were to compete for this type of labor, employment would be determined at the intersection of market demand and supply, where $Q_L = 6$. But equating the value of Marginal Product with Marginal Resource Cost (MRC) yields employment of only $Q_L = 5$.

What wage will be paid to the workers hired at $Q_L = 5$? The wage rate is read from the market supply curve. It is the wage at which $Q_L = 5$ labor units will be offered in this market. In Figure 7–6, the wage rate for $Q_L = 5$ is $w = \$3.00$, and the total wage bill is $Q_L \times w = 5 \times \$3.00 = \$15.00$. The total wage bill is represented by the rectangle formed beneath the supply curve at $Q_L = 5$ and $w = \$3.00$. Note that for a monopsony firm both the level of wages and the total wage bill are lower than would be true in free labor markets.

These are the circumstances that some economists believe justify a minimum wage law. Defenders of the minimum wage say that it forces monopsony firms to pay a wage comparable to the one that would be paid in free markets. Requiring firms to pay the competitive wage would change the supply curve to a horizontal line at the legal

Table 7–2 Resource Costs for a Monopsony Firm

Quantity of Employment (Q_L)	Wage Rate (w)	Total Resource Cost (TRC)	Marginal Resource Cost (MRC)
1	$1.00	$ 1.00	
2	1.50	3.00	$ 2.00
3	2.00	6.00	3.00
4	2.50	10.00	4.00
5	3.00	15.00	5.00
6	3.50	21.00	6.00
7	4.00	28.00	7.00
8	4.50	36.00	8.00
9	5.00	45.00	9.00
10	5.50	55.00	10.00

minimum, up to the point where it meets the market supply curve. The monopsony firm could hire any quantity of labor shown on the horizontal portion of the supply curve and pay the legal minimum wage. The actual level of employment would determine the total wage bill and the value of total production.

- Use a labor market model to determine the level of employment when a government-imposed minimum wage converts the labor supply curve to a horizontal line over part of its length. Explain your graph.

QUESTIONS

1. Explain various ways by which the minimum wage might work to increase or decrease total employment. Illustrate your explanation graphically.
2. Discuss the implications of the "baby boom" (1947–1961) in terms of worker productivity, the rate of unemployment, the direction of capital investment, the content of Gross National Product.
3. Discuss the pros and cons of a liberal immigration policy for the United States. What are the opportunity costs of enforcing strict limits on immigration?
4. Research the concept of "alienation" described by Karl Marx and show how it relates to work in the United States. What mechanisms are aimed at reducing alienation?
5. What are the advantages and disadvantages of organizations like workers' councils, work teams, and quality circles?
6. Use a labor market model to show the possible effect on wage rates and employment of reducing unemployment compensation. How might such action affect the Phillips curve? Explain your answer.
7. Illustrate graphically each of the minimum wage effects discussed on pages 185–86.
8. Distinguish between the efficiency and incentive effects of wage rates. Explain their significance for resource allocation and equity in the distribution of real income.
9. Consult the *Economic Report of the President* for information about trends in real wages over recent years. Illustrate graphically and explain your findings.

10. Explain the contention that free markets will eliminate unemployment. What factors make U.S. labor markets "not free"? How do these factors affect the Phillips curve?
11. Discuss the relative advantages and disadvantages of public service jobs and public works programs. What are the advantages and disadvantages of job training programs?
12. The text presents one reason unions give for supporting a minimum wage law. Consider the effect of the law on unionized workers and list as many other possible reasons as you can for their support.
13. Debate the proposals for removing the work disincentive effects of unemployment compensation.
14. Diverse changes in the structure of the labor force and the structure of the job market mean that some job seekers will be disappointed even though some jobs remain unfilled. What are some of the costs of *structural unemployment*? What are some of the remedies?

DEFINITIONS

Behavioral scientists study the environmental factors that influence human behavior.

A board of directors is an elected group charged with the responsibility of overseeing policy for a particular corporation.

Cost-of-Living Adjustments (COLAs) are labor contract provisions that guarantee workers an automatic wage adjustment for inflation.

The demand for labor is the quantity of labor that will be hired at various wage rates. A labor demand curve is based on the dollar value of labor's Marginal Product. It slopes downward because Marginal Product tends to decrease as more workers are added to a fixed quantity of capital resources.

Employee Stock Ownership Trusts (ESOTs) are means of encouraging employees to purchase ownership shares in the firms where they are employed.

The equilibrium level of employment is that at which all workers willing to work at the equilibrium wage will be hired.

A fixed cost is a cost that must be paid regardless of the level of operation of a firm.

Frictional unemployment is unemployment that results from movement from job to job. Frictional unemployment is generally short-lived.

Funded pension plans are those in which worker and employer contributions are invested, with the income to be used to pay retirement benefits.

Individual Retirement Accounts (IRAs) are tax-free contributions to a worker's retirement fund. When funds are withdrawn from an IRA, they are taxed at the owner's current tax rate.

Job training programs involve training in the skills needed for satisfactory employment. They may be financed by the federal government or by private firms.

The labor force is the adult population that is employed or seeking employment.

Marginal Resource Cost is the additional cost associated with employing an additional unit of a particular resource.

The minimum wage law requires most employers to pay at least a certain wage to all employees.

A monopsonist is an employer who is the only employer of a certain type of labor. Thus the monopsonist has a monopoly on the demand side of a labor market.

A Phillips curve shows the relationship between the rate of inflation and the level of unemployment.

Public service jobs are jobs in state and local governments, financed at least in part by the federal government.

Public works programs are programs to construct social overhead capital, financed at least in part by the federal government.

Quality circles are groups of workers in a particular firm with the aim of improving product quality.

Real wages are wages adjusted for the effects of inflation. If prices increase faster than current-dollar wages, real wages decline.

Structural unemployment is unemployment that results from differences between the composition of the labor force and the job market.

The supply of labor is the quantity of labor that will be offered for employment at various wage rates. A labor supply curve slopes upward because more labor will be offered at higher wages.

Tax-based income policies are agreements to hold wages to a certain rate of increase in return for certain tax advantages.

Trade associations are organizations of employers in particular industries that are set up to deal collectively with industry problems.

Unemployment compensation is payments to unemployed workers, financed by a tax on employers.

Unfunded pension plans are those in which worker and employer contributions are used to pay retirement benefits directly to retired workers.

Value added is the difference between the value of a firm's product and the cost of materials used to produce it.

The value of Marginal Product is the change in a firm's revenue that results from hiring an additional worker and selling his or her Marginal Product.

Work improvement councils are groups of workers in a particular firm with the aim of improving conditions of work life.

SUGGESTED READINGS

"Are the Unions Dead, or Just Sleeping?" *Fortune*, September 20, 1982, p. 98.

Auld, D. A. L. "In Praise of Markets: Wage Imitation and Price Stability." *Challenge*, September/October, 1982, p. 52

Collins, Lora S. "The Service Economy." *Across the Board*, November, 1980, p. 17.

———. "Straightening Out the Phillips Curve." *Across the Board*, March, 1980, p. 11.

"Concessionary Bargaining." *Business Week*, June 14, 1982, p. 66.

Edson, Lee. "Slaves of Industry." *Across the Board*, July/August, 1981, p. 5.

Feldstein, Martin, ed. *The American Economy in Transition*. Chicago: National Bureau of Economic Research, 1980, Chapter 5.

Fraser, Douglas. "Beyond Collective Bargaining." *Challenge*, March/April, 1979, p. 33.

Johnson, George E. "Do Structural Employment and Training Programs Influence Unemployment?" *Challenge*, May/June, 1979, p. 55.

"Labor Seeks Less." *Business Week*, December 21, 1981, p. 82.

Lubar, Robert. "Why Unemployment Will Hang High." *Fortune*, June 14, 1982, p. 114.

Main, Jeremy. "Work Won't Be the Same Again." *Fortune*, June 28, 1982, p. 58.

Mitchell, Daniel J. B. "Gain-Sharing: An Anti-Inflation Reform." *Challenge*, July/August, 1982, p. 18 and Audrey Freedman, "A Fundamental Change in Wage Bargaining," p. 14.

"The New Industrial Relations." *Business Week*, May 11, 1981, p. 84.

Nollen, Stanley D. "The Changing Workplace." *Across the Board*, April, 1980, p. 6.

Piore, Michael J. "American Labor and the Industrial Crisis." *Challenge*, March/April, 1982, p. 5.

_____. "Unemployment and Inflation: An Alternative View." *Challenge*, May/June, 1978, p. 24.

Ragan, James F., Jr. "The Failure of the Minimum Wage Law." *Challenge*, May/June, 1978, p. 61.

Raskin, A. H. "Can Management and Labor Really Become Partners?" *Across the Board*, July/August, 1982, p. 12.

_____. "From Sitdowns to 'Solidarity.'" *Across the Board*, December, 1981, p. 12.

Reubens, Edwin P. "The Services and Productivity." *Challenge*, May/June, 1981, p. 59.

Seligman, Daniel. "Who Needs Unions?" *Fortune*, July 12, 1982, p. 54.

Simon, Herbert A. "What Is Industrial Democracy?" *Challenge*, January/February, 1983, p. 30.

Staines, Graham L. "Is Worker Dissatisfaction Rising?" *Challenge*, May/June, 1979, p. 38.

Thurow, Lester. *The Zero-Sum Society*. New York: Basic Books, 1980, Chapter 3.

CHAPTER EIGHT

Income Distribution —and Redistribution

How Much Should We Share?

LEARNING OBJECTIVES

- To understand the basis for programs to redistribute incomes and their implications for efficiency and incentives.
- To use a market model to show income paid to a resource, when resource demand is based on marginal productivity.
- To consider Keynesian economic policies and recent questions regarding the efficiency-equality trade-off.
- To examine in detail current programs involving transfer payments and government purchases.
- To show how taxes redistribute income and how federal income taxes offset some of the inequitable effects of state and local taxes.
- To consider the effects of inflation on income distribution.

Imagine three men stranded on a desert island. One is strong and able and sets to work quickly to build a dwelling that is secure from the weather and comfortable for his hours of leisure. The second is not skilled but is able nevertheless to build a crude hut for his own protection. The third is blind and crippled and can build no shelter at all.

To what extent are the castaways responsible for easing the plight of each other? To what extent should the work of one be used to improve the life of another?

Under the circumstances described above, probably the first two would agree to assume a certain responsibility for the welfare of the third. Beyond this, it is not clear that the first would sacrifice the fruits of his own ability and effort to allow the second to live as well as he. When living standards depend on each individual's own personal adaptation to the surrounding environment, there may be no obligation to share one's product with another.

Other circumstances may yield other conclusions. Consider now the movement of the three castaways into a functioning society—a village or a nation with established customs and institutions for regulating social behavior. The joining of large numbers of people together in a group implies the existence of a **social contract.** A social contract is a set of implicit agreements among the people and between the people and their leaders that persons who assume certain responsibilities will receive certain rewards. Rewards may vary along a scale extending from material wealth to social status or political power. The effect of the reward system is to bind together members of the society in a framework that serves the common good. Thus, the social contract builds a kind of civilization in which the actions and interests of any member may at times be restrained in order to serve the interests of the community as a whole.

The precise arrangement of the social framework depends strongly on the ethical judgments of the people, as expressed in their political activity. And it depends also on the objective circumstances of the material environment. Primitive societies did not slaughter female babies because they disliked girl children, nor did they cast elderly people adrift on icebergs because they opposed grandparentage. Rather, their material surroundings were too poor to allow them to care for people who could not contribute to their own support. In such cases, a society's ethical values adjusted to *economic realities* of the environment.

Like any other society, our nation struggles continuously to use our material environment for serving people's needs. We struggle also to determine the ethical or moral justification for what we do. We have some particular advantages and disadvantages in the struggle. An advantage is that we are a *heterogeneous* society — one composed of many different talents, attitudes, skills, and aspirations. Our many differences help us to use our material environment efficiently—allowing some to farm, others to pursue crafts, and some to govern.

Our differences may also pose a disadvantage, in that we tend to disagree broadly on the ethics of what we do. Our heterogeneous society finds it difficult to agree on what policies actually do serve the "common good"— we find it difficult even to *define* the "common good." As individuals, we sometimes resist the restraints on our actions and interests that are intended to serve the interests of the community as a whole.

Production and distribution of goods and services are basic to the welfare of the community. Achieving maximum production depends on achieving maximum efficiency in the use of resources and incentives toward increased productivity. How we distribute goods and services can influence efficiency and incentives. Rewarding workers for efficient production may be expected to stimulate greater effort, shifting upward the production function and improving average living standards. Withholding rewards from unproductive people may have a range of consequences: from encouraging new kinds of productive activity, at one extreme, to gradually eliminating unproductive people through starvation, at the other. (On the other hand, certain kinds of distribution to unproductive people may be regarded as investments in human capital — aids toward development of productive capacity that may eventually reduce the level of dependency in these groups.)

Deciding on the correct policy for income distribution requires consideration of all these efficiency and incentive effects, as well as consideration of our ethical beliefs. In this chapter, we will explore the issue of income distribution and redistribution. First, we will look at recent trends that have raised average living standards while keeping income distribution rather unequal. Then we will discuss the implications of income inequality for increasing total production of goods and services. We will look at government programs that have the effect of redistributing income toward greater equality. We will want to evaluate current programs in terms of their effect on efficiency and incentives. Finally, we will look at two factors that have the effect indirectly of redistributing income: taxes and inflation.

TRENDS IN INCOME DISTRIBUTION

A look at history produces no evidence of public support for massive redistribution of income in the United States. Over the years since World War II (1947–1981) the distribution of earned income to households has remained roughly stable. Still, fairly steady growth of productivity has raised real income such that the percent of the population living in poverty has fallen.

The first important movement toward income equality in the United States occurred during the 1930s and early 1940s. One reason was a substantial increase in government spending. Government spending in the areas of education, agriculture, welfare, and relief increased economic opportunities and relieved the plight of poor people. Another reason was the progressive income tax. High personal exemptions and deductions reduced the tax bills of many low- and middle-income people and contributed to greater income equality. Since World War II, however, government spending has increased only enough to offset the reduced progressivity of the tax structure. Increased use of **tax "loopholes"** has excluded many upper-income families from taxation. At the same time, relatively smaller personal exemptions and the increase in regressive state and local taxes have raised the tax bills of low-income families.

There is a natural tendency for redistributive programs gradually to become rather neutral in their effects. Income taxes levied on one group can often be avoided by having more of income classified as untaxed fringe benefits, by taking advantage of tax "loopholes," and by increasing deductions and exemptions.* In the meantime, governments supplement their tax collections by taxing previously untaxed groups through sales, excise, and property taxes. Government spending programs tend to have a weakening effect on income distribution. Government services are provided first to the most needy groups, thus reducing inequality; but as programs grow and as new groups seek to qualify under various programs, the effect on inequality diminishes.

The second important movement toward income redistribution in the United States began during the administration of President Lyndon Johnson in the 1960s. President Johnson's "Great Society" programs were intended to provide temporary assistance during times of family emergency or financial crisis. It was expected that recipients would soon learn a skill or otherwise restructure their lives so as to move above the **poverty line.** Job programs and community revitalization plans were expected to provide the means for increasing economic opportunity. Many of these expectations were unfulfilled. Poverty was not eliminated, or course, and many participants in vocational training programs were unable to find jobs. Critics charged that Great Society programs were often begun by "do-gooders" with no expertise in administering costly and complex programs. They pointed to examples of waste and fraud in the administration of public funds. True, waste and fraud did occur, but probably no more frequently than it occurs in calculating personal income tax and business expense accounts.

When the Great Society programs began, a poverty standard of $3,000 was set for all families regardless of family size. In 1965, the poverty line was redefined to allow for families of different sizes living in urban and rural settings. The poverty line was set at three times the Department of Agriculture's estimated family food budget and is updated annually to reflect price changes.

About 18 percent of the nation's families earned incomes below the poverty line in 1960: 8 percent of white families and 30 percent of black families. By 1974, only 8.8 percent of families (6.8 percent of white and 26.9 percent of black) were below the official poverty line. Some analysts assert that the gains have actually been greater: that cash and in-kind benefits have actually moved almost all of the nation's families out of poverty. (At the end of 1981, the poverty population had increased again to 11.2 percent: 8.8 percent of white and 30.8 percent of black families.)

It is difficult to separate the effect on poverty of government redistribution programs from the effect of other economic factors. The number of poor families tends to fluctuate with economic activity: prolonged unemployment and the lapse of a worker's unemployment compensation force more families into poverty. This is particularly true of black and female-headed families, who constitute 28 percent and 48 percent, respectively, of the nation's poor (1980). Economic growth, improved education, and antidiscrimination laws and practices contribute much toward equality of opportunity for these groups.

---

*Morgan Reynolds and Eugene Smolensky estimate that the federal tax structure was slightly *regressive* by 1970. "The Fading Effect of Government on Inequality," *Challenge,* July/August, 1978, pp. 32-37.

Figure 8–1

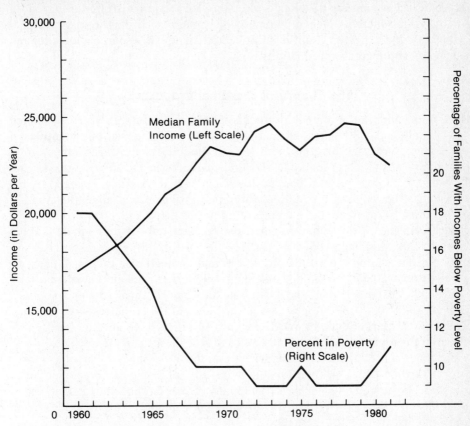

Figure 8-1 shows what has been accomplished in terms of increasing real income and reducing the incidence of poverty in recent decades. The upper line shows the trend in *median* family income in the United States: **median income** is the income of the family in the precise middle of the nation's income scale. Except for recessions, when median income has declined, the median income has increased fairly steadily. The lower line in Figure 8–1 shows the percent of the population below the poverty line. This measure appears to have stabilized at about 9 percent over the last decade.

THEORIES OF INCOME DISTRIBUTION

Theories and judgments about income distribution have changed over time along with changing economic and political circumstances. Writing in the eighteenth century, Adam Smith concentrated on the distribution of income among productive resources: labor, capital, and land. In the nineteenth century, Karl Marx introduced the concept of exploitation to explain the relative income shares of capitalists and workers. Toward the end of the nineteenth century, the **neoclassical economists** developed the theory of income distribution based on marginal productivity. When income is distributed according to marginal productivity, the expected result is improved efficiency in resource allocation and incentives to increase productivity.

The Theory of Marginal Productivity

Remember that Marginal Product is the change in Total Product associated with additional employment of a particular resource. When various quantities of a resource are used together with a fixed quantity of other resources, Total Product tends to increase first at an increasing rate, then at a constant rate, and finally at a decreasing rate. The result is a tendency toward decreasing Marginal Product. The value of a resource's Marginal Product determines the *demand curve* for that resource: the quantities that will be employed at various resource prices. Business firms employ a particular resource only up to the point that the value of its Marginal Product is equal to the cost of hiring the resource.

Resource *supply* depends on natural and demographic circumstances, as well as on available technology and capital resources. Resource owners offer a particular resource up to the point that the pay is equal to the resource's *opportunity cost:* opportunity cost is the value of using the resource in some other way. Market equilibrium determines resource price and the level of resource employment. Look at Figure 8–2 and note these values in the figure. Note also that the product of resource price times quantity employed is total *income* for that resource: Y_R = Total Income = quantity of a resource employed *times* resource price = $Q_R \times p_R$. This is true for any resource. Thus, the total income of labor is $Y_L = Q_L \times p_L = Q_L \times w$. Relative incomes among all resources determine income distribution for the nation.

If all resources were identical, their prices would be equal. If resource owners could adjust resource supplies, shifting supply away from markets with

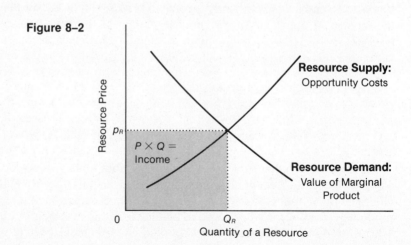

Figure 8–2

Resource Price

p_R

$P \times Q =$ Income

Resource Supply: Opportunity Costs

Resource Demand: Value of Marginal Product

0

Q_R

Quantity of a Resource

low prices and into markets with high prices, income distribution might be precisely equal. We know this does not happen in the real world. Differences in resource productivity make for differences in *demand*—business firms' willingness to pay more or less to employ certain resources. Differences in *supply* arise from particular resource characteristics — skills, location, or function — that cannot be precisely duplicated to take advantage of high demand. The result is substantial differences in resource prices and inequality of income distribution.

In general, the neoclassical economists resisted government programs to distribute income more equally. The reason had to do with the effect of income inequality on efficiency and incentives. Differences in resource prices, they said, encourage business firms to conserve the scarcest resources and to develop additional supplies of the most productive resources. Equality of resource prices would reduce incentives to increase productivity. In their view, forced movements toward income equality could be justified only on social or political grounds.

Imperfect Markets and Market Power

Economists of the twentieth century challenged the Marginal Productivity theory and the view that income inequality was necessary for economic efficiency. According to these critics, differences in resource prices are often caused by imperfections in market adjustments. Resource supplies may be slow to move from market to market, new skills may be slow to develop, and functions may be slow to adapt. Furthermore, owners of particular resources may contrive to create or maintain scarcity in particular markets, excluding competition and prolonging income inequality.

Market imperfections create price and income differentials without at the same time improving efficiency and incentives. In such cases, achieving economic efficiency would require government programs to improve resource mobility, encourage skill development, reduce market power, and, in general, smooth the operation of market forces. By ensuring a wider range of economic opportunities to all the people, government can increase incentives toward greater production.

The Emphasis on Consumption

You may have noticed that the emphasis of the early economists was on *production:* providing the appropriate quantities of resources for producing the maximum quantities of goods and services. By the time of the Great Depression, emphasis on production had given way to emphasis on *consumption*. Resources were readily available; in fact, farms, factories, and labor were idle across the nation. Economists began to wonder if income distribution might be significant for determining how incomes would be spent and, ultimately, whether business firms could operate profitably.

The followers of John M. Keynes concentrated on the distribution of income between consumption and investment. In Keynesian theory, national income (Y)

would depend on total consumer and investment spending (C and I) and the **multiplier effect** (k) of respending current incomes throughout the year. Thus, national income is a function of consumption, investment, and the multiplier effect: $Y = f(C, I, k)$.

In very general terms, Keynesian economists assumed that the income of labor (wages) would be spent for consumer goods and the income of capital (profits) would be spent for new capital investment. This made the allocation of income between wages and profits especially important. The correct share for wages would ensure sufficient spending for new consumer goods. The correct share for capital would ensure new capital equipment for future growth. If the supply of capital were to be too small relative to labor, the share of income to capital would increase, making additional investment possible. On the other hand, if the supply of capital were to be too great relative to labor, the share of income to capital would fall. The share of income to labor would rise and allow consumer spending to increase.

Keynesian economists recommended different government policies, depending on the desired level of current spending for consumption and the need for new investment. Policies to increase the income shares of labor or capital were expected ultimately to benefit both groups. An increasing share for labor would be expected to increase workers' living standards. An increasing share for capital would increase job opportunities and living standards in the future. Government could use tax and spending policies to influence relative shares. Other government policies might be used to offset market imperfections: the use of government regulation, for instance, might be used to enhance the share of either wages or profits.

The Efficiency-Equality Trade-off

The important cornerstones of Keynesian economic policy were progressive income taxes and outlays under various government programs. The effects of both have been to redistribute income from high- to low-income families, stimulating spending for consumer goods and services. Outlays under government redistribution programs have increased substantially in the years since the Great Depression. As more groups have come to enjoy the benefits of redistribution programs, critics have begun to worry about the possible trade-offs between equality of income distribution and efficiency in the use of productive resources.

When rewards are tied to the value of Marginal Product, resource allocation is said to be efficient. Tying rewards to resource productivity also increases incentives toward increased productivity. To the extent that income shares differ from contributions to total output, efficiency and incentives may be harmed. Workers may not be encouraged to develop new skills nor to exercise their skills fully. Other resource owners may not be encouraged to supply additional resources, and total productive capacity may fail to grow. Resource allocation may be affected, too, as business firms substitute capital equipment for workers diverted from private employment by government spending programs.

A general decline in resource productivity during the 1970s aroused public concern about the **efficiency-equality trade-off** and increased opposition to

Keynesian economic policies. Most voters continued to support income redistribution to truly needy families. But public sentiment began to shift away from increasing income equality toward encouraging capital investments that would increase the productivity of the nation's resources.

Some critics continue to complain about income inequality. Even exceptional ability, they say, is generally inherited and is not necessarily earned by its fortunate owner. Nature's rather arbitrary generosity should not be reinforced by public policies, but corrected through programs to redistribute the fruits of success. In fact, to perpetuate the existence of an "underclass" is dangerous and an "abiding insult to the spirit and mood of (our) nation."*

The next section will examine government redistribution programs in detail. As you read, ask yourself to what extent the transfer of real income to particular groups serves to increase efficiency of resource allocation and incentives toward increased productivity. Consider the possibility that the short-run effects of these programs may differ from their long-run effects. Consider also the moral or ethical implications of the various redistribution programs.

PROGRAMS OF INCOME REDISTRIBUTION

Government is involved directly in income distribution in two ways: transfer payments and purchases of goods and services.

Transfer payments include benefits paid through Social Security, Medicare, Aid to Families with Dependent Children (AFDC), unemployment compensation, and food stamps. Some transfer payments are awarded to persons within specific categories regardless of their other income: retirement income and unemployment compensation are examples. Other transfer payments are awarded on the basis of income: AFDC and other welfare and food stamps are examples. It is estimated that about 70 million Americans receive transfer payments of some kind. That number represents nearly one of every three Americans.

Government purchases frequently provide services for particular groups. Government expenditures for veterans' hospitals and farm subsidies are examples. Likewise, Medicaid provides health care for the poor; school lunch and other nutritional programs are aimed at poor families; public housing and housing subsidies provide shelter for the poor. Certain government outlays are actually "negative taxes"; for example, tax exemptions for the elderly are referred to as **"tax expenditures."**

After the end of World War II, the total of government transfer payments and purchases amounted to only about 13 percent of Gross National Product. By 1980, the total was 31 percent. Much of the growth in government outlays relative to GNP has been a result of increases in transfer payments, particularly unemployment compensation, food stamps, and the welfare portion of Social Security.

*Alvin L. Schorr, "Welfare Reform and Social Insurance," *Challenge,* November/December, 1977, pp. 14–22.

The growth of welfare-type transfer payments depends greatly on changes in the level of economic activity. In prosperous years, welfare benefits consume only about 13 percent of total transfers, but in recessions they grow to more than 20 percent. Transfer payments have helped stabilize personal income during recessions, cushioning what would otherwise have been a substantial drop in total spending power for the nation as a whole.

Social Security

The largest transfer program in the United States is the Social Security system begun in 1935. For its first 25 years, Social Security was primarily an insurance program, providing financial protection against certain hazards of life. A person did not have to be poor to qualify for Social Security benefits; one needed only to fall into one of the specific categories covered by the legislation.

Programs directed at specific categories of recipients are called **categorical programs.** Categorical programs under Social Security include separate benefit programs for old age, survivors, disability, and hospital insurance under Medicare. (Medicare consists of two parts, of which hospital payments are provided under Social Security and physicians' payments through general tax revenues.) More than 100 million covered workers and their employers now contribute 6.7 percent of wages up to $35,700 to the Social Security trust fund. At age 65, retired workers receive monthly benefits based on the size of their past contributions. Benefits are weighted to favor low incomes, so that low-income participants recover substantially more than their total contributions, and high-income participants substantially less. Dependent children of deceased workers receive benefits until age 18. Monthly Social Security benefits average about $300 per person or $450 per couple.

Since 1960, two changes have taken place, both of which have increased the cost and the complexity of the Social Security program. One change has been to adjust the structure of benefits to reflect more nearly a person's contributions to the Social Security trust fund. The result of this change has been a relative decline in payments to some groups and a compensating increase in the need for welfare programs: health care, food stamps, and AFDC. Benefits under these welfare programs depend on the recipient's own earned income. This means that social workers must determine whether or not the family is actually in need and withhold aid from persons who can care for themselves. For some welfare recipients, "need" has meant reduced incentives to seek productive employment. "Need" testing has also required a large and costly bureaucracy.

A second change involves the funding of the Social Security system. In the beginning, Social Security was funded like many other pension plans: workers' monthly contributions were invested, and income from investments was used to pay retired workers' benefits. But benefit obligations have tended to grow faster than contributions, so that the trust fund has been depleted. Under its present structure, Social Security is a procedure for transferring income from one generation to another. Moneys collected from working young people are paid directly to dependent elderly people or their survivors and dependents.

Providing adequate Social Security benefits depends on collecting adequate payroll tax revenues from large numbers of productive taxpayers. Currently, the payroll contributions of 3.2 workers and their employers support each beneficiary, a total income transfer that amounts to about $200 billion annually. Early in the next century, "baby boom" retirees will begin to swell the ranks of Social Security beneficiaries. Meanwhile lower birthrates in the 1970s and 1980s will have reduced the number of working contributors to the Social Security fund. The expected result is that each beneficiary will be supported by only three workers and their employers, a major increase in the payroll tax burden. By 1981, the maximum annual Social Security contribution had increased to almost $2,000 per worker (from $375 as recently as 1970).

The payroll tax burden on workers of the twenty-first century may be eased somewhat by incentives to postpone retirement. The result will be to increase contributions paid in and reduce benefits paid out. And, supposedly, capital resources constructed by "baby boom" workers during their productive years will be available for enhancing the productivity of their descendants, thus enlarging the quantity of real income available for redistribution. Finally, slower population growth will mean fewer requirements for education and child care, thus freeing funds for use by the elderly.

Concerns about the long-range health of Social Security have produced various recommendations for change:

1. Social Security insurance benefits could be adjusted to provide adequate retirement income to all covered workers. Persons not covered by Social Security would be guaranteed access to relief through Supplemental Security Income (SSI). Benefit schedules would be adjusted to ensure higher-income workers an adequate return on their past contributions.
2. Welfare and Medicare benefits unrelated to payroll tax contributions could be financed from income tax revenues. Slowing the growth of payroll taxes for Social Security would help hold down increases in labor costs and tend to reduce inflation.
3. Federal and some state and local government employees (not presently covered by Social Security) could be brought into the system. The effect of this change would be to reduce "double dipping" by retired federal employees who have worked briefly in the private sector in order to qualify for Social Security benefits at retirement.
4. Half of a recipient's Social Security benefits could be taxed as income, thus allowing a larger portion of Social Security benefits to flow to retired persons who have no other retirement income.
5. The retirement age could be increased to prolong the period of contributions to the fund and reduce the period of withdrawals. There are some problems with this proposal. Many early retirements are a result of poor health, such that continued employment would be a real hardship. And by working longer, retirees would also earn increased benefits and push the costs of the program up. Finally, longer years of work for the elderly will mean fewer job opportunities for the young.

6. Some changes might be made in the system of spouse's benefits. Instead of providing a dependent spouse one-half the covered spouse's benefits, a married couple could be treated as a single economic unit. Benefits earned by both partners would be considered as having been earned one-half by each, and benefits received would reflect equal participation in the system.

Disability Insurance

Disability insurance was added to Social Security in 1956 and today is one of the fastest growing programs for redistributing income. Liberal definitions of "disability" have enabled claimants to receive benefits for such problems as chronic headaches, "nerves," and lingering depression. Transfer payments under disability insurance are tax free and require no "need" test. Thus, payments may go alike to rich and poor, and there is little incentive for recipients to return to work. The result of generous disability benefits may be a redistribution of income from middle-income working people to healthy, but idle, people.

Supplemental Security Income (SSI) and Relief

Congress established the Supplemental Security Income (SSI) program to replace state and federally financed programs for the elderly poor, the blind, and disabled persons not covered by Social Security. Funds are administered by the Social Security Administration. About 5 million people receive Supplemental Security Income, more than half of whom are elderly and 40 percent are disabled. Monthly benefits average about $200 per person or $300 per couple.

In addition to SSI, state and local governments pay about $1.5 billion annually for general relief to needy families. The cost of relief varies with changes in the level of economic activity.

Aid to Families with Dependent Children (AFDC)

Aid to Families with Dependent Children (AFDC) was established along with Social Security in the 1930s. Financing is shared about equally between the federal government and the states, but benefits vary widely (from a low of less than $100 a month for a family of four in Mississippi to about $450 in New York). Payments may be limited to fatherless families, a restriction that frequently encourages fathers to desert their families.

More than 11 million people receive AFDC, of whom 8 million are children and only about 150,000 are adult men. In general, AFDC mothers are untrained and unskilled; still, about a third work at least part of the year. A full-time job at the minimum wage would still leave a family of four beneath the poverty level. Moreover, for many female heads-of-households, working leads to a reduction in AFDC benefits.

Medicare and Medicaid

Medicare and Medicaid were added to Social Security in 1965. Together, these two health care programs cost more than $40 billion annually and treat almost 40 million people.

Medicare provides hospital insurance to recipients of Social Security and to others who choose to purchase insurance protection. Medicare helps pay hospital costs, rehabilitation care, and related health costs. Participants in Medicare may purchase medical insurance for about $10 a month. Medical insurance helps pay for physicians' services, drugs, X-rays, and home visits.

Medicaid is a program of medical assistance for the poor. It is administered by the states and covers a range of health care needs, including full payment for nursing-home care and for drugs. Almost 100,000 doctors participate in Medicaid, some receiving hundreds of thousands of dollars annually for performing surgery and abortions, delivering babies, and treating patients. Medical laboratories are paid for performing tests, dentists for dental work, hospitals and chiropractors for patient services. Medicaid costs are the least controllable of the two programs, since expenditures are based on the actual price of service rather than set at a fixed amount.

In 1964, before the Medicare and Medicaid programs began, Americans visited physicians an average of 3.8 times a year. Poor people visited physicians an average of 4.7 times a year. By 1978, Americans in general were visiting physicians 5 times a year, and poor people 6.2 times a year. Among poor people, improved health care has brought a decline in infant mortality and lower death rates from influenza, pneumonia, tuberculosis, and diabetes. Among the population as a whole, improved health care has brought an increase in life expectancy — and a further increase in demand for health services.

The relatively fast growth of demand for health care has contributed to faster increases in the prices of health services than of other consumer goods and services. Hospital costs alone have increased about 3 percent faster than the Consumer Price Index. Price increases have the effect of reducing health services for persons not covered by Medicare or Medicaid. Thus, there has been a redistribution of health care resources from providing medical care to the general population to performing services for the poor and elderly. And there has been a redistribution of real income from the general population to those who provide health services.

Food Stamps and Other Nutritional Programs

The nation's food stamp program began in 1961 with federal outlays of less than one million dollars. By 1980, roughly 21 million persons in 5.6 million households were receiving food stamps. This number constitutes about 1 of every 11 persons in the nation. The cost of the food stamp program now runs about $7 billion annually, of which $500 million goes for administration. The program is administered by the Department of Agriculture and consumes about half its annual budget.

Elderly, blind, and disabled persons eligible for Supplemental Security Income are entitled to receive food stamps, as are recipients of other welfare programs. Other families may qualify after passing a "need" test. (If gross income minus estimated costs of child care, shelter, utilities, medical care, and work-related expenses is below the poverty line, the family is eligible.) Twice a year a recipient's food stamp entitlement is adjusted upward to compensate for inflation. Until 1979, food stamps were sold to recipients who redeemed them for an amount of food worth more than their purchase price. The typical food stamp allotment for a family of four is about $200 a month. Only about 60 percent of those eligible for food stamps actually receive them. The average family receiving food stamps contains three persons and has a gross monthly income of about $300. Almost two-thirds of recipient families are headed by females. Fewer than 4 percent of recipient households are headed by students, and striking workers constitute less than half a percent. One in five black households participates in the food stamp program, compared to one in twenty-five white households. About 8 percent of Southern households participate, compared to 6 percent of households nationwide.

Rising unemployment and rising food prices spur increases in the food stamp program. Every time the unemployment rate rises one percentage point, the number of people eligible for food stamps increases by 500,000 to 750,000. Many recipients receive food stamps temporarily to tide them through a family or financial emergency. Since eligibility depends on monthly income, a recipient's annual income may be substantially above the poverty level.

Some critics complain that food stamps are frequently spent for junk food or for nonfood items. Analysts agree that many poor families lack basic information on nutrition and budgeting—and that many have the same poor eating habits as the well-to-do!

The federal government subsidizes breakfasts in the nation's public schools at a cost of about $215 million annually (1978). Only about a fifth of schools participate. The 30-year-old school lunch program costs about $700 million annually. Meals on Wheels provides home-delivered meals to the elderly and disabled.

The federal government's nutritional programs have moved the nation far toward eliminating malnutrition. Not only do they represent transfer payments from taxpayers to low-income recipients, but the benefits of nutrition programs flow also to the agricultural sector, increasing the incomes of food producers.

Student Loans and Other Educational Programs

A variety of student loan programs have been available since 1958. Recipients pay no interest while in school and only 3 to 7 percent after graduation. Still, the default rate on student loans has been about 16 percent, compared with a rate of less than 3 percent on most commercial lending. Some defaults have been associated with vocational schools, some of which were established exclusively to receive borrowed tuition payments. A substantial number of medical and nursing students have also defaulted on student loans.

The Headstart program provides pre-school learning experiences to disadvantaged children. Headstart children have been found to reach higher levels of educational attainment than poor children outside the program. Headstart also provides medical and dental check-ups for needy children.

Impact Aid and Other Community Programs

During World War II, the federal government established Impact aid programs for communities with military installations. The objective was to help pay the cost of services provided to federal employees and their families. Today Impact aid goes to communities with almost any kind of federal facility, regardless of the community's own taxing capability.

Community mental health centers are provided to reduce crowding in state mental hospitals and enable patients to live more normal lives in a neighborhood setting. Often the centers are placed in rundown housing, however, where they are resented and feared by residents of the community.

The federal government provides housing assistance through rent subsidies to families whose rental payments constitute more than 25 percent of income and through grant programs to state and local governments.

Figure 8–3 shows the trends in federal budget allocations for various transfer and purchase programs over recent decades.

An Evaluation and a Proposal

How well do government redistribution programs work? One consideration should be the effect of redistribution programs on the level of living of poor families. When all welfare payments and in-kind services are taken together, small welfare families still fare worse than working families in many states. For families of four, however, total welfare aid may exceed earnings from work at the minimum wage. Some families may receive aid from 10 or 11 programs, while other needy families may receive little or no aid. Many states withhold aid from families unless the father is permanently disabled or missing.

Another consideration is the effect of redistribution programs on work incentives. A ten-year study of the incentive effects of welfare programs was completed in 1978. Under the test program, families in seven states were given a variety of aid and their reactions were measured. Male heads of households receiving aid were found to work 6 percent fewer hours than those not receiving aid. Their wives worked 17 percent fewer hours, and female heads of households 12 percent fewer hours. The work disincentive appeared to be about twice as high for blacks and Hispanics as for whites.

There were other effects on recipient families. Although increased financial security was expected to enhance family stability among aid recipients, their divorce and separation rate was 60 percent higher than among families not receiving aid. On the other hand, many recipients used their aid to seek vocational training or better jobs and eventually earned enough to make them ineligible for further benefits.

President Nixon was the first president to recommend a major change in the nation's programs for redistributing income.* Under his proposal, all poor families would receive a guaranteed income based on what has been called a

*The negative income tax has long been championed by economist Milton Friedman.

Figure 8–3

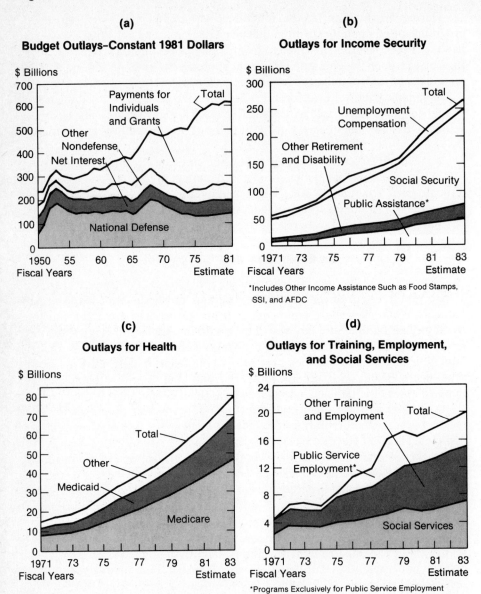

(a)

Budget Outlays–Constant 1981 Dollars

$ Billions

Payments for Individuals and Grants — Total

Other Nondefense

Net Interest

National Defense

1950 55 60 65 70 75 81
Fiscal Years — Estimate

(b)

Outlays for Income Security

$ Billions

Total

Unemployment Compensation

Other Retirement and Disability

Social Security

Public Assistance*

1971 73 75 77 79 81 83
Fiscal Years — Estimate

*Includes Other Income Assistance Such as Food Stamps, SSI, and AFDC

(c)

Outlays for Health

$ Billions

Total

Other

Medicaid

Medicare

1971 73 75 77 79 81 83
Fiscal Years — Estimate

(d)

Outlays for Training, Employment, and Social Services

$ Billions

Other Training and Employment — Total

Public Service Employment*

Social Services

1971 73 75 77 79 81 83
Fiscal Years — Estimate

*Programs Exclusively for Public Service Employment

"negative income tax." A comprehensive NIT program could be administered by the Internal Revenue Service, removing the need for the vast bureaucracy that now administers categorical programs. Consolidating all redistribution programs into a single program with uniform benefits for poor families would probably increase efficiency and reduce waste. Payments could be adjusted to achieve maximum work incentives, while ensuring adequate incomes for those unable to work or lacking marketable skills.

The version of the negative income tax finally adopted by Congress was the **Earned Income Tax Credit.** The Earned Income Tax Credit pays a percentage of earnings to families whose incomes are too low to require them to pay income tax.

In general, transfer payments and government spending programs have the effect of redistributing real income: from workers and taxpayers to dependent persons and social workers, from young people to old people, from one productive sector of the economy to another. Such programs should be evaluated in terms of *net benefits:* total benefits received less total costs paid. The public tends to support programs that achieve maximum social benefits with a minimum of administrative waste. The late economist, Arthur Okun, referred to this concept as a "leaky bucket." Some portion of total benefits transferred, he said, is lost in the transfer from giver to receiver. A certain amount of leakage is inevitable and tolerable. But programs that involve excessive leakage will ultimately lose public support. This means that redistribution programs must continually be evaluated and should be changed or abandoned if benefits fall short of costs.

INCOME REDISTRIBUTION THROUGH THE TAX SYSTEM

Payment of benefits is not the only way to redistribute income. The structure of taxes also has the effect of increasing or decreasing income equality. There are three fundamental kinds of taxes: a tax on what is produced (income tax), a tax on what is consumed (expenditure or sales taxes), and a tax on what is owned (wealth or property taxes). The combination of taxes at all levels of government determines the distribution of *disposable* income and affects resource efficiency and incentives to increase productivity.

The tax structure may be judged also in terms of equity or fairness. A nation's ethical or moral code influences its view of equity. In the view of most U.S. citizens, an equitable tax system has two main features:

1. It requires similar taxpayers to pay similar amounts; this feature is called *horizontal equity.*
2. It shares the tax burden according to ability to pay; this feature is called *vertical equity.*

If persons at the same income level pay the same taxes and if persons with higher incomes pay significantly higher taxes, the tax system is said to be equitable.

In general, state and local governments depend on consumption and property taxes. Consumption taxes impose a relatively heavy burden on low-income families, and property taxes impose a relatively heavy burden on owners and users of real property, regardless of income. Thus state and local taxes tend to violate the second equity feature listed above.

Considerations of equity are less important to state and local governments than collecting the necessary revenues to finance needed public services.

Moreover, state and local policymakers must consider the disincentive effects of taxes on the location decisions of business firms and individual taxpayers. For these reasons, state and local taxes tend to be based on *willingness to pay* (that is *ability to avoid paying*). Sales and property taxes are less easily avoided and, therefore, are the primary source of state and local government revenue.

The federal government depends primarily on income taxes. Income tax rates in the United States are progressive: that is, they take significantly more from high-income families than from low-income families. The effect is to satisfy the second principle of equity above. Also, the federal tax system allows taxpayers to deduct state and local taxes from their taxable income before calculating federal taxes owed. The effect is to equalize the total tax burdens of similar taxpayers across the nation, thus satisfying the first principle above. Hence, through its tax policy the federal government attempts to offset some of the inequitable effects of state and local taxes.

In recent years, the nation's existing tax structure has suffered criticism on the basis of inefficiency. Many critics blame declining productivity growth on the disincentive effects of progressive income taxes. Taxing high incomes at a higher tax rate, they say, discourages work effort and reduces the savings available for new investment. Property taxes, in effect, add insult to injury by taxing savings twice. The result of these disincentives is to distort resource allocation toward greater consumption and slower economic growth. Unless new incentives can be built into the tax structure, lower total production will eventually mean lower living standards for the nation as a whole.

Solving our efficiency and incentive problems might require a shift to new sources of tax revenues: in particular, to a nationwide sales tax.* A nationwide sales tax would tax not what a person *adds to* total production but what he or she *takes out*. Thus, whatever a person *saves* would not be taxed. Leaving savings untaxed would provide more incentive for saving and the means for making new capital investment.

A nationwide sales tax would not necessarily be inequitable, since those who acquire more goods and services would pay more. Rates could even be made progressive, giving greater emphasis to taxpayers' ability to pay. Furthermore, over a taxpayer's lifetime he or she would probably pay the same under a sales tax as under an income tax. (For a very young person, sales tax payments would exceed what the person would have paid as income taxes; then, as a productive working person, income taxes would far exceed sales taxes; finally, as a retired person, sales taxes would again exceed income taxes.)

Certain changes have been made in federal taxes in recent years to reduce taxes on investment income and stimulate savings. Under the capital gains tax, for instance, profits from the sale of productive assets are taxed at less than half the seller's personal tax rate. Also, tax-free Individual Retirement Accounts or IRAs and Keogh plans allow an individual to save from income without paying a tax. Congress has been slow to adopt a nationwide sales tax, however, in part

---

*Most European governments already depend on expenditure taxes, in the form of the Value-Added Tax, or VAT.

because the immediate effect would be a dramatic increase in consumer prices with a new burst of inflation.

INCOME REDISTRIBUTION THROUGH INFLATION

Income redistribution can take place with no apparent transfer at all, through inflation. Disproportionate changes in certain prices and wages may leave particular income classes poorer or richer than before. Consider each of the following income groups in terms of the prices they pay and the incomes they receive. Ask yourself if the resulting pattern of income distribution contributes to increased efficiency and incentives.

The lowest 10 percent of the income scale spends more than 100 percent of their income on necessities (through borrowing or the use of past savings). This makes low-income families particularly vulnerable to price increases on these necessary items. During the 1970s, prices of the four broad categories of necessities rose nearly half again as fast as prices of non-necessities in consumer budgets:

1. *Energy* prices led the way, following the actions of OPEC.
2. *Food* prices responded to rising worldwide food demand, as well as the rising costs of energy used in food cultivation and processing.
3. *Housing* prices were subject both to rising energy costs and to the rising cost of home financing.
4. Prices of *medical care* rose with the rising costs of hospital construction and equipment and with rising physicians' fees.

Rising prices for these items have worsened living standards for many poor families, as wages have failed to keep up with inflation. On the other hand, the very poorest of this group have access to Social Security benefits, food stamps, and other government programs that increase automatically with inflation. Moreover, since rental costs tend to lag behind other necessities, renters escape some of the inflation in housing costs.

The middle 70 percent of the nation's income scale spends about 70 percent of income on the four basic necessities. Purchase of basic necessities cannot generally be postponed. When their prices rise, middle-income families must either cut back other nonessential spending or increase their borrowing. On the other hand, home mortgage costs are fixed and represent relatively less of the budget of these families as inflation worsens. Moreover, middle-income families' share of national income tends to rise and fall with changes in total employment and total spending. The result is to help protect these families against inflation.

The top 20 percent of the income scale spends only about half of income on necessities, suffering less from the effect of inflation. On the other hand, incomes within this group may be strongly affected by inflation. A larger portion of income in this group comes from ownership of property: bonds, stocks, and other real or financial assets. Interest on bonds tends to rise with inflation, but inflation reduces the current market value of bonds as well as the real value of the bond at maturity. Moreover, interest earnings are taxed as personal income, so that the net result of inflation for bondholders may be a loss. The real value of stock dividends tends to fall with inflation because corporate profits (and taxes on corporate profits) are distorted by artificially low deductions for depreciation.* Rental income on real property tends to lag behind inflation. Finally, federal income taxes for this group tend to increase faster than inflation. This is because exemptions and deductions from taxable income are generally constant, so that inflated incomes are taxed at higher rates. All these different effects make it difficult to state precisely the effect of inflation on income distribution. It may be true that the effects of inflation differ between families within a single income group about as much as they differ between groups.

The effect of inflation on income distribution might depend more fundamentally on whether or not inflation is *expected*. People who expect inflation may be able to adjust their incomes and expenditures to protect against it. Buyers of financial assets may add an inflation premium to the guaranteed dividend or interest return on a new stock or bond. Owners of rental property may include an inflation adjustment clause in property leases. Home mortgage lenders may require that mortgage interest payments vary with inflation. All families may attempt to purchase durable goods in advance of expected price increases. In general, it is those who inadequately predict inflation, or who are unable to adjust for it, that are harmed most.

Some Conclusions and Recommendations

The status of the United States in the world community depends greatly on our economic success — on our ability to use our resources and to apply technology efficiently to produce goods and services. Our status also depends on the equity of our system: the fairness with which we distribute the benefits and costs associated with our economic growth. Occasionally, we find that success in achieving economic growth conflicts with our notions of equity. When this happens, we must choose the proper balance between emphasis on economic goals and emphasis on equity. In a sense, we must decide the proper combination of ethical and material considerations for maintaining our nation's status in the world community.

It is important not to exaggerate the trade-off between material and ethical goals, however. We began this text with a review of Adam Smith's projections of life under the market system. Remember that Adam Smith saw economic growth as a means toward improved equity. Material prosperity would enhance the prospects for fairness in the distribution of income and wealth. Thus, achieving economic success can help achieve our ethical goals as well.

---

*Corporations may deduct a portion of the initial cost of buildings and equipment from gross income over a certain number of years, thus reducing their taxable income and their tax bill. Inflation makes replacing buildings and equipment more costly, however, so that deductions for depreciation tend to be lower and tax bills higher than justified by real costs of production.

Further, Adam Smith emphasized that the econor
nity as a whole would depend to a large degree on the
Enhancing the productive capacities, the incentives,
smallest units of the society would be essential for
whole.

Special Case

Global Income Redistribution

The distribution of income among nations has some of the same implications as income distribution within a single nation. The system for global income distribution could improve efficiency and incentives and raise production possibilities for the world. Or income distribution could destroy incentives and retard development of productive capacity. Programs to redistribute global income may have positive or negative effects on productivity, both in the short and the long run.

During the 1960s, rising incomes enabled many industrialized nations to increase their aid to nations of the "fourth world"—the poorest nations with GNP averages of less than $370 per capita per year. Foreign aid was the means by which nations like India were helped to increase their agricultural production and move toward self-sufficiency in food.

By the 1970s, slower income growth in industrialized nations had reduced the flow of foreign aid. Currently, most foreign aid consists of bilateral cash grants, food, loans at less than market rates, and multilateral aid from the World Bank, regional development banks, and the United Nations. A United Nations goal for foreign aid has been 0.7% of a nation's Gross National Product. Noncommunist industrialized nations allocate an average of 0.35 percent of GNP to foreign aid; the United States contributes 0.20 percent. In real terms, the $7.7 billion the United States allocated for foreign aid in 1982 was less than half the amount contributed in 1955. Analysts at the World Bank estimate that only a third of the 17 billion dollars of foreign aid provided annually goes to the poorest nations. Most of U.S. aid goes to military clients like Israel, Egypt, Turkey, and Pakistan.

What makes entire nations poor? Poverty creates social and biological conditions that prevent improvement and perpetuate poverty. John Kenneth Galbraith has described a self-reinforcing process that causes economic stagnation:

1. With income low, saving and investment are virtually impossible.
2. Health, education, and technology are low and birth rates are high.
3. Land is scarce and held under social arrangements that are hostile to mass improvement.

According to Galbraith, the way out of poverty can be accomplished either by trauma or by education. Trauma involves famine, political oppression, or military force and is less preferred than education. Free and compulsory education can relieve the frustration and hopelessness associated with poverty and plant the seeds of industrialization.*

*John Kenneth Galbraith, *The Nature of Mass Poverty.* Cambridge, Mass: Harvard University Press, 1979.

r nations have broken the self-perpetuating cycle of poverty in other ways. pment of a cash crop, like rubber or cocoa, has enabled Asian and African nations crease income, accumulate savings, and invest in productive capital. European ustrialization during the 1800s was accomplished without widespread education. The ference between these experiences and today's problem nations involves centuries of economic and social progress, which laid the foundation for material growth.

In the fall of 1981, 22 developing and industrialized nations met in Mexico to discuss proposals for correcting the problem of poverty in poor nations. Poor nations were seeking cooperation in areas including food, energy, international lending, and trade. Participants included:

- *Industrialized Nations:* United States, Great Britain, Japan, West Germany, Canada, France, Austria, and Sweden.
- *Poor Nations:* Brazil, China, Guyana, Ivory Coast, Philippines, Saudi Arabia, Venezuela, Mexico, Algeria, India, Nigeria, Tanzania, Yugoslavia, and Bangladesh.

As was true in the past, migration is an important means of economic progress: it moderates population pressure on limited resources and increases opportunities for highly motivated workers.

QUESTIONS

1. Explain the basis for the diminishing progressivity of the U.S. tax structure over the years.
2. Consult the latest *Statistical Abstract of the United States* for recent data on the characteristics of the nation's poverty population. Illustrate graphically some trends in the incidence of poverty.
3. Discuss the merits of suggested recommendations for changes in Social Security.
4. What are the unintended side-effects of AFDC programs and how might they be corrected?
5. Discuss the merits of nutritional and educational programs for the poor. What are their disadvantages?
6. What factors make it difficult to measure precisely the redistribution effects of inflation?
7. Under what circumstances would incomes be equal under marginal productivity theory? How do the neoclassical economists regard the inequality that actually results?
8. What sorts of income policies would be recommended by followers of Adam Smith?
9. What changes in the theory of income distribution arose from circumstances of the Great Depression? How were these changes significant for economic policy?
10. As income support programs grow and include more groups, what are the likely effects on the psychology of recipients? How might such effects be favorable or unfavorable for the nation's long-range economic health? Discuss.
11. Debate the arguments for and against replacing income taxes with a nationwide sales tax.

DEFINITIONS

Categorical programs are aid programs for persons in particular categories of need.

The Earned Income Tax Credit is a payment to persons whose earned income is too low to require them to pay income tax. The credit is some fraction of the difference between earned income and a specified level of income.

The efficiency-equality trade-off refers to the expected loss in efficiency that results from programs that increase income equality.

Government purchases are expenditures for goods and services to be used by certain groups of the population.

The median income is the income of the family precisely in the middle of the nation's income scale.

The multiplier effect is the effect on a nation's income when an initial increase in spending is respent many times.

"Need" testing refers to certain low income standards that must be met if persons are to receive government benefits.

The neoclassical economists developed the Marginal Productivity theory of income distribution. They began their influence around the end of the nineteenth century.

The poverty line is officially defined as three times the cost of a nutritionally sound diet. The poverty line varies for rural and urban families and for families of different sizes. It is updated yearly to account for inflation.

A social contract is a set of implicit agreements to accept certain restrictions on one's behavior and receive certain rewards in return. A system of restrictions and rewards is essential for a healthy community.

Tax expenditures is a name given to negative taxes for certain groups.

Tax "loopholes" are legal ways to reduce taxes by taking certain actions approved by Congress. Some examples are the deduction from taxable income of mortgage interest payments and a lower tax rate on capital gains.

The theory of Marginal Productivity explains income distribution in terms of a resource's contribution to total production.

Transfer payments are payments made by government to persons in particular groups. Some examples are Social Security benefits to retired persons, Medicaid payments to poor persons, and farm subsidies to farmers.

SUGGESTED READINGS

Aaron, Henry. "Advisory Report on Social Security." *Challenge,* March/April, 1980, p. 12
———. "A Debate on Social Security, 2." *Across the Board,* July, 1980, p. 241.
———. "Social Security Can Be Saved." *Challenge,* November/December, 1981, p. 4.
Breckenfeld, Gurney. "Has Reagan Hurt the Poor?" *Fortune,* January 24, 1983, p. 77.
Capra, James R., et al. "Social Security: An Analysis of Its Problems." *Federal Reserve Bank of New York Quarterly Review,* Autumn, 1982, p. 1.
Coe, Richard D. "Welfare Dependency: Fact or Myth?" *Challenge,* September/October, 1982, p. 43.
Ehrbar, A. F. "Heading for the Wrong Solution." *Fortune,* December 13, 1983, p. 113.

Feldstein, Martin, ed. *The American Economy in Transition*. Chicago: National Bureau of Economic Research, 1980, Chapter 6.

Guzzardi, Walter, Jr. "Who Will Care for the Poor?" *Fortune*, June 28, 1982, p. 34.

Juster, F. Thomas. "Social Security Entitlements: The Economics and the Politics." *Economic Outlook USA*, Survey Research Center, University of Michigan, Autumn, 1982, p. 82.

———. "Social Security, Private Savings, and All That." *Economic Outlook USA*, Survey Research Center, University of Michigan, Autumn, 1980, p. 81.

Keeley, Michael, and Philip, Robins. "Work Incentives and the Negative Income Tax." *Challenge*, March/April, 1979, p. 52.

Morrison, Peter A. "Demographic Links to Social Security." *Challenge*, January/February, 1982, p. 44.

Rasmussen, David W. *Urban Economics*. New York: Harper & Row, 1973, Chapters 3 and 4.

Reuss, Henry S. "Inequality, Here We Come." *Challenge*, September/October, 1981, p. 49.

Robertson, A. Haeworth. "A Debate on Social Security, 1." *Across the Board*, June, 1980, p. 32.

CHAPTER NINE

Keeping Americans Well: The Health Care Industry

Who Should Pay?

LEARNING OBJECTIVES

- To consider the usefulness of benefit/cost analysis in questions involving provision of health care.
- To describe trends in health care, including especially the growth in private insurance programs and government health care programs.
- To use a market model to illustrate efficiency in the production of health services and the implications of externalities and third parties in the health sector.
- To examine cost trends in the health sector along with some of the reasons for rising costs and some policies for reducing costs.

Probably the most important person in the emergency room of a large metropolitan hospital—as important in many ways as the neurosurgeon, anesthesiologist, or radiologist—is the "triage nurse." The triage nurse may never treat a patient at all. He or she is there solely to allocate emergency room facilities among patients so as to yield the greatest total benefits: providing immediate care for some and deferring attention to others, and merely making others as comfortable as possible while they, inevitably, die.

These decisions are difficult, of course. Imagine a natural disaster that destroys homes and offices, disrupts transportation and communication facilities, creates havoc with public utilities. Hundreds of victims will be brought to emergency rooms for treatment of burns, crushed limbs, neurological damage, and unimaginable trauma. Without quick medical attention some will die, others will die in spite of heroic efforts to save them, and some will survive with little care at all. The triage nurse establishes priorities and rations out the hospital's limited resources to achieve maximum efficiency.

Few of us would envy the job of the triage nurse. But in a real sense, we practice triage all the time. Through our votes we influence the allocation of our nation's health care facilities, choosing the groups who will have free access to care and those who must survive or die without it. Although the choices are made in committee rooms and legislative sessions, the results are every bit as critical as the decisions of the triage nurse.

Deciding on the allocation of health care resources requires analysis similar to other economic decisions: that is, measurement of benefits and costs. Objectively applying benefit/cost analysis to human suffering is not easy. It is acceptable only because the available supply of health care resources is limited. Under such circumstances, the denial of extraordinary care in one case can greatly improve the quality of life for many others.

THE EVOLUTION OF HEALTH CARE IN THE UNITED STATES

In 1929, total expenditures for health care in the United States absorbed less than 4 percent of Gross National Product and amounted to $26 per year for each American citizen. Of each health care dollar spent, 88¢ was paid directly by the recipient of care. Over the next half century, health expenditures grew to absorb 8 percent of GNP. Annual per capita health care costs increased to about $500, of which only a third is paid by the user.* Federal, state, and local governments now pay 40 percent of health care costs, and private insurance plans pay about 25 percent.

Private health insurance plans collect premiums amounting to more than $50 billion a year. More than 190 million Americans have insurance coverage for their hospital and/or doctor bills; and 1,500 insurance firms, employing 900,000 people, compete for their business. Unions, health care organizations, and some corporations also provide health insurance. The largest private providers of health insurance are Blue Cross and Blue Shield. Blue Cross was established by the hospital industry and Blue Shield by medical societies to cover hospital and physicians' costs, respectively. It is estimated that 24 million Americans have no insurance at all, and another 20 million have inadequate coverage. At the other

---

*In constant dollars of 1929, the $500 figure is about $100, for a real increase of almost 3 percent annually.

extreme are those Americans who seek 100 percent coverage. Premium charges on 100 percent coverage are particularly high.

The federal government entered the health care field in the 1930s when Congress established the National Institute of Health and the National Cancer Institute. The role of these organizations was to conduct, finance, and coordinate research into the causes and cures of disease. During the next several decades, other institutes were established for other areas of biomedical research. Beginning with the Hospital Survey and Construction Act of 1946, federal money was paid to states for building and modernizing hospitals (the Hill-Burton Program). The Health Professions Educational Assistance Acts of 1963 and 1964 and Health Manpower Acts of 1971 and 1974 provided funds for schools and students in the health professions.

The culmination of several decades of increasing federal involvement in health care came in 1965 with establishment of Medicare and Medicaid. Medicare provides two kinds of health care to elderly and disabled persons and sufferers of chronic kidney disease: (1) hospital care financed by a payroll tax on workers and employers, and (2) physician and outpatient care financed by monthly premiums. Like private insurance plans, Medicare requires **deductibles** and **copayments**: a deductible is the amount the beneficiary must pay before receiving care; a copayment is a certain percentage of costs above some stated level that must be paid by the beneficiary. Currently, Medicare covers around 30 million people and pays an average of 45 percent of their total health expenses.

Medicaid provides free health care to the poor, blind, and disabled and to welfare families with dependent children. Medicaid replaced a variety of programs through which the federal government formerly assisted the states in financing medical care for the welfare population. Through Medicaid, states offer hospital, physician, and nursing home care free of charge. They share the cost with the federal government, whose share varies from 50 to 80 percent, depending on per capita income in the state. Medicaid coverage varies among persons and locations such that only about 50 to 60 percent of the nation's poor are covered at any one time.

Other federal-state programs provide maternal and child care, veteran and dependent care, and disease prevention services. Still, the following groups are not covered by any public health programs:

- Widows under age 65 and other nonelderly single persons.
- Most two-parent families.
- Families with a father working at a low-paying job.
- Families with an unemployed father (in 26 states) and families with an unemployed father receiving unemployment compensation (in other states).
- Medically needy families (in 21 states). Medically needy families are families with incomes too high to qualify them for welfare aid but too low to cover their medical expenses.
- Women pregnant with their first child (in 27 states).
- Children of non-AFDC poor families (in 36 states).

In 1965, before Medicare and Medicaid were instituted, the federal government spent $5 billion (4.4 percent of its total budget) on health care services. The federal government's health costs rose to $51.6 billion in 1980, almost 10 percent of total federal outlays. About half of this amount goes for Medicare and a fourth goes for Medicaid. The increase in federal health care outlays is in part a result of a higher level of inflation in medical costs than in other prices and in part a result of increasing benefits and extending benefits to more people. The result has been a 12 percent annual increase in real outlays for federal health care programs. Other sources of cost increases are the following:

- Federally sponsored research has increased to about 60 percent of total medical research.
- Federal outlays for training provide 15 percent of medical schools' revenues.
- Improved health care has lengthened life and increased the portion of the population eligible for Medicare.
- Although about a fourth of those eligible for Medicaid fail to enroll, the number of beneficiaries has increased substantially.
- Outlays per enrollee have increased, particularly among the poor, who frequently require more health services than middle-income people.
- Hospital costs have increased about 12 percent per year through additional lab tests, intensive care units, open-heart surgery, and other advanced medical procedures.

Figure 9–1 shows changes in recent decades in the portion of health costs paid by various parties. Note especially the substantial increase in payments by private insurance and government and the decline in direct payments and philanthropy. When the total volume of health care payments is corrected for inflation, the result is a sixfold increase over the period shown.

Public medical assistance programs have had remarkable success.* Whereas poor people formerly neglected health care or depended on private charity, improved access to health care has helped prevent or reduce the severity of disease. By the mid-1970s, poor children were visiting physicians almost as frequently as high-income children. Low-income pregnant women were seeking medical care almost as early in pregnancy as high-income women. Infant mortality declined 33 percent in the first decade of Medicaid, and infant deaths from influenza, pneumonia, and gastrointestinal disease declined 50 percent. Death rates of young children declined 14 percent, and age-adjusted death rates for the entire population declined 10 percent. Life expectancy for the population as a whole has risen to 73.2 years, up from 70.9 years in 1970.

There are still weaknesses in the system, of course. The health needs of the poor continue to exceed those of other groups, and many poor are denied access.

*Karen Davis, *Achievements and Problems of Medicaid*, Brookings General Series Reprint #318, Washington, D.C., 1977.

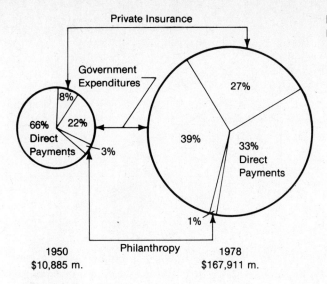

Figure 9–1
Health care payments.

Blacks, in particular, continue to experience higher incidence of elevated blood pressure, higher infant mortality, and higher death rates from diabetes, malignancies, and cardiovascular disease.

FREE MARKETS AND MARKETS FOR HEALTH CARE

The United States relies upon free markets to allocate resources according to the priorities of its people. Markets bring buyers of goods and services together with sellers. Figure 9–2 shows how decisions in free markets help to ensure efficiency in the use of scarce resources. The horizontal axis measures quantity of output, and the vertical axis measures the additional benefits and costs associated with quantities on the horizontal axis.

Market demand for the good or service is shown as the downward sloping curve, marked *MB*. Demand reflects the willingness of buyers to pay a certain price for a certain quantity of a good or service. The willingness of buyers depends on the additional benefits the buyer expects to enjoy from acquiring an additional unit. The additional benefits associated with a good or service are called *marginal utility*. Buyers will pay a price proportional to the expected marginal utility from acquiring the good or service.

A market demand curve slopes downward because of the **principle of decreasing marginal utility**. This is the principle that states that the more you have of a particular good or service the less are the added benefits from acquiring another unit. Decreasing marginal utility means that buyers are willing to buy more of a good or service only if its price is lower.

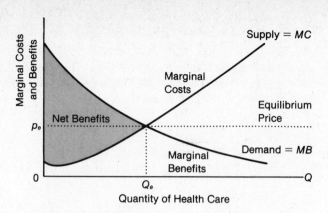

Figure 9-2
Free markets allocate resources efficiently.

Market supply is shown in Figure 9-2 as the upward sloping curve, marked *MC*. Supply reflects the willingness of sellers to provide a certain quantity at a certain price. The willingness of sellers depends on marginal costs. Marginal costs measure the added cost of producing an additional unit. Sellers will require a price that compensates for the marginal cost of producing the good.

A market supply curve slopes upward because of the **principle of increasing marginal costs**. This is the principle that states that producing larger quantities with some constant quantity of fixed resources eventually requires higher costs. Increasing marginal costs mean that sellers will require a higher price for producing larger quantities.

The interaction between market demand (*MB*) and market supply (*MC*) determines the market equilibrium price (p_e) and the equilibrium quantity (Q_e) of a good or service that will be sold. The equilibrium price is satisfactory to buyers because it reflects the value of expected benefits from acquiring the good or service. It is satisfactory to sellers because it reflects the added costs of production.

Total benefits (ΣMB) associated with any quantity of output are shown in Figure 9-2 as the area under the demand curve at that quantity. Total costs (ΣMC) are the area under the supply curve. Producing at Q_e yields total benefits equal to the entire area under the *MB* curve at Q_e; total costs are the area under the *MC* curve. The difference between the two areas is net benefits: **net benefits** $= \Sigma MB - \Sigma MC =$ the excess of total benefits over costs. Net benefits are greatest at Q_e, where $MB = MC$. Beyond Q_e, the area between *MB* and *MC* is negative, indicating that further production for this market would have the effect of reducing net benefits.

Free markets are said to be *efficient*: that is they allocate resources so as to achieve maximum net benefits. Equilibrium price equal to both marginal benefits and marginal costs means that resources are used for producing the things people want. Equilibrium quantity where $p = MB = MC$ means that precisely the right quantity is being produced. (One additional unit would cost more to produce than the value of its expected added benefits.) Therefore, the allocation of resources to a particular market is neither too great nor too small.

Free markets also produce *incentives*: that is, they encourage buyers and sellers to do desirable things. They encourage buyers to conserve—to use only the quantity of a good or service that yields positive net benefits. They encourage sellers to produce larger quantities of goods that yield positive net benefits. Together, these two characteristics of free markets can help achieve maximum total production of wanted goods and services.

Ethics and Externalities

Free markets have certain advantages over and above the advantages of efficiency and incentives. Free markets are devoid of ethical considerations.* They depend solely on the subjective judgment of buyers and the objective conditions of technology. This means that they allow buyers the maximum freedom to choose the allocation of their incomes, and they allow sellers the maximum freedom to choose the allocation of their resources. Neither buyers nor sellers are required to consider the moral or ethical implications of their choice. A free market system does not enforce a particular kind of moral choice on its people.

The amorality of free markets is appropriate for many buying and selling decisions.† Freely allocating resources according to individual choice yields production of such items as clothing, recreation and entertainment equipment, vehicles, and home appliances. Industries that produce these goods prosper by satisfying widely differing consumer tastes with widely differing production technologies. As our economy has developed and matured, however, material goods have become relatively less significant in consumer choice. The greater ease with which we now satisfy our material needs has made it possible to choose nonmaterial uses for available resources: for example, to produce health services for ourselves and others.

Decisions involving health care are not easily accomplished in free markets. One reason is the amoral character of markets. When buying and selling decisions involve life and death, ethical considerations inevitably intrude. Our ethical standards require us to evaluate the result of market decisions in terms of *equity*. We want to ensure that the allocation of health care resources is equitable, or fair.

Another consideration in the market for health care involves *externalities*. When producing a particular good or service brings added benefits to persons other than the buyer, we say that production yields external benefits, or positive externalities. Consider, for example, the broader social benefits associated with

---

*Free markets do involve ethical considerations in the sense that our value system regards free markets as generally fair, and therefore ethical.

†Amorality is not the same as immorality. Amorality means "without moral considerations," while immorality means "opposed to accepted moral standards."

immunizations against smallpox. The added benefits to a single buyer are not nearly as great as the benefits to all of that person's neighbors (whose risk of contagion is reduced). When there are externalities, the benefits of health care to an individual buyer may yield additional benefits to the society as a whole.

Our nation's great wealth enables us to consider the equity and externalities associated with allocation of health care resources. Consideration of equity and externalities requires us to make collective decisions about the price and quantity of health care. Our great wealth does not enable us to eliminate death, however, so we must choose the level of health care (and a corresponding level of ill health or death) that satisfies our ethical as well as our economic standards. The resulting price and quantity of health care services should be *efficient* — achieving maximum net benefits — and *equitable* — satisfying our moral obligations to our fellow men.

"Third Parties" in the Market

There is another fundamental difficulty with free market approaches to health care. Free markets depend on individual decisions as reflected in buyers' demand curves and sellers' supply curves. Since World War II, health care markets have come to be strongly influenced by **third parties** such as private insurance plans that pay almost a third of health care costs, and government programs that pay another 40 percent. The average consumer pays only about 30¢ of each health care dollar, with the result that the marginal cost of health care to individual buyers is much lower than the actual cost of producing the service.

A dashed line has been added to Figure 9–3 to reflect the lower payments actually charged to consumers.* The result of lower payments is a substantial increase in the equilibrium quantity of health care services. Thus, the effect of "third party" payments by private insurance or government is to shift the allocation of resources strongly toward increased production of health services. At the same time, the true costs of production are higher, as shown on the original *MC* curve.

There is another "third party" in the health care decision—the physician. Physicians are strongly motivated to provide the best care for their patients, to perform laboratory tests, utilize the most modern equipment, and seek the most specialized medical advice. Prolonging a patient's life frequently becomes a physician's primary objective, regardless of the cost. A dashed line has been added to Figure 9–4 to show the effect of physicians' demand for increased health care services. The result is another substantial increase in the equilibrium quantity of health care services.

To many physicians, life itself yields benefits worth achieving. Whether or not the life preserved is meaningful does not normally affect their recommendations. A physician's emphasis on preserving life (whatever the quality of

---

*Higher costs must ultimately be paid by consumers, of course, in the form of higher insurance premiums or higher taxes to finance public health programs.

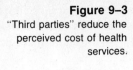

Figure 9–3
"Third parties" reduce the perceived cost of health services.

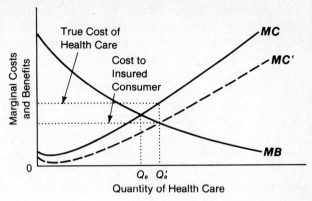

Quantity of Health Care

Figure 9–4
Physicians increase the perceived benefits of health services.

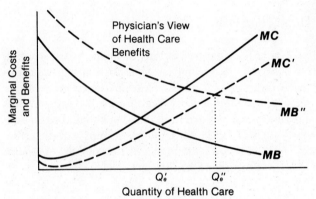

Quantity of Health Care

that life) would yield a relatively flat MB'' curve: that is, keeping more people alive longer would always yield added benefits. Some physicians are now beginning to question this assumption. They recognize that prolonging life for some patients may merely prolong suffering, while at the same time consuming resources that could greatly improve the lives of basically healthy people.

Finally, some physicians prescribe added health care services to patients in order to avoid a possible malpractice suit, in case the patient's condition worsens or the patient dies. All these factors work to lengthen and shift upward the curve representing the demand for health care services.

The Consequences

What is the effect of these circumstances on market efficiency and incentives? An upward shift in MB (to MB'') and a downward shift in MC (to MC') pushes the equilibrium level of health care services beyond equilibrium at Q_e. Production beyond Q_e yields negative net benefits so that the true marginal costs of health care are greater than the additional benefits received. Therefore, the allocation of resources to this market exceeds the efficient quantity. Incentives are harmed, too. The artificially low cost of health services discourages conservation; buyers are encouraged to purchase excessive quantities of the service. On the other hand, the high prices actually paid to suppliers of health services encourage excess production for this market.

Allocating too many of the nation's productive resources to the health sector has the effect of reducing production elsewhere in the economy. As a result, total production of goods and services in the economy as a whole is less than it might be otherwise. This is not necessarily a regrettable result. It is regrettable only if the loss of goods *not* produced exceeds the gains from improved equity and enhanced positive externalities from the production of health services. Judgments about the value of equity and externalities are difficult and imprecise and depend on the particular ethical standards of those making the judgments.

HEALTH CARE COSTS

Increasing the quantity of health care services has brought on substantial increases in costs. Figure 9–5 shows increasing medical costs along with increases in the Consumer Price Index for all items. Note the rapid increase in medical costs since the mid-1960s, when federal health care programs were established. Part of the cost increase can be attributed to rising hospital costs and part to the rising cost of health insurance. The following sections will describe cost behavior in each of these areas. Then we will look at the rising cost of health personnel, along with some efforts to reduce health care costs.

Hospitals

While physicians have been demanding more health services and public and private insurance plans have been financing the costs, hospitals have responded normally to market incentives.

Hospitals can earn more revenue by serving more patients. More patients come from increasing the number of physicians on the hospital's staff. Therefore, competition for staff doctors is vigorous. Many hospitals compete for staff doctors by providing the most advanced equipment and services possible. As a result, highly specialized medical equipment is made available by most hospitals, whether or not their normal patient load would justify the investment.

Duplication of equipment is wasteful and costly, since a few patients in any single hospital must assume costs that would normally be spread over a much larger volume. It has been asserted that Southern California hospitals own more CAT scanners (at a cost of $700,000 each) than the whole of England (where they were invented). Former President Carter's Secretary of Health, Education, and Welfare Joseph Califano estimated that there are at least 130,000 excess beds in the nation's 7,000 hospitals, costing as much as $2 billion a year.

Labor costs constitute almost half of hospital costs. Hospitals provide the staff for carrying out physicians' orders, for operating intensive care units and

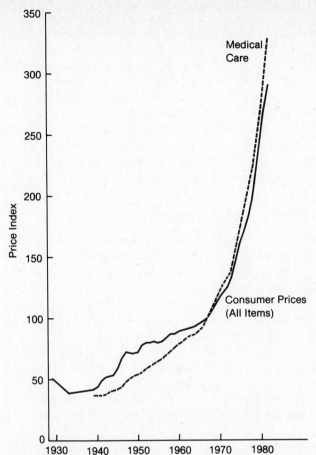

Figure 9–5
The escalating costs of health care.

performing coronary bypass surgery, therapy and rehabilitation services, and organ transplants. Patients tend not to question procedures ordered by their physicians, routinely performed by their hospitals, and paid for by someone else. The result is that some hospital services may be performed beyond the point where they are needed, at costs running into the tens of thousands of dollars. Sophisticated new medical procedures require highly skilled and costly technicians. Moreover, a rising minimum wage and rising wage demands of hospital unions are raising the costs of unskilled and semiskilled hospital workers.

In 1977, Congress was considering a hospital cost containment bill that would have held hospital price increases to 9 percent annually. In part to forestall passage of the bill, many hospitals held down their spending, postponing modernization and improvements until the threat of price controls had passed. Then, in 1980, increased capital expenditures and sharply rising labor and material costs pushed the average cost of a hospital room to more than $200 a day. Many hospitals increase their charges for regular patients to offset their losses on government-financed Medicare patients.

Health Insurance

Most private health insurance is provided through a person's place of employment.* Rising health care costs are pushing up premium rates for private health insurance by as much as 15 percent a year. Higher premium costs for employers mean smaller wage increases for employees. In fact, General Motors paid $1.4 billion for health benefits in 1979—an amount equal to $2,300 for each employee or $200 for every GM auto produced that year.

Some business firms encourage better health habits among employees through company gyms, dieting and antismoking seminars, and stress clinics. Others save money by setting up self-insurance plans that monitor workers carefully and discourage excessive insurance claims.

Health Care Personnel

The largest share of health care costs is the portion paid to health personnel. A scarcity of health personnel can have the effect of reducing competition and raising prices. Increasing the quantity of health personnel can help reduce the cost of health services and increase efficiency.

The following sections describe market conditions for the three largest groups of health professionals. As you read, consider the probable effect of trends in resource supply on the costs of health care.

Physicians. The number and size of medical schools in the United States grew considerably over the 1970s, such that the number of physicians grew more than 3 times faster than the population as a whole. The ratio of physicians to total population has increased from 156 for every 100,000 people in 1966 to about 200 per 100,000 in 1980.

Whereas we would expect that increasing the supply of a resource would drive its price down, this has not happened in the medical field. In fact, the increase in the supply of physicians has had the effect of increasing demand for their services. One reason is the fact that consumers have little control over demand for medical care. Once a consumer makes the decision to visit a physician, the physician generally makes all further decisions for tests, drugs, hospital treatments, and surgical procedures without weighing the costs. The increase in the number of medical specialists has increased the number of patient referrals, so that demand for services has increased even further. Health economists estimate that each new physician entering the market creates from $150,000 to $350,000 in additional health care expenditures annually.

One of the original hopes in the expansion of medical education was that new physicians would set up practice in rural areas and small towns where health care services are scarce. Regrettably, affluent urban and suburban areas have attracted more new physicians, even in communities where health services are already more than adequate.

---

*Many companies and other employers do not pay for the health insurance. Employees pay lower premiums because they belong to a group — because they are the workforce of a specific employer.

Much of the criticism of physicians arises from what has been also a source of medical progress: increased specialization in areas such as psychiatry, anesthesiology, aerospace medicine, allergies, pediatrics, teaching, and research. General practitioners are only one-seventh of the total versus one-half 30 years ago, even though 90 percent of health problems do not require specialty training. Today's 350,000 physicians are better trained and meet higher certification standards than ever before. Their salaries average about $90,000, the highest of any profession. There is little price competition among physicians. In fact, prices tend to be highest where there are the most physicians!

Surgeons.   The United States and Canada have more surgeons and more operations per capita than any other nations in the world. Twenty million operations are performed a year in the United States, one every two-thirds of a second. Inevitably, some surgery is unnecessary or innappropriate. A study by Blue Cross and Blue Shield found that of patients seeking a second physician's opinion before agreeing to surgery, one-fourth decided not to have the operation. Estimates of total unnecessary surgery are two million a year.

Of the nation's 100,000 surgeons, about 60 percent are certified to perform specialized surgery in obstetrics and gynecology, orthopedics, ophthalmology, and urology. Analysts estimate that the nation has a surplus of up to 40,000 surgeons. Still, their median income for 1981 was about $103,000, 15% above that of other physicians.

Nurses.   In contrast to physicians and surgeons, the supply of nurses may be less than adequate. Between 1968 and 1975, admissions to nursing schools grew faster than at any time since World War II. Since 1975, there has been no significant increase in the growth rate of admissions, and in 1978 there was an absolute decline in admissions. Moreover, in recent years substantial numbers of graduate nurses have left the profession. The National League for Nursing has projected a 2 to 3 percent per year decline in registered nursing graduates between 1980 and 1985.

One reason for the slow growth in supply is the decline in population growth, which reduced the number of high school graduates. Another is the decline in the proportion of high school graduates choosing nursing as a career. Low salaries may be a significant factor. The median wage for nursing professionals is about 15 percent below the median wage for the nation as a whole.*

A comprehensive campaign to reduce health care costs in the United States could have either of two effects for nurses:

1. Cuts in spending might cause many health care institutions to close, reducing the demand for nurses.
2. Rising costs for other health care professionals could shift more of patient care from highly paid physicians to nurses.

In either case, new technologies in the health field will increase the need for specialized skills among new nursing personnel.

---

*Walter L. Johnson, "Supply and Demand for Registered Nurses, Parts I and II," *Nursing and Health Care*, July/August and September, 1980.

COST DIFFERENCES FOR HEALTH CARE PERSONNEL

Members of the American Medical Association (AMA) generally agreed to maintain fees and avoid other forms of competition. The result is a degree of monopolization in health care services.

The effect of monopoly pricing is shown in Figure 9–6, which shows a demand curve relating hours of a physician's time to patients' ability and willingness to pay. Hours are measured along the horizontal axis. Price is measured on the vertical axis and reflects the value of added benefits patients expect to receive for additional hours of the physician's time. According to Figure 9–6, one hour could be "sold" for $100, the second for $90, the third for $80, and so on.

In free markets, equilibrium price and quantity are determined by the interaction of demand and supply. Services are provided up to the point where the value of added benefits to buyers is equal to the added costs to the seller. With a single equilibrium price, total revenue for the physician would be shown as the shaded rectangle formed by quantity sold (Q_e) and the single equilibrium price (p_e).

Monopoly control of the supply of health services enables sellers to practice **price discrimination**. Price discrimination involves setting different fees according to buyers' ability and willingness to pay. Look at Figure 9–7. Charging all patients what each is willing and able to pay enables the physician to collect total revenue represented by the entire shaded area under the demand curve (up to number of hours worked). In general, we would expect price discrimination to yield greater total revenue than would a single equilibrium price. Note also that a system of price discrimination enables physicians to serve low-income patients at low rates, in effect subsidizing low fees at one end of the demand curve with high fees at the other. The physician can do this because he or she can distinguish between patients on the basis of ability and willingness to pay and because the service cannot be transferred from lower-paying patients to higher-paying patients. With price discrimination, each patient pays according to his or her own ability to pay and the subjective value he or she places on the service.

The widespread availability of private insurance and public health care programs has changed the system of price discrimination. Nowadays, ability and willingness to pay extend over more of the population, so that physicians can set high fees for *all* their patients. Relieved from the obligation of subsidizing low-income patients, physicians may receive income represented by the shaded rectangle in Figure 9–8. In Figure 9–8, all patients are charged a standard fee, and physicians' incomes rise even higher than before.

These same circumstances apply to other suppliers of health care where the necessary elements of monopoly prevail:

1. There is a single seller of health services without price competition.
2. Buyers are unable or lack incentives to seek lower-priced care (because of the availability of public or private insurance funds).
3. The product is distinctive (without acceptable substitutes).
4. Buyers lack the information that would enable them to avoid the purchase.

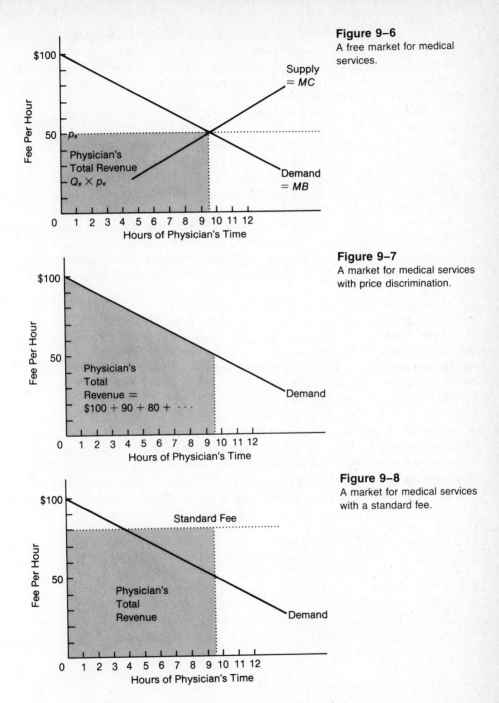

Figure 9–6
A free market for medical services.

Figure 9–7
A market for medical services with price discrimination.

Figure 9–8
A market for medical services with a standard fee.

The necessary elements of monopoly tend not to prevail in the market for nurses. In fact, for decades there were plentiful supplies of nursing services. Buyers were free to seek lower-priced care among many substitute workers in the nursing profession. These circumstances may now be changing, in part because of reduced incentives to enter the nursing profession.

We have pointed to wide differences between the salaries of physicians and surgeons, on the one hand, and nurses, on the other. At least part of the difference may be a result of differences in market power. To see why, assume that the following conditions are true:

1. Assume there is some total expenditure for health personnel the nation is willing to pay in a single year.
2. Assume also that physicians maintain a level of fees that absorbs some portion of total personnel costs. Because of the absence of competition among physicians, the level of fees tends to be higher than would be true in a free market, and the share of total expenditure paid to physicians is greater.
3. Finally, assume that other personnel in more competitive health care occupations must share the remaining health care revenues. As more health care workers enter the market, their average shares become smaller and real wages tend to fall.

Figure 9–9 illustrates the result of these assumptions: the demand curve shows the number of nurses employers will seek to hire at various wage rates. The supply curve shows the willingness of nurses to work at various wages. The equilibrium wage is w_e and quantity employed is Q_e.

An increase in demand for health services increases the demand for nurses, shown in Figure 9–9 as a rightward shift in demand to D'. The equilibrium wage rises to w_e'. But if cost pressures prevent an increase in nurses' wages, there will be no increase in quantity supplied. The difference between demand and supply at the constant wage is the shortage of nurses.

A shortage of nurses may be relieved by a tendency of qualified persons to move in and out of the market in response to changes in employment opportunities in other fields. When other employment opportunities increase, qualified

Figure 9–9

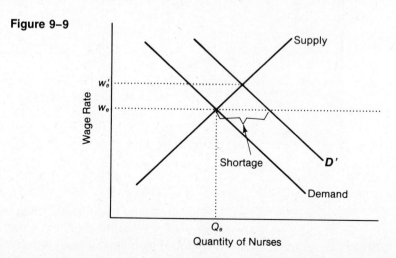

Quantity of Nurses

persons leave the market to take other jobs, and the supply curve shifts to the left. When other opportunities decrease, nurses return to the health care market, and the supply curve shifts to the right. Pencil in these events on Figure 9–9 and describe the results.

A NEW APPROACH TO HEALTH CARE

Concerned about their rising insurance costs, many business firms have looked for more efficient ways to provide employee health benefits. One new approach is the use of **Health Maintenance Organizations (HMOs).** Health Maintenance Organizations are medical facilities financed by regular contributions of members. They provide a range of medical and surgical care at no charge and encourage their members to treat minor ailments in the early stages before costly hospitalization is required. Health Maintenance Organizations have the advantage of teamwork, with peer consultation and review. Their fixed incomes provide incentives for efficiency in carrying out their responsibilities to members.

There are about 200 HMOs in the United States, with 7.4 million members. Most business firms located near an HMO must provide their employees the option of ordinary health insurance or membership in the HMO. Memberships cost about $100 a month, most of which is paid by employers. Members are usually covered for eye exams, immunizations, physical examinations, lab work, drugs, allergy treatment, surgery, and orthopedic reconstruction.

HMO physicians are paid a straight salary rather than a fee for service.* Thus, there is no incentive to perform unnecessary or excessive health services: they hospitalize patients about half as often as private physicians and attempt to ward off serious health problems before they occur. Joseph Califano estimated that HMOs can reduce outpatient visits by 15 percent and hospitalization by 30 to 60 percent. A nationwide reduction of only 30 percent in hospitalization would amount to savings of almost $25 billion annually.

POLICY PROPOSALS FOR IMPROVING THE HEALTH CARE SYSTEM

Proposals for improving efficiency and incentives in the health care sector range from one extreme to the other: that is, from providing even more comprehensive health insurance to relying more completely on free markets. Expanding private or public insurance would worsen the problems associated with "third parties" and tend to reduce efficiency in health care procedures. On the

---

*HMO salaries for various medical specializations are comparable to the earnings of an independent physician, net of overhead expenses.

other hand, complete reliance on free markets might violate ethical considerations and might have unacceptable external costs (in terms of the spread of disease).

The first extreme can be illustrated by Senator Edward Kennedy's proposed Health Care for All Americans Act. Senator Kennedy's proposal would provide full coverage for physician, laboratory, and hospital costs, to be financed from federal income tax revenues and from an additional payroll tax on employers and employees. The system would be managed by existing private insurance companies. In 1979, former President Carter proposed a more modest National Health Plan that would cover **"catastrophic" medical expenses**: catastrophic medical expenses are those over some amount, say $5,000, per family per year. The Carter program would have expanded Medicare and Medicaid and would have included incentives for disease prevention, as well as cash incentives not to overuse the public health care system.

Laurence S. Seidman of the University of Pennsylvania has suggested another approach that would avoid either of the extremes discussed above.* His proposal would reduce many of the disincentive effects of more comprehensive insurance while at the same time limiting an individual's medical costs to a reasonable fraction of his or her income. Seidman's proposal calls for health care *credits* against a family's personal income tax bill. A tax credit is an amount to be subtracted from tax owed. Thus it represents a kind of cash rebate to the taxpayer.

To illustrate, suppose a family with gross income of $30,000 pays medical bills of $7,500 in a single year. Under Seidman's proposal, the family would have to bear some portion of its medical expense outright: say, 5 percent of income or $1,500. The family's outright payment would correspond to the "deductible" in private insurance plans:

outright payment = some percent of income = 0.05 x $30,000 = $1,500.

Then the family would apply for a tax credit equal to some fraction of the remaining medical expense: say, 80 percent of the remaining expense.

tax credit = some percent of (total expense − outright payment) =
0.80 × ($7,500 − $1,500) = $4,800.

Under this plan, the family's total medical expense would be the outright payment of $1,500 plus 20 percent of the remainder:

total medical expense = outright payment plus some percent of remaining medical bill
= $1,500 + 0.20($6,000) = $2,700, or
medical bill − tax credit = $7,500 − $4,800 = $2,700.

*Laurence S. Seidman, "Hospital Inflation: A Diagnosis and Prescription," *Challenge*, July/August, 1979, pp. 17–23.

The 20 percent paid would correspond to the "copayment" in private insurance plans. Above some fraction of family income, say 30 percent, a family would receive a tax credit equal to the excess amount of health care costs. For the family described above, 30 percent of income is $9,000. Any medical expense over $9,000 in a single year would be described as "catastrophic" and would be returned to the family in the form of an additional tax credit. Thus, for a medical expense of $10,000 in a single year, the family would pay a "deductible" of $1,500 plus a "copayment" of 20 percent of ($9,000 − $1,500) = $1,500 for a total of $3,000.

Deductibles and copayments could be adjusted to various income levels by varying the percentages (5, 20, and 30 percent above).* In this way the level of individual responsibility for health care costs could be adjusted to a family's ability to pay. The result would satisfy certain equity considerations regarding health care. Moreover, since all families would have to bear some fraction of costs, they would be encouraged to decide carefully on the quantity and quality of health care to purchase. They would compare marginal costs with the benefits of additional care and seek a level of health care services that provides maximum net benefits.

Seidman adds that only out-of-pocket medical costs should be eligible for the tax credit. A person who purchases insurance to avoid paying any medical expenses at all would not be entitled to a tax credit. A person who receives health insurance as a fringe benefit at the workplace would be required to pay income tax on the benefit. Many firms would stop providing health insurance and pay insurance premiums to workers as income. Thus, to the extent that a worker remains healthy or utilizes efficient health care services, his or her spendable income would increase.

A policy for sharing costs between individuals and government would also affect producers of health care services. Patients might be expected to demand that physicians and hospitals operate efficiently. In turn, hospitals, health professionals, and medical clinics might be expected to specialize in a particular type or quality of service geared to different participants in the market. The result might be a reduction of duplication and waste and lower health care costs.

SOME CONCLUSIONS AND SOME FURTHER QUESTIONS

The goal of improved access to health care for all Americans is a noble one. But our health care goals must be considered within the broader context of all our social goals. Exclusive emphasis on achieving one policy objective inevitably involves an *opportunity cost*: a sacrifice of other programs, projects, or enterprises we might have had. Policymakers should carefully evaluate the expected

*A family with income of only $15,000 and medical expenses of $7,500 might pay only 4 percent of income and only 10 percent of the remainder up to 25 percent of income. The family's total medical expense would be 4% of $15,000 = $600 plus 10% of ($3,750 − $600) = $315 for a total of $915.

benefits and costs of achieving each goal and pursue any one goal only to the point where the expected gain in net benefits exceeds the gain in net benefits of others. This is clearly a difficult task, similar to the job of "triage" we mentioned earlier.

Questions of ethics are a necessary part of policy decisions. Our ethical codes make especially difficult the denial of health care to any individual. On the other hand, resource limitations mean that satisfying a particular need requires neglect of another. Is it ethical, for instance, to prolong the life of a diseased person and neglect disease prevention in a healthy one? Should equality of health care services extend to persons who knowingly abuse their own bodies—through use of alcohol and tobacco or through overeating and lack of exercise? To what extent should health care resources be focused on a particular disease that brings unimaginable suffering to only a small minority of the population? When is *enough* attention to health care finally *enough*?

These are the kinds of questions society must answer. Through our elected representatives we must determine the allocation of health care resources that is most efficient and the distribution of health service that satisfies our views of equity.

Special Case

The Occupational Safety and Health Administration

In 1970, Congress passed and President Nixon signed legislation establishing the Occupational Safety and Health Administration (OSHA). The role of OSHA is to establish and enforce health and safety standards at the workplace. The agency has written thousands of rules requiring changes in procedures and equipment that can cause accidents or illnesses among workers.

Many of OSHA's regulations have been costly. They have reduced the profitability of U.S. firms, in some cases driving firms out of business and depriving workers of jobs. They have reduced the measured rate of productivity in industry, raised prices, and affected the competitiveness of U.S. goods in international trade. They have made new investment riskier and lowered the rate of return, thus discouraging investment and slowing economic growth.

The results have not all been bad, of course. Under OSHA regulations, business firms (and, more correctly, consumers of their products) must bear the costs of work-related illnesses, costs that were formerly distributed rather arbitrarily among workers. New health and safety procedures have added days and years to the lives of productive labor resources, thus enhancing the nation's long-range growth potential. Health and safety regulations have encouraged the development of new industries that produce equipment required to make workplaces safe. Moreover, even firms not directly affected by OSHA's rules may have been encouraged to improve their work environment so as to forestall new kinds of regulation.

The issues surrounding OSHA are similar to other health care issues. They involve choosing the level of regulation at the workplace that achieves the greatest total benefit at the minimum cost. Critics complain that OSHA's hastily devised rules have penalized conscientious employers without ensuring lowest-cost solutions to safety problems. They suggest that rather than drawing up new rules, OSHA should set *performance standards* and let firms achieve the standards in ways consistent with their own technological and financial circumstances. Other critics contend that OSHA's reach is still too limited, that serious health hazards persist and that many workers and employers are unaware of the serious dangers they face. These critics recommend increasing OSHA's budget substantially and increasing its enforcement powers. (Currently, fewer than 3,000 inspectors are responsible for about 5 million places of business with about 65 million employees.)

Some form of benefit-cost analysis is certainly called for in occupational health and safety regulation. All social benefits and social costs should be included in the analysis. And finally, firms should be encouraged to achieve health and safety goals at lowest cost.

- Some analysts have proposed replacing occupational safety and health regulation with a requirement that firms purchase insurance to cover work-related accidents and illnesses. The cost of the insurance would depend on the firm's experience with health and safety. Evaluate this proposal.
- Another regulatory agency concerned with public safety is the National Highway Traffic Safety Administration. When speed limits were reduced from as high as 75 miles per hour to 55 miles per hour nationwide, the NHTSA reported a significant reduction in highway deaths. What is the logical conclusion of this report (at what speed would deaths be zero?) and how might benefit-cost analysis be applied to policy decisions?

Special Case

Britain's National Health Service

Britain was the first nation to establish a National Health Service (NHS), in 1948. Today, Britain's National Health Service employs more than a million people and has an annual budget equivalent to $20 billion. This amounts to about $325 for every person in the United Kingdom. Still, per capita medical cost is lower in Britain than in the United States, Sweden, France, and Canada and higher only than in Japan and Italy (among industrialized nations). Britain's health record in terms of infant mortality and life expectancy is better than that of the United States.

Persons in the NHS select their own general practitioner who, in turn, may agree to serve or not. Most of the cost of service is paid from general tax revenues, but patients pay a weekly tax. Both patients and physicians can choose to operate outside the NHS if they wish. Physicians in private practice receive their medical training in the NHS, however. When necessary, NHS patients are referred to outside specialists.

Almost every year total expenditures by NHS have grown faster than the rest of the British economy, such that medical expenditures amounted to almost 6 percent of GNP by the late 1970s. Physicians in the NHS receive a salary that amounts to about 2.5 times the annual male wage. They work four days a week and serve an average of 2,300 patients. Their pay is based on number of patients served rather than the kinds of services performed.

By 1980, a number of factors had combined to increase substantially the cost of Britain's NHS: rising prosperity and rising public expectations, more complicated and costly equipment and procedures, the growing numbers of elderly citizens who need more care. Also, some patients abuse the Health Service, so that their excessive demands raise the costs associated with treating other patients. Policymakers in Britain have been forced to apply benefit-cost analysis to health care, denying care to some whose advanced age or disease reduces the effectiveness of treatment.

- What is the likelihood of the establishment of a National Health Service in the United States? How would the medical profession react, and how would the public respond? Can such a system be combined with a private system?

Mathematical Supplement

Deciding to Be a Doctor

Training to be a medical professional is long and costly. If a person is to make such an investment in "human capital," he or she must expect to be fully compensated for the sacrifice at some time in the future. In economic terms, the *opportunity costs* of early years of sacrifice must be offset by later years of prosperity.

The tradeoff between sacrifice and reward is made more complicated by the fact that the sacrifice occurs now and the reward much later. Suppose, for example, a medical student plans to invest $20,000 in training for each of the next five years, after which earnings from professional services are expected to follow the pattern shown below:

C: Current Year Outlay	F: Future Cash Flows (in thousands of dollars)									
	Years									
	1	2	3	4	5	6	7	8	9	10–40
−20	−20	−20	−20	−20	+25	+30	+40	+50	+60	+70 (every year)

Since all but the first payment and all the receipts occur in the future, each must be *discounted* at a rate determined by the interest yield on financial investments (r) and the distance in the future (t) the payments occur.* Discounting the figures above for $r = 15$ percent reduces their value as shown below:

*Discounting was explained in chapter 2.

Discounted Cash Flows at 15 Percent

C: Current Year Outlay	F: Future Cash Flows (in thousands of dollars)									
	Years									
	1	2	3	4	5	6	7	8	9	10–40
−20	−17.39	−15.12	−13.15	−11.44	+12.43	+12.97	+15.04	+16.35	+17.06	+115.35

Figure 9–10 illustrates the cash payments and receipts by bars above and below a horizontal line. The dashed line marks the value of cash flows after discounting at $r = 15$ percent.

Figure 9–10

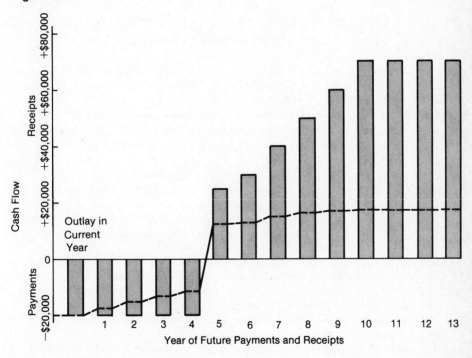

Deciding on an investment in human capital is very much like deciding on any other kind of investment.* The potential medical student must compare the net value of all future cash flows (discounted according to r and t) with the necessary outlay in the current

---

*The discussion in this section is not intended to deny the nonmeasurable benefits medical personnel enjoy from their work in the health field, such as the social rewards associated with following a respected profession and the psychological rewards associated with serving humanity.

year. In Figure 9–10 it is obvious that the positive flows outweigh the negative flows and that the investment should be made. In other cases, the decision would depend on the size of the negative and positive flows and on the interest rate of return available on other investments. If the interest return were as high as $r = 25$ percent, for instance, five annual $20,000 purchases of financial investments would yield almost precisely the same income as would the professional training in this problem.

This example illustrates the importance of high professional incomes as incentives to acquire the necessary training. Even very high incomes far in the future, when discounted at high interest rates, may not be enough to offset the high cost of training. For physicians who specialize, training is even longer and more costly than for those who go into general practice. Thus, balancing off heavier negative cash flows requires even greater income in the future.

- How would the guarantee of substantial fees from Medicaid affect a potential medical student's decision?

QUESTIONS

1. Discuss the advantages and disadvantages of government financial support for medical research and training. What are the corresponding advantages and disadvantages of private philanthropy for these purposes?
2. What is the meaning of the assertion that free markets are "amoral"?
3. Explain the apparent paradox between the increased supply of physicians and surgeons and their higher costs. Can there be resource surpluses and shortages at the same time? Explain.
4. Name other professions that require substantial opportunity costs that are not fully compensated by future material rewards. What other forms of compensation may justify the current sacrifice?
5. Consult the latest *Statistical Abstract of the United States* for recent data on death rates for various diseases, trends in life expectancy by sex and race, and infant death rates. Illustrate graphically and comment on your findings.
6. Debate the two "extreme" approaches toward changing the nation's health care system. What are the efficiency and ethical implications of each?
7. What is the significance of a "deductible" and a "coinsurance" payment for either private insurance or government health care plans?
8. Cite possible reasons for OSHA's failings in its first decade and recommendations for improvement in the future.
9. Opposition to HMOs has come from physicians and the American Medical Association. Can you account for the opposition?

DEFINITIONS

Catastrophic medical expenses are expenses that are greater than a certain percentage of a family's annual income.

A copayment is the portion of a medical expense after deductibles that must be paid by the insured.

A deductible is the direct payment an insured patient must pay before his or her insurance policy begins to take effect.

Health Maintenance Organizations (HMOs) are organizations of health care personnel that provide basic health services in return for a monthly fee.

Market demand shows the quantities of a good or service that will be purchased at various prices. The decision to purchase a particular quantity is based on the relationship between the expected added benefits from the purchase and the purchase price.

Market supply shows the quantities of a good or service that will be offered for sale at various prices. The decision to offer a particular quantity is based on the relationship between the expected gain from making the sale relative to the expected gain from an alternative use of the good or service.

Net benefits are the difference between total benefits and total costs of a particular quantity of a good or service.

Price discrimination is the practice of charging different prices to different consumers on the basis of their ability and willingness to pay.

The principle of decreasing marginal utility states that the more of a particular good or service one acquires the less is the added utility from acquiring another unit.

The priniciple of increasing marginal cost states that the more of a particular good or service that is provided in a market the higher is the additional cost of another unit.

"Third parties" are persons or groups that influence buying and selling decisions in a particular market. In the market for health care, third parties include insurance companies, government health care programs, and private physicians.

Total benefits are represented by the entire area under a demand curve up to the quantity that is acquired.

Total costs are represented by the entire area under a supply curve up to the quantity that is provided in the market.

SUGGESTED READINGS

Adams, Sally. "How the British Health Service Is Doing." *Across the Board*, January, 1980, p. 45.

Daley, John Charles, et al. "National Health Insurance: Now, Later, Never?" *Across the Board*, May, 1980, p. 54.

Fralick, James. "RX for Treatment of Hyper-Health Care Costs." *Across the Board*, April, 1982, p. 64.

Moore, Geoffrey H., and Robert Austin Milch. "How to Reduce the Cost of Medical Care." *Across the Board*, November, 1981, p. 79.

Shapiro, Edward. "Controlling Health Care Expenditures." *Challenge*, September/October, 1980, p. 40.

"The Spiraling Cost of Health Care." *Business Week*, February 8, 1982, p. 58.

CHAPTER TEN

Feeding the World's People: The Agricultural Sector

Will We Have Enough?

LEARNING OBJECTIVES

- To describe trends in agricultural production and policies for guiding production.
- To use a production function to illustrate the theory of food production and the implications of population growth for real per capita living standards.
- To show the effect of inelastic supply and demand on farm incomes and the effect of government price supports on efficiency and incentives.
- To examine in detail the characteristics of various farm commodities and the regulations governing their production.
- To consider ways for shifting upward the production function in agriculture and raising average product.
- To show how hedgers and speculators help stabilize farm prices.

A prospective buyer was being shown a home in a newly developed subdivision in California. Noting the absence of grass and shrubs, she asked, "Is this soil fertile enough for me to have a flower garden?" "Madam," replied the agent, "you are standing on some of the richest agricultural land in all the world."

He was probably telling the truth. Much of the world's population now depends on food grown on the North American continent. And some of the best farmland is also the most attractive for residential development. Near major U.S. cities land that is worth, say, $4,000 an acre as farmland may be worth as much as $100,000 an acre for condominiums. Analysts estimate that farmland lost annually to development would form a half-mile wide strip across the continent from California to New York.

Residential development is not the only reason for the decline in arable land. Increased cultivation of hilly land has aggravated the problem of soil erosion. In the United States, an estimated five to six billion tons of topsoil are lost every year to wind and water erosion.

The United States has experienced several decades of food abundance, but such good fortune is unique in human history. Mankind has consistently struggled to produce enough food to survive. Our abundance has enabled us to satisfy our own needs lavishly and to provide food to other people around the world. The issue now is whether these conditions can endure, and what we can do to improve the production and distribution of food.

In this chapter, we will discuss some characteristics that distinguish the agricultural sector from other parts of the U.S. economy. Those characteristics and the vital significance of food products for world security appear to call for a degree of government intervention. In fact, some combination of government policies and individual incentives may be necessary for achieving efficiency and increased production in agriculture. Designing agricultural policy is a critical responsibility of our elected representatives.

THE PROBLEM

The year 1973 was a kind of watershed year for the world community. In the years since World War II, food production had been increasing almost 2 percent a year. New high-yield seeds and scientific breeding had enabled U.S. farmers to produce more food with less land and labor resources. The farm population had dwindled from 23 percent of total U.S. population in 1940 to 3 percent in 1973. Every U.S. farmer was able to feed 75 people, compared to only about 10 people for each Soviet farmer.

New technologies had created almost embarrassing abundance in the United States. The use of agricultural chemicals and sophisticated new farm equipment had dramatically increased agricultural productivity and enabled the farming sector to pile up huge surpluses. Exports increased, to the extent that more than half the world's trade in wheat, corn, barley, oats, and sorghum was grown in the United States. Under Public Law 480 (the "Food for Peace" law), the United States made concessional sales at below-market prices to poor countries that were unable to obtain enough food from their own production or from commercial imports. By 1973, global food production was enough to supply the minimum health requirements of all the world's people.*

---

*This does not mean that malnutrition and starvation did not occur, due to the unequal distribution of total food supplies.

Annual surpluses of certain food products are stored as a kind of *reserve* on farms and in warehouses around the world. A **food reserve** acts as a cushion against agricultural disasters, moderating sharp increases in prices when food is scarce. Until 1973, world reserves of food grains had fluctuated between 100 and 155 million metric tons, amounts equivalent to 30 to 50 days of total world consumption.

Despite severe droughts and floods and civil unrest around the world, new production records were set in 1973 for certain crops and animal products. Still, steadily rising population and uncertain growing conditions were beginning to raise questions about food supplies for the future. Three events of 1973 heightened concerns about a coming food crisis:

1. Disastrous crop failures in the Soviet Union, China, India, and Brazil led to record grain purchases from the United States.
2. A severe drop in the anchovy catch off South America reduced supplies for livestock feed; the suspected cause was overfishing in these waters in the 1960s and early 1970s.
3. The oil embargo and rising energy prices increased the cost of nitrogen-based fertilizers necessary for expanding crop production.

Beginning in 1973, declining growth in world food production began to reduce the annual surpluses for adding to the world's food reserve. By 1974, the world as a whole was only 27 days away from depletion of grain reserves. Food prices began to rise, an especially serious problem for poor nations heavily dependent on food imports. Even in the United States, per capita food consumption declined about 1 percent in 1973, largely through substantial cuts in consumption of animal products.

Storing grain is not the only way to maintain a food reserve. Since the farm legislation of the 1930s, the U.S. government has limited the amount of acreage used for agriculture as a means of reducing production and supporting farm incomes. Roughly 50 million acres were kept idle during the 1960s. But by 1973, rising food demand had brought virtually all the nation's arable land back into production, thus eliminating this source of additional supply.

Beginning in 1974, a 67-nation United Nations-sponsored World Food Conference has considered the problem of world food supplies and has looked for ways to stabilize world grain markets. Participating nations agreed on a general framework for purchasing grain reserves and influencing grain production. But the Conference could not agree on the details for carrying out their recommendations regarding the prices at which governments would buy farm products, the distribution and total volume of grain reserves, and the amount of food aid to be granted the less-developed nations.

For the remainder of the 1970s, U.S. farm production increased at about 1⅓ percent annually. Agricultural production in the world as a whole grew at about 2 percent annually, with most of the gain occurring in the less-developed countries. In 1977, the world enjoyed the first buildups in grain reserves since 1973. Both developed and less-developed countries increased production by about 3 percent. Then in 1979 and 1980, bad growing conditions cut world production sharply, with the severest drops in East Asia and Africa. More seriously, crop yields in the United States fell sharply from the highs reached in the late 1970s. Idle cropland has virtually disappeared, and soil erosion and expanding residential development are eliminating fertile acreage. Heavy dependence on food production in a few areas of the world increases our vulnerability to freak disasters.

FARM POLICY

Until 1973, U.S. farm policy emphasized government control of crop production and price supports on farm commodities. Through the Commodity Credit Corporation, the federal government purchased surplus farm commodities at the **support price** to keep prices from falling and to protect farm incomes. In 1973, real net income of the farm sector peaked at $25 billion (in constant dollars of 1967).

The emphasis of farm policy changed in 1973. In 1973 the federal government sold its food storage facilities, and the Secretary of Agriculture urged farmers to plant from "fence post to fence post." Under the farm law of 1973, **target prices** were set for certain farm commodities (grains, rice, soybeans, cotton, milk, sugar, peanuts, and tobacco) at about the cost of production. If ample supplies put downward pressure on food prices, prices were allowed to fall, and farmers were paid an income supplement. Or farmers could store surplus farm commodities on the farm and obtain low-interest government loans to tide them over until prices rose. When the loan matured, the farmer could either sell his crop in the market and repay the loan or default on the loan and turn his crop over to the government.

Following the 1973 farm legislation, U.S. agricultural production expanded. Increasing supplies pushed farm prices down, while farmers' costs of production rose above the target price. Plunging farm profits pushed farmers to desperation. A farm "strike" was called, and angry farmers marched to Washington to demand a more generous farm policy. When the Farm Bill expired in 1977, however, constraints on the federal budget and competing demands for welfare and defense expenditures called for a compromise on farm policy. New target prices and loan levels were set between what the farmers wanted and what the President was willing to grant. For farmers to receive income-support payments on farm commodities, they would have to "set aside" a certain percent of acreage not to be cultivated. No farmer could receive more than a total of $50,000 for all commodities.

Under the 1977 law, farmers were allowed to store surplus grain and receive loans from the Commodity Credit Corporation. Grain not sold at the time of maturity of the loan could be added to a national grain reserve, from which sales would be made in years of food scarcity. In general, the aim of farm policy was to raise food prices and cut production only slightly, while guaranteeing a basic minimum food reserve and ensuring a minimum income to farmers.

Drought and declining farm incomes in 1980 led President Carter to increase farm target prices, and Congress increased loan levels on stored commodities. Still, except for milk, loan rates on farm commodities remained well below market prices, so that most crops were sold in the open market. In 1981, pressure began to build for increasing target prices for corn, wheat, and cotton. President Reagan was worried about the federal budget and recommended a 10 percent reduction in milk support levels, but Congress passed a 5 percent reduction. Congress also raised sugar support prices.

Income supplements and commodity loans to farmers cost taxpayers more than $3 billion annually. Income-supplements are not directly inflationary because food prices are set by supply and demand in free markets. But commodity loans can be inflationary, since loans enable farmers to refuse to sell until prices rise above the government loan rate. Furthermore, if farmers turn over their surpluses to the grain reserve, government must pay to store it. Don Ratajczak of Georgia State University estimates that government price support programs add 1.5 to 2 percent to the nation's food bill, now about $325 billion a year.

Parity Pricing

One consistent demand of farmers is for 100 percent parity pricing. **Parity** is a ratio of prices on farm products the farmer *sells* relative to prices on manufactured goods the farmer *buys*:

$$\text{parity ratio} = \frac{\text{prices the farmer receives}}{\text{prices the farmer pays.}}$$

Using dollars of 1910–1914 for computing a price index, average farm prices were 538 in 1981 and manufactured prices were 744. Thus, the parity ratio was equal to

$$\text{parity ratio} = \frac{538}{744} = 72 \text{ percent.}$$

Farm prices returned to the farmer only 72 percent of the 1910–1914 purchasing power of farm prices. Farmers would like to continue receiving real income equivalent to that of 1910–1914: that is, 100 percent parity.

To tie farm prices to an index of other prices would be inefficient. Improved technology has vastly increased farm yields and reduced average production costs. Lower food costs should enable more consumers to enjoy larger quantities. Also, fixing the price of farm commodities interferes with the market's ability to adjust production to changes in demand and supply. Artificially high prices would encourage producers to allocate too many of the nation's resouces to food production. Moreover, 100 percent parity pricing would eliminate the United States' low-cost advantage in the export of farm commodities.

Agricultural economists estimate that the cost of 100 percent parity pricing would be more than $55 billion in government outlays. Consumers would be hit twice: first through higher food prices at the supermarket, and second through taxes to pay income supplements to farmers. Furthermore, higher prices for grain would increase production costs for meat, as well as activate Cost-of-

Living-Adjustment clauses (COLAs) in wage contracts. The result would be worsening inflation.

THE THEORY OF FOOD PRODUCTION

For any specific period of time, certain of the earth's resources are fixed: for example, usable land and capital equipment and the technology for using them. Applying various amounts of labor to the earth's **fixed resources** yields increasing, constant, and decreasing Marginal Product. Extreme quantities of labor relative to fixed resources yields negative Marginal Product or, what is the same thing, decreasing Total Product.* The typical behavior of production when certain resources are fixed is shown in Figure 10–1a. Increasing total product is associated with increasing, constant, and decreasing (but positive) Marginal Product.

The important consideration for human welfare is Average Product, shown in Figure 10–1b. Average Product is Total Product divided by quantity of labor: Average Product of Labor $= AP_L = TP/Q_L$. Average Product is a measure both of labor productivity and real income. Thus, Average Product is the basis for real per capita income and living standards.

The horizontal dashed line in Figure 10–1b indicates the **subsistence level of production;** that is, the average level of production that is necessary to sustain life. When Average Product is above the dashed line, per capita living standards are greater than the subsistence level, and the population may enjoy prosperity. If Average Product falls below the dashed line, some members of the population will suffer deprivation and die.

History's most famous student of food-population linkages was Thomas Malthus (1766–1834). Malthus made some gloomy predictions about trends in the world's ability to feed itself. According to Malthus, prosperity would cause population to grow until Average Product reached the point of subsistence (Q_s in Figure 10–1b). Then population would tend to stabilize. If population were to expand beyond the point of subsistence, Average Product would be too little to support life: disease and starvation would reduce population. On the other hand, if population were to fall below the point of subsistence, prosperity would extend life expectancy: population would grow again until it reached subsistence. Malthus was not very optimistic about changing these results. He had little hope for achieving permanent improvements in levels of life.

A major flaw in Malthus' argument was his disregard for the ability of human actions to correct what seemed to be inevitable trends. In fact, humans have used their intelligence to expand technology, thus shifting upward the Total and Average Product curves of Figure 10–1. Investors have added to fixed quantities of capital equipment—and even usable land—to expand the range of increasing Average Product. Also, many nations of the world promote policies to discourage population growth, reducing the pressure of population on fixed resources.

*The student may want to review the explanation of this model that appears in chapter 1.

Figure 10-1

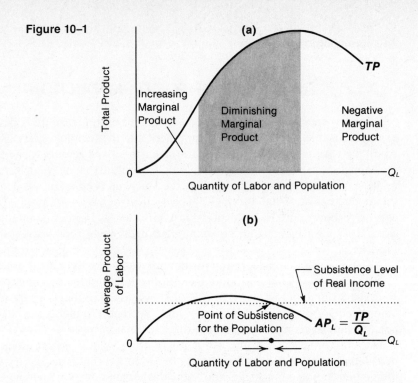

(a)

Total Product

Increasing Marginal Product

Diminishing Marginal Product

Negative Marginal Product

TP

0 — Q_L

Quantity of Labor and Population

(b)

Average Product of Labor

Subsistence Level of Real Income

Point of Subsistence for the Population

$$AP_L = \frac{TP}{Q_L}$$

0 — Q_L

Quantity of Labor and Population

The important issue now is to what extent these efforts can be successful in the future. There is, after all, some final limit to the earth's supply of usable land and even lower limits on transportation facilities to reach the land. There are limits also on applications of new technology. Some of our new technologies have been found to damage the environment. Investments required to protect our air and water reduce the funds available for investment in industry. At some point, there may be no more gains from new technologies. Then increasing Average Product will come to depend only on reducing population growth. Slowing population growth can help ensure a comfortable level of real income for all the world's people.

The problem of ensuring adequate real income is complicated by differences in the distribution of Total Product. Wealthy and productive nations such as the United States enjoy a favorably low level of population relative to resources, such that Average Product may far exceed the subsistence level. Poor and less developed nations like Bangladesh have populations far beyond Malthus' maximum population for subsistence.

A free and open market system would work to transfer food from countries with food surpluses (and low food prices) to countries with shortages (and high food prices). To a degree, this is what happens. However, many poor nations lack sufficient resources for producing items for exchange and are unable to participate in world food markets. They have become more and more dependent for food on gifts from nations with surpluses. Indeed, the world as a whole has become increasingly dependent on the production of a few areas with high productivity and frequent surpluses. A natural disaster, political turmoil, or transport failure could cut off vitally needed food supplies and create a major food crisis for many of the world's people.

Policy for a Food Reserve

One way to ensure dependable food supplies is through establishment of a food reserve. We have seen that a reserve can take the form either of stored grain or of idle productive capacity, ready to be used quickly when shortages threaten. These two objectives do tend to result from U.S. farm policies of the last half century. To see why, look at Figure 10–2 which shows the market for a particular farm commodity. The demand curve measures quantities buyers are willing and able to buy at various prices. The supply curves measure current production for the market. Equilibrium between demand and supply determines the market price (p_m) and the quantity that will be sold (Q_e). At market equilibrium, farm income is represented by the rectangle formed by Op_m and OQ_e.

Now suppose that new technology and favorable weather conditions combine to increase farm output. At every price, the quantity of food offered for sale increases. As a result, the supply curve shifts to the right to S' and the market equilibrium price falls to p_m'. What is the effect of the increased supply on equilibrium quantity sold and on income paid to farmers? According to Figure 10–2, quantity demanded increases only to OQ'. Farm income falls to the area of the rectangle formed by price Op' and quantity OQ'.

Compare the new income rectangle with the income rectangle before the benefits of new technology and favorable weather increased food supplies. The smaller size of the second rectangle suggests that improved growing conditions have actually reduced the incomes of farmers! In fact, this result is not surpris-

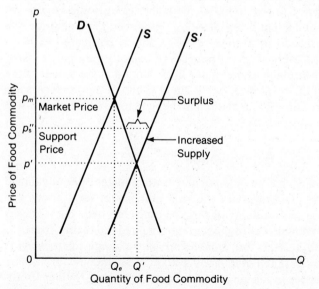

Figure 10–2

ing. The reason has to do with elasticity of demand for farm products. Remember the definition of price elasticity of demand:

$$\text{price elasticity of demand} = \frac{\text{percent change in quantity demanded}}{\text{percent change in price}} = \frac{\%\Delta Q_d}{\%\Delta p}$$

If percent change in food quantity demanded is less than percent change in food prices, the value of the elasticity ratio is less than one and we say that demand is inelastic.

In general, demand for farm products is price inelastic: purchases do not increase or decrease substantially with changes in price. We do not buy much less milk if milk prices rise, nor much more cake if wheat prices fall. With inelastic demand, farmers cannot sell enough additional output to offset their lower prices, and total farm income falls.

Under these conditions, many farmers would have to go out of business. Some farmers would remove forever their productive capacity from the agricultural sector. The loss of productive capacity would make the world more vulnerable to shortages in case of crop failure. Government price supports help avoid this possibility. A government price support at p_S'' raises farm incomes to a level adequate for financing farm operations. At the support price of p_S'', buyers purchase the quantity shown on the demand curve, and farmers supply the quantity shown on the supply curve. The difference between quantity supplied and quantity demanded at the support price is the farm *surplus*. The surplus can be added to reserves for future use. The procedure for accumulating farm commodities may vary from actual government purchase and storage (prior to 1973) to granting loans to farmers for on-the-farm storage (since 1973). In either case, a reserve built up in years of surplus can help relieve shortages when crops fail.

In Figure 10–3, poor weather has reduced food supplies from S to S', causing the market equilibrium price to rise to p'. At the higher price some buyers are forced out of the market and might face starvation. However, the high price will encourage farmers to sell food from their reserves and to cultivate idle land. Increased quantities will then push the supply curve back to the right, causing prices to fall. Pencil in these changes on Figure 10–3. Note that the extent of the price decline depends on the magnitude of the supply shift. If food reserves are plentiful, the supply curve can shift far enough to the right to bring prices down to their level in favorable crop years.

An Evaluation

United States farm policy has advantages and disadvantages. One advantage has been greater stability of farm prices. Greater stability of farm prices has benefited U.S. consumers, and stability of farm incomes has helped maintain a healthy farm sector. Dependable food supplies have enabled the United States to sell surplus grain in export markets for valuable foreign exchange and to provide food aid to starving nations. On the other hand, a guaranteed income for farmers may have reduced efficiency in farming. A guaranteed income provides incentives to keep resources in the agricultural sector that might be better employed

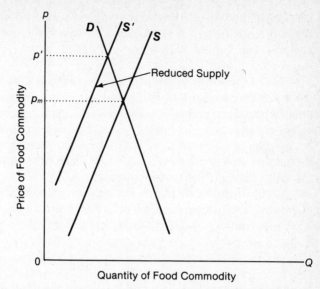

Figure 10–3

elsewhere. Moreover, the farm program is costly. Through their taxes, U.S. citizens are called on to pay the cost of ensuring adequate food supplies for other nations. Whether the benefits of farm policies exceed their costs may depend on whether other nations are helped thereby to become more productive. If this does happen, other nations may soon be able to help solve the world's food problems.

FARM PRODUCTS

We have described trends in world food production, along with the policies that have influenced agricultural markets. We have looked at the theory of food production and shown how building a food reserve helps stabilize food supplies and prices. There is an ominous theme that runs throughout our discussion: that is, the slowing growth of world food production and the threat of future shortages.

In the sections that follow we will look more specifically at the major food crops produced around the world. We will describe current production arrangements and projections for production in the future. As you read, consider the effect of world food policies on efficiency and incentives in food production. Ask yourself what policy changes might be expected to yield additional benefits for the world's people.

Grains

More than 235 million hectares worldwide are planted in wheat (1 hectare = 2.47 acres). The largest producers are Australia, Canada, China, France, India, Turkey, the Soviet Union, and the United States. The United States and the European Economic Community (the Common Market) tend to export wheat, and China and the USSR tend to import wheat. For the last twenty years, total wheat production has been on an upward trend, amounting to about 1.85 tons per hectare. The United States holds about 25 million tons of wheat in a grain reserve.

Half of the world's corn is produced in the United States. About a fourth of the corn is exported, and half is fed to livestock. Production of beef requires about 8 pounds of grain per pound of meat, pork requires 4, and poultry 2. Corn yields per acre have increased about 4 percent annually since 1950. But since corn requires substantial rainfall, the corn crop is especially vulnerable to drought. When production falls, nations dependent on corn for livestock feed are forced to reduce their consumption of meat.

Along with wheat, rice is the major source of calories in less-developed countries. The primary producers of rice are India, Indonesia, Bangladesh, Thailand, Vietnam, Japan, Korea, and China.

Soybeans

The United States is the world's foremost producer of soybeans. Since 1950, additional acreage has steadily moved into soybean production, but yields per acre have only increased by about 1 percent a year. The soybean plant has its own built-in supply of nitrogen and is not very responsive to increased applications of nitrogen fertilizer.

Soybeans are a principal source of protein for livestock feed as well as for feeding more than a billion people in East Asia. (Price differences between soybeans and grain play a large part in determining their use as animal or human food.) Soybeans are the leading U.S. export, exceeding wheat and corn and even jet aircraft and computers in dollar value of sales.

Dairy Products

Six hundred farmer-owned cooperatives control 80 percent of the nation's raw milk supply, and some are beginning to move into milk processing as well. Protected by law from the antitrust regulations, dairy cooperatives maintain prices and allocate supplies to protect dairy farmers' incomes. Concern about cholesterol has led Americans to consume less milk and only slightly more processed milk products.

The government support price for milk is held at a minimum of 70 percent of parity to keep milk prices rising with general inflation. A support price of about $12 per 100 pounds of milk in 1981 meant a retail price of about $1.10 per half gallon.

Meat

The rise of affluence around the world is increasing the demand for meat. Meat and other animal products are important, but inefficient, sources of protein. This is because the animal itself must consume substantially more grain protein than it yields to the human consumer.

World meat production has been leveling off but still reached record levels in 1980. Substantial increases in poultry and pork production offset continuing declines in beef and veal. Beef herds in 1980 were in an expansion phase, however, suggesting that supplies would be greater by 1982. Hogs and poultry have shorter reproductive cycles, so that supplies respond more readily to demand, and prices tend to be more stable.

The major producers of meat for export are Australia, New Zealand, Central America, Mexico, Argentina, and Uruguay. The European Common Market countries support beef prices at about twice the world price, causing surpluses to develop and allowing for substantial exports at subsidized prices. Meat producers in the United States are "protected" by import quotas that limit supply and raise prices.

Grazing lands for beef production are now almost fully utilized, so that production cannot increase significantly. Rising meat prices have prompted consumers to substitute other animal products, such as cheese, in their diets. Changing feed prices also affect the quality of beef. Normally about 70 percent of U.S. beef cattle are fed grain to produce "marbled" steaks and top-quality roasts. High feed prices prompt livestock producers to shift to grass for cattle food, producing leaner, lower-quality cuts. The ability to change livestock feed gives producers greater flexibility and ensures that the market can allocate resources toward areas of greatest need: to direct human consumption or to livestock. Livestock are increasingly being produced in "animal factories" under scientifically controlled conditions from birth to slaughter.

Sugar

Demand for sugar has increased substantially, particularly in the less-developed countries and the centrally planned economies. Americans consume almost 100 pounds of sugar per capita a year, about half of which is imported. About one-third of domestically produced sugar is from cane and two-thirds is from beets. World production of sugar has not grown as fast. The Soviet Union has suffered poor growing conditions for sugar beets, and Brazil has diverted part of its sugar cane crop to production of gasohol. Production problems in Cuba have also reduced Cuba's export potential.

United States sugar producers are protected by import taxes that keep the price at about 16¢ per pound, almost twice the world price. Lower wages abroad help foreign growers produce sugar for about two-thirds of the cost of production in the United States. Although sugar producers constitute fewer than 1 percent of all U.S. farmers, sugar production is dominated by large corporations with considerable lobbying power in Washington.

High U.S. prices result in high consumer prices as well as considerable storage costs for surplus sugar. It is estimated that a 1¢ per pound increase in sugar prices adds $225 million a year to consumer expenditures for sugar and raises production costs for Coca Cola, the country's largest buyer, by $20 million.

Sugar exports are controlled by the International Sugar Agreement. Major producing nations who are parties to this commodity agreement limit their exports when sugar prices fall below 13¢ per pound (1981). Then, when prices rise above 23¢, producers sell sugar from accumulated stockpiles. The effect is to stabilize the quantity and price of sugar in world markets.

Coffee, Tea, and Cocoa

Disastrous growing conditions in Brazil in the mid-1970s reduced world supplies of coffee and pushed prices up to $3.34 a pound in 1977. Since then prices have moderated. The International Coffee Agreement is a commodity agreement to hold prices within a $1.15–1.55 range through export quotas agreed to by member nations.

India, Sri Lanka, China, and Kenya are the largest exporters of tea, with production gains generally about equal to increased consumption, such that prices have remained fairly stable. Producing nations have grown concerned about the low rate of return on tea production and have looked for ways to regulate total production. Although tea faces increasing competition from coffee and soft drinks, it is still the cheapest and most popular drink in the less-developed countries.

World demand for cocoa has been falling due to increased use of cocoa substitutes, high sugar prices, and declining income growth in consuming countries. Supplies have been increasing and prices falling. Brazil and Malaysia are the principal sources of cocoa, along with Ghana and the Ivory Coast. The International Cocoa Agreement is a commodity agreement to hold cocoa prices between $1.10 and $1.50 per pound.

Special Case

Food from the Sea

The harvesting, processing, and distribution of fish is an important business in the United States. But it is a business primarily of small entrepreneurs with little influence in Washington. Still, in 1976 Congress passed the Fishery Conservation and Management Act extending U.S. authority over all fishing—domestic and foreign—up to 200 miles off our shores. The law establishes four categories of fish:

a.   those that can be taken without limit;
b.   threatened species that may *not* be taken;
c.   fish of prime importance to U.S. fishermen;
d.   fish of little importance to U.S. fishermen but of substantial importance to foreigners.

Regional Fishery Management Councils determine how much of each class may be taken and the fraction that should go to U.S. fishermen. The Councils also set fishing limits in terms of geographical area and types of equipment. Foreign governments are required to inform the United States when they have taken their quotas, and foreign fishermen are required to record their catches for review by the Coast Guard.

The fishing industry is fragmented; 90 percent of fishing firms employ fewer than five people, of whom many are members of a single family. A typical commercial fisherman owns a 50- to 100-foot boat and works a 13-hour day. Fish nets scoop up the fish, and the crew sorts them out for sale or discard. Half of the catch belongs to the owner of the boat, and half to the crew. The owner must pay interest and principal on a boat costing as much as half a million dollars.* During the fishing season, boats may stay at sea as long as 10 days at a time, and crew members may earn up to $2,000 a week. Then during the winter the crew may be unemployed. Winter is the time for repairing the boat and overhauling the engines.

Fishing is risky. The sea is treacherous, and the catch is uncertain. Storing the surplus is not generally a fisherman's option!

Some new investments in the fishing industry are being made by foreigners and some by large food processing corporations. The Japanese and Soviet governments own "fish factories" that ply U.S. coastal waters and process the catch on board. Such "superboats" may remain at sea for as long as a year. Both the increase in foreign fishing and overfishing by U.S. fishermen have depleted valuable species. Some foreign vessels use closely woven nets that capture even the immature fish.

Scientists are studying "fish farming"—the cultivation of fish under controlled conditions. There has been some success with salmon cultivation, but shellfish have not responded well to cultivation.

- What are the differences and similiarities involved in farming and fishing?
- Can you suggest new technologies that might be developed in fishing?

INCREASING AVERAGE PRODUCT

If the world is to avoid a food crisis, ways must be found to shift upward the production function for agriculture. Shifting upward the Total Product function can increase Average Product and raise the level of real income. In general, increasing production possibilities depends on increasing the quantity and quality of resources and improving agricultural technology. Research and development efforts around the world have this important objective. The spread of information about scientific farming can help, too. Efforts of this kind are necessary to offset the pressure of population growth on world food supplies.

In the following sections we will look at some of the factors that contribute to increasing or decreasing production possibilities in agriculture.

Agricultural Research

Agricultural research differs from the popular view of discovery. There are few startling revelations that suddenly blast their way into public knowledge. Most developments in food production occur after years of costly experimentation, with results roughly proportionate to the level of investment expenditures

---

*United States fishermen are required to use U.S.-made boats, which are normally more costly than foreign-made vessels.

for R&D. This was certainly true of the "Green Revolution," spearheaded by biologist and Nobel laureate Norman Borlaug in the 1960s.

Achievements of the 1970s have continued to add to the world's capacity for food production. New varieties of poultry were bred to eat less grain and mature earlier. Chickens and turkeys were bred to have a larger proportion of white meat. Some chickens were bred to remain small; they lay the same size eggs but require less food and take up less space. Dairy cows were bred to yield three times as much milk as in the 1950s (Average yield is 1,175 gallons, but specially bred cows have produced as much as 6,550 gallons.) Cows today have stronger legs and are better suited for life in a concrete dairy barn and for the use of milking machines. Embryonic transplants can enable a prize cow to produce substantially more offspring than in the past. Researchers are working on the job of increasing pig litters, and in England scientists have successfully developed embryo transfer techniques for sheep, cattle, and horses. Vegetables have been bred for easy picking by machine and for greater resistance to disease and insect pests. Researchers are working on production of plants that can tolerate salty soil and on producing perennial corn—corn that will grow year after year without replanting. Others are attempting to create new plant strains that will produce their own nitrogen and plants that will absorb more light and, therefore, grow faster. And finally, new processes are underway for increasing the sugar, oil, or protein content of various vegetables.

The benefits of agricultural research have only recently extended to the less-developed countries (LDCs). Although LDCs farm 70 percent of the world's arable land, they use only 25 percent of the world's agricultural machinery and only 10 percent of the fertilizer. A United Nations subagency, the Consultative Group on International Agricultural Research, is now working to spread scientific farming techniques to these nations. Local research and agricultural extension programs help provide information to small farmers. Because of their ample supplies of labor, emphasis on labor-intensive agriculture is appropriate in the LDCs. To transplant agricultural techniques directly from developed to less-developed countries would be inefficient.

Chemical Fertilizer

One of the important reasons for increased agricultural productivity has been the increased use of chemical fertilizers. Chemical fertilizers were a major part of the "Green Revolution," adding significantly to crop yields per acre. The OPEC oil price increase raised the cost of petroleum-based fertilizers substantially and threatened to put an end to this source of increased food production. Nevertheless, fertilizer production has resumed growth at about 10 percent a year, with the greatest increases in the less-developed countries. Growth in supply has caused prices to moderate, and surpluses have appeared for nitrogen, phosphate, and potash. Most countries are expected soon to be self-sufficient or nearly so in fertilizer production. The Soviet Union and China are moving toward self-sufficiency.

Increased use of fertilizer in the LDCs has almost doubled their agricultural output over the past decade. New strains of wheat and rice used in Asia have responded particularly well to applications of fertilizer. The chief obstacles to greater fertilizer use have been government policies that reduce incentives in farming, outmoded practices on the farms, and the scarcity of foreign exchange for importing supplies.

(Each year Americans spread 1.3 million tons of fertilizer on lawns, golf courses, and cemeteries, an amount that could be used to produce grain for 65 million people.)

Weather

Little conclusive research has been done on the possible effects on food production of changes in the world's weather. Scientists are divided over whether a continuation of long-term trends will cause a drop in global temperatures* or whether increased burning of fossil fuels has caused an increase in atmospheric carbon dioxide and a tendency toward warmer temperatures.† In either case, the significant factor for agricultural scientists will be the *variability* of weather, since plant and animal strains can be developed for a particular kind of weather but not for *all* kinds.

The Soviet Union is more vulnerable to weather changes than much of the world. In the Soviet Union, government pressure to expand farm output has meant that only a small portion of arable land can be left "fallow," or unplanted for one or more growing seasons. In parts of the United States, a third to a half the arable land is left fallow. **Fallow land** is tilled to remove weeds and is left to accumulate moisture. When fallow land is returned to cultivation, yields per acre tend to be greater. The failure to leave land fallow in the Soviet Union means that a dry season will remove all available moisture from the land and sharply reduce crop yields.

The United States experienced severe droughts of about four years' duration in the 1930s and 1950s. Some scientists believe that the world is subject to 20-year drought cycles and that the 1970s may have been the beginning of another periodic dry spell. United States agriculture is less vulnerable to drought today because of the development of improved irrigation and drought-resistant varieties of grain. Other scientists believe there has been a southward shift of rain-bearing winds around the globe. In Africa, the southward shift of winds is causing an expansion of the Sahara Desert to the south by as much as 30 miles a year. In Asia, wind changes have caused a shift offshore of needed monsoon rains.

*Similar to the "little ice age" that occured in Europe from the thirteenth to the nineteenth century. Even a 1°F. drop in temperature reduces growing seasons by a week to 10 days. Dust particles in the air also deflect some of the sunlight from earth and reduce solar heat.

†Carbon dioxide in the atmosphere allows sunlight to reach the earth but prevents the escape of infrared heat waves that radiate back from the earth's surface. Scientists call this result the **greenhouse effect.**

The first major manifestation of an expansion of the Sahara was prolonged drought in pasture and farmlands stretching across Africa. Fast population growth in the 1960s had increased the human and livestock population beyond the fragile capacity of the area. A failure of rain in 1972, combined with overgrazing of pastures, forced livestock herds and starving herdsmen into areas already suffering from crop failure and overpopulation. Disease spread rapidly among the crowded and ill-nourished people. Death rates rose, and the survivors will bear the physical scars of deprivation for their entire lives.

The United States has a number of distinct climatic zones, making us less susceptible than many nations to particular climatic changes. Moreover, some U.S. climate zones can support two crops a year. This means that at least one crop may be unaffected by poor growing conditions. Still, a decline in farm production means higher food prices, higher Cost-of-Living Adjustments (COLAs) in wages, and generally higher inflation. Also, food prices tend to rise easily but seldom fall as much when growing conditions improve.

Population

The positive results of improved resources and technology can be only temporary if population growth outstrips advances in agricultural productivity. Moreover, population and economic growth increase pressures on natural resources, disturb the delicate balance of nature, and create problems of waste disposal. All these factors affect agriculture, food supplies, and food requirements. The growth of agriculture itself worsens the general problem of coordinating the use of global resources.

World population is expected to grow by 200,000 a day, from 4 billion to 7 billion people by the end of the century. Southern Asia, Africa, and Latin America continue to experience rapid population growth, while population in Western nations and Japan will soon stabilize or perhaps decline. In certain less-developed nations, efforts by the West to encourage population control are looked on as "imperialistic" strategies to perpetuate control of weak nations by strong nations. This is certainly a subject that requires greater public education and policies sensitive to the cultural and political concerns of other nations.

FOOD PRICE FLUCTUATIONS

Whereas prices of industrial products tend to be stable (or to rise fairly steadily), agricultural prices tend to fluctuate widely from year to year and even month to month. One reason has to do with price elasticities, both in the short and the long run. In particular, demand for farm commodities tends to be relatively price inelastic over very long periods. This is because of our inability to consume substantially more or substantially less food, regardless of price. Supply of farm commodities tends to be price inelastic in the short run and more elastic in the long run. This is because changing the quantity supplied is difficult

Figure 10-4

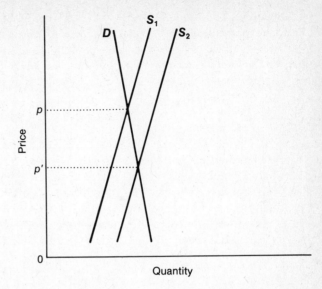

in one growing season but easier when idle capacity can be returned to production in the next. (An increased demand for strawberries or sirloin steaks cannot be satisfied in the short run as easily as increased demand for T-shirts or record albums.)

Farmers' responsiveness to high or low food prices may work to aggravate tendencies toward price fluctuations. Look at Figure 10-4, which shows the market for a particular food product in the short run. Inelastic demand and supply yield a relatively high market equilibrium price at p_1. But the high price encourages farmers to use idle capacity and to transfer existing capacity into production of the high-priced food. For food products that can be produced relatively quickly, supply curves move quickly to the right, and prices stabilize at a level high enough to cover costs of production. A moderate shift of supply yields price p' on Figure 10-4.

Some food commodities may require several years to produce, so that supply remains limited and price high for a relatively long time. Beef is a commodity that requires time to produce; it takes up to six years to build a cattle herd. This means that beef prices may remain abnormally high for considerable time, encouraging substantial movement of farmers into beef production. When new beef supplies are finally brought to market, the drop in price may be quite sharp.

Pencil in a third supply curve with an abnormally low equilibrium price, p'', on Figure 10-4. The effect of abnormally low prices is a substantial reduction in production plans for the coming period and a new backward shift in supply. Then, high prices cause a repeat of the cycle and a continuing tendency toward price fluctuations.

The pricing theory behind Figure 10-4 is called the **cobweb theorem** because surpluses ultimately appear at high prices, driving price down until shortages

Figure 10–5
Price behavior over time.

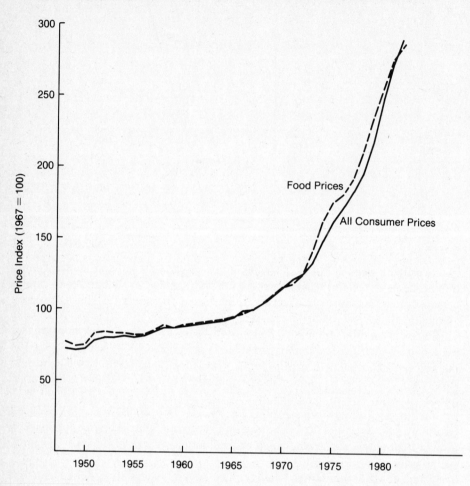

occur at low prices. The pattern of price changes oscillates around equilibrium in the shape of a cobweb. Locate the surplus that appears at price p in Figure 10–4 and the shortage at p''. Then show how an eventual leftward shift of supply will cause a repeat of the price cycle.

Figure 10–5 is a time series graph of all consumer prices since 1947 with a corresponding graph of prices for unprocessed food. Rising food prices since 1973 have pulled up the index of all consumer prices. Still, consumer prices in general are more stable than food prices. Food prices are strongly affected by beef prices, which tend to move in 9- to 10-year cycles corresponding to the building and depletion of cattle herds.

Special Case

Hedging and Speculating in Farm Commodities

Hedging and **speculating** in farm commodities provides a degree of stability—or at least predictability — to farm prices. The actions of hedgers and speculators enable producers and users to lock in a price for a commodity to be traded in the future. The system works through **futures contracts.**

Suppose a farmer expects to bring 10,000 bushels of wheat to market in three months. He learns that three-month wheat futures are selling at $4.00 a bushel, an acceptable price. By agreeing now to sell at $4.00, the farmer protects himself against a drop in wheat prices. The buyer of the farmer's wheat contract—for example, a major baking company—protects itself against a possible rise in wheat prices over the next three months.

Farmers and cooperatives, large agribusiness firms, and food processing firms use the futures market every day to "hedge" against future uncertainties. To "hedge" is to buy or sell futures contracts for crops that will be needed or will be available in the future.

Other participants in futures markets do not expect to have nor do they want agricultural commodities: such traders are called "speculators." Speculators participate in the exchange of futures contracts for the sole aim of making a profit. To illustrate, suppose the price of wheat actually rises to $4.25 during the duration of the farmer's contract in the above example. If a speculator had anticipated the price rise and bought the farmer's contract, he would have a cheap source of grain to sell to a final user. By selling the contract at a price somewhat below the current market price of grain, the speculator would make a profit. He would also help hold down the price of grain sold to processing firms.

Now suppose a commodities speculator expects the market price of wheat to fall to $3.75 over the life of a three-month futures contract. This time he would contract to sell grain at the current futures price of $4.00. He hopes to "cover" his contract in three months by buying grain cheaply and reselling at a profit.

Speculators' purchases and sales are described as "long" or "short" positions. When a speculator purchases a contract for something he does not want, he is said to have taken a "long" position. When he sells a contract for something he does not have, he has taken a "short" position. Profits on long and short trading depend on actual price movements relative to expected movements. If prices move as expected, the speculator gains. If not, he loses.

Speculators are sometimes accused of unjustly profiting from losses borne by farmers and users of farm commodities. More correctly, speculators accept risks of price changes and are compensated for accepting risk. Without speculation, buyers and sellers would be more vulnerable to the vagaries of the market. There is another advantage of speculation. Speculation is a free-market activity: speculators respond to market incentives as opposed to government mandates. The combined decisions of many knowledgeable and motivated speculators may achieve more efficient results than would a single major decision of government.

- In what ways are the actions of speculators similar to government policy for stabilizing farm prices?
- Can the actions of speculators be destabilizing?

Special Case

World Hunger

If there is one thing the average American is *not,* it is hungry. In general, our food problems arise less from scarcity than from overindulgence. We spend more for appetite suppressants, diet books, and weight loss clinics than many entire nations spend for all their basic food requirements.

This was not always the case. During the 1930s and 1940s, poor children in the rural South suffered from a variety of diseases due to malnutrition:

- Rickets is caused by a deficiency of vitamin D and produces soft, deformed bones.
- Pellagra appears in corn-eating populations where a deficiency of animal protein prevents the body from utilizing the protein in corn; pellagra is said to lead to the four Ds—dermatitis, diarrhea, dementia, and death.
- Beriberi occurs in rice-eating populations deficient in vitamin B_1 and affects the heart, circulatory system, and brain.
- Anemia results from a deficiency of iron, protein, and vitamin B_{12} necessary for the formation of blood hemoglobin and red blood cells.

Probably two-thirds of the world's population now have an inadequate food supply, and half a billion people are chronically hungry. The press of people on scarce land makes it necessary to plant foods high in calories (rice, corn, cassava, and wheat) instead of foods high in vitamins (leafy vegetables and fruits).

Vitamin deficiency affects infants and children more critically than adults, leading to swollen abdomens, lesions on the face and body, apathy, and arrested development. Some primitive cultures still adhere to ancient traditions in which fathers and mothers have priority over children in the distribution of food. In some cultures, religious taboos forbid the consumption of certain healthy and nutritious foods.

Malnutrition has permanent effects on children. At least 80 percent of brain growth occurs between conception and age two years. Without proper nutrition, children cannot develop the capacity to function as adults. Humans die less frequently from starvation than from the diseases that attack weakened bodies. Lack of food causes the body to consume its own fat, muscles, and tissues, leaving it especially vulnerable to disease.

The food problem is as much a problem of distribution as of production. Affluence in part of the world increases food demand and raises food costs for the poorer areas. Areas of food crisis today include northeastern Brazil, Bangladesh, Ethiopia, Chad, Niger, Mali, Mauritania, Senegal, Vietnam, New Guinea, Upper Volta, Bolivia, Angola, Zambia, Tanzania, Kenya, Uganda, and India. Even generous food aid cannot help many of the world's starving people. Transportation and distribution systems are inadequate for moving food, and storage facilities are poor. It is estimated that one-fourth of the world's food is wasted to insects, rats, fungus, and mildew.

- Is the concept of "triage" (discussed in chapter 9 relative to health services) relevant to the problem of world hunger? is triage efficient?

QUESTIONS

1. What circumstances contributed to making 1973 a "watershed" year for agriculture worldwide?
2. Consult the *Economic Report of the President* for data on resources used in farming over recent decades. Chart trends and interpret your findings.
3. Explain the basis and procedure for "target pricing." How is a "target price" policy different from price supports? What are the significant issues for farm policy in the 1980s? Discuss.
4. Discuss the advantages and disadvantages of parity pricing. What other producing groups in our economy seek parity incomes?
5. How are trade barriers for meat and sugar significant for meat and sugar prices in the United States? What is the significance for U.S. inflation?
6. What new agricultural technologies may have costly side-effects?
7. Discuss the interrelationships between population growth, agricultural land, productivity, and environmental pollution. What strategies might be successful for reducing the negative feedbacks of these variables? How can agriculture be made more efficient?
8. Consult the latest *Statistical Abstract of the United States* for data on farm sales relative to average acreage. Comment on trends: then determine sales per acre for farms of various sizes. What can you conclude about scale economies in farming?
9. What potential problems exist in the fishing industry? How are these problems similar to those of agriculture?
10. What specific technical advances in the United States have contributed to an upward shift of the total product function for agriculture? Consult the *Economic Report of the President* for data on farm productivity. Compare changes in productivity with population growth, and comment on your findings.

DEFINITIONS

The cobweb theorem explains the tendency of farm prices to fluctuate widely above and below an equilibrium price that would just cover farmers' costs of production. The wide fluctuations are a result of farmers' response to high or low prices for a product that requires a relatively long time to produce.

A commodity agreement is an agreement among producing nations to limit their exports of a particular product in years of surplus in order to maintain an agreed price. Surplus stocks are to be sold in years of shortage.

Fallow land is land that is held out of production to allow nutrients and moisture to return to the soil.

Fixed resources are quantities of land and capital equipment that remain constant over some period of time.

A food reserve is a stock of food stored to use in periods of food shortages. A reserve can be accomplished also by keeping land out of production but ready for movement back into production when food shortages appear.

Futures contract are contracts for delivery of a commodity at some time in the future at an agreed price.

The "greenhouse effect" is the effect on climate that results from the burning of hydrocarbons. As hydrocarbon waste accumulates in the earth's atmosphere, radiation from the sun cannot escape and contributes to a warming of the earth's climate.

Hedging is the purchase or sale of contracts for delivery of food commodities some time in the future. Farmers sell their crops and users buy supplies for future delivery at an agreed price.

Parity is the ratio of prices farmers receive to prices farmers pay. A 100 percent parity ratio is recommended by many farmers. This would mean that farm prices would maintain the same purchasing power as in a certain previous year.

Speculating is the purchase or sale of contracts for future delivery of food commodities by persons who do not have or need the product. The purpose is to resell the contract later at a gain.

The subsistence level of production is a level of Average Product that is just sufficient for sustaining the life of the population.

A support price is a price below which market price may not be allowed to fall. It is the opposite of a price ceiling. Government maintains a support price by buying surplus food products and taking them off the market.

Target prices are legislated prices for food commodities. They are set at about the cost of production. If market prices fall below the target price, government pays an income-supplement to farmers.

SUGGESTED READINGS

Breimyer, Harold F. "Agriculture: Return of the Thirties?" *Challenge*, July/August, 1982, p. 35.

Brown, Lester R. "Global Food Prospects: Setting the Record Straight." *Challenge*, November/December, 1982, p. 48.

———. "Global Food Prospects: Shadow of Malthus." *Challenge*, January/February, 1982, p. 14.

Schultz, Theodore W. "Knowledge Is Power in Agriculture." *Challenge*, September/October, 1981, p. 4.

Simon, Julian L., and William J. Hudson. "Global Food Prospects: Good News." *Challenge*, November/December, 1982, p. 40.

CHAPTER ELEVEN

Regulated Industries: The Transportation Sector

What's the Best Way to Go?

LEARNING OBJECTIVES

- To note the particular characteristics of transportation that distinguish it from other kinds of economic activity and necessitate some form of government regulation.
- To show how a single transportation firm can select price and volume of service so as to enjoy economic profit and how negative economic profit can be offset by government subsidies or price discrimination.
- To explain the most efficient level of transportation service according to Marginal Social Product (including external benefits) and Marginal Social Cost (including external costs).
- To describe the progress of transportation in the United States and the various forms of government intervention in the transportation sector.
- To analyze location decisions of business firms in terms of transportation costs.

Ever since Paul Revere galloped his trusty steed over the darkened roads of Massachusetts, no sector of the U.S. economy has been influenced more by government than the transportation sector. Governments financed much of the early building of roads and canals and contributed greatly to the construction of railroads. Governments continue to build roads, maintain waterways, and direct air traffic. Perhaps more important, governments regulate practices in all the forms of public transportation by air, water, or highway.

Where would we be without government intervention in transportation? This is a worrisome question, particularly since our highly developed, diverse, and interdependent economy is so dependent on efficient and reliable transportation for moving goods and people. Our ability to enjoy labor-intensive services, our freedom to consider quality of life in making policy, our capacity to extend prosperity to more regions and more people all depend on our ability to satisfy fundamental needs cheaply. All this requires cheap transportation — with regional specialization and exchange and with the confident expectation that the things we want will be there when we need them.

The importance of transportation for our well-being makes policy decisions especially critical. Both for managers of individual transportation firms and for policy makers in government, the goals of policy should be efficiency—the use of scarce transportation resources to produce the maximum gains in total goods and services—and equity—the fairest possible distribution of the benefits and costs of an effective transportation system.

SOME PRINCIPLES OF TRANSPORTATION

Transportation firms are similar in many ways to firms that produce other goods and services. They are different in other ways, ways that justify some sort of government intervention in the transportation sector. The following sections describe some of these similarities and differences. As you read, consider the ways that, say, railroads differ from manufacturing firms. Think about the cost considerations facing both kinds of firms and the factors that influence their pricing decisions. Then consider the advantages and disadvantages of government regulation in one market and not the other.

Costs and Pricing Policy in Transportation Firms

Transportation illustrates two principles of economic policymaking at the level of the individual transportation firm and at the level of the nation as a whole:

1. For a single transportation firm, market equilibrium may occur at a level of service at which **average total cost** per unit of service is different from the **marginal cost** associated with an additional unit. With ATC $\neq$ MC, a single transportation firm may collect positive economic profits. On the other hand, a firm may continue in operation even though current operations yield negative **economic profit** (or loss).
2. For the nation as a whole, the sum total of all benefits and costs of transportation may differ from the benefits enjoyed and costs paid by individual users of transportation services. In this case, the occurrence of *external benefits and costs* may provide the basis for government intervention in the industry.

Differences Between Average and Marginal Costs.   To provide transportation services requires substantial initial investment in capital equipment before business can begin. High capital requirements limit the number of firms that can enter the transportation sector and limit competition between them. Once in place, transportation equipment can continue to provide service over many years. Canals that have been constructed, ports that have been dredged, and rivers that have been deepened require minimum maintenance to accommodate ship and barge traffic. Railroad tracks and rights-of-way, terminal buildings and freight yards, and electronic and locomotive equipment are costly but long-lasting. The same is true of superhighways, bridges, and air traffic control systems.

High initial capital costs make average costs per unit of service very high if only a small volume of service is produced. This is because the cost of capital equipment must be shared by a small number of buyers. When the volume of service increases, the cost of capital shared by each unit of service falls sharply. Furthermore, a larger volume of service can usually be provided with very little increase in other costs: fuel, maintenance, terminal handling, and so forth. All these factors contribute to the emergence of a few large firms in the transportation sector, each with substantial market power.

The difference between *fixed* and *variable costs* is especially significant for transportation firms. **Fixed costs** are the contractual costs of business that must be paid over a certain period of time. The fixed costs of transportation include the costs of rights-of-way, automotive equipment and terminal facilities, property taxes, administrative salaries, dividends on preferred stock, and interest on bonds and loans. Fixed costs also include *normal profit*. Normal profit is a necessary payment to entrepreneurs for assuming the risks of operating in the transportation sector.* Normal profit may consist of dividends to holders of common stock and minimum acceptable payments to other owners and managers.

The level of fixed costs depends on the size of the enterprise; fixed costs do not vary with the volume of service sold in the short run. As a result, a larger volume of service can usually be produced without increasing these costs. In fact, given some level of fixed costs, the average fixed cost per unit of service declines as larger and larger quantities are produced.

Variable costs are costs that change with the volume of service produced during a certain period of time. The variable costs of transportation include wages of crew and maintenance workers and the costs of fuel and terminal services. Typically, total variable costs increase slowly as volume of service increases from zero. This is because crews and equipment can be operated more efficiently with small increases in volume of service. Thus, average variable cost per unit tends to fall over a range of service from zero to some quantity.

---

*Entrepreneurs may receive more or less than **normal profit,** depending on actual conditions in the market for particular goods or services. We call a return that is greater than normal profit *economic profit*. Economic profit is an amount over and above the minimum amount necessary to persuade the entrepreneur to remain in the business. We will have more to say about economic profit later in this chapter.

At some level of operation, existing transportation equipment will be providing just the volume of service for which it was designed. Average variable costs of crew, fuel, and terminal service will be at their minimum. In fact, over some range of service for which the firm's fixed capital was designed, total variable costs will increase at some constant rate as the volume of service increases. This range is the **optimum range of plant utilization.** Beyond the optimum range of utilization, total variable costs will normally rise more sharply. This is because crews tend to become overworked or excessive, equipment load capacities tend to be exceeded, and additional stops tend to be required for loading and unloading. All these factors will cause average variable costs to increase.

The graphs of Figure 11–1 illustrate the various cost categories for a single transportation firm in the short run. Quantity of service is measured on the horizontal axis, and costs on the vertical axis. Fixed costs are shown as a constant amount in Figure 11–1a, whatever the quantity of service. **Average fixed cost** is determined by dividing fixed costs by quantity of service: $AFC = FC/Q$. Average fixed cost declines over the entire range of volume, as shown in Figure 11–1b. Total variable costs rise first at a decreasing rate as volume approaches the optimum range, then at a constant rate, and finally, beyond the optimum range of

Figure 11–1
Categories for a transportation firm in the short run.

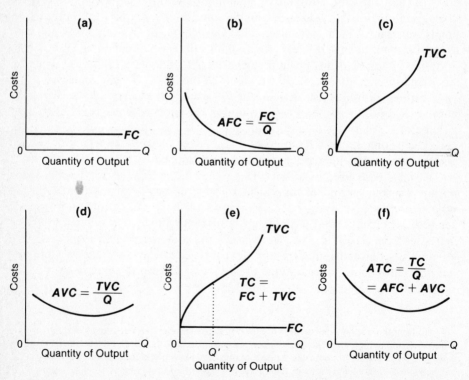

plant utilization, at an increasing rate. Look at Figure 11–1c and confirm the behavior of total variable costs. **Average variable costs** are total variable costs divided by quantity of service: $AVC = TVC/Q$. Average variable cost declines as volume approaches the optimum range of output and increases beyond that range. The behavior of average variable costs is illustrated in Figure 11–1d. Figure 11–1e shows **total costs,** the sum of the firm's constant fixed costs from Figure 11–1a and total variable costs from Figure 11–1c. Finally, Figure 11–1f shows average total costs, the sum of average fixed cost and average variable cost at every level of output: average total cost $= ATC = AFC + AVC = (FC + VC)/Q$. The behavior of average total cost is determined by the initial decline of AFC and AVC and the eventual increase in AVC.

Economic Profit

The goal of a profit-maximizing firm is to produce the quantity of output that maximizes the difference between total revenue and total cost. The difference between total revenue and total cost is *economic profit*. Economic profit differs from normal profit, which is a necessary payment to entrepreneurs and is included in total cost. When there is competition, price is normally forced down to a level that eliminates economic profit. With market power, on the other hand, a single transportation firm can set price high enough to collect economic profit.

The maximum-profit level of transportation service is the level at which producing a single additional unit adds the same amount to total revenue as it adds to total cost.* We say:

Marginal Revenue = Marginal Cost means maximum Economic Profit.

Marginal revenue is the change in total revenue associated with a unit change in quantity of service; marginal revenue depends on characteristics of demand for the service. Marginal cost is the change in total cost associated with a unit change in quantity; marginal cost depends on characteristics of production costs. Let us look at these concepts in detail.

Marginal Revenue. Demand for transportation service reflects the usefulness (or utility) of the transportation service to consumers. A transportation demand curve has a typical downward slope, indicating that larger quantities will be bought only at lower prices. The reason is that larger quantities provide decreasing marginal utility. Equilibrium price depends on quantity supplied in the market. If many firms were to compete to sell transportation services, supply would be the sum of quantities supplied by all firms. Market equilibrium would

---

*The truth of this statement is easy to see if you first imagine it were not so. If an additional unit of service adds more to total revenue than to total cost ($MR > MC$), production should be increased. If an additional unit adds less to total revenue than to total cost ($MR < MC$), production should be cut back. Only if $MR = MC$ is the firm collecting maximum Economic Profit.

Figure 11–2

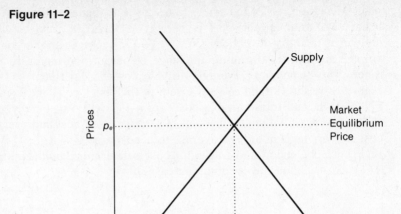

establish a single price to apply to all firms. Thus, for all firms in the market, **marginal revenue** would be the same as price. In this case, the profit-maximizing level of output for a firm in competition is the level at which market equilibrium price = marginal revenue = marginal cost for that firm. Total quantity is the sum of all quantities produced and sold by all the firms in the market. Market equilibrium is illustrated in Figure 11–2.

The result is different if only one large firm (or cooperating group of firms) provides the entire quantity of service in the market. A single firm that produces all the output for a particular market is called a **monopoly.** When a single transportation firm faces the entire demand curve for the service, there is no market equilibrium price. The single monopoly firm can select any price and corresponding quantity that satisfies the firm's own profit goals. Normally, the firm will select the profit-maximizing quantity at which marginal revenue is equal to marginal cost. But for the single monopoly firm, marginal revenue is *not* the same as price. The monopoly firm must choose a price that yields marginal revenue equal to marginal cost. Stated differently, the monopoly firm must choose a point on its demand curve at which the quantity produced and sold will increase the firm's revenue by just enough to offset its increase in costs.

Figure 11–3a shows a demand curve for a particular kind of transportation service. The demand curve slopes downward, indicating that the single monopoly firm must reduce price if it is to sell additional units of service. However, applying a lower selling price to all units of service means that additional revenue for additional sales is less than price. Thus, the marginal revenue for a monopoly transportation firm is less than selling price.

The marginal revenue associated with increasing sales volume has been calculated and drawn below the demand curve in Figure 11–3a. For the monopoly

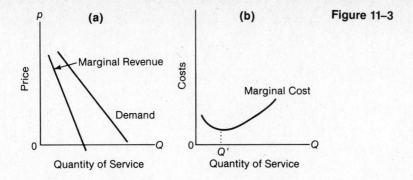

Figure 11–3

firm, maximum profit occurs at the level of service at which marginal revenue is equal to the transportation firm's marginal cost.

Marginal cost. Look back at Figure 11–1e to determine marginal cost. Marginal cost is defined as the change in total cost that results from a unit change in quantity of service. In Figure 11–1e, marginal cost is the *slope* of total costs as service expands by small increments moving from left to right along the horizontal axis. The steep slope as TC leaves the vertical axis indicates high marginal cost for the first units of service. The slope of the total cost curve tends to decline with larger volume until some level of service Q' at which the slope is lowest and, therefore, marginal cost is also lowest. Beyond this level of service, existing fixed capital is insufficient for expanding volume as readily as before. Therefore, marginal cost tends to rise, and the slope of the total cost curve increases. A marginal cost curve with these characteristics has been drawn as Figure 11–3b.

The Profit-Maximizing Output. Figure 11–4 combines demand and marginal revenue curves with marginal and average total cost curves necessary for selecting the **profit-maximizing level** of service for a monopoly transportation firm. The profit-maximizing quantity occurs where marginal revenue is equal to marginal cost at the level of service shown by Q''. For this firm, OQ'' units of service can be sold for a price of Op'', read from the demand curve. Total revenue for the firm is the area of the shaded rectangle formed beneath the demand curve at price p'' and quantity Q'': Total Revenue = price times quantity = $Op'' \times OQ''$. Unit costs at this level of output are read from the average total cost curve as Oc''. Total cost is shown as the rectangle beneath ATC: Total Cost = average total cost times quantity = $Oc'' \times OQ''$. The difference between the total revenue and total cost rectangles is the firm's economic profit.

The curves in Figure 11–4 are drawn so that there is, indeed, positive economic profit. Whether economic profit is achieved in the real world depends on the positions of demand and average cost curves. For the transportation sector, average total costs tend to fall rather sharply, as we have seen. This makes positive economic profit a strong possibility for a monopoly transportation firm.

Figure 11–4

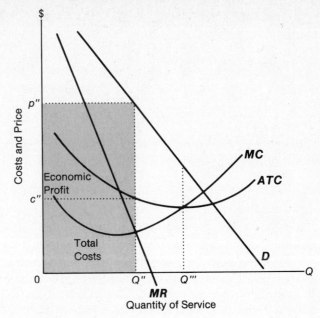

Quantity of Service

The Question of Efficiency

Look again at Figure 11–4 and particularly at the average cost curve at the profit-maximizing level of service for the monopoly firm. Note that the profit-maximizing level of service occurs along a portion of the average total cost curve where *ATC* is falling. This is typical of cost behavior in industries with high initial capital requirements and a few large firms. Producing in the range of decreasing *ATC* means that the firm is not operating at maximum efficiency. To expand production to the level of service shown at *Q'''* would be most efficient, since at *Q'''* the average total cost curve reaches its lowest point. However, at *Q'''* the profit rectangle is smaller than at *Q''*, and the profit-maximizing firm will not normally choose this level of operation.

One reason for government intervention in transportation markets is to require a monopoly transportation firm (or group of similar firms) to expand service to a more efficient level. The role of a public regulatory commission is frequently to require a firm to move down its demand curve, set a lower price, and produce a larger volume of service. The firm will still collect normal profits and may collect economic profits as well; but profits will generally be lower than without government intervention.

There is another possibility, illustrated in Figure 11–5, where exceptionally high costs for fixed capital and exceptionally low variable costs combine to yield an *ATC* curve that falls over the entire range of service shown. Marginal costs are also lower than *ATC* as additional units of service are provided with smaller and smaller increases in variable cost. Notice that under the conditions shown, no level of service demanded by consumers would mean lowest cost, most efficient operation.

Figure 11–5

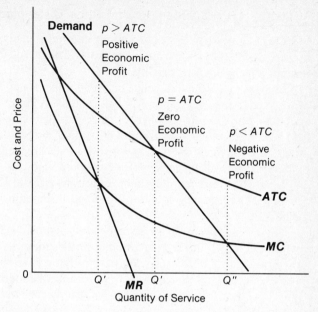

Suppose the firm in Figure 11–5 were to expand production to the largest volume at which selling price just covers average total cost. This volume is shown as Q', where price read from the demand curve is equal to average total cost. With $p = ATC$, economic profit is zero. A firm is not likely to choose a zero economic profit level of output unless required to do so by a public regulatory commission. At the volume of service indicated at Q', the firm can pay all its fixed and variable charges, including interest and stock dividends, wages and salaries, utilities and materials, and normal profit. But there is no economic profit, over and above the necessary payment to productive resources.

There is still a third possible result of government intervention in transportation markets. Look again at Figure 11–5 and note that MC lies below ATC over its entire length. This means that *additional* costs (not including fixed costs) for expanding service are less than average costs (including fixed costs). This result is typical of industries with high initial capital costs relative to variable operating costs. Because the necessary plant and equipment are already in place, the additional costs associated with expanding volume are not very great. In this case, a public regulatory commission may require that the transportation firm (or firms) provide a level of service at which selling price just covers *additional* costs: that is, where MC crosses the demand curve at Q''. Producing at Q'' is the most efficient level of operation, given the demand and cost conditions shown in Figure 11–5. Thus, it provides maximum benefits at lowest costs for this market.

A single firm is not likely to choose the level of output shown at Q''. At this volume, total revenue is less than total costs, as represented by their respective rectangles, and economic profit is negative. A firm can provide this level of service only if revenue from sales is supplemented from another source.

Subsidies and Price Discrimination

There are two ways government can help ensure sufficient revenue to a regulated transportation firm. One way is through a direct subsidy, and another is through discriminatory pricing.

In Figure 11–5 the difference between total revenue and total cost at Q'' units of service is negative economic profit, or loss. A direct subsidy equal to negative economic profit would enable the firm to pay all its fixed costs: rent for necessary land resources, wages for trained personnel, interest and preferred stock dividends to owners of capital, and profits to entrepreneurs and common stock holders. Unless all these resources are paid amounts comparable to what they could earn in other employments, they may leave the transportation sector, causing service quality to deteriorate and threatening abandonment of service facilities.

There are certain disadvantages with a subsidy. If firms are guaranteed a payment equal to negative economic profit, they may be slow to adopt cost-saving innovation or to seek ways of improving operating efficiency. Equity may be harmed, too, because a subsidy is paid from general tax revenues. Thus, all taxpayers contribute to the subsidy while only certain taxpayers actually use the service. Whether all taxpayers should be required to contribute may depend on whether the benefits of efficient transportation extend broadly over the community, indirectly improving the living standards of all taxpayers. A more equitable source of funds for the subsidy might be a **user tax** levied only on those who actually use the service. A user tax would be similar to a price increase in that it would discourage less essential uses of transportation resources. The result would be to allocate transportation services more toward buyers whose needs are most urgent and who are willing and able to pay the cost. On the other hand, the higher price would also have the effect of reducing quantity demanded. The result would be to reduce the volume of service produced and raise the average total cost of each unit sold.

The second way of ensuring sufficient revenue is through price discrimination. Price discrimination involves setting different fees for different users of the service. This means that price discrimination is possible only where markets can be separated. Otherwise, buyers would be able to buy the service cheaply in one market and resell it in another, thus eliminating the firm's advantage. In general, the transportation firm will set high prices where the need is most urgent and buyers are most willing to pay. Prices will be set lower for less urgent consumer needs.

The effect of price discrimination is to enable the firm to collect all — or a substantial portion of — the revenue under the demand curve. The public regulatory commission may agree to a level of price discrimination such that total revenue is sufficient to pay total costs. Few users of the service will pay a price equal to actual production costs. In fact, the firm will use high prices collected from some buyers to **cross-subsidize** other buyers at low prices A familiar example of this kind of price discrimination is rate-setting for electric power. In general, homeowners, whose need for electric power is particularly urgent, are charged higher rates than are industrial firms, who may have the option of producing their own power if rates are set too high. Can you explain why the electric power industry is similar to the transportation industry in this respect?

There are some disadvantages with price discrimination. Setting different prices for different buyers may be inequitable, or unfair, particularly when the price is set on the basis of need. Also, a public regulatory commission may be subject to political pressure to favor particular groups in setting up the rate structure. And finally, the system of cross-subsidization may cause the service to be used inefficiently. Buyers who enjoy low rates may tend to overuse the service relative to less-favored buyers.

External Benefits and Costs

Some costs and benefits of transportation services are simple to calculate: a shipper of farm equipment pays the cost of service and receives transportation benefits equal to costs; a business or vacation traveler receives benefits equal to the cost of his or her ticket. (Otherwise, he or she wouldn't travel.) In both these cases, the benefits of transportation services are received by the users, and the users pay the costs.

There are other benefits and costs that result from a well-developed transportation system. The entire community receives benefits from the trade that transportation makes possible: job opportunities, a wider variety of consumer goods, and investment possibilities. Likewise, the entire community suffers the costs of pollution, congestion, and depletion of natural resources that transportation services may bring.

We have referred to these broader effects of economic activity as *externalities*—external benefits and external costs. External benefits and costs occur outside the market for a particular good or service. We say that external benefits and costs are *nonexclusive:* persons cannot be excluded from enjoying the external benefits or paying the external costs just because they have not purchased the service.

When all consumers can enjoy external benefits without purchasing the service, individual consumers may be reluctant to pay for it. Similarly, when producers can shift some of the costs of production to the community as a whole, individual producers will resist paying them. The community will expect to enjoy all the external benefits of increased trade, but it will not be able to escape the external costs of pollution, congestion, and resource depletion.

When there are external benefits and costs, the free market may be unable to allocate resources to ensure efficiency. Remember that the sum of all direct costs and external costs from increased production is called Marginal Social Cost; the sum of all direct and external benefits is Marginal Social Product. Maximum efficiency occurs where Marginal Social Product is equal to Marginal Social Cost.* Expanding production to the level where $MSP = MSC$ yields maximum Net Benefits. Stated differently, if $MSP/MSC > 1$, production should be expanded to increase Net Benefits. If $MSP/MSC < 1$, production should be cut back. If $MSP/MSC = 1$, production is efficient.

*This concept was applied to the issue of health care in chapter 9.

Whatever external benefits and costs occur in the production of transportation services should be included in the above calculations. Thus, if $MSP/MSC = 1$, production is efficient, in the sense that the community as a whole enjoys maximum Net Benefits from the production of transportation services.

The existence of externalities is the second major reason for government intervention in the transportation sector. An agency of government is normally given the responsibility of considering external benefits and costs and directing production so as to achieve maximum total benefits (including external benefits) relative to total cost (including external costs).

Implications for Government Regulation

We have discussed two principles of policymaking that affect the transportation sector: the difference between average and marginal costs for firms with high fixed costs and the occurrence of external benefits and costs. These two characteristics have important implications for the transportation sector. They create conditions that lead to government regulation or even government ownership. We have seen how high fixed capital requirements may result in economic profits or losses and that competition may not work to eliminate economic profit or loss. Government regulation may be needed to establish rate schedules that do not unfairly penalize certain groups of users. Government subsidies may be needed to finance a money-losing transportation firm and preserve the benefits of transportation service for the community involved. And finally, we have seen how external benefits and costs flow over the community without the requirement that costs be paid equal to benefits received. Government regulation or ownership may be necessary to pay full costs (commensurate with benefits) from the community's tax revenues. Transportation thus becomes a subject for public decision-making based on a consensus on community needs for long-range development or on its long-term resource availability.

THE PROGRESS OF TRANSPORTATION IN THE UNITED STATES

Transportation is closely bound up with the process of economic development. Transportation enables communities to pass beyond the stage of self-sufficiency to specialization in production. As a result of improved transportation, early peoples were able to begin the process of division of labor and mass production for a larger market. Large-scale production meant lower unit costs and higher rates of return on new investment—all leading to improved material standards of living.

In his *Stages of Economic Growth*, W. W. Rostow listed a well-developed transportation network as one of the necessary "preconditions" for economic growth. Transportation is essential for the exchange of ideas, materials, and goods. The construction of a transportation network may be regarded as "social overhead capital" — productive capital constructed by and for the use of the society as a whole. It is the necessary **infrastructure**—the foundation on which private enterprise can build capital for profitable production. The early settlers in North America realized this. They pooled their efforts to construct roads, bridges, and port facilities. Later they taxed themselves to finance the building of canals and tramways.

The development of the steam locomotive provided new opportunities for integrating the growing industrial centers of the Northeast with the vast agricultural lands of the Midwest. In the early 1800s, cities and counties sold bonds to finance railroad building. They offered railroads a guaranteed monopoly, special banking privileges, exemption from taxation, and even convict labor to encourage railroad building. In the process, some rail lines were overbuilt. Where capacity was excessive, some railroads went broke and defaulted on their loans.

As commerce resumed after the Civil War, the federal government grew interested in further development of transportation. The value of rail transport had been demonstrated during the war. Earlier, the controversy over states' rights had prevented the federal government from intervening in local needs, but the tremendous sums required for railroad construction made federal help necessary. United States government bonds were sold to provide up to $48,000 per mile of roadbed. Rights-of-way and terminal sites were provided from public land. Railroads were given land along their routes to be sold or mortgaged to finance construction. In return for federal aid, the railroads were obligated to carry U.S. mail, troops, and government property at preferred rates.

Regulation in the Transportation Sector

We have seen how certain characteristics of transportation gave rise to various forms of government regulation: first, high fixed costs that permitted the emergence of monopoly firms and, second, external benefits and costs of transportation for the society as a whole. Other characteristics were also important. Duplication of service in some areas and lack of service in others contributed to inefficiency in the allocation of transportation resources. All these factors seemed to call for government intervention in the transportation sector.

The states tried to regulate rail transportation, but differences between the states made enforcement difficult. The federal government began regulation of rail transportation in 1887 with establishment of the Interstate Commerce Commission. Regulation was extended to other forms of transportation throughout the first half of the twentieth century.

In recent years, critics have begun to question whether continued regulation is efficient or equitable. Some of the initial characteristics that gave rise to regulation may no longer be true of the transportation sector. Whereas once it may have been possible for a particular kind of transportation service to establish a monopoly, today, competition among all kinds of transportation services is vigorous. Railroads compete with airlines, and trucks compete with water transport. With competition, there may be no need for regulation to protect the public against monopoly pricing. In fact, competition has pushed economic profits down to zero for many transportation firms and has created losses for others.

Where there are losses, critics of regulation recommend that transportation firms be allowed to abandon service and shift their resources to more efficient uses. The result would be improved efficiency and increased total production. Also, removing regulation from the transportation sector would allow firms to compete on the basis of operating performance. Competition would have the effect of encouraging innovation and reducing costs. In the 1970s, Congress began deregulating the transportation sector.

In the following sections, we will look briefly at each of the major forms of transportation, roughly in the order in which they developed in the United States. As you read each section, keep in mind the fundamental characteristics of transportation that have prompted government intervention: the high fixed costs and the usual domination by a single firm (or cooperating group of firms); the low marginal costs that determine the profit-maximizing quantity of output; and the occurrence of external benefits and costs for the community. Then consider the strategies employed by regulatory commissions to increase efficiency, ensure adequate revenue, and promote quality service for many parts of the country. Ask yourself: what are the expected external benefits from government intervention? What have been the costs, particularly in terms of efficient resource allocation? Are the actual benefits received sufficient to justify the costs? What are the likely consequences of deregulation?

Railroads

The oldest regulatory body established in the United States to serve broad community interests was the Interstate Commerce Commission (ICC), established in 1887 to regulate rail traffic. The ICC was given authority to decide what routes *must* or *must not* be served by the various rail companies and to regulate the rates they could charge. At one point the ICC had the power to regulate earnings and distribute "excess" earnings of strong carriers to weak ones. Protecting weak lines was believed to be necessary in an interconnected system of rails spanning broad geographic areas.

Rail was appropriate for hauling large quantities of bulky commodities over long, uncongested rights-of-way. A typical freight train with three locomotives can pull a million ton-miles a day, about a hundred times more than a truck can carry. Freight trains carrying bulky agricultural and industrial commodities continue to operate profitably today, especially where there is little competition from trucks, barges, and other railroads.

Circumstances have changed in the industrial Northeast, however, where production of small, high-value goods has reduced the advantage of freight transport by rail. Increased competition from lower-cost barge and truck carriers has so reduced rail profits that in 1970 the nation's largest railroad, the Penn Central, declared bankruptcy. Six other lines in the Northeast followed quickly. In 1973, Congress passed the Regional Rail Reorganization Act, which combined parts of the seven bankrupt lines into a government-owned freight system called Consolidated Rail Corporation, or Conrail. Conrail was given authority to abandon unprofitable routes, consolidate lines and terminals, lay off surplus workers, and upgrade rail facilities. The rehabilitation program for northeastern rails was expected to take about 14 years and cost $7 billion.

Passenger rail service was also in trouble in the 1970s, suffering from competition with air travel and the private automobile. In 1971, money-losing passenger trains were combined into the National Rail Passenger Corporation, or Amtrak, to operate government vehicles on rails maintained by private rail firms. The objective of Amtrak was to preserve a limited number of passenger routes and to remove this unprofitable responsibility from private companies. Amtrak requires a considerable subsidy every year (more than $700 million in 1982, or about $35 for each Amtrak passenger). But Congress has concluded that the national interest justifies preservation of rail passenger service. Cutbacks in the federal budget in 1981 threatened to cut funds for Amtrak, but strong pressure from constituents kept the subsidy coming. Amtrak's defenders believe the system is on the verge of breaking even, with improved cars and schedules and substantial increases in passenger loads.

Some of the problems of the railroads were not of their own making. Whereas air and highway transportation are heavily dependent on government-owned facilities, the railroads must finance their own capital construction and maintenance. Since maintenance costs comprise a significant part of rail budgets, maintenance has often been neglected, such that about 50,000 miles of rail are in disrepair. Poorly maintained rails have meant costly delays and derailments, with a further reduction in demand for rail transport. Moreover, the ICC has required railroads to serve unprofitable routes, cross-subsidizing money-losing routes with high charges on other routes. The effect of cross-subsidies has been to drive the high-priced freight to competing forms of transportation and leave the railroads with the unprofitable traffic.

In 1980, Congress passed the Staggers Rail Act, giving railroads more flexibility in setting rates and more authority in establishing routes. Eventual deregulation of the rails will allow rates to be set by the market. Bulky freight particularly suited to rail will probably have to pay higher rates: then railroads will be able to use their higher revenues to purchase specially made equipment for carrying bulky freight more efficiently. Unregulated rail firms will be able to abandon unprofitable lines, consolidate and coordinate service, and compete on the basis of quality of service. Where the public interest clearly favors continuation of an unprofitable service, a subsidy may be paid to preserve it.

The energy shortage may prove to be an advantage for railroads, which consume less fuel than other forms of transportation. Moreover, high oil prices have increased demand for railroads' principal freight — coal — particularly low-sulphur coal mined in the West and used to produce electricity in the Northeast. Rail transport is generally cheaper than transport by truck and causes less congestion and environmental pollution. Many railroads have increased the use of "containerized" cars in order to reduce loading and unloading costs. Freight carriers are increasingly "intermodel" systems, transferring freight between various transportation modes to take advantage of the strengths of each mode. "Piggy back" containers can go directly from truck to rail to barge with little handling required. Preserving a relatively efficient low-cost rail transport system with little or no subsidy may be in the national interest after all.

Shipping

The United States merchant fleet is one of the most heavily subsidized industries in the country. In fact, the first U.S. Congress established a precedent by imposing higher customs duties on imports delivered by foreign ships as a means of protecting the shipping industry.

United States ship operators claim that government subsidies are necessary to enable them to compete with government-operated freight lines in the Soviet Union and other Communist countries. By law, all freight moving between U.S. ports must be carried on U.S. ships, whatever the cost advantage of competing service. Operating subsidies to 16 ship operators and 8 ship builders amount to more than half a billion dollars a year. The shipping industry in the United States utilizes waterways maintained by the Army Corps of Engineers and calls on ports maintained at public expense. The result is a kind of subsidy that gives intracontinental barge traffic a substantial cost advantage over rail transportation.

The reason for such lavish federal support has been concern for national security and preservation of jobs in the shipping industry. On the other hand, protection from competition may have impaired the efficiency and quality of water transport. In fact, many shipowners prefer to operate foreign ships because of their lower wage costs and better operating performance.

Investment in shipping can be particularly risky, since ships built for one kind of cargo—oil or grain, for example—cannot easily be converted for carrying another kind. A decline in a particular class of freight or an increase in competition can run a small carrier out of business. Ships ordered in years of expanding trade may not be delivered until a recession year when capacity is already excessive.* Some operators have attempted to establish a kind of cartel in which all members would share the cost of junking some amount of shipping capacity in order to keep freight charges from falling.

Some shipping firms are fighting high costs and competition with a move to "containerization." Special containers are designed for refrigerated, liquid, or powder cargo. The use of containers reduces terminal handling at both ends of the shipping line. By 1979, about half of suitable cargo was being shipped by container, leaving substantial room for increasing efficiency for the future.

Trucking

Until the 1950s, trucks carried less than 20 percent of intercity freight, but over recent decades trucking has gained in market share and now carries almost as much freight as the nation's railroads. Trucks have an advantage over rails in

*There is a parallel here to the problem in agriculture of making the supply of beef correspond to the demand. See chapter 10.

that they are more flexible for reaching out-of-the-way places, for short hauls, and for carrying less-than-carload sized lots.

The main cost advantage of trucks is their low fixed costs relative to rail transport. Also, the right-of-way used by trucks is built and maintained at public, rather than private, expense.* As a result, freight charges for truck transport may be lower than freight charges for comparable rail service. Low freight charges have diverted many users from rail to truck transport, severely damaging rail revenues. In recent years, the increased cost of fuel and reduced speed limits on the nation's highways have reduced the advantages of shipping by truck. Still, lobbyists in the auto, petroleum, rubber, and cement industries continue to press the interests of trucking in Washington.

Trucking came under federal regulation by the Interstate Commerce Commission in 1953. The ICC was given power to decide who can enter the industry, the routes they can serve, and the commodities they can carry. Through rate bureaus immune from antitrust prosecution, truckers set uniform prices to be approved by the ICC. The lack of competition tends to aggravate inflation and has probably stifled innovation in the trucking industry.

In 1980, Congress passed the Motor Carrier Act, giving truckers more freedom to raise and lower rates and removing certain restrictions on entry to the industry and routes served. The pace of deregulation has been slow, however, partly because of opposition within the industry. Industry analysts predict the following changes in the trucking industry:

1. Deregulation will accelerate the trend toward large firms carrying full truckloads from source to user. Full truckload service does not require heavy investment in terminal facilities and may be quite profitable. Smaller firms carrying less-than-truckload traffic have substantially higher terminal costs. Without cross-subsidization from truckload service to less-than-truckload service, all freight charges will have to reflect their true costs, and many rates will rise.
2. Deregulation will permit company-owned trucks to hire out to other firms on the backhaul after delivering company freight. Since the return to base is costless, the freight charge can be set low enough to undercut small trucking companies and drive them out of business. The result will be a substantial loss of jobs in the trucking industry.
3. Deregulation will deprive small towns of service. Since carrying freight to a small town may result in an empty backhaul, truckers will refuse to carry it.

In general, supporters of deregulation maintain that deregulation will force trucking firms to compete on the basis of price and quality of service. The result will be more efficient use of transportation resources. Forcing small firms out of business or merging them with larger firms will improve efficiency.

The ICC has power to enforce Congress' new law, but enforcement depends on the composition and philosophy of the seven-member commission. President Reagan appointed a new chairman to the commission and set forth a new

---

*Trucks do pay a truck-fuel tax to a fund for maintaining the highways.

philosophy of deregulation. Surprisingly, an administration that campaigned on a platform of reducing government intervention in business began to turn around the process of deregulation in trucking. Campaign promises to the Teamsters Union and the truckers' association were blamed for the reversal.

Highways and Mass Transit

The United States owns a vast system of superhighways, built to knit together producers and consumers over broad areas of the nation's economy. Highways have rearranged American life, brought profits to new industries, provided new opportunities for work and recreation, and created lively new cities and residential areas. On the other hand, an efficient highway system has worsened the economic problems of central cities, fragmented once-robust neighborhoods, and disturbed or destroyed woodlands and streams. Today, environmental impact studies are required before new interstate highways can be built.

Interstate highways are 90 percent financed by the federal government under the Federal Aid Highway Act of 1956. States must contribute $1 for every $9 paid by the federal government. The system is expected to be fully complete (with some modifications) by 1983. Estimates of the total cost for the 42,500 miles of highways range from $80 billion to $100 billion. Federal funds for highway construction come from user taxes collected on gasoline sales. State and local taxes also finance highway construction and maintenance.

The Federal Highway Act of 1973 gives city and state governments the opportunity to cancel proposed highway construction and use federal funds instead for improving mass transit. The "Metro" system in Washington, D.C., and rapid-transit systems in Boston and Atlanta are examples of systems financed in this way. However, cities are running into exceptionally high construction costs, particularly for subways. High costs result from high labor costs and a lack of standardization in transit equipment. Many cities are finding buses cheaper and more flexible for satisfying special transportation needs.

In addition to the federal construction subsidy paid mass transit systems, many local governments pay an *operating subsidy* to hold transit fares below the average variable costs of the service. Subsidies of more than $1 billion in 1980 contributed more than an eighth of transit operating revenues. Payment of the subsidy is based on the external benefits that flow from a workable transport system and on the fact that many transit riders are poor people. Without subsidies for paying a portion of operating costs, high fares would place the service beyond the reach of its most needy users. On the other hand, subsidies may have discouraged efficiency in transit management, and the Reagan administration plans to phase out federal operating subsidies by 1985.

In some cities, transit ridership is beginning to increase, as more commuters turn away from private transportation. In others, deteriorating transit service is prompting manufacturing firms to move out of the city to low-density suburbs closer to workers' homes. Costs are rising fast, particularly labor costs, as transit labor unions have become more aggressive. Fares now pay less than half of mass transit costs.

Airlines

Since 1938, U.S. airlines have been regulated by the Civil Aeronautics Board (CAB). Regulation of air fares and routes was intended to prevent "ruinous" competition and ensure air transport service throughout the country. Under the CAB, a form of price discrimination was used to subsidize costly short hauls with revenues collected on more heavily traveled long hauls. The result, according to industry analysts, was too high fares on long hauls (to guarantee profits to major carriers) and too low fares on short hauls (discouraging the entry of new, smaller carriers). Critics of the CAB feared that fare regulation would reduce profits and cause the airlines to "eat up their capital," as the railroads did.

In 1978, the CAB began to relax its control over fares and routes, and Congress passed the Airline Deregulation Act, phasing out the agency entirely.* Fares began to fall, and passenger traffic on major airlines increased by an estimated 10 percent. Airlines that had been flying barely half full were able to fill almost 65 percent of their seats. Higher load factors reduced the average unit cost of service and contributed to substantial profit gains.

The greatest change brought by deregulation has involved the arrangement of the air travel industry. Air transport employs what is called the "hub and spoke" principle. Short spokes feed into major transportation hubs for connecting with the long spokes between hubs. Three kinds of air carriers travel through the system:

1. *Trunk lines* fly large, wide-bodied jets from coast-to-coast; they maintain costly terminal facilities in major hubs. Until deregulation, they also flew short spokes to feed passengers into their long flights between the hubs.
2. *Regional lines* fly intermediate routes between hubs; they use smaller jets and frequently employ nonunion workers.
3. *Commuter lines* bring passengers from small communities into major transportation centers for connecting flights.

In general, the three types of firms coordinate ticketing and baggage handling so as to simplify travel arrangements for passengers.

Since deregulation, many of the trunk lines have abandoned the short spokes to concentrate on beating the competition between major hubs. This has resulted in new opportunities for regional and commuter lines to increase their share of traffic. Smaller planes and terminals and generally lower wages have given these lines cost advantages in the kinds of traffic for which they are best suited. The smaller airlines have more flexibility for adapting service to changes in demand and have probably improved the efficiency of air transport.

*Safety regulations remain the responsibility of the Federal Aviation Administration (FAA).

Fuel price increases in 1979 and a recessionary decline in air travel in 1980–1981 worsened airline earnings. Some analysts feared that cutthroat competition would run some carriers out of business, and, in fact, in 1982 Braniff International declared bankruptcy. Other airlines were forced to sell off assets to satisfy their debt obligations. With fewer airlines operating in many markets, some prices rose and some services were cut. Still, policymakers hoped that sufficient competition would remain in the industry to ensure service quality.

Special Case

A New Future for the Auto Industry?

One in seven U.S. jobs is tied directly or indirectly to the automobile business. When auto sales slump, work slows in steel mills, rubber plants, resort hotels, residential construction, and a host of industries related to travel by automobile.

For years, the U.S. auto industry enjoyed increasing demand, with rising stock prices and hefty profits. The lack of effective competition probably contributed to a reduction in efficiency and certainly stifled incentives toward innovation. When the fuel crisis hit in 1973, U.S. auto manufacturers began to lose the domestic market to smaller, more fuel-efficient European and Japanese cars. By 1980, foreign car sales captured almost a fourth of the U.S. market. (Low import restrictions in the United States and higher restrictions abroad also contributed to an imbalance in international car sales.)

Redesigning American cars and retooling to produce them will cost tens of billions of dollars at a time when two of the three major auto makers (Ford and Chrysler) are already running in the red. In the fall of 1979, Chrysler announced staggering losses that would force bankruptcy unless the U.S. government would provide financial assistance. Congress weighed the costs of a Chrysler failure (widespread unemployment and financial losses) against the costs of federal aid (a continuation of inefficiency and a further erosion of the U.S. competitive position in world markets). The final decision was to guarantee $1.5 billion in loans if Chrysler could raise $2 billion in credit from banks, other lenders, stockholders, suppliers, dealers, labor unions, and management. Chrysler hoped that sales of its revolutionary new "K" car would finally put the company back on the road to profitability.

Critics of the Chrysler "bail out" argue that the free enterprise system depends on the possibility of failure as well as success. If all the risks are removed from business, firms will become complacent and productivity will suffer. Declaring bankruptcy would force Chrysler to cut unprofitable models, fire excess personnel, and generally improve efficiency. The result would be a smaller, leaner firm, engaged in producing only the products for which it is most suited.

Supporters of Chrysler point out that real competition in auto production requires the existence of three healthy firms. Some claim that the high cost of government-mandated mileage and air-emission standards brought on Chrysler's collapse; therefore, government had a responsibility to help Chrysler. Moreover, government subsidies provide rather lavish advantages to other transportation firms: Lockheed is an example. Low profits in transportation have led foreign governments to take over some transportation firms entirely.

Some analysts believe that the only hope for the auto industry is a painful shake-out, with finally only three or four firms surviving worldwide (General Motors, Ford, Volkswagen, and "Japan, Inc"). If fewer firms supplied the entire world market, there could be significant economies of scale. Global firms could purchase materials and parts from specialized suppliers around the world and assemble cars near strategic international markets. Selling to international markets could help offset the swings in demand that tend to occur in a single domestic market. Furthermore, more efficient allocation of global resources will provide the profits for making necessary design changes. And finally, unless auto manufacture becomes global, there is the danger that nations will erect trade barriers to protect domestic firms, even at the cost of reduced efficiency.

Steps toward global manufacture have already been taken by the major auto firms. Through coproduction arrangements, leasing and technical cooperation, and export agreements, many auto firms already operate internationally. "Turnkey" factories built around the globe have helped create pools of technical personnel. Producing larger quantities of a single model has helped reduce costs and increase profits.

Producing cars in less-developed countries has particular advantages. Labor costs tend to be lower than in the developed countries. Cars can be designed to satisfy special needs of local buyers. Many developing countries offer incentives to new industry in the form of tax advantages or export credits. And markets in less-developed countries tend to accept products made in other less-developed countries more readily than those made in developed countries.

- What are some possible disadvantages of global auto manufacture? Are there advantages not mentioned here?
- Discuss the pros and cons of the Chrysler "bail-out." To what extent was government regulation at fault? Is there basis for the claim that government mileage standards may have prevented an even worse result?

Mathematical Supplement

Transportation and Regional Development

What determines the location of economic activity? Efficient transportation can have an important effect on the prosperity or poverty of a region. Ease of transportation permits separation of economic activities:

1. *Extractive* activities can be carried on in areas rich in minerals, fuels, and timber.
2. *Agricultural* regions can provide basic commodities for food processing and manufacturing.
3. *Manufacturing* regions can produce the finished consumer goods and capital goods needed by our economy.
4. *Residential* areas require complex human services.
5. *Recreational* activities require open spaces and pleasant surroundings.

Transportation allows us to divide areas according to their suitability for the activity at hand: an efficient transportation system enables us to exchange the goods and services of one region for those of another. A variety of transportation modes enables us to use the most suitable form for carrying the various kinds of traffic.

Manufacturing industries tend to develop in areas where production costs are at a minimum. Typically, production costs include materials, labor, land, and processing costs. But an important element of total costs is transportation costs—transport costs of material inputs to the manufacturing site and transport costs of finished products to consumer markets. A manufacturing firm will normally locate at a point between its source of raw materials and the market for finished goods.

The costs of transporting material inputs may differ sharply from the cost of transporting finished goods. Bulky or heavy materials will be costly to transport over long distances. Firms using such materials will locate close to the source of supply: steel mills and sawmills are examples. Fragile, perishable, or sensitive products will be costly to transport because of the risks of breakage or spoilage. Manufacturers of such goods will locate close to markets: dairies, auto assembly plants, and meat packers are examples. Some material inputs are widely available in many locations and would be foolish to transport; this is why soft drink bottlers, who use water as a principal ingredient, locate close to consumer markets.

Figure 11–6 is a model of transport costs for materials and finished goods. The horizontal scale is measured in miles separating material inputs (at the left) from consumer markets (at the right). The curves represent transport costs associated with locations at any point on the scale. At A, for example, material transport costs would be zero and product transport costs would be quite high. The reverse is true at point B. For any other location, total transport costs are the vertical sum of the distances under both curves, shown as the dashed line on the figure. The most efficient location for this manufacturer is at point A, where total transport costs are lowest. In Figure 11–6, transport costs of material transport are shown to rise sharply with distance, making the preferred location at the material source.

When economies of large scale are significant for an industry, firms will tend to locate in one central area and ship the product in all directions. Economies of scale explain the concentration of steel production in the Northeast, chemicals in the Southwest, and aircraft in the Central and Western states. Highly centralized manufacturing will incur low average production costs and relatively high transport costs. The reverse will be true of

Figure 11–6

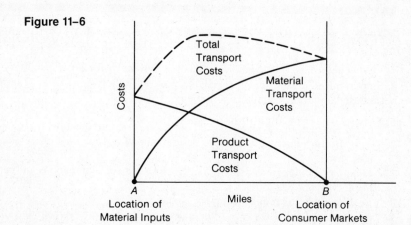

Figure 11–7

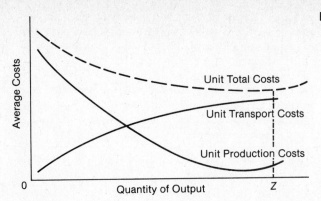

industries with few opportunities for scale economies. Such industries will be more decentralized, will be located near population centers, and will pay higher unit production costs than transport costs.

Figure 11–7 is a model of a firm that experiences economies of scale. The horizontal axis measures productive capacities of plants of all sizes. The average production cost curve declines to show lower unit costs for plants of larger size. The transport cost curve slopes upward, since more concentrated production will require that the finished product be transported over longer distances. The dashed line shows the sum of production and transport costs for plants of all sizes. The most efficient plant size is the one at which total unit production costs plus unit transport costs are lowest, as shown at point Z. In Figure 11–7 production costs are drawn to diminish more sharply than transportation costs increase, making the preferred plant size quite large.

For all kinds of manufacturing firms, the problem of transport costs diminishes at longer distances. This is because of the difference between *terminal* and *moving* costs. Terminal costs are the costs of handling the freight at the point of origin and the point of destination. Moving costs are the fuel, labor, and equipment costs along the route. A short haul will incur both terminal and moving costs. A haul that is ten times as far will not cost ten times as much, since terminal costs are charged only once. This makes it possible for many industries to concentrate in areas far removed from urban markets. Efforts to reduce terminal handling through containerized cargoes and piggy-back cars have further reduced terminal costs and, therefore, the cost of long hauls.

Figure 11–8a is a model of terminal and moving costs. The horizontal axis is measured in miles of transport. All shippers must pay a constant terminal charge, shown as the horizontal line drawn at *t*, plus a moving charge per mile, shown as a curve rising at a constant rate with distance traveled. Total transport cost is shown as the dashed line. Transport costs per mile are calculated by dividing the sum of terminal and moving costs by number of miles traveled, as has been done in Figure 11–8b. Reducing terminal costs would be shown in Figure 11–8a as a downward shift of the horizontal line at *t* and a corresponding downward shift of transport cost per mile.

The structure of transport rates can also have implications for the economic development of regions. During the most vigorous period of railroad building, manufacturing and rail service were centered in the Northeast. The northeastern monopoly of manufacturing and transport permitted firms to charge high prices on finished consumer goods and guaranteed favorably low rates on freight originating in northern cities. The agricultural South suffered from the high prices of manufactured goods brought into the region and high freight rates for raw commodities shipped out. As a result, southern business firms

Figure 11–8

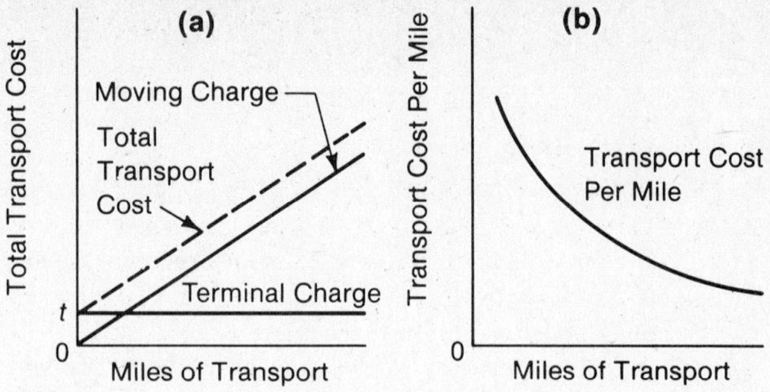

were unable to accumulate economic profits for expansion and for investment in improved technology. Some historians compared the economic situation of the South in the 1800s with that of the colonial possessions of imperial nations.

QUESTIONS

1. In transportation, what two possibilities follow from the difference between marginal costs and average total costs? How does this difference affect the need for government intervention in the transportation sector?
2. List external benefits and costs associated with various transportation modes.
3. Distinguish between normal and economic profit. Describe the circumstances under which economic profit (both positive and negative) might persist for a transportation firm.
4. Explain the basis for requiring a transportation firm to provide service for a price equal to marginal cost when marginal cost is less than average total cost.
5. Explain the conditions under which a government subsidy might be necessary to pay dividends to common stockholders of a transportation firm.
6. Explain the circumstances under which price discrimination is effective. Why does this apply in the transportation sector?
7. List disadvantages of subsidies and price discrimination.
8. Define "infrastructure" and explain its significance for economic development. Explain how government and private investment are interrelated in the construction of a nation's infrastructure.
9. Define *Conrail* and *Amtrak* and discuss their similarities and differences.
10. What circumstances in transportation frequently lead to a cumulative downward spiral of profits? How might a downward spiral be reversed?
11. What are some innovations that are increasing the efficiency of the transportation sector and reducing unit costs?
12. Describe the various requirements under regulation that had the effect of reducing transportation profits and that are now being eliminated.
13. Explain the fear that airlines might "eat up their capital." Why is this a problem for transportation industries in general?
14. Discuss the cost considerations that have determined the locational patterns of particular industries: chemicals, food processing, auto manufacture and auto assembly, building materials.

DEFINITIONS

Average fixed cost is total fixed costs divided by units of output: $AFC = TC/Q$. For any period of time in which certain costs are fixed, the unit share of fixed costs declines with increases in volume.

Average total cost is the unit cost of producing a good or service. It includes the unit share of fixed cost and variable costs of production: $ATC = TC/Q = (TC + VC)/Q$.

Average variable cost is total variable costs divided by units of output: $AVC = TVC/Q$. Average variable costs tend to decrease as a few units are produced and to increase as output increases beyond the optimum range of plant utilization.

Cross-subsidization is the use of revenues from sale of one product to allow sale of another product at a price lower than it costs to produce. Cross-subsidization is possible only where there is price discrimination.

Economic Profit is the difference between total revenue and total cost at the firm's level of production, where total cost includes the normal profit to be paid to entrepreneurs. Economic profit may be positive or negative. Negative economic profit is economic loss.

Fixed costs are costs that must be paid regardless of the firm's level of operation.

Infrastructure is the social overhead capital provided for the use of the society as a whole.

Marginal cost is the change in total costs that results from increasing production by one unit. Marginal costs include only variable costs, since fixed costs do not increase with quantity of output.

Marginal revenue is the change in total revenue that results from selling an additional unit of output. For competitive firms, marginal revenue is the same as price, since all units are sold for the market equilibrium price. For a single monopoly firm, marginal revenue is less than price, since selling an additional unit requires the firm to reduce price on all units.

A monopoly is a single firm (or cooperating group of firms) that supplies the entire output for a particular market. A monopoly firm can set price so as to collect economic profit.

Normal profit is a necessary return to entrepreneurs. It is included in total costs of resources used in production.

The optimum range of plant utilization is the range at which average or unit variable costs are the lowest.

The profit-maximizing level of output is the level of output at which marginal revenue is equal to marginal cost: $MR = MC$ means maximum economic profit. The reason is that this level of output adds the same to total revenue as it adds to total cost.

Total costs are the sum of all fixed and variable costs.

A user tax is a tax collected from the users of a public good or service.

Variable costs are costs that vary with volume of output. Typically, variable costs rise slowly as a few units are produced and more rapidly as volume of output increases beyond some optimum range of plant utilization.

SUGGESTED READINGS

"America Rediscovers Itself." *Business Week*, August 23, 1982, p. 66.

"Delta: The World's Most Profitable Airline." *Business Week*, August 31, 1981, p. 68.

"Deregulation: A Fast Start for the Reagan Strategy." *Business Week*, March 9, 1981, p. 62.

Kahn, Alfred E. *The Economics of Regulation,* Volumes I and II. New York: John Wiley and Sons, 1970.

Kraar, Louis. "Putting Pan Am Back Together Again." *Fortune,* December 28, 1981, p. 42.

"Railroading for Fun and Profit." *Business Week,* November 30, 1981, p. 80.

Rasmussen, David W. *Urban Economics.* New York: Harper and Row, 1973, Chapter 7.

Reich, Robert B. "The Fourth Wave of Regulation." *Across the Board,* May, 1982, p. 4.

Stuart, Alexander. "Boeing's New Beauties Are a Tough Sell." *Fortune,* October 18, 1982, p. 114.

Tabb, William K. "Government Regulation: Two Sides to the Story." *Challenge,* November/December, 1980, p. 40.

Thurow, Lester R. *The Zero-Sum Society.* New York: Basic Books, 1980, Chapter 6.

"Upstarts in the Sky: Here Comes a New Kind of Airline." *Business Week,* June 15, 1981, p. 78.

"U.S. Auto Makers Reshape for World Competition." *Business Week,* June 21, 1982, p. 82.

Weidenbaum, Murry L. "Weidenbaum Analyzes Benefit-Cost Analysis." *Across the Board,* February, 1982, p. 66.

CHAPTER TWELVE

U. S. Global Interests: The International Economy

How Shall We Share the Pie?

LEARNING OBJECTIVES

- To consider global production and distribution of goods and services, particularly with respect to efficiency and equity.
- To use an economic model to show the equilibrium level of production and consumption for a closed economy and for a trading economy.
- To explain the Balance of Payments and its significance for measuring flows of goods and services and financial assets among nations.
- To describe policies and institutions that aim toward improved efficiency and equity in international relations.
- To learn how currency exchange rates affect currency flows, worsening an imbalance or helping to bring currency flows into balance.
- To understand the domestic economic consequences of massive petrodollar flows and the policies for dealing with them.

A poet once said, "No man is an island," and most of us believe that. Most of us recognize our interdependence with our neighbors. We know that our own security and well-being depend to a large extent on the security and well-being of our community and our nation. Decay in any small sector of our economy can quickly spread to others until finally it affects us all.

The awareness of our interdependence with *other nations* came more slowly. In fact, for much of our history we have had a conscious policy to avoid "entangling" relationships with other countries. Through assorted laws, tariffs, and doctrines, we isolated ourselves from contact with the rest of the world, hoping to escape the various "evils" we associated with other cultures and other governments.

Isolation from the world community was a more realistic aim in years past when clipper ships sailed the oceans and armies fought hand-to-hand, when messages took weeks for delivery and language barriers slowed communication. Such circumstances are no longer true. Technological changes of the last decade alone have speeded transportation and communication such that events in one country have immediate effects in another. Moreover, having seen the benefits of travel and trade around the world, people are unlikely ever to reduce their expectations as to what constitutes a good life. From fearing and avoiding foreign entanglements, we have come increasingly to welcome them.

Closer relations with other nations have brought new sources of valuable raw materials and have opened new markets for our agricultural and industrial products. The result has been wider opportunities for growth of production and for consuming a wider range of consumer goods and services. International trade has helped to increase efficiency in the allocation of resources. Growth of production has made possible more equitable distribution of global wealth. We have enjoyed certain positive externalities of international cooperation, too: a greater appreciation of diversity, with improved tolerance of new ways of living and increased incentives to learn from others.

In this chapter we will explore some international concerns of the United States. We will look first at conditions of production and exchange that increase or decrease opportunities for economic growth. Then we will consider various ways for balancing nations' external economic relations with their domestic economic goals. We will be especially concerned with currency values and the effects of changing currency values on trade patterns. Finally, we will discuss the problem of redistributing global wealth as a result of the oil crises of the 1970s.

We will find an overriding concern in all our relations with other nations: that is, the strategic or defense implications of foreign involvements. Relations with other nations can occur in a climate of conflict and hostility, thus threatening our own security. Or international relations can yield such mutual benefits that all parties find their security improved. A goal of foreign policy should be to build an international environment most conducive to healthy and peaceful cooperation and growth.

GLOBAL PRODUCTION POSSIBILITIES

Nations are very much like people, and controversies among nations are like controversies among people. Most controversies involve fundamentally the distribution of the "economic pie": the total quantity of goods and services available for use. International controversies are especially complex because the global economic pie is complex: it includes high-technology manufactured goods from Germany and Japan, simple manufactures from Brazil and Hong Kong, agricultural products from Argentina and Australia, fuel and minerals from Saudi Arabia and Zaire, tourism and financial services from the Bahamas and Switzerland. Measuring the global economic pie and satisfying claims against it are enormously complex tasks.

The diversity of the global economic pie reflects the diversity of people and cultures around the world. Diversity of climate and physical features, of native customs and capabilities, of historical experience and political arrangements makes possible the wide variety of goods and services we produce and enjoy. Diversity has another effect: people who differ widely in custom and experience may differ also in their attitudes and expectations about distributing the economic pie. For this reason, dealings among nations require much greater sensitivity to diversity than do dealings among like peoples.

Some controversy over the distribution of the economic pie is inevitable. If controversy is to be held to a minimum, however, the economic pie must grow faster than the growth of claims against it. In a sense, we are talking about growth of **global production possibilities**—the maximum quantities of all goods and services that can be produced worldwide. Increasing global production possibilities depends on increasing the quantity and quality of global resources and improving the technology for organizing and using them; this is especially important as new resource supplies become scarce. One way of increasing global production possibilities is through specialization and exchange on the basis of *absolute* or *comparative advantage*.

Absolute Advantage and Comparative Advantage

Diversity of physical and social features around the world leads to absolute or comparative advantage in the production of different goods and services. *Advantage* is measured in terms of resource costs of production: **absolute advantage** means lowest unit costs relative to other nations in producing a certain good or service; **comparative advantage** means lower unit costs relative to other goods and services that could have been produced. To illustrate this, the world could be divided into two nations, Alpha and Omega. Each nation owns certain resources for producing food and machines. Alpha has good land and climate for agriculture and can produce more food per unit of resource employed than Omega. Omega has factories and skilled labor and can produce more machines per resource unit. We say that Alpha has absolute advantage in the production of food and Omega has absolute advantage in the production of machines. The existence of absolute advantage suggests that Alpha should produce food for export to Omega and Omega should export machinery to Alpha. **Specialization** permits both nations to improve technology and enjoy economies of scale. The result is greater total output and greater real per capita income for the people of both nations.

Now let us change our conditions and assume that both nations produce machines cheaply in terms of resources employed and neither produces food cheaply. How should production be decided? Under these conditions, each nation should produce for sale the product that requires the least sacrifice of the other good *not* produced. The quantity of one good given up to acquire another is the familiar *opportunity cost*.

For example, suppose that a unit of resources in both countries includes land, labor, capital, and entrepreneurship. Using one resource unit, Alpha can produce either 5 units of food or 10 units of machines. Thus, for each food unit produced, Alpha must give up 10/5 = 2 units of machines. Using one resource unit, Omega can produce either 5 units of food or 15 of machines. For each food unit, Omega must give up 15/5 = 3 units of machines.

	Food	Machines	Opportunity Cost of Food
Alpha	5	10	$^{10}/_5 = 2$
Omega	5	15	$^{15}/_5 = 3$

Note that the opportunity cost of growing food is lower in Alpha than in Omega. Therefore, Alpha has comparative advantage in food production. Omega has comparative advantage in the production of machines, since the opportunity cost of machines is lower in Omega.*

The world economy is most efficient when nations export goods or services in which they have absolute or comparative advantage and import those in which other nations have advantage. The result is global specialization, with each nation's resources used for producing the goods or services for which they are best suited. Global specializaton means greater total output and also greater interdependence among nations for the goods and services appropriate for a good life.

Domestic Economic Policy

Spreading technology has extended the benefits of specialization to more and more nations of the world, such that the global economic pie has tended to grow. At the same time, population growth has increased the demands on the economic pie, making continued growth necessary. Further growth in global production depends on increasing the capabilities of world resources, both in terms of quantity — developing new lands, producing new machines — and in terms of quality — training better workers, finding better raw materials, producing more efficient machines. Avoiding conflicts over the distribution of the pie depends on producing adequate shares for all claimants.

Much of national economic policy in the United States and cooperative policies with other nations aim toward increasing the quantity and quality of productive resources. Still, nations are constrained in their policymaking by

---

*Can you prove this? For each unit of machines, Omega must give up 5/15 = 1/3 unit of food; Alpha must give up 5/10 = 1/2 unit. Therefore, Omega's opportunity cost is lower.

purely domestic considerations. When the international goal of global economic growth conflicts with domestic employment goals or with domestic price stability, national governments tend to set aside their cooperative arrangements with other nations. Instead of promoting specialization on the basis of comparative advantage, they set up **barriers to free trade** to ''protect'' domestic industries against competition from lower-cost producers abroad. Some examples of protectionist policies are:

1. *Tariffs and other barriers to imports.* A tariff is a tax added to an imported good or service. The effect of a tariff is to discourage sales of foreign goods in domestic markets. Other barriers to imports include quotas and labeling or quality standards that effectively exclude foreign goods.
2. *Capital controls.* Capital controls may take the form of credit restrictions or of direct control of earnings on exports. In either case, they act to limit the free flow of investment funds internationally.
3. *Currency manipulation.* A nation's central bank may buy or sell domestic currency in order to affect its international exchange value. The effect is to influence citizens' ability to purchase imports.
4. *Embargoes and boycotts.* Embargoes and boycotts prohibit certain kinds of trade or trade with certain nations. The objective is to deny exports to a nation whose international policies are contrary to those of the exporting nation.

All these interferences with trade work to obscure absolute and comparative advantage, disturb production arrangements, and diminish the effects of specialization. The effect is a smaller global economic pie and a tendency toward more heated conflicts over its distribution.

Other government policy may also influence the growth of global production possibilities. For example, one nation's policy to stimulate domestic employment or to reduce inflation has international effects. *Stimulative policy* involves an increase in total spending, with additional spending flowing into international markets as well as domestic markets. Increased spending stimulates new capital investment and promotes growth in production worldwide. It may also contribute to rising prices, both in the domestic economy and abroad. Policy to reduce inflation reverses these effects and slows the growth of trade. Thus, the employment and price effects of one nation's economic policies are felt in other nations, helping or hindering their own efforts toward full employment and price stability.

The 1970s brought a whole new set of problems affecting global economic growth. The energy crisis and worsening scarcities of other resources raised production costs and reduced business profits in many developed nations. New investment expenditures fell, and growth of global production possibilities slowed. The problem was particularly severe for less-developed countries, whose exports of raw commodities were too small to finance needed imports of energy and capital equipment. To make matters worse, an accelerating arms race between the United States and the Soviet Union diverted resources from investment in capital goods and heightened tensions over resource supplies.

SPECIALIZATION AND THE RATE OF EXCHANGE

Production of material wealth depends on the quantity and quality of resources and the technical and organizational procedures for using them. For a closed or isolated economy, total production and consumption are limited by resource capabilities in the nation alone. Figure 12–1 is a model of production possibilities for a single nation, together with citizens' preferences for particular goods and services.* The production possibilities curve shows maximum quantities of agricultural and industrial products that can be produced in the nation, given its available resources and technology.

The slope of the production possibilities curve reflects the marginal rate of substitution in production for the goods on the two axes: slope = Marginal Rate of Substitution in Production $= MRS_p = -\Delta Q_i/\Delta Q_a$. The curve has an increasing slope because of limitations in the supply of certain fixed resources. With fixed resources, a move toward total specialization in either agricultural or industrial production would cause the marginal cost of that good to increase.

Citizens' preferences for goods and services are shown by indifference curves. The slope of the indifference curves in Figure 12–1 reflects the marginal rate of substitution in consumption: slope = Marginal Rate of Substitution in Consumption $= MRS_c = -\Delta Q_i/\Delta Q_a$. Indifference curves have a decreasing slope because of the law of decreasing marginal utility. Acquiring larger and larger amounts of one product involves smaller gains in total utility.

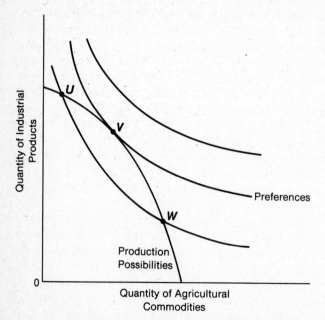

Figure 12–1
Production and consumption for a closed or isolated economy.

*Derivation of this model was explained in chapter 4 with respect to decisions about military and civilian production.

Equilibrium for a Closed Economy

The goal of a closed or isolated nation should be to achieve the highest level of total utility possible with available resources and technology. This goal is satisfied by producing the combination of agricultural and industrial products where the production possibilities curve touches the highest possible indifference curve, shown at V in Figure 12–1. Producing at the point of tangency is *equilibrium* production for the closed or isolated nation.

At equilibrium, the slopes of production possibilities and the indifference curve are equal. This means that the Marginal Rate of Substitution in Production is equal to the Marginal Rate of Substitution in Consumption: $MRS_P = MRS_c$. Stated differently, the ratio of marginal costs for the two goods is equal to the ratio of their marginal utilities.

Equality of marginal costs and marginal utility is essential for efficiency in the allocation of resources. This is easy to see if we first imagine it were not so: say, $MRS_c > MRS_P$, as is true at point U. (We know this because the slope of the indifference curve is greater than the slope of the production possibilities curve at U.) With $MRS_c > MRS_P$, it must be true that the ratio of marginal utilities is greater than the ratio of marginal costs: that is, people's desire for a particular good is greater than the cost of producing it. If the ratio of marginal utility is greater than the ratio of marginal costs, it would be efficient to reallocate resources toward additional production of the good with greater marginal utility. In this case, it would be efficient to move down the production possibilities curve to production of more agricultural goods at V. Producing additional units of agricultural commodities would add more utility than is lost by producing fewer units of industrial products.

The reallocation of resources toward more efficient production is shown by a movement along the production possibilities curve toward the axis representing agricultural products and toward tangency with a higher indifference curve. Select another disequilibrium position, say the one at W, and explain the circumstances that would move the nation's economy to equilibrium at V.

Equilibrium at V in Figure 12–1 represents the highest level of material consumption for a closed or isolated national economy. The average level of living in the nation would depend on total population in the nation.

The Terms of Trade

International specialization according to absolute and comparative advantage means lower production costs and increased production worldwide. Then international exchange enables citizens of all nations to consume a wider variety of goods and services, according to their particular preferences.

International exchange is governed by the **terms of trade,** which measure the quantity of goods received in trade relative to the quantity of goods paid out. Simply stated, the terms of trade are quantity of imports per unit of exports:

$$\text{terms of trade} = \frac{\text{quantity of imports}}{\text{quantity of exports}}$$

The absolute value of the terms of trade ratio depends on production costs of the two goods and the strength of world demand for each.

To illustrate the terms of trade, remember our two imaginary nations, Alpha and Omega. Assume that Alpha produces an agricultural commodity that is in great demand among consumers around the world. Omega produces an industrial good with insignificant demand worldwide. The characteristics of Alpha's product mean favorable terms of trade for Alpha: a large quantity of industrial imports can be bought per unit of Alpha's agricultural exports. The reverse is true of Omega. With unfavorable terms of trade, Omega must export large quantities of its industrial products in order to earn even small amounts of agricultural imports.

The terms of trade between Alpha and Omega can be described by a line on a graph. Look at the dashed line on Figure 12–2. The slope of the line measures quantity of industrial products relative to quantity of agricultural commodities. Its steepness indicates a large quantity of industrial products per unit of agricultural commodities and, therefore, favorable terms of trade for Alpha.

To understand this, pick a point A on the dashed line. Then move down the line to point B. Note the large quantity of industrial products (bc) that is given up to acquire a smaller quantity (de) of agricultural commodities. The reason is the relatively low cost of industrial products and the low level of world demand, relative to agricultural products.

Changes in the Terms of Trade

Changes in production costs or in global demand for particular goods would change the terms of trade and change the slope of the dashed line on Figure 12–2. The terms of trade would become *steeper* if:

1. Agricultural productivity falls, raising average production costs in agriculture and reducing Alpha's surplus available for export;

2. Worldwide preference for agricultural commodities increases relative to preferences for industrial goods.

In both cases, Alpha would require larger quantities of industrial imports in exchange for each unit of agricultural exports.

The terms of trade would become *flatter* if:

1. The technology of industry advances more slowly than the technology of agriculture; industrial production would grow more slowly and Omega's surplus available for export will be less;

2. World demand for industrial goods increases, so that consumers the world over are willing to sacrifice more agricultural commodities per unit of industrial goods.

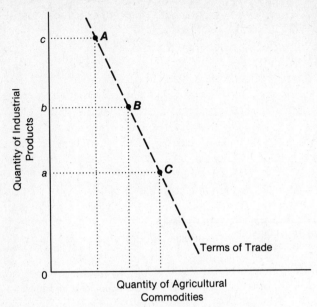

Figure 12–2
The terms of trade: the slope
of the terms of trade depends
on production costs and the
strength of world demand.

In these cases, Omega would require larger quantities of agricultural imports for each unit of industrial products exported.

Changes in the terms of trade enable citizens of the favored nation to increase their material standards of living while the living standards of people in the other nation fall.

Equilibrium for Trading Nations

The terms of trade line from Figure 12–2 has been combined with the production possibilities curve in Figure 12–1 to demonstrate the process by which trading nations make their production decisions. See Figure 12–3. The terms of trade line has been drawn tangent to production possibilities at X. Point X identifies the level of production at which the international terms of trade justify the corresponding allocation of productive resources in the domestic economy.

At the point of tangency the slope of the terms of trade is equal to the slope of domestic production possibilities:

$$\text{terms of trade} = \frac{\text{quantity of industrial imports}}{\text{quantity of agricultural exports}} = MRS_p$$

A trading nation is in equilibrium when it can gain no more through domestic production of a particular good than it gains through specialization and exchange.

Let us add indifference curves to the model in Figure 12–3 to determine the level of consumption for the trading nation. This has been done on Figure 12–4. Remember that one goal of trade is to achieve the highest possible level of total

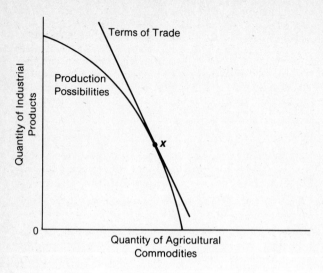

Figure 12–3
Resource allocation for a trading nation.

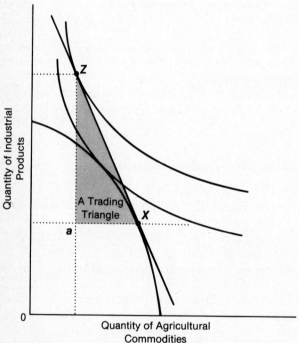

Figure 12–4
Equilibrium for a trading nation.

utility. When a national economy is opened to trade, consumption possibilities are no longer limited to domestic production possibilities. The terms of trade provide the basis for exchange to reach higher levels of total utility. In Figure 12–4 equilibrium production in the nation is indicated by tangency of the terms of trade with the nation's production possibilities curve. Consumption in the nation is indicated by tangency of the terms of trade with the highest possible indifference curve. Thus, specialization enables the nation to produce the combination of goods at X. Then by exchanging aX units of agricultural commodities for aZ units of industrial products, the nation achieves total utility represented by Z.

The triangle formed by aX, aZ, and the terms of trade may be called a **trading triangle**. A trading triangle can be constructed for any nation's production possibilities curve and any combination of global preferences (as reflected in the terms of trade). Then the nation may choose a quantity of both goods consistent with its own preferences. Average levels of living in the nation depend on global resource productivity, global preferences for both goods, and population of the trading nation.

The student should illustrate a variety of production possibilities and consumer preferences with a corresponding trading triangle. Begin by drawing a production possibilities curve showing greater capacity for producing agricultural products than for industrial products. Use the terms of trade line from Figure 12–3 to show equilibrium production for the nation: the combination of domestic production at which MRS_P is equal to the terms of trade. At equilibrium, the nation can gain no more through domestic production than it can gain through specialization and trade. Now draw an indifference curve that reflects citizens' preferences for the two kinds of goods. Construct a trading triangle and explain the process by which decisions are made.

BALANCE OF PAYMENTS

Transactions between nations are recorded in a **balance of payments statement**. A nation's balance of payments statement reflects what that nation puts into the global economic pie and what it takes out. Taking out no more nor less than the nation puts in is essential for international peace and harmony. Putting into the pie a greater total of goods and services each year is essential for global economic growth. The balance of payments is a way of measuring this relationship.

The balance of payments can be divided into two parts by a horizontal line. Above the line are recorded **real transactions** which measure exchange of real goods and services, exchange of real and financial properties, and personal or government transfers for which a compensating transfer is not expected. Below the line are recorded **settlement transactions** for bringing the statement into balance.

Settlement transactions are necessary whenever exchange of real goods, services, and property is one-sided: that is, if a nation has withdrawn from the global economic pie more or less than it has contributed. Settlement transactions take either of two forms. They may be claims for real goods, services, or property earned in the current period and held as reserve assets. Or they may be newly issued debt to be paid off at some time in the future. The effect of settlement transactions is to balance a nation's withdrawals from and contributions to global production over the long term.

Table 12–1 is a simplified model of the balance of payments. Notice that all transactions above the line involve transfers of real or financial assets. Transac-

Table 12–1 The Balance of Payments

International Purchases and Sales	
Merchandise Trade	Investments in Financial Assets
Exports (wheat, airplanes, computers)	Government Securities
Imports (autos, textiles, petroleum)	Corporate Stocks and Bonds
Trade in Services	Mortgages
Exports (insurance, consulting)	Net Income from International
Imports (tourism)	Investments
Investments in Real Property	
Capital Exports (factories, plantations abroad)	
Capital Imports (hotels, auto assembly	
plants in the U.S.)	

Settlement Transactions
Changes in Reserve Assets
Increase
Decrease
Issuance of New Debt

tions below the line involve changes in national holdings of reserve assets (monetary gold and foreign currencies) or issuance of new debt. Settlement transactions are necessary whenever above-the-line transactions yield **balance of payments deficits** (imports greater than exports) or **surpluses** (exports greater than imports).

For several decades after World War II, exchange was, in fact, one-sided. War's destruction had left much of the developed world unable to supply its own needs, and heavy U.S. exports of agricultural and industrial products were necessary to fill the gap. The United States enjoyed trade surpluses year after year and earned substantial claims against the future production of other nations.

Eventually, the construction of technically advanced productive capacity abroad enabled other nations to satisfy their own domestic needs and even to increase their exports. The heavy U.S. exports of the 1950s were replaced by heavy imports in the 1960s. The United States began to experience trade deficits and soon exhausted all its reserve claims against other nations. Certain other nations with deteriorating industrial capital and accelerating domestic demand continued to require more imports than they were able to contribute to world production. Along with the United States, they were obliged to issue new debt against future production.

For many nations, below-the-line settlement transactions were necessary year after year, with issuance of more and more debt to be settled at some future date. Debts of heavy importers began to pile up as reserve assets in the hands of heavy exporters. (Specifically, debts of the United States, Great Britain, and Italy began to pile up in the hands of Germany and Japan.) More important, debts issued in one year were not generally cancelled out by exchanges made soon after. Policymakers realized that finally satisfying the heavy burden of outstanding debt would so deplete a nation's current production as to require unacceptable sacrifices from its people.

Early in the 1970s, representatives of trading nations met to discuss the problem of increasing imbalance in world trade. The result of their discussions was new policies toward exchange, which, they believed, would automatically bring international accounts into balance without need for settlement transactions. Under the new system, all exchange would take place above the line. Balancing above-the-line imports with above-the-line exports would eliminate the need for long-standing debt and the accompanying threat to national well-being.

The new policy was, in fact, a return to a policy that had governed trade to some degree before the Great Depression disrupted global trade relations in the 1930s. It involved international currencies and, in particular, their values relative to each other. In the quarter-century after World War II, the exchange rate between currencies was fixed at an agreed-on level, but the new policy was to allow currency values to be determined in free markets. Free currency markets can help relieve the problem of accumulating debt and eliminate the need for settlement transactions.

FREE MARKETS FOR FOREIGN CURRENCIES

Before exchange can take place, traders must acquire the necessary foreign currency. Foreign currencies are traded in **foreign exchange markets**, which are similar to markets for goods and services.

Market demand for a currency reflects the desire of consumers and investors worldwide to purchase the exports of the nation that issued it. A currency demand curve shows the quantities that will be demanded at various price levels. The demand curve slopes downward because at lower prices more currency will be demanded for purchasing goods and services, real property, and financial assets in the issuing nation. The shape of a currency demand curve depends on the attractiveness of the issuing nation's goods, services, property, or financial assets at various currency exchange rates.

Market supply of a currency reflects the willingness of its holders to exchange it for another currency. Holders may be citizens of the issuing nation who wish to acquire other currencies to pay for purchases abroad, or holders may be world traders who have received the currency in exchange for goods and services. A currency supply curve shows the quantities that will be supplied at various price levels. The supply curve slopes upward because at higher prices more holders will be willing to provide the currency for exchange. The shape of a currency supply curve depends on the attractiveness of foreign goods, services, real property, and financial assets relative to those of the issuing nation.

Equilibrium determines the market rate at which all demanders of a particular currency are satisfied. That is, all persons who wish to purchase goods, services, real property, and financial assets in the issuing nation are satisfied by persons who have purchased goods, services, real property, and financial assets abroad. Stated differently, above-the-line transactions that involve exports are satisfied by above-the-line transactions that involve imports. With purchases

Figure 12–5

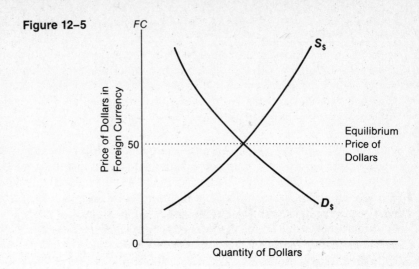

equal to sales in the issuing country, there is no need for settlement transactions.

Figure 12–5 is a model of the market in which U.S. dollars ($) are exchanged for foreign currencies (*FC*). The demand curve for dollars represents the desire of persons the world over to exchange foreign currencies for dollars for purchasing goods and services, real property, or financial assets priced in dollars. The supply curve represents the desire of holders of dollars to exchange dollars for foreign currencies. Market equilibrium determines the *exchange rate* between dollars and other currencies: that is, the price at which all demanders of dollars are satisfied by suppliers of dollars. The free market exchange rate of dollars is shown in Figure 12–5 as $1.00 = 50 FC$.

When free markets determine currency exchange rates, there is no need for settlement transactions. All transactions take place above the line. Persons who have sold goods or property in the United States receive dollars; their holdings constitute the supply of dollars in currency exchange markets. Persons who wish to buy goods or property in the United States need dollars; their need for dollars constitutes demand for dollars in currency exchange markets. At market equilibrium the supply provided by the first group satisfies the demand of the second group.

Now suppose that sales to the United States increase so that there is a net outflow of dollars. In terms of the balance of payments, imports to the United States exceed exports. Under the former policy, the exchange rate for dollars was fixed at an agreed-on rate. In this case, a net outflow of dollars would have to be settled by below-the-line transactions to increase the foreign debt of the United States. With free **market exchange rates,** this is not necessary. In fact, whenever supply or demand is temporarily greater in foreign exchange markets, the pressure of excess supply or demand will push the dollar's exchange rate up or down until supply and demand (and thus exports and imports) are again equal. Figure 12–6 shows an increase in the supply of dollars. The increase in supply is a result of an increase in the desire of holders of dollars to acquire other currencies.

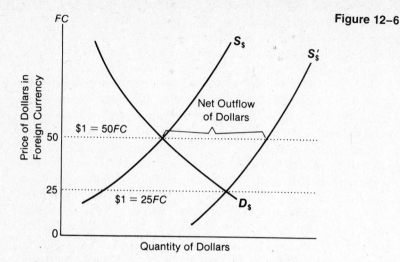

FC

Figure 12–6

Price of Dollars in Foreign Currency

Net Outflow of Dollars

$1 = 50FC

50

25

$1 = 25FC

$D_\$$

$S_\$$

$S_\$'$

0

Quantity of Dollars

In terms of the balance of payments, the increase in supply is a result of increased imports in the United States, for which payment is made in dollars.

If the exchange rate for dollars is held constant at $1.00 = 50\,FC$, the supply of dollars in currency exchange markets will exceed demand. The United States will experience a net outflow of currency that must be settled by below-the-line transactions. However, notice the result if the exchange rate of the dollar is allowed to fall. A drop in the equilibrium price of dollars to $1.00 = 25\,FC$ causes buyers to move down their demand curves and purchase more dollars. The larger quantities of dollars will be used to purchase goods and property priced in dollars, helping to increase U.S. exports and reversing the flow of dollars abroad. At the same time, the lower price will cause holders of dollars to move down their supply curves and supply fewer dollars. In terms of the balance of payments, this means that fewer U.S. citizens will be seeking to acquire foreign currencies for purchases abroad. The result is to reduce U.S. imports and, again, to reverse the flow of dollars abroad.

Consider the opposite situation from the one explained here. Suppose, for example, that U.S. products become significantly more attractive to consumers in other nations. What would be the effect of this kind of change, both with respect to the nation's balance of payments and with respect to the dollar's exchange rate? Would you describe these developments as favorable or unfavorable for the United States?

The Consequences of Free Market Exchange Rates

We have demonstrated how changes in a currency's exchange rate affect the level of purchases and sales recorded above the line in the balance of payments. *More imports than exports* causes an outflow of domestic currency, increasing its supply in currency markets and causing its exchange rate to fall. Then, a cheaper domestic currency encourages foreigners to buy the nation's exports and brings accounts into balance again. *More exports than imports* increases the demand for domestic currency and increases its exchange rate. This time, a stronger domestic currency encourages local citizens to buy foreign imports and helps bring accounts into balance. In the meantime, the opposite changes would be occurring in other countries; countries with relatively high-priced currency would be reducing exports and/or increasing imports, also contributing to balance in trade accounts.

Freely fluctuating exchange rates were expected to help achieve international balance in trade accounts. Simply stated, fluctuating exchange rates would work to balance contributions to and withdrawals from the global economic pie. There have been some less desirable side-effects. In fact, fluctuating exchange rates have brought increasing prosperity to certain nations and worsening poverty to others. To see why, consider a heavy exporter whose currency is in great demand and experiences an increase in value. A rising exchange rate enables that nation's manufacturers to purchase foreign currencies cheaply. The result is to reduce the costs of raw materials purchased abroad and to reduce the production costs of their own manufactured goods. Lower selling prices for manufactured exports make their goods even more attractive to foreign buyers, such that exports continue to increase and the currency's exchange rate continues to rise. The opposite is true of heavy importers: when excessive imports cause an excess supply of a nation's currency, its value falls. The result is to raise the price of foreign currencies and raise the domestic cost of needed imports. Higher production costs reduce the country's ability to sell manufactured goods abroad, such that heavy imports continue and the currency's value continues to fall.

Freely fluctuating exchange rates have also affected workers and consumers in the various nations. Nations with rising currencies have enjoyed greater job opportunities and rising consumer incomes. Nations with falling currencies have suffered a loss of jobs and a decreasing capacity for purchasing internationally traded goods and services. Policymakers have looked for ways to achieve domestic employment and price goals while allowing international accounts to come into balance. But the job is difficult and complex.

Groups of nations have entered into cooperative agreements for coordinating domestic economic policies toward more balanced global production and more equitable distribution of global wealth. Some gainers from fluctuating exchange rates have arranged loans and grants to less-favored nations in order to enhance their participation in world trade.

INTERNATIONAL ORGANIZATIONS FOR PROMOTING TRADE AND DEVELOPMENT

The gap between living standards of rich and poor nations has aroused international concern and prompted establishment of international organizations to deal with trade problems.

The International Monetary Fund (IMF), established in 1946, helps ease the flow of funds for trade, providing short-term loans to settle payment deficits for heavy importers. A subsidiary of the IMF is the International Bank for Reconstruction and Development, often called the World Bank. The role of the World Bank is to make long-term loans to help deficit nations build industrial capacity for increasing their own exports. In addition to contributions from participating governments, the World Bank acquires funds for lending from investors in the United States and abroad who expect to earn a satisfactory return on investment. Therefore, its loans are described as "hard loans": loans for building major industrial projects (like electric power plants and steel mills) that are expected to earn sufficient revenue to repay the loan with interest.*

Another IMF subsidiary, the International Development Association (IDA), makes "soft loans": loans for education and rural development that help create a social environment conducive to economic development rather far in the future. The IDA loans carry a smaller borrowing charge and may be repaid in the currency of the borrowing government. The International Financial Corporation provides venture capital for productive enterprises in less-developed nations. The Asian Development Bank, African Development Bank, and Inter-American Development Bank also provide subsidized loans to developing nations.

Typically, U.S. loans to developing nations result directly in U.S. exports. Former Secretary of the Treasury, G. William Miller, estimated that U.S. contributions to the World Bank in 1977 and 1978 resulted in about 50,000 more jobs for Americans, $2.7 billion in additional output, $1.1 billion in exports, and $720 million in additional federal revenue. Thus, growth in other nations contributes directly to growth in the United States.

For 13 years (1968–1981), the president of the World Bank was Robert McNamara, Secretary of Defense in the administrations of Presidents John F. Kennedy and Lyndon Johnson. Under McNamara's leadership, the Bank expanded its loans to raise living standards directly and respond to human needs of developing countries. Some examples were loans for agriculture and small manufacturing, rural roads and water systems, education and population control. The transfer of wealth from rich to poor nations was intended to accelerate tendencies toward economic development, increase productivity, and improve poor nations' capacity for trade.

Controversy over the lending policy of the World Bank has been building in recent years. Poor nations have been seeking more generous loans at the same time that rich nations have been cutting back their contributions to lending organizations. Lending nations want to ensure that credits are used efficiently to strengthen the economies of borrowing nations. At a conference of rich and poor nations in Cancun, Mexico, in the fall of 1981, the U.S. representative recommended that further lending by the IMF and its subsidiaries be limited and that private investors be encouraged to make up the difference. The position of the U.S. representative reflects both the Reagan administration's commitment to free market principles and budgetary considerations of the federal government.

The new World Bank president, A. W. Clausen, formerly president of Bank of America, believes that developing nations should do more to reform their own

---

*In 1980 the World Bank loaned about $12 billion and earned net income of $500 million on total assets of $28 billion.

economies. For instance, in some countries that are heavy importers, governments have imposed price ceilings on food products. Price ceilings favor urban consumers of food but also reduce incentives in agriculture as well as agricultural exports. In other countries, governments have held currency values artificially high, a practice that reduces their ability to sell goods abroad and stunts the growth of manufacturing industries.* In many less-developed nations, a tendency to rely on government to provide the resources for development has strained government budgets and drawn resources away from private enterprises.

Defenders of the World Bank doubt that private investment will actually increase sufficiently to replace government aid to poor nations. Furthermore, to refuse further lending to some countries may slow the progress of development and force borrowers to default on past loans. And finally, slowing growth in developing nations will reduce export markets and endanger materials sources for the developed nations.

One way to help developing nations would be to remove certain barriers to their exports to developed nations. The U.S. tariffs and quotas on sugar, shoes, textiles, steel, meat, and television sets limit export earnings of developing nations and slow their industrial growth. Japanese and European governments subsidize their own exports or grant their manufacturers low-interest loans in order to undercut developing nations' exports in world markets. Packaging and labeling regulations in many nations also work to exclude products of developing nations.

Participants in the General Agreement on Tariffs and Trade (GATT) meet periodically to negotiate reductions in trade barriers. Regular, reciprocal removal of trade restrictions has helped liberalize world trade, while easing unemployment problems in developing nations. Still, when recession hit in 1980, business leaders in many developed nations began pressuring their governments for increased protection against low-priced imports from developing countries.

THE PROBLEM OF PETRODOLLARS

The last decade has brought enormous problems of financial adjustment in the international economy. Beginning with the oil price increase of 1973, large payments have flowed to members of OPEC, the international oil cartel. Industrial nations require large oil imports to sustain economic growth; less-developed nations require oil and oil-related products for beginning the process of economic development. Nations either paid for their oil with dollars earned through their own export sales or borrowed from international financial institutions. When these sources were exhausted, acquiring the dollars for continued oil imports became a real problem.

*Why might a nation contrive to sell its currency at a value higher than the equilibrium value established in free markets? An artificially high currency value enables the nation to buy goods more cheaply abroad. Thus, a high currency value favors those who import capital equipment, raw industrial commodities, or luxury consumer goods.

Dollars paid to finance petroleum imports are often called **petrodollars**. The flow of petrodollars peaked in 1975 at about $32 billion, following a quadrupling of the price of a barrel of oil in 1973–1974. Since 1975, high domestic prices for petroleum products have forced consumers to move up their demand curves and purchase smaller quantities. Business firms have substituted more energy-efficient technologies, and new domestic sources of energy have been exploited. Then in 1979 and 1980 oil prices increased again and the flow of petrodollars accelerated.

By 1981, the cumulative trade surpluses of OPEC nations amounted to about $300 billion. Beginning in 1974, oil exporters used their oil revenues to purchase from the industrial nations goods and services such as food and durable consumer goods, vehicles and capital equipment, and materials and technicians for building and operating factories, ports, and airports. Petrodollars were also used to purchase real property (homes, hotels, and other business firms) in other nations. Such purchases are classified as *direct investment*, since the owner is directly involved in operating the asset. And finally, petrodollars were used to purchase **portfolio investments**. Portfolio investments are financial claims against the assets of business firms or governments: long-term bonds, stocks, and government securities.

All the above purchases constitute above-the-line transactions, since they involve exchange of goods, services, real property, or financial assets. In each case, the buyer is motivated by the superior quality of items available in the selling nation. Other uses of petrodollars are less motivated by quality of goods or property in the selling nation. In fact, some holders of petrodollars use their funds for purchase of short-term financial claims in whatever nation offers the highest interest return. Bank balances and certificates of deposit are examples of short-term financial claims that pay interest at current market rates. Such purchases are, by nature, temporary, responding quickly to changes in interest rates around the world.

Short-term capital flows are often called **hot money** because of their tendency to move abruptly from one nation's banks to another's. They add to the demand or supply curves of currencies and affect equilibrium exchange rates. Moreover, they influence commercial bank deposits, thus affecting a nation's domestic money supply. All these effects complicate international trade and investment practices, as well as domestic economic policies. Efforts are being made to persuade oil exporters to use their petrodollars in ways less disruptive to the international economy.

Adjusting to Flows of Petrodollars

Rising oil prices of the 1970s caused a massive transfer of wealth from consumers to producers of oil. Deficits in U.S. trade accounts placed more and more claims to U.S. wealth in the hands of oil-exporting nations. Exercising their dollar claims would necessarily require sacrifices from American workers, consumers, and business firms. How a sacrifice is shared depends on the economic policies chosen to deal with it.

The first result of the oil price increase was a general increase in prices for all goods that require energy in production or distribution. The rise in consumer and producer prices triggered worker demands for wage increases at least equal to the increased cost of living. Rising labor costs then aggravated energy cost increases and worsened price inflation.

There were other structural effects. Higher wage costs caused business firms to move back up their labor demand curves and hire fewer workers. Furthermore, the rising wage bill reduced business profits and left fewer funds for investment in new plant and equipment. For consumers, higher prices for petroleum products left less income remaining for purchasing consumer goods and services. Reduced spending power meant unwanted inventory accumulation and idle capacity for business firms. The nation entered recession.

Government economic policy could have taken either of two directions. One direction would have been toward *reducing* total spending, forcing the nation to accept a sacrifice of wealth. Slower growth in consumer spending and lower price inflation would have enhanced the price competitiveness of U.S. exports and helped finance necessary oil imports. Lower government spending and reduced government borrowing would have freed private savings for new investment spending. One result of these kinds of policies would have been some domestic sacrifices to accommodate the immediate transfer of wealth: in particular, a policy of lower total spending would have caused a substantial decrease in domestic employment. The distribution of sacrifice from lower spending would have depended on the kinds of policies adopted to achieve these results.

Another direction of policy would have been toward *expanding* total purchasing power through income supplements to unemployed workers, lower personal income taxes, and low-interest loans for business investment. Increased purchasing power would enable imports of oil to increase. Expansionary policy would, in a sense, accommodate the initial oil price increase and protect the domestic economy against an immediate sacrifice of wealth. In fact, expansionary policy was used. Whatever sacrifices were actually suffered were suffered by those whose incomes were unaffected (or reduced) by expansionary policies.

The choice of expansionary policies was dictated in part by political considerations. Expansionary policies sustained the illusion that sacrifice could be avoided. Expansionary policies reduced the painful effects of the energy crisis and allowed consumer spending to continue almost as before. On the other hand, the accompanying inflation and fears of new energy crises discouraged new investment, so that productivity growth slowed. Our nation's capacity to produce goods and services failed to keep pace with our rising material expectations.

The policy decisions of the mid-1970s illustrate a fundamental dilemma of a nation engaging in international trade. When changing trade relationships disturb the balance of international payments, policymakers may choose general economic policies that correct the imbalance. Such policies frequently disturb *internal* economic relationships, however: in particular, domestic prices and the level of employment. To balance *external* accounts at the expense of *internal* prosperity is not a happy choice for a government. This is why governments frequently postpone the hard choices that are necessary for balancing international accounts.

Nevertheless, the conditions that initially disturbed the balance did not peacefully go away. By the end of the 1970s, policymakers were leaning toward policies more appropriate for enforcing the sacrifices from reduced oil imports and more appropriate for increasing domestic saving and investment. The United Kingdom and West Germany, in particular, established policies to slow the growth in total spending. And the administration of President Reagan instituted a mix of policies intended to spur economic growth and reduce inflation in the United States.

Special Case

A Return to the Gold Standard?

The petrodollar problem of the 1970s has reawakened concerns about equity in the distribution of the world's wealth. Many governments have adopted new policies to protect their own citizens from sacrifice: they have adopted policies to stimulate consumer spending, erected trade barriers to promote their own exports and to limit imports, and intervened in exchange markets to manipulate their currency's value to their own advantage.

Self-serving policies toward international trade distort trading relationships and reduce the potential gains from trade. Some economists began looking for ways to stabilize exchange rates and to ensure that distribution of the world's wealth would be based on contributions to production. One proposal was to return to an international gold standard.

The gold standard governed international currency values from the late 1800s until the 1930s. Under the gold standard, currency values were measured in terms of gold. The national treasury stood ready to buy and sell gold for paper currency at the stated value. Tying paper money to a rare commodity like gold helps maintain a stable value. It limits a government's ability to create new money, since too much outstanding currency threatens to exhaust the Treasury's holdings of gold. Thus, the gold standard limits a government's tendency to adopt expansionary spending policies.

Under the gold standard, it was expected that gold production would rise or fall along with production of goods and services, automatically adjusting the supply of money to the needs of trade. The result would be a tendency toward full employment and price stability in nations on the gold standard. If the supply of money in a country should rise more slowly than the supply of goods and services, spending would decline, unemployment would increase, and prices would fall. Stated differently, the purchasing power of money would rise. Supposedly, the rising value of money would encourage discovery and production of new gold for sale to the national treasury. Then the supply of money would increase, consistent with the increased supply of goods, and prices would rise to a more normal level. In the meantime, the increasing supply of money would help to maintain total spending and employment at the maximum possible level of total production.

On the other hand, if the supply of money should rise faster than the supply of goods, then spending, employment, and prices would tend to rise. The declining value of money would discourage gold production for sale to the treasury. This time the effect would be slower growth of money, consistent with slow growth in the supply of goods, and falling employment and prices. In either case, the gold standard would adjust the supply of money to the needs of trade and help stabilize prices and employment.

The automatic adjustment qualities of gold were expected to apply also in international dealings. Gold would flow between nations—away from nations with rising prices and toward nations with falling prices — so that prices would stabilize worldwide. To summarize, adherence to the gold standard would stimulate maximum total production and ensure equitable distribution of global wealth.

How well did the gold standard actually work? Discovery and production of gold tended to be more erratic than expected, and prices and employment fluctuated more widely than expected. When gold flowed out and a nation experienced lower spending and recession, governments tended to react by issuing **fiat money** not backed by gold. Thus, their citizens were able to avoid (temporarily) the sacrifices required by excessive imports.* Failure to "follow the rules" resulted in more currency outstanding than could be redeemed in gold, and nations finally abandoned the gold standard.

To adopt the gold standard again today would require, first, establishment of the "correct" gold price. Too high a price for gold would encourage individuals to exchange gold for paper currency, thereby increasing the money supply and worsening inflation. Too low a price would encourage individuals to buy gold, depleting the Treasury's stock and reducing the money supply, prices, and employment. Second, monetary authorities would have to resolve the dilemma over irregular (or declining) production of gold and a fairly steady need for money. If authorities should decide to ignore the supply of gold and adjust money creation to production of goods and services, there would be no real need for the gold standard.

Most economists recommend some sort of control of a nation's money supply, independent of gold. They recommend either steady growth equal to growth of production possibi'ities or adjusted growth to offset changes in the level of real production. Furthermore, they worry about tying the nation's money to a commodity whose production is dominated by the Soviet Union and the Union of South Africa.

- Explain how petrodollar flows would have affected a nation on the Gold Standard. How would the distribution of wealth have been affected?
- What are the weaknesses of arguments favoring a new Gold Standard?
- What are the disadvantages of tying the money supply to a commodity whose production is concentrated in a few areas of the world?

Special Case

Trade as a Weapon

Citizens of the world today have lived their lives through years of turmoil, disruption of established order, and mounting concerns about future security. It is difficult to imagine the relative stability the world enjoyed prior to, say, 1914. True, even then there were rich nations and poor ones; but whatever the distribution of the global economic pie, certain

*Even so, between 1880 and 1914, the heyday of the Gold Standard, the U.S. suffered 10 recessions, broader and deeper than those of recent years. (National Bureau of Economic Research)

nations had the power to enforce the *status quo*, to ensure continuation of policies that favored some and perpetuated the poverty of others.

In the old world dominated by Western powers, certain nations were looked upon as "export markets" and "suppliers of raw materials" to the developed nations. They were not expected to participate as equals in trade with the West. World politics have changed dramatically, such that today, few nations submit willingly to practices they regard as unfair. In the world of today, less-developed nations are demanding a "new world order," a shift of the balance of world economic power to favor their interests. Political leaders the world over seek increasing shares of the world's wealth for their own constituencies. Instead of a feeling of interdependence among the world's people, we are seeing sharper divisions and more bitter conflicts. Trade has become both a means toward achieving power and a reflection of power.

In the past, military conflict has generally been accompanied by economic warfare. Trade between warring parties and their allies virtually stops, as governments enforce *boycotts* on particular nations and *embargoes* on particular commodities. (Embargoes and boycotts are completely effective only if they involve a strategic commodity unavailable from other sources.) Regardless of the outcome of military actions, economic warfare has generally been unsuccessful. This is because nations isolated by boycotts are motivated to increase their own productive capabilities, secure from foreign threats.

In peacetime, economic warfare may have the goal of achieving a certain political objective. Member nations of OPEC used economic warfare in the 1970s. They used their oil exports to enforce their demands — both economic and political — on nations grown dangerously dependent on cheap oil. In 1980, the U.S. grain embargo against the Soviet Union was an attempt to punish the Soviet government for its invasion of Afghanistan.* Critics of the grain embargo doubted its effectiveness, since many of the world's suppliers failed to cooperate. While it probably did impose costs on the Soviet Union, the costs to U.S. farmers may have been at least as great, and the U.S. balance of trade went further into deficit. Furthermore, whereas the embargo may have united the Soviet people in defiance of the United States, it also seriously divided Americans on the equity of the policy itself.

A tendency to impose embargoes and boycotts might have the unintended effect of isolating the United States from the world economy. Seeing the United States as an unreliable supplier, our trading partners may seek to develop other more dependable sources.† The United States could lose forever its competitive advantage relative to other exporting nations. Economic warfare probably does have some positive effects: it spotlights actions deplored by the world community, and it provides a means—short of actual warfare — of expressing disapproval of aggressive acts.

A FINAL NOTE

Interdependence in the world community makes solving global economic problems especially urgent. International policies to increase the efficiency of world production can increase the quantity of goods and services and make possible more equitable distribution.

---

*The United States cancelled the sale of about 15 million metric tons of grain and suspended shipments of sophisticated technology to the Soviet Union.

†Following the Soviet grain embargo, the Soviet Union turned increasingly to Argentina for its grain supplies.

This chapter has emphasized the significance of free markets for improving economic efficiency:

- Free markes allow nations to produce on the basis of absolute and comparative advantage;
- Free markets allow nations to trade on the basis of freely fluctuating exchange rates.

Free markets provide the incentives to behave efficiently. Free markets encourage growth of the economic pie and help to achieve balance between a nation's contributions to and withdrawals from the pie.

The result of free markets may not be entirely equitable. Just as was true of the domestic economy, distribution of global wealth may not be regarded as fair. Disputes over the distribution of wealth can be settled by war, with war's destruction of much of current production as well as much of the capacity for production in the future. A more healthy approach to distributional disputes is through cooperation and negotiation. International institutions and organizations provide ways to influence the distribution of global wealth so as to ensure more equitable participation in the world economy.

Mathematical Supplement

Speculating in Foreign Exchange

Currency markets are complicated by the actions of hedgers and speculators. Hedgers and speculators are typically uninterested in exchanging goods, services, real property, or financial assets in the current period. They enter currency markets only to acquire currencies, generally for use at some future date. Thus, their transactions take place in futures markets, and their actions affect future trends in a currency's value.

Hedgers enter currency markets to lock in the value of a currency needed in the future.* A dealer of Japanese Toyotas, for instance, would enter the futures market for yen to ensure some quantity of yen to pay for Toyotas when they arrive in the United States. He or she might purchase a futures contract from a supplier of soybeans to Japan, who expects to receive some quantity of yen in the future. The price of the futures contract would reflect the current yen value plus or minus a risk premium to cover expected changes in the yen's value.

Currency speculators enter markets to take advantage of expected changes in a currency's value. By purchasing or selling futures contracts, speculators lock in a certain value on a currency to be received or paid out in the future. Speculators who expect a currency to increase in value would normally buy futures contracts at the current price plus risk premium; if the currency's value does increase, the contract can be sold for a

*Refer to chapter 10 for a discussion of hedging as it applies to agricultural commodities.

profit. Speculators who expect a currency to fall in value would sell futures contracts; if the value does fall, speculators can buy currency cheaply to satisfy their obligation and retain a profit on the transaction.

Frequently, speculators finance their futures transactions through borrowing. Borrowing is practical only if the interest cost on the loan is less than the expected gain in the currency's value. To illustrate, suppose interest rates in England and the United States are $i_{GB} = 12\%$ and $i_{US} = 16\%$, respectively. The exchange rate for the dollar is $r_\$ = r_\pounds = \$1.00 = \pounds0.5$, and the exchange rate for the pound is (dividing by 0.5), $r_\pounds = r_\$ = \pounds1 = \$2.00$. A currency trader could borrow $\pounds50$ in England and use the loan to purchase $\$100.00$ for lending in the United States. After a year the trader would have a total of $\$100.00 \, (1.16) = \$116.00$. Converting $\$116.00$ to pounds would yield $\$116.00 \, (\pounds0.5) = \pounds58$ for paying interest and principal of $\pounds50 \, (1.12) = \pounds56$ with a currency gain of $\pounds2$.

Thus, a gain is possible whenever

$$\frac{X_\$}{r_\$}(1 + i_{US}) \neq \frac{X_\pounds}{r_\pounds}(1 + i_{GB})$$

where $X_\$$ and $X_\pounds$ are equivalent quantities of dollars and pounds and the r's are taken from the exchange rate equations above. In the example given, the left side of the inequality is greater, indicating that a trader should borrow in England and lend in the United States for a net gain.

Now suppose the dollar's value is expected to fall by 10 percent over the year, so that the future exchange rate is $r_\$' = r_\pounds' = \$1.00 = \pounds0.45$.* Borrowing $\pounds50$ today and relending $\$100$ at interest would yield $\$116.00$, as before. But converting $\$116.00$ to pounds at the expected future exchange rate would yield only $\$116.00 \, (\pounds0.45) = \pounds52.2$. The trader is unable to pay interest and principal on the loan and suffers a net loss. In this case, the inequality above should be changed to

$$\frac{X_\$}{r_\$'}(1 + i_{US}) \neq \frac{X_\pounds}{r_\pounds'}(1 + i_{GB}),$$

where the r's represent the expected exchange rate for the currencies in the future. A 10 percent reduction in the value of the dollar yields

$$\frac{\$100}{\$1}(1.16) \neq \frac{50}{0.45}(1.12)$$

and $116 \neq 124.32$. This time, the right side of the inequality is greater, indicating that a trader should borrow in the United States for lending in England. Borrowing $\$100$ in the United States and lending $\pounds50$ in England would yield $\pounds56$, which converts to $\pounds56 \, (\$2.20) = \$123.20$ for repaying the loan and enjoying a gain.

Very often a nation with a rising currency value relative to interest rates will experience an increase in currency demand from speculators who expect to gain from currency transactions. In foreign exchange markets the result is a rightward shift of demand and an increase in the currency's exchange rate. Speculators will gain, and the nation will enjoy the prosperity associated with a "strong" currency. This would have been true of Great Britain in the last example.

In the meantime, speculators who expect a currency's exchange rate to fall will be selling futures contracts. They will be borrowing the depreciating currency and convert-

---

*A 10 percent fall in the value of the dollar implies a corresponding 10 percent rise in the value of the pound, for $\pounds1.00 = \$2.20$.

ing it to other currencies for relending in other countries. This time the result is a rightward shift in currency supply and a fall in the exchange rate. Speculators "cover" their futures contracts by buying currency cheaply to repay the original loan. Speculators gain, but the nation suffers the increasing poverty associated with a "weak" currency. This would have been true of the United States in the example.

The extreme results of currency speculation were most harmful under fixed exchange rates. Under fixed rates, excess currency demand or supply tended to persist over a substantial period before governments would finally agree to change the currency's value. Speculators would purchase currencies for which the market equilibrium value was substantially above the fixed price. Their increased demand increased that nation's payment surplus further and ultimately forced a large increase in its currency's value. Likewise, speculators would sell currencies for which the market equilibrium value was below the fixed price, worsening the nation's payments deficit and forcing a large drop in the exchange rate. Under fixed exchange rates, large payment deficits and surpluses tended to accumulate until a massive readjustment of exchange rates finally became necessary.

Speculation has become more risky under freely fluctuating exchange rates. Under market rates, a currency's value is free to fluctuate in *both* directions. Temporary deficits and surpluses tend to be eliminated by short-term changes in currency values. Without massive deficits and surpluses to force an eventual change in exchange rates, speculation has become less certain and less profitable.

- Use a model of foreign exchange markets to demonstrate the effects of currency speculation when exchange rates are fixed.
- Discuss the risks associated with currency speculation when exchange rates are allowed to fluctuate according to market demand and supply. What circumstances bring losses to currency speculators?

QUESTIONS

1. Discuss current economic policies whose effect is to increase or to decrease global production possibilities. What are the policymakers' motivations in each case?
2. What is the significance of equality between MRS_p and MRS_c? Explain how free domestic markets help to achieve equilibrium for a closed or isolated nation.
3. Suppose Youngland has comparative advantage in production of tropical fruits and desperately needs machinery for building an industrial base. How does trade enable Youngland's people to live better?
4. Explain the significance of the horizontal line in the Balance of Payments statement. What circumstances make below-the-line transactions risky?
5. What are the advantages and disadvantages of a currency that falls in value? What steps might a government take to preserve its currency's value?
6. The statement was made that rising oil prices required a "massive transfer of wealth." Under ordinary circumstances, how might such a transfer take place? How is it possible to avoid (temporarily) the transfer?
7. In an international transfer of wealth, discuss each of the following in terms of the effects on the sacrifice involved.
   — increased transfer payments
   — reduced personal income taxes

— faster growth of the money supply
— reduced military spending

8. What are the advantages and disadvantages of the Gold Standard? Do you think a renewed Gold Standard would be more or less effective than the Gold Standard of the past? Explain.
9. In what ways might trade be a valid instrument of international conflict?

DEFINITIONS

Absolute advantage is the ability to produce a good or service more cheaply than the good or service can be produced in other countries.

A balance of payments statement measures the flows of goods and services, real property, and financial assets among nations and a corresponding flow of currency.

Balance of payments deficits occur when the outflow of a nation's currency exceeds the inflow in international transactions.

Balance of Payments surpluses occur when the inflow of currency exceeds the outflow of a nation's currency in international transactions.

Barriers to free trade interfere with specialization and exchange. Tariffs, quotas, capital controls, currency manipulation, embargoes, and boycotts are examples.

Comparative advantage is the ability to produce a good or service with a smaller opportunity cost in terms of other items not produced.

Currency speculators are persons who deal in futures contracts for foreign currencies, with the expectation of profiting from a change in a currency's value.

Fiat money is a system of money in which the value of a nation's currency is determined by the willingness to accept it in exchange.

The foreign exchange market is a place for exchanging one nation's currency for another's.

Global production possibilities are the various combinations of goods and services that can be produced worldwide, given global supplies of productive resources and the level of technology.

The gold standard is a system of money control in which the value of a nation's currency is determined in relationship to the value of gold.

Hot money is money that flows from nation to nation in response to changes in interest earnings.

Market demand for a currency indicates the quantities of the currency that will be purchased for various quantities of other currencies. Market demand reflects the desire of consumers the world over to purchase goods and services priced in that currency.

The market exchange rate is the equilibrium rate at which one currency will exchange for another.

Market supply of a currency is the quantity of the currency that will be offered in exchange for various quantities of other currencies. Market supply depends on currency holdings of persons the world over who have acquired that currency in trade.

Petrodollars are flows of dollars to sellers of petroleum.

Portfolio investments are purchases of stocks and bonds.

Real transactions are exchanges of real goods and property that are listed "above the line" in the balance-of-payments statement.

Reciprocal trade agreements are agreements to reduce barriers to trade in return for a corresponding reduction on the part of other nations.

Settlement transactions are exchanges of debt claims used to satisfy outstanding obligations from exchange of real goods and property. Settlement transactions are listed "below the line" in the balance-of-payments statement.

Specialization is the emphasis on production of particular goods or services in which a nation has absolute or comparative advantage.

The terms of trade measure the quantity of imports per unit of exports. Terms of trade depend on domestic cost of production and global demand for the traded good.

A trading triangle identifies the quantities of goods paid out relative to goods received. The ratio of quantities depends on the terms of trade.

SUGGESTED READINGS

"At the Summit: Reagan Stands Firm on Reaganomics." *Business Week*, June 7, 1982, p. 100.

DeVries, Rimmer. "Urgent Tasks on the International Scene." *Challenge*, March/April, 1981, p. 42.

Feldman, Robert A. "Dollar Appreciation, Foreign Trade, and the U.S. Economy." *Federal Reserve Bank of New York Quarterly Review*, Summer, 1982, p. 1.

Feldstein, Martin, ed. *The American Economy in Transition*. Chicago: National Bureau of Economic Research, 1980, Chapter 3.

Hein, John. "Paging Adam Smith—" *Across the Board*, January, 1981, p. 44.

Moore, Thomas. "Trying to Restart the Engine." *Fortune*, November 29, 1982, p. 52.

"New Restrictions on World Trade." *Business Week*, July 19, 1982, p. 118.

Pearson, Charles, and Wendy Takacs. "Should the U.S. Restrict Auto Imports?" *Challenge*, May/June, 1981, p. 45.

"A Return to the Gold Standard." *Business Week*, September 21, 1981, p. 114.

Rolfe, Sidney E., and James L. Burtle. *The Great Wheel*. New York: McGraw-Hill, 1975.

Schott, Jeffry J. "Can World Trade Be Governed?" *Challenge*, March/April, 1982, p. 43.

Volcker, Raul L. "The Recycling Problem Revisited." *Challenge*, July/August, 1980, p. 3.

Whalen, Richard. "No American Business Is An Island." *Across the Board*, July, 1980, p. 40.

"A World Economy Ready to Struggle Back." *Fortune*, August 23, 1982, p. 56.

"Worry at the World's Banks." *Business Week*, September 6, 1982, p. 80.

CHAPTER THIRTEEN

Government Policies Toward the Economic System

Is There a "Crisis of Competence" in Government?

LEARNING OBJECTIVES

- To review the role of government in promoting efficiency and equity and in the production of positive externalities.
- To describe changes in the political environment that hinder progress toward solution of economic problems.
- To use the circular flow to illustrate flows of spending, production, and income, along with the changes that affect the size of the circular flow.
- To describe demand-management, supply-side, and monetarist policies for promoting stable growth of the circular flow.
- To analyze the factors that have contributed to indecision and stalemate in government.

Once, political decisions in the United States were made in "smoke-filled rooms." Leaders of the two major political parties met regularly to define their fundamental principles, establish priorities and outline policies, select representatives to carry their banner before the public (and finance their campaigns), and finally work toward carrying out their party's programs. There was a clear thread of responsibility binding members of one party to its goals and to its success or failure in achieving them.

A clearly defined delineation of political power was possible when issues were broad and inclusive. A person's own sympathy for ''big business interests'' or ''the common people'' rather clearly determined his or her political affiliation. For the nation as a whole, alternating periods of control by one or the other party gave government a kind of balance over the long run that helped achieve the goals of both.

In recent decades, changes in our economic environment have brought on political changes that may have weakened our government's ability to respond effectively to today's issues. Resource allocation and income distribution, for example, are issues that tend to develop constituencies fiercely committed to protecting their own interests. **Single-issue constituencies** are often unwilling to compromise their positions. They join together in **coalitions** to support or veto proposals that enhance or contradict their special goals. All of this makes broad policy consensus almost impossible and thwarts any moves toward concerted action in the economic arena.

The problem is made more acute by the growing interdependence of national economies and of national economic issues. When a particular national issue has wide-ranging international effects, it becomes especially necessary for government to act promptly and effectively. Programs to deal with individual issues must be integrated into a coherent strategy that serves broad interests as well as single interests. Otherwise, individual programs may be inconsistent with each other or with long-range economic goals.

This chapter will consider broadly the role of government in dealing with microeconomic issues such as the ones discussed in this text and the macroeconomic issues of unemployment and inflation. We will focus on the political processes of deciding policies and on changing circumstances that have interfered with effective decision-making. And finally, we will suggest some possible implications of a failure to work toward constructive solutions of our economic problems.

THE ROLE OF GOVERNMENT: MICROECONOMIC ISSUES

In general, the role of government is to do for people what they are unable to do for themselves. As citizens, we call on government to provide collectively certain goods and services that we are unable to purchase individually. Goods and services produced by government are called **public goods and services** and include things like national defense, public education, highways, and agricultural research. Through our taxes, we expect to pay some portion of the cost of providing public goods and services.

This text has stressed the role of government in helping to achieve efficiency in private production and equity in income distribution. In particular, when market power distorts the use of productive resources or the income shares of resource owners, we expect government to intervene in free markets. We do not expect government to eliminate income inequalities that result from real differences in economic performance. We know there are trade-offs between efficiency and equality, and we want to reduce income inequality only to the point that income distribution seems fair.

Finally, we call on government whenever externalities interfere with efficiency and equity. We want government to promote activities that yield positive externalities and discourage those that yield negative externalities.

In each of the chapters in this text, we considered issues that threaten the efficiency and equity of our economic system and that produce positive and negative externalities. We discussed the role of governments at all levels in dealing with the questions raised by these issues.

- In chapter 1 we showed how prosperity can increase human capacities for equity and benevolence. We explained how achieving the goal of increased productivity requires incentives and efficiency in the use of productive resources. We showed how market power tends to distort resource allocation and disrupt incentives, and we discussed acts of government designed to improve efficiency and equity.

- Chapter 2 described the importance of new capital construction for increasing productivity and real per capita income. Construction of capital requires, first, saving from current income and, second, an acceptable rate of return on new investment. The uncertainties associated with inflation, goverment regulation, and fluctuations in consumer spending increase the risk and reduce the quantity of new investment spending. Adequate new capital construction may depend on changes in government policies to encourage greater saving and investment.

- Chapter 3 explored the effects of the energy crisis on productivity in U.S. industry. After World War II, the United States enjoyed several decades of increasing productivity, in large measure because of cheap and plentiful energy. During the 1970s, however, rising energy costs forced a substitution of labor for energy, with the result that worker productivity declined and average living standards fell. Government policies have tended to discourage innovative activity in the energy sector, keeping demand and supply curves relatively inelastic. In general, government intervention in free markets is inefficient. But if markets themselves are inefficient or if there are externalities or inequities, government intervention may be necessary.

- Chapter 4 explored the allocation of resources for civilian or military production. Efficient resource allocation for the nation ensures production of the maximum possible quantities of goods and services the people want. Wants are described in terms of the marginal rate of substitution in consumption. Equality between the marginal rates of substitution in production and consumption determines the most efficient combination of military and civilian production. Efficiency in military production depends on strategic planning and budgeting and on choosing the appropriate combination of human labor and military equipment for achieving strategic goals.

- Chapter 5 showed how the structure of governments in the United States was intended to promote the efficient use of resources and the flow of positive externalities between states and regions. Policies of the federal government have aimed at achieving equity in the distribution of the nation's wealth. Limited jurisdictions and administrative costs reduce the taxing ability of state and local governments and reduce their ability to provide needed services; but federal revenue-sharing programs help equalize service quality among regions. Moreover, federal tax policies aim at promoting horizontal and vertical equity among taxpayers nationwide.

- In Chapter 6 we used the concepts of Marginal Social Product and Marginal Social Cost to evaluate policies for economic growth. We showed that maximum Net Benefits from growth occur when the ratio of Marginal Social Product to Marginal Social Cost is equal to one.* Many economists believe that market-oriented policies toward the negative externalities of growth yield more efficient and equitable solutions than rigid rules. Inequitable distribution of the benefits and costs of growth can create conflicts, both among regions and internationally.

- Chapter 7 considered labor, our most abundant resource. Combining labor with other productive resources yields the goods and services necessary for a good life. In free markets, wage rates and the level of total employment are determined by the dollar value of labor's Marginal Product and the quantity of labor supplied. Free markets ensure efficiency and incentives and ensure against (involuntary) unemployment. Most markets are not perfectly free, such that unemployment may occur together with wage inflation. Government has not been very successful in correcting the problems of excessive unemployment and accelerating inflation.

- In Chapter 8 we focused on the distribution of income in the United States. We found that average income has grown, but the level of inequality has remained about the same since World War II. Income inequality may be necessary to promote efficiency in employment and incentives toward higher productivity, but beyond some point income inequality offends our national sense of equity. Moreover, extreme inequality of income distribution may threaten profitability in the private business sector. In addition to purchases and transfer payments, government affects income distribution through the tax structure and through policies toward inflation.

- Chapter 9 explored circumstances in the health care sector that interfere with the operation of free markets. Free markets perform badly in the health sector because of ethical considerations and because of positive and negative externalities. Also, "third parties" in the health sector have the effect of reducing apparent costs to buyers and increasing the demand for health service. One result is a tendency for the production of health services to exceed the most efficient level where Net Benefits are greatest. Another result is a tendency for the cost of health care services to increase. Current proposals in the health sector include providing health services for the needy while encouraging conservation of scarce health care resources.

---

*When both are weighted by their probabilities and discounted according to the time in the future they are expected to occur.

- Chapter 10 considered the most basic of all economic activities, the production of food. Food production in the United States is enhanced by favorable natural resources and by generous government policies. Surplus farm production in good years contributes to a food reserve for sale in bad years when food is scarce. Global population growth puts pressure on world food supplies and calls for policies to shift upward the production function in agriculture. Agricultural research and the use of chemical fertilizers have this objective, but changes in weather may offset tendencies toward increased productivity.

- Chapter 11 suggested that transportation has characteristics that call for government regulation: (1) the high fixed costs and low variable costs of transportation services enable monopoly firms to collect economic profit; and (2) transportation services provide positive and negative externalities for which individual consumers are unable or unwilling to pay. Critics of regulation in the transportation sector argue that continued control of routes and fares is no longer efficient, stifles innovation, and destroys competition. The process of deregulating transportation has begun in rail, air, and truck transport.

- Chapter 12 showed how an integrated world economy yields advantages of specialization and increased production, along with the potential disadvantage of interdependence. A growing global economic pie helps ensure adequate shares of material goods and services for more people. Policies promoting specialization and trade include "hard" and "soft" loans by international development agencies and the removal of national barriers to trade. Imbalances in trade may be corrected by an easing of financial arrangements between nations.

In each of these economic sectors, there are opportunities for government to provide public goods and services and to develop policies for affecting efficiency, equity, and externalities. Acts of government yield benefits to certain groups and costs to others. The frequent result is conflict over the precise design of government policy. In the United States, such conflicts must be resolved through the political processes. In recent years, changes in the U.S. political climate have made conflict resolution especially difficult.

The Politics of Microeconomic Issues

Microeconomic issues like the ones discussed in this text call for actions of government to increase efficiency and/or improve equity. Actions of government imply a degree of coercion. Thus, government decisions require us to change our behavior in ways that reduce our individual well-being for the sake of the community as a whole.

Coercion is contrary to the fundamental principles of our system. In general, we believe that free choice results in the greatest possible total benefits at the lowest total cost. We accept coercion only when we are satisfied that we will be compensated by gains elsewhere: we adhere to local traffic regulations in return for the gain of safe and secure streets, we pay state taxes in return for the gain of clean and pleasant recreational areas, we accept the risks associated with conducting business enterprises in return for healthy and prosperous markets for our products.

Deciding the degree of government coercion and the distribution of gains is the responsibility of voters and their elected representatives. Still, as voters, we feel strongly about only a limited number of public issues. We spend the time, the effort, and frequently the money to become informed about a particular problem; black-lung disease, the loss of farmland, and urban decay are some examples. Then we pressure our elected representative to design policies that favor our special interests. When all voters concentrate on single issues, the result is a collection of uncoordinated government programs. Each separate program benefits a single interest group, while the costs of each are paid by all of us.

Concentrating on a single issue makes it difficult to evaluate programs in terms of their overall effect. Thus, some of us support programs like low-interest loans to college students without thinking about the higher taxes others will have to pay. Others oppose such programs without considering their effect on the level of productivity and employment in the nation as a whole. In general, we tend to favor programs that promise short-range benefits and tend to ignore their long-range costs. At the same time, we avoid paying short-range costs for programs whose benefits are uncertain and far in the future.

When a number of single-issue groups combine in support of a particular interest, the political effect is called **logrolling**. Single-issue groups combine to achieve a majority on one issue, then separate and combine in different ways to achieve a majority on another. The effect of a freely swinging majority is to reduce consistency in government programs and to divert attention from long-range economic goals—the goals of maximum production and efficiency and an acceptable level of equity in distribution.

Logrolling can be effective also for vetoing proposals that conflict with the interests of well-organized groups. Economic, social, and environmental problems continue to worsen while opposing factions debate the appropriate remedy. Stalemate in government weakens our nation's capacity to deal with worsening crises. Logrolling makes it more difficult to make the painful decisions that would begin constructive change and more difficult to develop coherent strategies to guide policy.

A divided and short-sighted electorate poses problems also in terms of macroeconomic stability, the subject of the next section. Single-issue politics and logrolling make it especially difficult to plan effectively for the long-range health of our economic system as a whole.

THE ROLE OF GOVERNMENT: MACROECONOMIC ISSUES

Most of the issues described in this text have been *microeconomic* issues; that is, they concern a particular sector or industry, as opposed to the economic system as a whole. Nevertheless, in every chapter we have referred frequently to

Figure 13
The circ
goods

macroeconomic issues: the problems of price inflation ₐ
extend through all sectors and influence our ability to dea
microeconomic, issues. We referred to the use of govern
for dealing with macroeconomic problems, along with the
vantages associated with their use.

In this section, we will consider macroeconomic pc
We will find that macroeconomic problems are compl
down. The complexity of the problems makes correcti
means that analysts will see the problem differently and favor different remedies.
Lacking a scientific laboratory for testing causes and effects, policymakers will
tend to base their decisions on nonscientific information, such as the political
implications of the decision. Political pressures hardly guarantee correct policy.
In fact, the pressure of political interests may so confuse government policy that
the actual results are the opposite of those intended.

The Circular Flow of Spending, Production, and Income

Simply stated, the goals of macroeconomic policy are: (1) the fullest employment of the nation's resources in productive work, (2) reasonable price
stability, and (3) healthy growth in the production of goods and services. Success
in these goals requires maximum efficiency in the use of productive resources
and establishes the potential for improved equity in the distribution of income.
We expect that pursuit of these goals will yield positive externalities greater than
whatever negative externalities may also occur.

Progress toward our macroeconomic goals can be explained in terms of a
simple diagram. In Figure 13–1, the various kinds of economic activity are
classified under either of two headings: *consumption* or *production*. Consumption (C) is carried on by households—families, groups, or single individuals—
who share at least some of the goods and services necessary for a good life.
Production is carried on by business firms—from large corporate manufacturing
firms through small partnerships to individual entrepreneurs producing a wide
variety of goods or services for sale. In Figure 13–1, the lower arrow between
households and business firms indicates the flow of consumer expenditures in
one direction and a corresponding flow of newly produced goods and services in
the other.

Business firms employ resources for carrying on productive activity: *land*
for building or growing crops, *labor* for operating equipment and performing
services, *capital* equipment for aiding work, and *entrepreneurship* for organizing
and guiding the use of other resources. Resources are owned by households and
are supplied to business firms in return for incomes in the form of rent (r), wages
and salaries (w), interest on capital (i), and profit for entrepreneurship (π). The
flow of resources and a corresponding flow of incomes is shown as the upper
arrow in Figure 13–1.

The total value of all goods and services produced for sale is called Gross
National Product, or GNP. This is, in its simplest sense, the value of the lower
arrow on the diagram. Moreover, the total value of new goods and services is also

–1

ular flow of spending, production, and income. The circular flow represents production of
and services for sale.

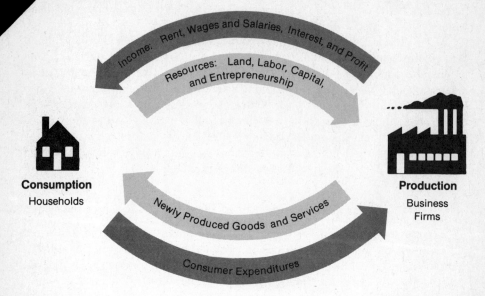

the value of the upper arrow. This is because the value of any product is the sum
of the resources used to produce it. Thus, the total of all income payments to
owners of resources is equal to the total value of all newly produced goods and
services.

The diagram in Figure 13–1 is called **the circular flow of spending, production,
and income**. Within the flow, spending circulates from buyer to seller, consumer
to producer, household to business firm and back again—all the while stimulating
economic activity and adding to the nation's total supply of wealth.

The diagram in Figure 13–1 is not quite complete. A complete model of
economic activity would include also the process of saving and investment and
the activities of governments. The next two sections describe these activities in
the context of the circular flow.

Saving and Investment

Savings of both households and business firms are shown in Figure 13–2 as
arrows (S) flowing out of the circular flow into financial markets. Household
savings typically flow into financial institutions—commercial banks, savings and
loan associations, mutual funds, insurance companies—for lending to potential
investors. Business savings are retained profits and depreciation allowances,
often used to purchase short-term securities issued by governments or by other
business firms.

Investment (I) is the use of savings to purchase new capital resources:

Figure 13–2
The effect of saving, investment, taxes, and government purchases on the circular flow. The total of consumer expenditures, business investment, and government purchases is gross national product, or GNP.

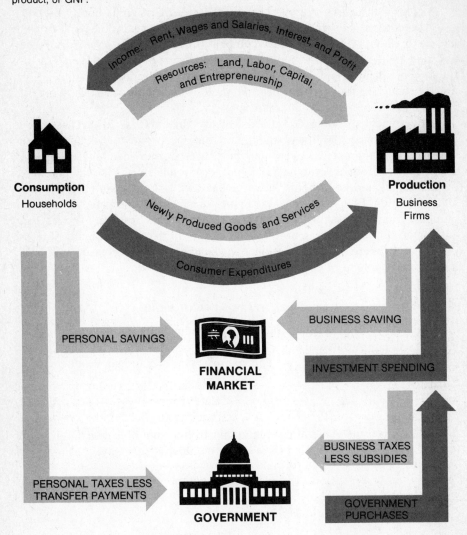

homes, buildings and equipment, and inventories of component parts or finished goods. Thus, investment is shown as a flow from financial markets into business firms for purchasing capital. Construction of new capital is essential for increasing productive capacity for the future. Not generally included under investment but important for future productivity, nevertheless, is the construction of human capital—education and skills for performing work. Investment spending is added to consumer spending and constitutes the second component of Gross National Product, or GNP.

Government Spending and Taxes

The principal economic activities of government are taxing and spending. Taxes (T) are collected from business firms and by households, shown in Figure 13–2 as arrows flowing to government. Some business firms and households receive negative taxes from government in the form of subsidies and transfer payments such as unemployment compensation and welfare benefits. When negative taxes received are subtracted from taxes paid, the result is **net taxes**— the flow of spending power to government. Net taxes represent claims against newly produced goods and services and, therefore, the allocation of resources to government to be used for public purposes.

Government spending (G) is the use of government funds to purchase public goods and services. Military equipment, buildings, and the skills of public employees are examples. Government purchases are shown in Figure 13–2 as an arrow flowing from government back into the circular flow. Like the purchases of individuals and households, government purchases stimulate employment and production. Like the purchases of investors and business firms, government purchases may also stimulate construction of new capital resources (both human and material) for increasing productive capacity in the future. Finally, government purchases are added to consumer and business expenditures and constitute the third component of Gross National Product, or GNP.

Changes in the Circular Flow

The total value of all goods and services produced for sale is Gross National Product. Since the value of sales is the sum of consumer (C), investor (I), and government (G) purchases, we can express Gross National Product as the following equation:*

$$GNP = C + I + G.$$

Moreover, since the value of production is also the sum of wages (w), rent (r), interest (i), and profit (π) paid to resource owners, we can say:

$$GNP = w + r + i + \pi.$$

Combining the two equations yields:

$$C + I + G = GNP = w + r + i + \pi.$$

GNP is at the same time the value of current production and the size of the circular flow. The left side of the equation above represents total spending for newly produced goods and services, and the right side represents current income to productive resources.†

---

*For simplicity, this explanation omits the effect of foreign purchases and sales.

†Production is always equal to sales because of the effect of inventory accumulation. Any portion of current production that is not sold to final users is in effect "purchased" by the firm that produced it and held in inventory.

The size of the circular flow is important because it represents the quantity of new goods and services available for use. It is the basis for the standards of living for the nation's people. A large and growing circular flow is essential for achieving large and rising real per capita incomes. Moreover, steady increases in the circular flow are essential for employing a growing labor force and achieving price stability.

Look again at Figure 13–2. Arrows leaving the circular flow represent outflows from spending. Saving and taxes are the portions of income that are not spent; they escape from the circular flow and tend to reduce its size. Arrows returning to the circular flow represent new inflows into spending. Investment and government spending flow back into the circular flow and tend to increase its size.

The combined effect of savings and taxes $(S + T)$ and investment and government spending $(I + G)$ determines whether the circular flow will tend to expand or contract. Thus, we can say:

> if $S + T > I + G$, the circular flow will tend to contract;
> if $S + T < I + G$, the circular flow will tend to expand;
> if $S + T = I + G$, the circular flow will remain the same.

These relationships make the behavior of savers, investors, and government critical for the level of employment, price stability, and healthy economic growth.

Tendencies Toward Unemployment or Inflation

Many production decisions depend on steady growth in spending for consumer goods and services, capital equipment, and public goods and services. Steady increases in the circular flow help ensure increased job opportunities and steady growth in the quantity of new goods and services. The ideal growth rate of total spending depends on growth in the nation's productive capacity: the quantity and quality of its resources and the organizational and technical arrangements for using them. Using productive capacity fully ensures maximum total production and maximum living standards for the nation's people.

Coordinating growth in total spending with growth of productive capacity is not easy. In fact, growth of the circular flow depends strongly on the independent decisions of households and business firms. Frequent changes in the level of consumer spending (C), in decisions to save (S) or borrow, and in business investment plans (I) all work to disturb the circular flow. When total spending declines or fails to grow, there may be declining job opportunities and slower growth of real production. On the other hand, when total spending increases too fast, there may be excess demand for workers, excess demand for materials and equipment, and rising prices for goods and services. In either case, the result will be inefficient use of the nation's productive resources.

Irregular growth in total spending may bring on either the problem of rising unemployment or the problem of price inflation.* Table 13–1 lists data on Gross

*There are other causes for both problems, as we have seen throughout this text.

National Product over the most recent two decades. Column 1 shows the level of total spending and production for the year (adjusted for inflation), and Column 2 shows the yearly growth rate of total spending. Columns 3 and 4 list values of unemployment of all workers and inflation, measured as percent change in the price index for GNP. During roughly the first half of the period shown, faster-than-average growth in GNP was associated with lower unemployment and increasing inflation. Slower-than-average growth was associated with higher unemployment and lower inflation. The last half of the period has been characterized by slower growth (or negative growth) of GNP and rising values of *both* unemployment and inflation.

Unemployment is a waste of productive resources and contributes to a deterioration of human and material capital. Thus, unemployment reduces total production both in the current period and for the future. Inflation distorts economic relationships and disturbs the allocation of resources. The frequent result of inflation is increasing risk of economic activity and, ultimately, economic collapse. Avoiding unemployment or inflation is the objective of much of U.S. government policies.

Table 13–1 Irregular Growth of Gross National Product Leads to the Problem of Unemployment or Inflation

Year	GNP ($1972)	% change in GNP	Rate of Unemployment	% change in GNP price index
1960	$ 737.2	2.2	5.5	1.6
1961	756.6	2.6	6.7	.9
1962	800.3	5.8	5.5	1.8
1963	832.5	4.0	5.7	1.5
1964	876.4	5.3	5.2	1.5
1965	929.3	6.0	4.5	2.2
1966	984.8	6.0	3.8	3.2
1967	1,011.4	2.7	3.8	3.0
1968	1,058.1	4.6	3.6	4.4
1969	1,087.6	2.8	3.5	5.1
1970	1,085.6	− .2	4.9	5.4
1971	1,122.4	3.4	5.9	5.0
1972	1,185.9	5.7	5.6	4.2
1973	1,254.3	5.8	4.9	5.8
1974	1,246.3	− .6	5.6	8.8
1975	1,231.6	− 1.2	8.5	9.3
1976	1,298.2	5.4	7.7	5.2
1977	1,369.7	5.5	7.1	5.8
1978	1,438.6	5.0	6.1	7.4
1979	1,479.4	2.8	5.8	8.6
1980	1,474.0	− .4	7.1	9.3
1981	1,502.6	1.9	7.6	9.4
1982	1,475.5	− 1.8	9.7	6.0
Average Rates		3.2	6.0	5.0

Source: *Economic Report of the President*, February, 1983.

POLICIES TOWARD UNEMPLOYMENT AND INFLATION

An important aim of U.S. economic policy is to maintain steady growth in the circular flow so as to ensure full employment and price stability. There are a variety of policy tools toward this goal (and some that interfere with achieving it, as we have noted throughout this text). Most economic policies include some elements of many kinds of government programs, differing only in the different emphasis placed on particular tactics. We will refer to three broad policy strategies as *demand management*, *supply-side economics*, and *monetarism*. As we describe each kind of policy, you will notice many similarities and some differences of emphasis.

Demand Management Policies

The emphasis in demand management policies is on total spending for newly produced goods and services. Total spending is shown in Figure 13–2 as arrows flowing into the circular flow. Total spending is also shown in our algebraic equation as the left side: $C + I + G = $ GNP. Government policies can affect all of the variables in the spending equation. For example, government tax policies affect the size and direction of consumer and investment spending (C and I). Higher taxes reduce the portion of income available for both consumer and investment spending; tax deductions for interest charges encourage borrowing for both kinds of spending; higher taxes on interest earned discourage saving and contribute to higher spending. Government purchases of public goods and services affect government spending (G) directly.

Government tax and spending policies are called **fiscal policies**. Fiscal policies involve the government budget, essentially taxes received by government (T) and purchases made by government (G).

A demand management strategy calls for changes in tax and government spending policies, depending on the behavior of private spending. If private spending is expanding too fast, a demand management strategy would call for higher taxes and lower government spending to draw purchasing power out of the circular flow. This kind of policy is called *contractionary* fiscal policy. Contractionary fiscal policy is expected to hold down spending growth and reduce tendencies toward inflation. On the other hand, if private spending is expanding too slowly, a demand management strategy would call for lower taxes and increased government spending to pump more purchasing power into the circular flow. This kind of strategy is called *expansionary* fiscal policy. Expansionary fiscal policy is expected to stimulate spending and increase job opportunities.

For fiscal policy to be truly effective, it must be put into place quickly when irregular growth begins. During too-fast growth, a delay in imposing contractionary policy may mean that taxes are raised and government spending is reduced when the circular flow has already begun to shrink. In this case, higher taxes and lower government spending would worsen existing tendencies toward rising unemployment. During too-slow growth, a delay in imposing expansionary policy may mean lower taxes and increased government spending at a time when the circular flow has already begun to expand. In this case, lower taxes and increased government spending would worsen tendencies toward inflation.

In fact, correct timing of demand management policies is extremely difficult, since Congress must debate and compromise and the President must agree before any change in fiscal policy can take place. Furthermore, agreement to *reduce* taxes and *increase* government spending is generally easier to achieve than the reverse. A frequent result is a tendency toward accelerating spending growth, with rising employment, rising wage rates, and price inflation.

Supply-side Policies

The emphasis in supply-side policies is on increasing the nation's capacity to produce goods and services. Whereas demand management policies assume that a rising level of final sales will stimulate capital investment, supply-side policies aim to stimulate investment directly. Thus, supply-side tax and spending programs focus more precisely on business firms. Increased tax deductions for new investment encourage investment spending; government-sponsored research and development programs stimulate innovation; low-interest loans encourage small business expansion; reduced government regulation reduces some of the risks of new investment. When business firms increase their investment spending, the result is increased job opportunities, higher incomes, and finally greater total spending for goods and services.

In a sense, supply-side policies may be said to focus on the right side of the algebraic equation for GNP: $GNP = w + r + i + \pi$. By increasing the after-tax rate of return on business investment (i) and profits in ongoing enterprises (π), supply-side economists expect ultimately to increase the growth rate of the circular flow.

Supply-side policies may also be applied to individual households. Most households receive income in the form of wages and salaries, rent, and interest (w, r, and i). Personal taxes must be paid from income, and the remainder is available for spending or saving. Supply-side economists recommend lower tax rates on personal income so that households can increase their saving.* Greater savings flows can provide low-interest loans for capital investment, again helping to increase the nation's productive capacity.

Monetarism

Neither demand management nor supply-side strategies can take place without **money**. An adequate supply of money is necessary for carrying on government spending and for conducting business and consumer spending. *Money* is defined as the total of cash held by the public and checking accounts in banks and other financial institutions. In the United States, money is supplied by the

*In fact, supply-side economists recommend reduced tax rates for high-income families who are most likely to save their added incomes.

Federal Reserve system. The Federal Reserve supplies money by providing reserves to the nation's commercial banks. **Reserves** are cash deposits that banks keep in their accounts in the Federal Reserve Bank. Banking regulations permit an individual commercial bank to hold checking accounts equal to some multiple of the bank's reserve account. Thus, at any point in time the commercial banking system as a whole will hold total checking accounts equal to a multiple of the reserves provided by the Federal Reserve. Along with cash held by individuals and business firms, total checking accounts constitute the nation's money supply.

A portion of commercial bank checking accounts are cash deposits made by bank customers. Checking accounts are convenient means for making payments for goods and services. However, much of commercial bank checking accounts are not cash at all but are new deposits created to satisfy the needs of bank borrowers.

Whenever a bank holds total checking accounts less than the permitted multiple of reserves required by banking regulations, the bank may create additional accounts. It does this by making a loan to a borrower. A borrower signs a promise to pay the loan with interest and receives in return a checking account at the bank. The result is an expansion of total checking accounts and, likewise, an increase in the nation's supply of money. The borrower will probably use the created account to purchase goods and services, thereby contributing to the size of the circular flow.

The Federal Reserve system can increase or decrease the nation's money supply by providing more or less reserves to commercial banks. In general, the Federal Reserve supplies more reserves by *buying* outstanding U.S. Treasury securities from individual holders or from commercial banks themselves.* When the sellers of Treasury securities deposit their receipts in commercial banks, bank reserves increase. Then the banking system may increase total checking accounts by a multiple of the increase in reserves.

The Federal Reserve supplies less reserves by *selling* U.S. Treasury securities to individuals or banks. When buyers pay for their securities, they draw down their checking accounts at commercial banks, and bank reserves fall. A decline in reserves limits banks' abilities to create new loans and reduces bank checking accounts.

Changes in bank reserves affect banks' ability to make loans. Often banks adjust their new lending by increasing or decreasing the interest rates charged to borrowers. A greater willingness to lend is reflected in lower interest charges and an increase in created accounts. Borrowers use their new checking accounts to purchase consumer goods and services or capital investments.

Federal Reserve policy toward the money supply can take either of two forms. The two kinds of policy can be described as either "leaning against the

---

*The Federal Reserve has two other means for changing banks' ability to create new loans. It can change the terms of lending additional reserves to commercial banks or it can change the level of required reserves banks must hold. However, the principal means is through purchase and sale of government securities, as explained here.

wind" or "steady as you go." "Leaning against the wind" involves variations in the money supply opposite to the current needs of the economy. If total spending is expanding too slowly so that unemployment is increasing, the Federal Reserve would increase the money supply faster to stimulate new spending and accelerate growth. If total spending is expanding too fast so that inflation is increasing, the Federal Reserve would reduce the money supply (or reduce its rate of growth) to discourage spending and slow the pace of economic activity. By "leaning against the wind" Federal Reserve policy helps reverse unwanted tendencies in the size of the circular flow. In general, both demand management and supply-side economists recommend variations in money growth to accompany government tax and spending policies.

Another group of economists, called Monetarists, tends to favor a "steady as you go" monetary policy. Monetarists recommend regular year-by-year money growth equal to expected growth in the nation's productive capacity. Growth in capacity averages about 4 percent annually: half of this is the result of increased capital equipment and half is the result of labor force growth. A steady 4 percent growth of money would allow total spending to increase regularly in line with capacity to produce goods and services. Steady growth in spending would promote steady growth in job opportunities as well as steady increases in funds for new investment.

"Steady as you go" policies might also promote stable prices. If prices should begin to rise, the constant supply of new money would not be enough; spending would slow and prices would fall. On the other hand, if prices should begin to fall, the constant supply of new money would be too much; spending would increase and prices rise again. Most important, according to the Monetarists, a steady monetary policy achieves all these desirable results automatically. It does not depend on the good judgment, forthright analysis, and prompt action of economic policymakers. Thus, it is not subject to many of the political problems we described earlier in this chapter.

An Evaluation

The plentiful supply of macroeconomic policy tools does not guarantee success in achieving macroeconomic objectives. In fact, the complexity of the economic environment and the changeable nature of economic variables guarantees at least a degree of failure. Whatever the quality of the strategy and the precision of the policy tools, the results will seldom satisfy completely the full employment/price stability goals.*

There is another consideration in the failure to ensure steady growth: that is, the significance of human behavior for the level of economic activity. Not only are human beings instrumental in economic relations, but they express their judgments about government policy through political activity, influencing for better or worse decisions about taxing and spending. The next section will look at the politics of macroeconomic issues.

*The preceding chapters in this text provide ample evidence to the truth of this statement.

THE POLITICS OF MACROECONOMIC ISSUES

Our discussion up to this point suggests a fundamental failure of our democratic society to achieve a coherent strategy for dealing with mounting problems of inflation and unemployment. In one sense, our failure in macroeconomic policy is worsened by our successes in other aspects of our national life. Our technical successes have increased our ability to communicate more information to more people. Access to communications media for more people has broadened their understanding of macroeconomic issues and sharpened their disagreements on policy proposals. Ironically, improved communications have tended both to unite us in a cultural sense and to divide us politically. Improved education has had a similar effect, increasing our awareness of the possible effects of economic policy decisions on our own living standards.

Our successes have worked also to increase our expectations of even greater successes in the future. The remarkable achievements of recent decades may have led us to expect too much and to blame others when our expectations are unfulfilled. The frequent object of blame is, of course, government.

One of the nation's leading political scientists, Samuel P. Huntingdon, has pointed to a fundamental gap between what we as U.S. citizens expect of life and what we actually achieve.* Early in our education we learn to recite a Pledge of Allegiance to a nation that promises "liberty and justice for all." The words are easy to say and the concepts inviting. Nevertheless, achieving "liberty and justice for all" is a monumental task, not easily achieved in even the wealthiest, best-intentioned nation. The goal of liberty and justice implies that each of us will be able to live life as we choose: we will have challenging and satisfying job opportunities, rising income and living standards, and increased freedom in our personal lives. For many of us, the gap between the promised ideal and the grim reality will generate frustration. We will tend to blame government for the failure to fulfill its lofty promises.

Professor Huntingdon divided the promises of U.S. citizenship into four categories. According to Professor Huntingdon, our understanding of and reaction to these promises actually make it more difficult to achieve them. Let us look at each of the four promises in detail.

1. *Liberty.* The promise of liberty implies that we should be free of government restrictions. Expecting perfect liberty, we tend to limit the size and responsibility of government.
2. *Individualism.* Our individualism causes us to demand economic and political freedom. We want to be able to run our own business, for instance, but we also want the right to conduct our own affairs without restrictions. In fact, these two kinds of freedom may be incompatible.
3. *Democracy.* Our democratic foundations guarantee the broadest possible participation in government. However, we tend to exercise our participatory

American Politics: The Promise of Disharmony, Cambridge, Mass.: Belknap Press of Harvard University Press, 1982, and *The Crisis of Democracy:* New York University Press, 1975.

responsibility in a negative direction: that is, to get government "off our backs."

4. *Equality.* Whereas our system promises only equality of opportunity and not equality of results, we tend to expect the latter. Furthermore, the belief in personal equality encourages each of us to assume we know as much as the experts or officials about matters of national policy.

All these tendencies contribute to feelings that are antigovernment and to a reluctance to allow significant powers to government. The frequent result is a government too weak to accomplish the goals we expect of it. Other nations are less subject to these limiting tendencies. For European nations and for Japan, the influence of the state is firmly imbedded in the established institutions of society. Whereas the actions of these governments are highly coordinated with other activities throughout the society, Americans make a special point of not allowing government to "take root." We limit its power and then blame it for ineffectiveness.

The Need for Leadership

Many of us can recognize these contradicting tendencies in our own attitudes and behavior. Similar attitudes among all citizens can produce indecision and stalemate in macroeconomic policy. In critical periods of the past our democratic society has been able to mobilize behind a coherent strategy. The essential element for this to occur (and that may be lacking today) is effective leadership. Past crises have provided the environment for emergence of leaders who can establish goals, evaluate alternative strategies, and persuade the public to accept their programs.

The role of a leader is to frame single issues into a broad context and state them in terms of the national interest. A leader should propose broad national goals and explain the importance of individual programs for achieving overall goals. A leader should not "run against government." After all, the role of a leader is to *use* government more effectively to deal with problems involving the national interest. Criticism should come from *outside* the current government, from those who would propose more effective policies than the current ones.

Citizens will continue to disagree on the priorities of various national goals and on the appropriateness of government's role in achieving them. An effective leader can persuade individuals to tradeoff single-issue interests for the sake of the broader national interest. He or she can create a climate of compromise in which citizens believe their concerns will be heard and dealt with when conditions permit. Can such leaders come from democratic electoral procedures? The answer is not clearcut. A seriously divided electorate may not be willing to concentrate that much power in the hands of a single individual. In fact, there is the danger that a potential leader might act to create a crisis (or worsen an existing crisis) as a means of concentrating popular support.

The Diminishing Significance of Political Parties

In the past, leaders have arisen from the membership of political parties. Typically, political parties are formed by groups of citizens joined together according to their confidence in government as a potential source of solutions to economic problems: a left-to-moderate group might be willing to allow a degree of government intervention in free markets and a right-to-moderate group might be less willing to do so. Members of each group will agree in general on fundamental approaches to macroeconomic issues. And they will agree to subordinate their individual interests to the broader interests of the party as a whole.

A decline of political parties has probably been a factor in the indecision and stalemate we are now experiencing. A decline in party leadership in the U.S. Congress can be dated about 1961, when a new procedure for selecting congressional committee chairmen was instituted. Before 1961, committee chairmen rose through the ranks and achieved their leadership positions as rewards for long service in the political party. In such persons, years of experience had developed the capacity for compromise and consensus. Long-standing associations among leaders in the legislative and executive branches helped ease the process of decision and action. Since 1961, committee responsibilities have been more widely diffused, with each member of the majority party awarded a major committee assignment as well as a subcommittee chairmanship. Proposed new legislation is assigned to several committees who report out conflicting versions; then a compromise must be worked out in long public sessions, where single-interest pressure tends to dominate. Wide participation in legislative power has reduced the leadership's control of new legislation and diminished the significance of party loyalty.

The influence of political parties has been further reduced by ordinary election procedures. Instead of campaigning as representatives of a particular party, candidates today run as representatives of diverse, well-organized, single-interest groups. Campaign funds are provided by special interests, and representatives defend those interests while in office. New legislation is decided by coalitions whose make-up differs on every issue before the Congress. Without party discipline to coordinate economic policy, there is a tendency toward inconsistency, producing a hodgepodge of programs popular with particular groups but serving no overall strategy.

Inconsistency in the Congress extends also to the executive branch of government through our processes of election. Because the President and Vice-President are elected separately, they may not share the same policy goals as the Congress. In fact, they may represent totally different constituencies with different aims and expectations relative to the role of government.* Their differences may make it impossible for the President to put into effect the programs on which his election campaign was based. A President cannot fairly be blamed for failing to achieve a program in the face of Congressional opposition. Nor can Congress

*During almost half of the last seven administrations (1946-1980), the President's party did not hold a majority of both houses of Congress.

be blamed for obstructing the President while carrying out legislators' proper roles as representatives of a legitimate constituency. Thus, there is a tendency toward stalemate, with no clear emergence of a consistent economic program.

Parliamentary governments of European nations and Japan are less troubled with this problem. Their chief executive is also a legislative leader, chosen from the legislature by members of the parliamentary majority. Cabinet members are also chosen from the majority party, and the party as a whole is responsible for forming and conducting the government. Members of the majority party must support the party's program or risk the loss of career opportunities in government. If the legislature rejects a key part of the majority party's program, it can call for a vote of "no confidence" to decide the government's future course. Under a parliamentary system, voters know whom to praise or blame for the success or failure of the government's program.

A CONCLUSION AND A WARNING

Throughout this text we have confronted major issues and minor subissues that divide the American people and that require solutions. The critical issues of today demand clearly defined proposals, objective evaluation of alternatives, and purposeful enactment of policy decisions. Failure to deal with important national and international questions can endanger our nation's standing as a world leader and threaten our own individual prospects for a good life.

Both in the realm of microeconomic issues and macroeconomic issues, there appears to be a "crisis of competence" in government for achieving fundamental goals. This is true at all levels of government, but particularly true at the level of the national government. Our government appears to be less than effective for ensuring efficiency, equity, and positive externalities and for achieving full employment, price stability, and healthy growth.

To some, incompetence in government is neither troubling nor surprising. In their view, free markets should make all the fundamental decisions for allocating resources and distributing benefits and costs. They believe that free-market decisions will automatically achieve the proper microeconomic and macroeconomic goals and that the costs associated with failure to achieve maximum objectives are offset by the benefits in added freedoms associated with independent decision-making. In this view, weakness and incompetence in government serve correctly to reduce government's role in the economic system.

The implications throughout this text suggest another point of view: that a government of informed citizens can design and carry out policies more favorable to the nation's long-range interests than the unrestricted acts of free and independent markets. We have pointed out a fundamental flaw in this approach, however. We have suggested that our government lacks the power and the leadership to carry out its responsibilities effectively.

In the words of President Woodrow Wilson: "Power and strict accountability for its use are the essential constituents of good Government." For the United States today, the complexity of modern issues and the spread of knowledge and communications have diffused and diminished political power. Inconsistency in government has limited accountability. The issues of the past have been resolved in spite of these flaws, but success in the future is not assured. In fact, as our economic problems become more complex and we become more interdependent, the cost of failures may rise substantially. As a nation, we may pay dearly for the inability of our government to deal promptly and consistently with problems that threaten our economic health.

QUESTIONS

1. Construct a chart with 12 rows and 4 columns. Label the rows with the subjects of chapters 1 through 12. Then in Column 1 list public goods and services (if any) associated with government action in the chapter topic. In Column 2, note actions of government to achieve greater efficiency; and in Column 3, note actions of government to achieve greater equity. In Column 4 list positive and negative externalities associated with government actions regarding the chapter topic.
2. Select a single issue of special concern to your town or neighborhood. Point out the costs and benefits associated with the problem and with proposed government actions to correct it. Evaluate the efficiency and equity of various proposals.
3. Discuss the consequences of "logrolling" for achieving coherent national policies. How is logrolling similar to and different from coalition building?
4. What is the basis for the statement that total spending for newly produced goods and services is equal to total incomes paid to owners of productive resources? Distinguish between such spending and spending for items like a used car, a Treasury security, or a plot of land. Do such expenditures contribute to national income for the year? Explain your answer.
5. Suppose the circular flow is expanding at a healthy rate: that is, the nation is enjoying full employment and price stability. Explain the effect of each of the following:
    (a) Consumers reduce their savings and increase borrowing to purchase larger quantities of goods and services.
    (b) Military spending increases, and taxes are raised to finance the greater government expenditures.
    (c) Business leaders become concerned about the level of sales and reduce their investments in inventory.
    (d) Technological development requires substantial new construction of capital goods.
6. The table below gives data for computing Gross National Product for the years 1979 through 1981. Net foreign purchases of U.S. goods and services are included, and all amounts are expressed in constant dollars of 1972.

	GNP	Consumption (C)	Investment (I)	Government Purchases (G)	Net Foreign Purchases
1979	$1,479.4 b	$927.6 b	$236.3 b	$278.3 b	$37.2 b
1980	1,474.0	930.5	208.4	284.6	50.6
1981	1,502.6	947.6	225.8	287.1	42.0
1982	1,475.5	957.1	196.9	291.2	30.3

Calculate the growth rate of GNP over the three periods shown in the table and the growth rates of the individual components of total spending. Interpret your results.

7. Distinguish between expansionary and contractionary fiscal policy and explain the effects on the circular flow. Describe the problem of correct timing of fiscal policy.
8. Discuss the two approaches to monetary policy and explain how each would be carried out.
9. The total of cash and checking accounts owned by the public is defined as "M–1." Consult the *Economic Report of the President* for information regarding yearly changes in M–1 over the last decade. Then, on a single graph, chart the annual change in M–1 and annual changes in GNP. Comment on your results. What does your graph tell you about causality: that is, the cause and effect relationship between M–1 and GNP?

DEFINITIONS

The circular flow of spending, production, and income is a diagram that represents the flow of spending and real goods and resources among consumers and producers in the economy.

Coalitions are combinations of groups organized to support or oppose a particular public policy. The make-up of coalitions varies from issue to issue, so that there is a tendency toward inconsistency in political decisions.

Fiscal policies involve the government budget: they are the tax and spending policies of government. Contractionary fiscal policies are increases in taxes and reductions in spending that together help hold down the level of total spending in the economy. Expansionary fiscal policies are cuts in taxes and increases in spending that help increase the level of total spending.

Logrolling is the practice of joining together in support of a particular issue in return for others' support of one's own particular issue.

Monetarism is the economic philosophy that levels of total spending in the economy can best be controlled by controlling the quantity of money in the system.

Money is the total of cash and checking accounts owned by the public.

Net taxes are the difference between total taxes collected by government and negative taxes paid out by government.

Public goods and services are items provided by government for use of all the citizens. Some examples are public education, defense, highways, and public health.

Reserves are accounts of commercial banks held in the Federal Reserve Bank. Commercial banks are allowed to increase their checking accounts up to a certain multiple of their reserve accounts.

Single-issue constituencies involve the division of citizens into small groups, each of which feels strongly about only one of a variety of economic issues.

SUGGESTED READINGS

"America's Restructured Economy." *Business Week*, June 1, 1981, p. 55.

Bergston, C. Fred. "Can We Prevent a World Economic Crisis?" *Challenge*, January/February, 1983, p. 4.

Danziger, Sheldon, and Robert Haveman. "The Reagan Budget: A Sharp Break With the Past." *Challenge*, May/June, 1981, p. 5.

Diebold, William, Jr. "Industrial Policy as an International Issue." *Challenge*, January/February, 1981, p. 30.

Drucker, Peter F. *The Age of Discontinuity.* New York: Harper & Row, 1969.

Eckstein, Otto. "Economic Choices for the 1980s." *Challenge*, July/August, 1980, p. 15.

Ehrbar, A. F. "Reagan Steps Back from Reaganomics." *Fortune*, February 21, 1983, p. 67.

Eichner, Alfred S. "Reflections on Social Democracy." *Challenge*, March/April, 1982, p. 33.

"The Fed's Plan for Economic Recovery." *Business Week*, December 13, 1982, p. 90.

Feldstein, Martin, ed. *The American Economy in Transition.* Chicago: National Bureau of Economic Research, 1980, Chapter 2.

Fiedler, Edgar R. "A Whiff of the Thirties." *Across the Board*, April, 1982, p. 22.

Hale, David. "Thatcherism." *Across the Board*, December, 1981, p. 48.

Heilbroner, Robert L. *An Inquiry into the Human Prospect.* New York: W. W. Norton and Co., 1974.

Hein, John. "Le Supply-Side: Plus ça Change. . ." *Across the Board*, October, 1981, p. 10.

Hodgson, Godfrey. "The Overloading of the Presidency." *Across the Board*, December, 1980, p. 54.

"How Strong a Recovery?" *Business Week*, January 31, 1983, p. 88.

Jameson, Kenneth P. "Supply-Side Economics: Growth versus Income Distribution." *Challenge*, November/December, 1980, p. 26.

Juster, F. Thomas. "The Economics and Politics of the Supply-Side View." *Economic Outlook USA.* Survey Research Center, University of Michigan, Autumn, 1981, p. 81.

Kahn, Alfred E. "Liberals Must Face the Facts." *Challenge*, November/December, 1981, p. 25.

Kindleberger, Charles P. "The Economic Aging of America." *Challenge*, January/February, 1980, p. 48.

Lekachman, Robert. *The Age of Keynes.* New York: McGraw-Hill, 1975.

Musgrave, Richard A. "What Will the Tax Cut Accomplish?" *Challenge*, May/June, 1981, p. 55.

Phillips, Kevin P. "America in the 1980s — A Weimar Analogy." *Across the Board*, November, 1982, p. 46.

Rohatyn, Felix G. "Strong Medicine." *Across the Board*, May, 1980, p. 3.

Rostow, W. W. "Working Agenda for a Disheveled World Economy." *Challenge*, March/April, 1981, p. 5.

Steger, Ulrich. "Piling Up Social Dynamite." *Challenge*, May/June, 1982, p. 28.

Stein, Herbert. "A Dangerous Time for Economic Policy." *Fortune*, December 27, 1982, p. 68.

——. "The Chief Executive as Chief Economist." *Across the Board*, January, 1982, p. 62.

Thurow, Lester. *The Zero-Sum Society.* New York: Basic Books, 1980, Chapter 8.

Tobin, James. "Supply-Side Economics: What Is It? Will It Work?" *Economic Outlook USA.* Survey Research Center, University of Michigan, Summer, 1981, p. 51.

Index

Absolute advantage, 299–301, 303, 319; definition of, 323
Accelerated depreciation, 48; definition of, 53
Africa, 263–64
Aged or elderly, 207–8, 210–11
Agricultural research, 114, 326, 329
Agriculture, 169–70, 201, 212, 248–70, 291, 299, 329
Agriculture, Department of, 202, 211
Aid to Families with Dependent Children (AFDC), 15–16, 207–8, 210, 225
Aircraft industry, 292
Airline Deregulation Act, 289
Airlines, 389–90
Aleutian Islands, 83–84
Allocative efficiency, definition of, 85
Alternative energy sources, 66–68, 76–78, 163
American Federation of Labor (AFL), 192
American Medical Association (AMA), 236
Antitrust Division, Department of Justice, 15
Antitrust laws, 15, 25, 71, 258, 287
Apparel industry, 173–74, 188; unions in, 192
Armament industry, 103
Arms sales, 103–4
Army Corps of Engineers, 286
Articles of Confederation, 109
Asia, 251, 258, 263–64
Automatic stabilizers, 44
Automobiles, 147, 173–74, 184, 188; unions, 192, 285, 290, 292
Average cost of production, 279–82; with learning curve, 76–78
Average fixed cost, 273–74; definition of, 295
Average product, 57, 143, 148–49; in agriculture, 253–54, 261; definition of, 8–25; graph of, 10; historical data on, 19, 46
Average total cost, 272, 277; definition of, 295
Average variable cost, 273–75; definition of, 295

"Baby boom," 50, 175, 185, 190, 209
Balance of payments, 174, 297, 307–9; definition of, 323
Balance of trade, 319
Bangladesh, 254, 258, 268
Banking regulation, 147
Bankruptcy, 290
Barriers to trade, 201, 317, 329; definition of, 323
Baumol, William, 69
Behavioral scientists, 186–87; definition of, 196
Benefit-cost ratio, 152–53; definition of, 165
Bills, U.S. Treasury, 127; definition of, 138
Block grants, 114–15, 127; definition of, 138
Blue Cross and Blue Shield, 224, 235
Boards of directors, 187; definition of, 196
Bombers, 97–98
Bonds, 45, 51, 217–18; corporate, definition of, 53; revenue, definition of, 217–18; U.S. Treasury, 127–28
Borlaug, Norman, 262
"Bottom line syndrome," 69; definition of, 79
Boycotts, 301, 319
Braniff International, 290
Brazil, 75, 250, 259–60, 268, 299
Britain, 146, 173, 188, 220, 321–22; National Health Service, 243–44

Califano, Joseph, 232, 239
California: tax revolt, 125–26; water shortage, 160
Capital: consumption allowance, 26, 43–44; controls, 301; deepening, 46; definition of, 53; definitions of, 5, 25, 52; resources, 27–28, 37, 41, 43–45, 48, 51, 84, 91, 124–25, 144, 146, 186, 206–7, 273, 285, 289, 301, 332–33, 335–36
Capital gains tax, 39, 48, 216; definitions of, 53, 138
Capital-intensity, 83, 99, 188
Capitalism, definitions of, 83, 106